PRESS GANG.

THREESCORE YEARS:

AN

AUTOBIOGRAPHY,

CONTAINING INCIDENTS OF VOYAGES AND TRAVELS,

INCLUDING

SIX YEARS IN A MAN-OF-WAR.

DETAILS OF THE WAR BETWEEN THE UNITED STATES AND THE ALGERINE GOVERNMENT, BOMBARDMENT OF ALGIERS BY LORD EXMOUTH, AND ITS SUBJUGATION BY THE FRENCH.

ALSO,

TWO YEARS IN CALIFORNIA,

A VISIT TO THE CRIMEA DURING THE BOMBARDMENT AND CAPTURE OF SEBASTOPOL, JOURNEY THROUGH ASIA MINOR, SYRIA, PALESTINE AND EGYPT.

WITH ILLUSTRATIONS.

BY SAMUEL F. HOLBROOK.

BOSTON:
JAMES FRENCH AND COMPANY,
78 WASHINGTON STREET.
1857.

PRESS OF S. CHISM,
FRANKLIN PRINTING HOUSE,
BOSTON.

PREFACE.

I am aware that a preface is seldom read, unless it is very brief. I wish however to say a few words to the reader before he commences reading the narrative, which is, that I have used my own style, endeavoring to write, just as I should talk, if telling a story. In some cases, I have suppressed names, as the parties are now living, and probably would not like to see themselves in print. It is possible that I may in some instances have been mistaken in dates, but this I do not conceive to be of much importance so long as the subject is correct. And not to crowd too much matter in this volume, I have avoided descriptions of countries, as much as could be done without abruptness, excepting only where it appeared to be indispensable.

I have quoted much, relative to Mr. Fulton, which appeared to me to belong to the narrative, and which I think will interest the reader. I have also made other quotations, which appeared to me to be applicable to the place where they are inserted. Chapter 15, consists entirely of matters relative to the capture of the U. S. frigate, Essex; as I consider it to have been the most sanguinary battle that occurred during the late war with England. At the commencement of the chapter, I have given my reasons for its insertion, which may be a sufficient apology for the digression. The bombardment of Algiers, by Lord Exmouth, is also a subject which must interest the world, and though obliged to condense it, the subject has not suffered by the contraction.

It is indispensable that a book writer should be well acquainted with the language in which he writes,—also his subject.

The responsibility, or success of this volume, I throw upon those of my friends who have urged me to write it, as the following extract will show.

"I don't know of anything that would give me more pleasure, than to read the narrative of your life. Mr. J——d observed to me after you left Washington, that if you would give him your manuscript, he would publish it immediately. I hope you will collect your journals and pencilings, and let us have them in the shape of a book."

Extract from the reply:—"You caused me to smile when you spoke about writing the history of my life. You know book writers, in order to be successful, must be popular. If the President of the United States was to write his autobiography, every body would read it, on account of the author. But when a man in the ordinary walks of life attempts it, his book must run the risk of anything more than an ordinary reception. Another objection, my style probably would not suit the sentimental reader. There would not be flourish enough about it, no beautiful display of emotions on leaving my native shore, no romantic description of the broad expanse of ocean; no detail of catching a dolphin with a vivid admiration of his dying hues; no capturing a Mother Cary's Chicken with a pin-hook; (the bird's name you would be sure to have in Latin,) then the dreadful effect it had on the minds of the superstitious sailor, who esteem the death of a Mother Cary's Chicken ominous of some fearful catastrophe; nor any paroxysm of delight on beholding Albion for the first time; besides a catalogue of first impressions, which always looks to me to be very flat."

Throughout the narrative I have not been personal, except only where individuality required it. Perhaps I should apologize to the reader for the abbreviated words, which in conversation would rank under the category of profane, and hesitated some time before I felt willing to insert them in their present form; but upon conclusion, felt that as I have aimed at the *verbatim* in all colloquies and conversations; the reader would pass lightly over in this narrative what would on any other occasion have been considered an error.

The story of a smuggler I give just as I had it on my journal, as I have also done with everything of which I was not an eyewitness. I may have omitted quotation marks where they properly belonged, which I hope may be excused as an oversight.

Egotism in an autobiography is unavoidable, and if on the whole, the style meets the approbation of the reader, then the highest wishes and expectations have been realized by the author.

S. F. H.

TO THE READER.

It was my intention at the commencement, to have included all within the limits of five hundred pages. In order to do this, I found it would be necessary to contract the narrative, so much as to injure it; although I did not intend to dwell upon the description or localities of countries, and much other matter that would more properly belong to a history, than an autobiography. Have accordingly concluded to issue another edition or volume, which will contain much of an amusing and entertaining character, besides the showing up of certain *personages* which have been omitted for want of room. In the preface, I have apologized for the style, and begged the reader to excuse the blunders. As I have now become somewhat initiated into the complicated modus operandi of following up the various functionaries required in getting up a book, the next edition will show whether I have improved by my bought experience.

Respectfully, The Author.

Still question'd me the story of my life
From year to year; the battles, sieges, fortunes,
That I had passed.
I ran it through, even from my boyish days,
To the very moment that I was bade to tell it;
Wherein I spoke of most disastrous changes,
Of moving accidents, by flood and field,
Of hairbreadth 'scapes 'i imminent, deadly breach;
Of being taken by the insolent foe
And held a prisoner of my redemption thence,
And with it all my travel's history,
Wherein of countries vast, and deserts wild,
Rough quarries, rocks, and hills, whose heads touch heaven,
It was my hint to speak.

SHAKSPEARE.

CHAPTER I.

Birthplace. — First act of mischief. — Punishment. — Object for relating it. — Narrow escape from drowning. — Slight reference to New York sixty years ago. — Description of my first school and my first whipping. — Removal to Worcester, Roxbury and Boston. — Remarks on Boston in 1798. — My father enters into partnership. — Is defrauded. — Return to New York at the solicitation of my maternal grandfather. — Come back to Boston for education. — Enter school. — Comparison between then and now, respecting school advantages. — Cruelty of the masters, and description of the punishment. — Unpleasant affair. — Leave school. — Had been much injured by keeping bad company. — Quarrel between boys of different grades. — Frequent fights, not condition that makes the man. — Folly of personal resentment. — Narrow escape from injury. — Good counsel from a good boy. — Forsake my bad companions, and lead a different life. — Punishment of offenders by public whipping. — A lesson for me.

IT MAY be immaterial to the reader, where, and when I was born, but in order to make a beginning, my birthplace was New York City, July 16, 1793. The first act of my life, of which I have a distinct recollection, was voluntarily taking up a stone, and breaking an earthern vessel belonging to an old lady, residing in the same house with myself. I was then about three years of age. Now what could have induced me to commit this mischievous trespass on the old lady's property I cannot tell, excepting only that I wanted to see if I could hit it, at a certain distance ; in which, unfortunately for me, I succeeded, for on complaint of Mrs. Morrell, my father took me across his knee, and the concussion of his brawny hand made me resolve never to break another "*old lady's jug.*" I name this trifling incident, to illustrate the truth of what is sometimes called, innate sin, or an inherent disposition or propensity in children, to do wrong. All who have brought up families are well acquainted with this matter, and see the necessity of watching the incipient developments of their children, and to check everything that is wrong, following the precept of the Bible, "*Train up a child in the way he should go.*"

Many who have suffered an ignominious death upon the scaffold, while standing with the halter about their necks, have declared to the gazing crowd, that had their parents discharged their duty, in correcting them for the first lie, or the first petty theft, they in all probability would have been saved from this untimely end. And so with the other sex. How many there are, now leading lives of infamy and disgrace, who attribute their downfall to errors in early education.

The next event of my early life which is indelibly fixed on my mind, is the sensation of drowning, when about four years old. I went with some boys to see a dead animal thrown into the river; and in my eagerness to view the launch, fell overboard, and as the distance from the top of the wharf to the water rendered it impossible for any one to reach me, I remained in the water until rescued by means, the particulars of which I never knew.

It so happened that, notwithstanding the river is always running rapidly, either one way or the other, the place where I fell was a short eddy, just around the corner of the wharf. Had I been out only a few feet further, the tide would have swept me away, and of course, that would have been the last of me. I remember to this day as though it were but yesterday, while struggling under water trying to get up as I thought, the recollection of playing on the wharf, the swallowing a large quantity of salt water, and a perfect knowledge that I was drowning. I was taken from the water, resuscitated, and carried home, but knew nothing more until consciousness returned. How many times since have I regretted being taken from the river. Had I have drowned, how much anguish would have been averted. But this is all wrong, since our lives belong to God. He takes them when and how he pleases. Every man was born for something, known only to Him who created us; and as for trouble, that man or woman is a coward who expects to get through life without it in some shape. Campbell, in his overland journey to India, refers to these beautiful lines:

> "This world, what art thou?
> Thy school O misery; our only lesson in it is,
> To learn to suffer; and he who knows not that
> Was born for nothing."

New York, in those days, was a different looking city from what it is now. Then it was scarcely half as large, and, what were then fields and orchards, are now splendid squares and parks.

Around and in the vicinity of the Battery, was the court end of the city. John Jacob Astor was then a thrifty and enterprising merchant, living in very modest style; and the few aged millionaires who now survive, and many who have long since gone to their final resting place, and whose vast property, if it had been kept together, would have amounted to an incredible sum; many of these were then sellers of nuts and apples, waiters in kitchens, small retailing grocers, and some of the descendants of these thrifty men, are now grappling with abject poverty; and often may be seen with bloated faces and tattered garments.

Yellow fever and small pox prevailed nearly every summer, although at some seasons very much mitigated. These sickly summers were generally succeeded by intensely cold winters, which was the cause of much suffering among the poor. The city depended on Connecticut sloops and other small vessels for fuel, and when the East and North Rivers were frozen, which they were sometimes for four or five weeks, wood then became both dear and scarce. Coal as fuel was scarcely known; anthracite, or any other than imported coal, had not yet been discovered, so that the poor were for many days, and in the most inclement part of winter, without a particle of fire. It was on one of these occasions that the corporation ordered a long row of wooden buildings, which stood on the Battery, to be torn down and distributed among the most destitute.

These buildings had been formerly used as barracks in

the Revolutionary War, and it may be said that for once they kept up a brisk fire. Another incident occurred when I was about five years of age, which has also made a lasting impression on my mind, and from which, I have in subsequent life drawn many useful illustrations. I was put to school to an old man, who taught us in an old dilapidated garret. The old fellow wore a large white wig, an old-fashioned coat with "buttons down before," greasy breeches, and large shoe buckles; he kept a good sized stick which might have answered well for an illustration of perpetual motion. One day he undertook to flog me, but by various convolutions and twistings, I got off almost "unscathed." But, oh, for human weakness; I was simple enough to tell him he didn't hurt me after all. "Aha!" said he, "didn't hurt, eh? then I'll try again," so suiting the action to the word, gave me a regular thrashing, which I guess hurt a little. However, the credit of making a man of me was not to devolve on him.

In the summer of 1798, we removed to Worcester, Mass., it being the birthplace of my father and of my paternal grandfather, it was then but a sparse village. Could some of my old relatives get out of their graves, and be placed in a populous street, they would be sadly puzzled to find their way back again.

In the autumn of the same year we came to Roxbury. The same remarks apply to this city, as to New York and Worcester, it having also undergone a metamorphosis, and is now one of the prettiest little cities in Massachusetts. Here my father commenced his business, as a worker in ivory and tortoise shell. We remained one year in Roxbury, and then removed to Boston. Shortly after our location in Boston, I came very near drowning again. I had gone in to bathe near the house, and before I was aware, got beyond my depth, and would have drowned had not a man accidentally come near the water-side and pulled me out.

And but a few days after this, an Irish boy with whom I had a short time previous disagreed with in play, came behind me with a large, sharp stone, and struck me with such force as to deprive me of my senses. His name was McNiel, and whenever I come across this name I always feel the wound in my head. But "*I guess I paid him off.*"

My father established his factory at the south part of the town, then called Washington street.

At that time, and for some years after, what is now called Washington street was then the Main street, and from the old Fortification, which was near the mansion of the late J. D. Williams, Esq., on the neck, down to a little north of State street, it was divided into Washington, Orange, Newbury and Marlborough streets, and below that, to the market, Cornhill, and Dock Square.

Boston, since 1798, has undergone a remarkable change, both in beauty and convenience. There is hardly a portion of it, of any magnitude, that has not been extensively improved. Then, where Charles street now is, was a gravelly beach extending from the bottom of the Common to Cambridge bridge. This beach was overlooked by a steep hill, called "Mount Whoredom," on the summit of which was a powder house, and around that vicinity, and on the northern slope, there was a collection of negroes, and characters of the worst grade.

In 1805 and 1806, the top of this hill was dug away, and removed by a railway, to build Charles street. Philanthropic and enterprising capitalists then commenced the purgation of this filthy place, by erecting handsome brick dwellings, and laying out regular and convenient streets. And it is now one of the most beautiful portions of our city. Then, from Fort Hill to Long Wharf, was little else than a beach; no India, or Central wharves until several years after; but 'tis not my intention to enter upon the history of Boston, therefore I have merely alluded to a few among the many valuable improvements that our city has undergone.

My father's business succeeded well, and would, no doubt, have continued well, had he not unfortunately formed a connection with two unprincipled villains who nearly ruined him. These two scoundrels, one named Richards, and the other Robbins, proposed a partnership, pretending to have a knowledge of the business. They were also to furnish a certain amount of capital, which, it afterwards appeared, they did not possess. After being together about a year, by which time they had acquired a considerable knowledge of the business, they persuaded my father to take a lot of manufactured articles to New York, and establish a branch there; and himself to manage it, while they carried on the concern in Boston. This all appeared so plausible, and my father, not suspecting treachery, readily consented, and a quantity of goods were packed up, and as there was no other mode of conveyance between Boston and New York than the mail stage, and Hingham packets, my father chose to go by land to Connecticut, with the intention of selling the goods he had with him, and also of obtaining customers in the towns through which he might pass. He had been absent only a few days, when these cloven-footed villains came out with their scheme, which was to rob my father. My mother was not aware of what they were doing until it was too late to prevent it. They had collected the most valuable part of the stock, and what cash they could get hold of, and then went off. Before they went, however, my mother, understanding what they were about, demanded an explanation. The reply was, that the partnership was broken up, and that my father had his portion of the property with him. All this she knew to be false, and before she could obtain assistance from any one, they were off, and I believe we never heard of them afterwards. They no doubt met their deserts, as all such villains are sure to do. My father was apprised of the whole affair, by letter, immediately, but did not get the letter until some weeks after they had gone off. It was sad news for him, but taking the whole matter into consideration, as the prospect for business was good in New York, and as they had taken all, and probably there were some demands against the concern, he arranged matters so that it was not necessary for him to return to Boston. In the following spring he sent for his family. We put our household stuff on board a Hingham packet, which plied between Boston and New York, and sailed on the 20th of May, 1801, and arrived there in eleven days, all well, and were soon comfortably located. After being in New York about eleven months, my maternal grandfather sent for me to return to Boston for the benefit of my education, as the New York schools were very much inferior to those of Boston.

My parents being willing, I returned to my grandfather's family, and was put to school. At that time there were separate schoolhouses for each department of scholarship, so that the attendance was half the day to each, during the summer months, both for boys and girls, the latter not attending school during the winter; and then the four classes were divided into two parts, the first and third made one, the second and fourth the other. The reading and grammar schools that I attended were the old Bingham, at the head of Nassau street, under charge of Dr. Asa Bullard, and the other was at the head of West street, and commanded by Rufus Webb, Esq.

I often look back at my school days, and compare the advantages of that time with those of the present day. Then, the books of the first class consisted of the American Preceptor, a small edition of a dictionary, a very diminutive grammar, called young ladies' accidents, and a little paper geographical catechism, containing about twenty-five pages. The contents of the latter I can repeat at the present time, nearly word for word.

We afterwards had an abridged history of England, and a new grammer by Peter Cochran, but notwithstanding the apparent scarcity of school books at this period, some of the most active and intelligent merchants of Boston, New York, New Orleans, and in most of the seaports of the United States, had no other school education than what they received at the Boston public school.

There are also those who are now enjoying, and those who have filled high and responsible positions, and one of the most popular of our modern poets, (whose poetic talents are known throughout Europe,) who were classmates with me, and I believe never attended any other school.

Then there were not half so many attractions to lure the youthful mind as at the present time; the reading was more of an instructive character, than much that falls into the hands of young persons now. Although it is certain, that the numerous associations, composed entirely of young men, such as Lyceums, Public Libraries, Scientific Lectures, and a host of moral and intellectual institutions, cannot fail of producing men of superior attainments.

My comparison was only intended to show that close application to anything, no matter what the difficulties or deficiencies may be, will, with few exceptions, come out successfully. At the early time of which I am speaking of my own education, the discipline and punishments were severe, and in some cases cruel, but visited only on those who were delinquent in their studies, or unruly in their conduct. Mr. Haskell, who was usher, when I first joined the school, was removed and made the principal of another.

He was succeeded by a tall, raw boned, sallow looking, New Hampshire man, named Peter Cochran, author of the new grammar. His very appearance struck a terror into those who were to be under his charge, of which, unfortunately, I was one. On his first appearance and after the school had been called to order, he took a position near his desk, and when all was silent, and every eye fixed on him, he gave a glance round with his fierce, snaky eyes and commenced his inaugural. "Boys, if you are attentive to your studies it will be well, but if not, I shall be very severe with you, be seated." He provided himself with a hugh rattan full four feet long; he then measured off two lines upon the floor, parallel with the wainscoting, one about two feet, and the other about thirty inches, this was intended as an inquisitorial punishment for those who were inattentive to their studies.

The application was as follows: the delinquent, if a tall boy, was made to stand with his right foot on the thirty inch line having the wall on his right, he then raises his right arm, and with open hand falls against the wall, thus forming an acute angle, his body the hypothenuse, the floor a base, and the wall a perpendicular; in this painful position he must stand during the pleasure of the inquisitor. A sharp lookout was kept, that he did not reduce the length of the base, if he did, he had a rap on the legs with the big rattan. The two-feet-line, was for smaller boys; I had the painful pleasure of forming this trigonometrical figure several times, but much rather preferred the incipient demonstration of two parallel lines, that is, if my body was to form any part of a geometrical figure. Another mode of punishment, as a sort of change, was to hold out a whole, or half brick, at arms length, during the pleasure of this modern Nero—this, I also tried and should prefer carrying the brick in my hat, than having to hold it in this most painful manner. The career of this fellow was short. His cruelties were disallowed by the head master, and he was discharged. I afterwards heard of a Cochran that was sentenced to the State Prison, in Maine. I wonder if it was this fellow? He was succeeded by another tall, gaunt-looking creature, who was truly the mathematical demonstration of a straight line "length without breadth." He was from New Hampshire also, and it might well be said that he stepped into Cochran's shoes. He had the same rattan, but was not allowed to continue Cochran's tortures. He was noway backward with his rattan, as my head and shoulders could well testify. He seemed to take a peculiar pleasure in flogging me; whether he thought there was a balance due me from Cochran, and the account had been transferred to him for settlement, I cannot say; for hardly a day passed that I did not get a rap and not for negligence either, for I always had my lesson and was as far ahead as any boy in the class.

One day, one of the largest boys in the lower division, for some misdemeanor was severely punished, he watched his opportunity and ran out of school. He soon returned with his father, a stout, red-faced man, armed with a large cane, And when Pierce and his father had entered the door "where is the fellow?" cried old Pierce, then walking up to Bradley with his cane uplifted, the latter, pale as ashes, stood still. Immediately I sprung out of my seat, the other boys following; we formed a dense ring around him, thus warding off old Pierce.

The head master now interfered, when the old man and his son retired peaceably from the school. After this affair I observed a marked change in Bradley towards me, very much in my favor; he never struck me again, and once he deigned to greet me with a smile.

Notwithstanding the severity of our treatment I continued to improve and was placed in the first class under charge of Dr. Bullard. Soon after my promotion to the first class, Bradley was dismissed, and was succeeded by Mr. Shaw (the present Judge Shaw) and so different was his conduct that there was not a boy but loved him. He was mild, amiable, and energetic, and very seldom resorted to punishment. I became a medal scholar and progressed in my studies. But an unpleasant affair occurred which caused me to leave school nearly a year before the usual time. The particulars are briefly, as follows:

A boy of a highly respectable family, and one of my classmates, wishing to have some fun, put a dead rat in the master's desk, unseen by any one. After the school had commenced, the master lifted the lid to get his rattan, and, as soon as he saw the rat he fixed his eye on me; and I was immediately called out and ordered to remove it. I could not avoid laughing, while I assured him I knew nothing about it. He grew furious; took me by the collar and drew me towards the desk, and ordered me again to take the rat out; he was in a violent passion. I however took the tongs from the fireplace, and held the rat up by the tail, which caused the boys to laugh; threw it out of the window and was going to my seat, when he clenched me again by the back of the neck and commenced whaling me with his rattan. I felt that I was unjustly whipped, and would not stand it. So I clenched him, and sung out "murder" at the top of my voice. The whole school was now in an uproar, I had him fast by the legs; he was unable to strike me again, so we scrabbled together a few minutes, when I let go my hold. He was so exhausted that he fairly panted for breath. The boy* for whose crime I was receiving the punishment had not magnanimity enough to rise and own the deed but calmly looked on and saw me receive his punishment.

*Since dead, and for many years held a responsible situation under the State Government.

At the closing of the school as I was going from my seat, Bullard ordered me to stop, and he then forbade me entering the school-room again. I just replied, that he need not be troubled about that, for I never intended to come again, neither did I wish ever to have anything more to do with him, adding: you have whipped me for the act of another, who was too cowardly to own it, and I think I can point him out. But remember Sir, that this affair remains between you and I to be adjusted at another time. As I was passing down the centre aisle of the school-room, the usher met me, saying, "I wish you to remain a few minutes after the school has retired," and requested me to step into his desk. Accordingly, after all had gone out, he very affectionately expressed his regret at what had happened. I assured him of my innocence of the affair, which he fully believed, shook me by the hand and wished me well. I went immediately home and acquainted the family with what had occurred, showed them the scars upon my legs made by the rattan. All seemed much affected on account of my undeserved punishment, and also much indignation towards the boy who was the cause of it. I continued my studies at home and probably lost nothing by leaving school. I regretted this affair very much, and felt it more sensibly than I should have done had it occurred a few months previous, as the following story will show. Unfortunately for me on my return from New York, I became associated with several very bad boys, although they belonged to respectable families, and were smart, intelligent lads, yet their habits were very bad; using much profane language, and were very fond of boxing, and on some occasions absenting themselves from school. All these bad habits I imbibed and became one of them. My language at times was awfully profane, and I was frequently engaged in a fight; sometimes I got well whipped and then again have flogged boys much larger than myself. Our gang, as we were called, were notorious for all kinds of mischief, not of thieving, however, or of doing any one an injury, but of playing tricks on boys, and of doing many things for sport that could be called by no other name than mischief. We often got into difficulties, some of which were of a serious character.

At this time there existed a feud between a class of boys denominated the aristocracy, and boys who did not come under this category, and between these two classes there was little association.

One day four of us went over to the bottom of the Common to have a swim; the water then came up to the foot of the knoll west of the great tree, and by wading out twenty yards, was deep enough for bathing. We selected a clean spot, where we undressed, and had just thrown off our clothes, when four of the above described chaps came down also for a bath. They commenced with their feet, kicking our clothes aside to make room for themselves. We demanded of them what right they had to meddle with our clothing One of them, in a very haughty manner, replied, "*Inferior should move for their superiors.*" "Do you hear that?" say one of our party. There were four of us and four of them but they were much the stoutest boys. However, we consulted the matter a few minutes, and determined to fight them We were all undressed, and in a good trim for a battle. was to commence by attacking the largest, who was alread in the water. I waded out and clinched him, but soon foun he was too many guns for me; his arms were so much longer than mine that I could hardly get a chance to hit hin The others sung out for quarters. They then apologized fc the insult, and we were ever after good and recognizabl friends. Another of these gentry, a fellow older and muc heavier than myself, grossly insulted me in the school yar one day, which ended in a fight. I whipped him in goc fashion, and to his perfect satisfaction. He belonged to wh: was then called one of the first families in Boston, and w afterwards a talented and distinguished lawyer. His fath was one of our most prominent statesmen, and as I have b fore observed, the sons of these rich men assumed a sort superiority over those of the lower and middling classe and scarcely would they ever mingle with them in play.

This foolish pride was often punished, and many a spru young gentleman had to walk home with a black eye or lamaged face, and on almost every occasion they commenced :he difficulty themselves, by assuming haughty airs, and try-ng to exercise a superiority over those who were not so well lressed.

One day a party of us were engaged in a game of cricket ın the Common, and it so happened that there were three of hese upper class on one side, and we wanted one more to nake even sides, so we took in a first rate boy, who was an xcellent scholar and of good deportment, when one of the hree just alluded to, threw down his bat, declaring he would ot play if this boy was chosen; for, said he, in a sneering ıanner, "*look at his dress.*" Now his dress was tidy and lean, though the cloth probably was not so fine as his who bjected to him. The boy felt hurt at the remark, but we ısisted that he *should* play, and any one who objected to im might leave the ground. The game went on and e had a good time. This boy afterwards became a very ealthy and successful merchant in New Orleans. The ·ader may possibly suppose that the objection on the part of .e rich boys to associate with those of the poorer class as, that they were vulgar and of low breeding.

This however was not the case, for there were boys whose ırents were poor and industrious, who were exemplary in eir deportment, good scholars, and many of them to my ıowledge became men of fortunes; many have filled high .d honorable positions in the navy, army, and in the gen-ıl government. And I have lived to see some of those ιo were born with a silver spoon in their mouth, dragging ›ng their lives in poverty and destitution.

> "Honor and shame from no condition rise;
> Act well your part, there all the honor lies."

I have spoken several times of resenting personal insults en a boy, but since I have become a man I have thought .t it was far more magnanimous to pass by than to avenge m, although it often caused a hard struggle to do so. It vritten of Bonaparte that while on the Island of Elba he lared to a friend that he never had resented a personal insult. But a personal injury is quite another matter. He who injures me in either my property or reputation, may create a pang in the bosom of my family that may not be removed until the grave encloses them; and he who does this must expect his recompense; for the Almighty hath said, "*Vengeance is mine, I will repay, saith the Lord.*"

Once more I came near losing my life in a very foolish manner. I had a large bow gun with a very strong bow, and an arrow fitted with a long sail needle projecting over three inches from the end. One of my companions out of mere sport, deliberately took up the gun and shot the arrow into my back, standing only about five or six yards from me The needle entered just above the kidney, probably a half an inch, and it was with much difficulty that we pulled i out. The doctor pronounced it a miraculous escape. Had i entered the kidney, in all probability it would have cause my death. Thus was I spared again, and it was eviden my time had not yet come.

I had as a classmate an intimate acquaintance, a la about my own age; who was both amiable and exemplar and was received as a member of Dr. Baldwin's (Baptist church, at the age of eleven years. He came to me one da in an affectionate manner, saying he wished to have som conversation with me, and commenced by asking if I eve thought of death and of the judgment, and if I thought was prepared to die. To all of which I answered in tl negative; but immediately felt the weight of these impo tant interrogatories. He then in the most friendly ar sympathizing manner, alluded to the bad company I ke and the profane language he so frequently heard from m I was much affected, and thanked him for his kind repro He then invited me to go with him to an old barn where was accustomed to go every day for secret prayer. I cc sented, and the next day went with him. He knelt, a desired me to kneel by his side, and then, in the most f vent manner, prayed that I might be led to see the error my ways and to seek repentance and forgiveness throu Jesus Christ. I also made an attempt to offer up a pra myself. I now felt a determination to break off from former associates, and also from my bad habits, embrace religion and follow the precepts of the Bible. My kind and faithful friend whom I will now introduce to the reader was the Rev. James Colman, who died on his passage to India, whither he was going to join the Burman Missions. James continued faithful, evincing towards me a truly brotherly affection.

I found it rather hard to disengage myself from my old associates, but was frank and open, telling them that I had seen my errors and was determined to forsake them. At this they sneeringly replied that as I had now turned Methodist, I had better go and preach. A good opportunity offered on the first Saturday of each month, for seeing the result of bad company and early vices. At the head of West street, and near to our writing school, right against the gate leading to the Mall, the public whipping post was erected; (at that time there was no House of Correction,) the whipping commenced at eleven o'clock, A. M., just about the time our school was dismissed. I have seen many a poor fellow stripped to the bare skin, and receive from twenty to one hundred lashes with the cat o' nine tails, the number depending on the magnitude of the crime. One man who was sentenced to stand in the pillory for a fraud against an insurance company, made a confession of the many crimes he had committed, attributing his vicious life to bad company in his boyhood. His confession was very affecting, and certainly could not fail of making a deep impression on many who heard him. I had been a reformed boy nearly three months, when the unpleasant school affair took place. My friend James understood the whole matter, and was well satisfied who the offender was, so my reputation did not suffer in his estimation. We continued our visits to the barn, and spent much of our leisure time together. I continued my studies at home, mingling no more with boys at play. I had access to a carpenter's shop, and was quite handy with tools. Much of my time was spent in making small articles for the neighbors, such as chests, benches and clothes horses, &c., which kept me well supplied with spending money.

CHAPTER II.

Determined to go to Sea, — Prospect of a voyage, — Severely injured and could not go, — Obtained another, — First attempt at cooking, — Severity of the Captain, — Arrival at Rotterdam, — Occurrence, — Sail for home, — Boarded by English Cruisers, — Severe gale on George's bank, — Captain intoxicated, — Captured and carried to Halifax, — Insults, — Arrival of the English fleet, — Affair of the Chesapeake, — Whipping through the fleet, — And execution of the deserter, — Occurrences at Halifax, — Description of the Execution, — And previous behavior of Sam Jackson, — Execution on board the St. Mary's at Vera Cruz.

For some years previous, and up to this time, I had been much inclined to read voyages, and travels, which created a strong desire for going to sea. And as I was then about fourteen years of age, the usual time for boys to choose their future profession, was *determined* on going to sea, although my friends were much opposed to it at first. They at length yielded to what they saw was my fixed determination.

I was acquainted with a Mr. Wilson, who was also intimate in our family, he was then mate of the brig Sally belonging to Nehemiah Parsons, Esq. She was then under repairs receiving new rigging, &c., and when ready for sea was bound to the Mediterranean. Mr. Wilson procured a chance for me as cabin-boy. I went on board and was set at work with the riggers. On the third day after I had joined her, a man in the maintop having a seven pound maul in his hand, driving the eye of a shroud down over the mast head, let the maul slip while making a blow with it, his hand being greasy, it came down and struck on the top of my head, knocking me senseless for a few moments. They took me up, dressed the wound and carried me home.

This accident prevented me from going the voyage in her. But when I had recovered from the wound I commenced again searching for a voyage. It was not an easy matter then for a boy to get a voyage, as most shipmasters had their apprentices; and besides, it was not then as it is now with respect to ships; then, there were comparatively few to what we see now. Scarcely could a ship be found over three hundred tons, and it was also very rare to see a coppered vessel. At length after much searching obtained a chance on board a small barque of one hundred and sixty tons, bound to Rotterdam in Holland. When I went on board to enquire for a situation I was directed to the Skipper, who was seated on a hen-coop on the quarter-deck; he looked at me rather quzziingly when I asked him if he wanted a boy, and then began to enquire if I was not some runaway, and whether my parents were willing that I should go to sea, and various other questions of this sort which led me to think he had taken a nipper. I soon satisfied him who I was and invited him up to my grandfather's house. As all my uncles were at sea, had no one to arrange for me.

It was settled, however, that I was to go this voyage, and if I still persisted in going to sea then, he was to take me as an apprentice. The captain took me to a sailor's clothing store and rigged me out in a sailor's dress, with which I was much pleased. I now went on board for duty and my master informed me that he always made his boys cook on their first voyage. So my first business was to go into the galley and put everything to rights in the cooking department. He at the same time told me that in the mate's state-room there was a beef bone hanging up, with which I must make some soup for the people's dinner.

The crew being shipped were now to live on board. So I took the bone on deck and with an axe smashed it up, and threw it into the copper. Now I was in a quandary what kind of water to use for the soup, having the impression that sailors made soup with salt water. I did not like to ask for information, and as the fresh water pump was some distance up the wharf I decided on using salt water drawing it from along-side. There were plenty of vegetables of which I was no way sparing, but I don't think that a lady with a delicate stomach, on seeing my modus opperandi of preparing this savory dish, would have eaten much of it; I forgot to rinse the potatoes and turnips before putting them in, and washing the beef bone slipped my mind also, for as in the case of the salt water, some how or other I got the impression that sailors must eat dirt anyhow.

I felt some small degree of uncertainty about the success of my first attempt at soup making, neither did I venture to say anything about the salt water; but thought I would leave the event as the proof of the soup would be in the eating.

At 12 o'clock the mate came to the galley to know if dinner was ready. I told him it had been boiling three hours, and I thought it was done. "Well, give the men their dinner, then go and set the table in the cabin." In the meantime he took a quid about the size of a musket cartridge from his mouth, and holding it in his left hand took out a ladle full of the boiling beverage, and after blowing and sipping a few minutes, turned round to me saying, "you young dog, you have put in too much salt, but it's good soup though, don't put in so much next time." "No sir."

So I came to the conclusion that soup should be made with fresh water, although I heard no grumbling from the sailors.

Our cargo being on board and everything ready for sea we sailed on the first of June, 1807, for Rotterdam. The next day I was quite sea-sick and could hardly crawl to the camboose house. I began to have some suspicion that our captain was what old sailors call a "horse," and I also discovered that it was his intention to be very severe on me, for I was so sick that I could hardly hold up my head, he sent me to look for what he called a creeper, a cooking utensil generally called a spider.

I had never seen it among the galley fixings; yet in a tyrannical manner he ordered me to find it.

I began to wish myself back again, for when drunk,

which was nearly half the time, he would grin and show his teeth like a monkey, threatening to flog me declaring it was the only method of making a smart man of a boy.

In a few days my sea-sickness had disappeared, and I was all right again.

The ship's bill of fare, the following of which is a true copy, was stuck up in the cabin, and from the orthography of the bill, it will seem to be evident, that the schoolmaster was not *on board.*

Sundy—bef and pork and podins and peters.

Mondy—bef and pork and peters.

Tusdy—pork and bens.

Wensdy—salt fish peters and pork fat.

Thusdy—bef and pork and podins.

Fridy—pork and bens.

Saterdy—salt fish peters and pork fat.

The first line of this remarkable document would read thus, in the English language:

Sundays—Beef, Pork, Puddings, and Potatoes.

Besides my duty as cook, cabin-boy, and steward, I had to loose and furl the royals, and as we had but one top-mast studdingsail, and but one boom, it devolved on me to shift the latter from side to side as occasion required, which was no easy job when she was rolling heavy, a trick she was well accustomed to. In tacking ship it was my duty to let go the fore-sheet, and shift over the middle stay-sail-sheet. One day when we had tacked, and after I had let go the fore-sheet, I jumped below to secure a can of molasses that I had just drawn; I was not below more than half a minute, the captain saw me go down and came to the hatchway with the end of the top-sail buntling in his hand, waiting for me to come up, and as soon as my head was above deck he commenced, and I am sure I shall never forget that *rope's ending.*

It may almost be set down as a proverb, and I have seen it verified in my commerce with men, that we as often get punished for doing our duty as for neglecting it.

My good captain seemed to labor under the impression

that flogging was a very necessary and indispensable branch of discipline in my education for a sailor. And whether he considered that the use of a rope's end was a vulgar mode of punishment, and wishing to treat me with some degree of refinement, I cannot say, for he had a nice cat o' nine tails made by one of the seamen, nicely pointed and grafted, and pretty enough to hang up in a museum; the elaborate finish of this cat the skipper looked upon as the profoundest test of skill in seamanship. After taking a stiff glass of grog, he called me into the cabin, and with his usual monkey grin, held out this pretty plaything, and commenced his address:

"*You see this, don't you?*"

"Yes, sir."

"*Well, when you first come aboard, I liked your looks, but know'd I should have a job to cook you. Look out now.*"

He then hung it up against his state-room door, and told me to be off. He never had the pleasure, however, of using his man-maker upon my back, for that night it disappeared, and was never seen afterwards; and what was very singular, he did not inquire for it. But I rather suspected that he had some idea where it went.

We had been out forty-two or three days, and were drawing nigh to our port of destination, and not once was I found to be remiss in my duty. I was not allowed a moment of time, even to mend my clothes.

Our cargo was coffee, and every night while taking it in, the sweepings of the deck, in which was some considerable quantity of coffee, were placed in barrels, and kept for ship use, and when my cooking was done for the day, I had this coffee to pick, and I have often shut myself up in the camboose, in order that I might have an opportunity to read a chapter in my Bible.

Things now began to be more favorable. I got through with my various duties without difficulty, although a sailor knocked me into the lee scuppers one day for refusing to rinse out his tin pot. I picked myself up, and had not the mate interfered, I think it doubtful whether he would ever have struck another.

I am sorry to acknowledge it, but to this day I find it hard to forgive an injury. I know it is unchristianlike, and contrary to the precepts of the religion of Christ, and earnestly hope that God will give me grace to overcome it.

And while I am now writing, (1856) my mind involuntarily glances over the past, when a recollection of the wrongs and impositions that I have suffered, flits before me, I find it necessary to lay down my pen until the perturbation ceases.

We arrived at Helvcot-sluys in forty-four days from Boston; took a pilot and proceeded up the river, stopping at Dort, Scravendale and Schiedam, and then to Rotterdam, hauling in to Glasshaven to discharge our cargo.

While lying at Rotterdam our captain lived on shore, which gave me rather more latitude than if he had been on board. I frequently went on shore with the sailors in the evening, and as the general resort of sailors are bad houses, and their habits tending to drunkenness, my accompanying them was of no benefit to my morals, for on one occasion they got me quite intoxicated on anise seed, which made me very sick all next day.

I did not go on shore again, but spent my time in reading, after my work was done.

There was now a general armistice throughout the continent of Europe. Joseph Bonaparte was king of Holland.

After receiving our homeward cargo, we sailed for Boston.

American vessels were at this time subject to much annoyance from English and French cruisers, but more particularly from the former, as they were very abusive to our flag, frequently bringing vessels to, insulting the captains, and in many instances impressing the seamen.

The French had issued the Berlin and Milan decrees, by which all vessels, of whatever nation, having enemy's goods on board, were considered as lawful prizes, and dealt with accordingly.

The English, on the other hand, had their orders in council, which also confiscated all vessels having enemy's property on board. American masters, in foreign ports, were often insulted by British officers, and I recollect a laughable incident that occurred in Gibraltar, and was well acquainted with the captain who was the hero of the story, and tells it so humorously. His name was Breck, but usually pronounced Brick.

One day, while at the Crown and Anchor hotel, in company with several American shipmasters, who were all seated in the principal room, enjoying themselves over a bottle of wine, there came in some British naval officers, who, finding the table occupied, went out grumbling, and from one of them was heard the epithet, " —— Yankees."

" Did you hear that ?" says Breck, to the others. They all heard it, and Breck jumped up, and following the officers into the hall, inquired which of the gentlemen it was that made use of that insulting language, and to whom it was addressed.

The British officer, who by the way was a captain in the navy, looking rather indignantly on Breck, who was rather short, though very stout, while the Englishman was a tall, raw-boned fellow, replied: " To you, if you take it up."

Breck immediately threw off his coat, put his fist in the captain's face, and told him to defend himself.

By this time a number of spectators had gathered around, and the noble Englishman finding himself in rather an awkward position, replied that he was not going to make a blackguard of himself.

" My name," said he, " is Clay, of His Majesty's brig Ranger, and I will give you any satisfaction you wish, in a gentlemanly manner."

" Well," says Breck, with his fist still clenched, " if your name is Clay, my name is Brick, and I'm already baked, and I want satisfaction now."

This created such a roar of laughter all around, that the by-standers as well as the British officer, insisted on settling it on the spot over as much champagne as all could drink, and the Englishman insisted on paying the bill. Thus ended this humorous affair.

We were boarded several times in the North Sea, and also in the English Channel, and were each time politely treated. Our crew were examined, and as all had protections but two we had no difficulty with the British officers, excepting once;

then the boarding officer was very impudent, speaking very *scurrilously* of American protections. This, however, we took no notice of, and the fellow went off on board his frigate.

With respect to the two men who had no protections, in order to save them from impressment, (as they were actually deserters from a British man-of-war,) they were entered in the ship's log-book, as having fallen from the maintop-sail yard while reefing; and when a man-of-war hove in sight, they were both snugly stowed away, and as we were apparently weak-handed, no attempt was made to impress any of the rest.

The captain had now materially relaxed his rigid conduct towards me. I had picked all the coffee, and had plenty of leisure time; our passage homeward was rather rough. On George's bank, we encountered a severe gale; it commenced in the morning, and by noon it blew furiously, and continued to increase until the following midnight. Our good skipper during this gale was sewed up below; at one ime, during the night, the mate came down and tried to get he captain up, as we were fast drifting on to the shoal, and by the mate's calculations were very near it; but all he ould get was a grunt; indeed, it was a fearful gale, but we ode it out nicely; the next day was fine and clear, and the ld man came on deck looking quite sheepish.

On that same afternoon while we were all busy in geting hings to rights and preparing for bending cables, a British Cruiser hove in sight, and was soon upon us. She be-onged to the Halifax Station, and was cruising in Boston ay for vessels coming from Europe; as in many cases, they ere found to have prohibited goods on board.

After detaining us two hours, and closely examining our apers, they declared us a prize to his Brittanic Majesty;—ccordingly we were ordered to get our traps up, and be all eady to go on board the man-of-war, when her boat re-urned with the prize crew.

The captain was permitted to remain on board the barque. n the return of the man-of-war-boat with the prize master nd crew, we were all bundled into the boat and put on oard the Cruiser. On getting on board we were ordered on the quarter-deck, until disposed of. The two unfortu nate fellows, who were lost off the maintop-sail yard, wer immediately seized as deserters, but by entering again noth ing more was said about their desertion.

I saw one of these same fellows a year afterwards in Bos ton; he had deserted again, and by a perilous adventur had succeeded in reaching Portland, and then came to Bos ton.

Soon after our arrival on board the man-of-war, the cap tain ordered the prize master, who was then on board th barque, to fill away for Halifax, while the Englishman con tinued on her cruise.

We were not confined, but put into watches for duty.

The barque having filled away, ran down under the man of-war's stern, and when within talking distance, my captai very earnestly requested of the English commander that h might have his boy returned to him. I stood near him, an said I did not wish to go back. "Never fear my lad, yo are not going," said he, and made no reply to the captain request; he ordered the prize master to strip the prize in mediately on his arrival at Halifax. We then squared awa standing S. E., and the barque proceeded on her course fo Halifax.

On this first night, I came near making a hole in the wate I was sent out on the foreroyal-yard, to stop a small portic of the sail that had got loose, and while out on the lee-ya arm, the foot rope was so long, that it brought my chin again the yard, and I could not have got into the bunt again, ha it not been that a tall Canadian had just come up, it bein his lookout at the mast head; he got hold of my arm an assisted me in: otherwise, in all probability, I must ha let go.

We continued our cruise along the Southern coast, an spoke a ship from Norfolk, bound to Cadiz; we next spoke schooner from Thomaston, bound to Barbadoes, with lin potatoes and onions. The captain was asked if he would bri on board some of his vegetables, which he did, and for whi he was well paid. We requested the boat's crew to report us aken, on their arrival in the U. S., which they promised to lo; we also gave them our names.

We now stood to the eastward a few days, and not falling n with anything, squared away for Halifax, and arrived here about ten days after the arrival of the Barque, encountering a smart gale the night before.

As soon as we appeared off the harbor, our captain, who 'as permitted to visit the barque when he pleased, as she 'as in charge of the admiralty officers, went on board nd hoisted the American ensign; this being contrary to he common usage of prizes, an officer was immediately depatched from the guard-ship, with a most indecent message o the captain, ordering him to haul down that ——— ankee flag. He at first positively refused claiming the ight, as an American, to show his colors, but he was over-owered and obliged to submit.

The Barque's sails were unbent, and much of the running igging unrove; the crew were sent ashore from the man-of-'ar, but I was sent on board the Barque, to wait on the ing's officers, as they were called; there were two of them, n Irishman and a blue-nose, and both of them regular sots; hey had access to the gin, of which they drank freely, and ere often drunk.

Prizes came in every day, although on our arrival, there as but one there. She was a long, rakish, Baltimore clipper, taken by the Cleopatra frigate. The prize was from 'era Cruz, with a large amount of specie on board, bound Baltimore, and under what pretext she was taken I could ot learn.

In three weeks from our arrival, there were twenty-five merican vessels sent in as prizes. A large portion of the en belonging to these prizes were impressed and claimed British subjects, and no doubt many of them were.

The people of Halifax, and more particularly, the naval ficers, seemed to have a very contemptible opinion of merican sailors. Calling them grass combers, lubberly shermen, and log haulers, saying also, that were it not for nglish sailors, our ships could not pursue their voyages.

On this subject I shall have something to say at anoth time.

Our trial was to commence on the thirtieth day from t] libel; but by compromise, our captain was to pay a certa sum, which, by so doing, we could leave Halifax as soon we could get ready; but if we stood trial, should, in a probability, be detained through the winter. And in ord to meet this proposition, we were permitted to land, and se a quantity of gin free from duty. Accordingly, we haul into the wharf for this purpose, also to get the Barque rea for sea.

On the day that we hauled in, the English fleet arriv from Hampton-roads—after the fracas with the U. S. Fri ate Chesapeake. And that night, such was the invetera hatred towards Americans, the rabble came down the wha along-side the barque, insulting us, by throwing stones ar brickbats upon our deck. We of course were obliged to su *mit to this patriotic indignity.*

A particular and correct account of the Chesapeake affa may be found in the books treating upon the origin of t late war with England. But as it may be, that the read cannot obtain such a book, I will briefly relate it, accordi to the best of my remembrance.

The British fleet consisted of the Leopard, 50, Ca Humphreys, Frigates, Jason, Melampus, and Chichester. H ifax and Squirrel, sloops of War. This fleet, and the U. frigate Cheaspeake lay together in Hampton-roads. T Chesapeake commanded by Com. Barron, was destined for t Mediterranean, to join the American fleet off Tripo Three men from one of the English boats, deserted while Norfolk, and to obtain money for a frolic, shipped at the S. rendezvous under assumed names.

The recruiting officer afterwards positively declared th when he shipped these men, he did not know that they we English deserters; for if he had known it he should r have received them. And even after they had entered, a proper application had been made to him they wou have been released; and if necessary, he would have tak the loss of the advance money upon himself.

It appeared that one of the deserters, Jenkin Ratford, ·ossly insulted one of his officers in the street at Norfolk, ıd I think it was reported that he struck the officer. All ree were sent on board the Chesapeake, after their liberty ıd expired.

As soon as Captain Humphreys had received official infor- ation that these men were on board the Chesapeake, he ldressed a note to Commodore Barron, requesting that the en might be returned to their ship. To this request Com- odore Barron would not consent, and on the following orning got his ship under way and when abreast of the ɜopard, the latter gave her the contents of one division ɔm the main deck, and every gun was shotted.

As the Chesapeake was not in a condition to fight, her bles having been hauled out of the tiers and strung along the main deck guns, they were taken up to make room ·r a quantity of provisions intended for the fleet in the ɜditerranean, and had not yet been put below. Under ese circumstances, and to prevent bloodshed, Barron order- the colors to be struck, at which the firing ceased. A at came immediately from the Leopard to the Chesapeake which was her first lieutenant, with a note from Captain ımphreys, sincerely regretting the course he felt himself der the necessity of pursuing in order to recover his ɜn.

The lieutenant anxiously inquired if there had been any ɜ hurt, and appeared much pleased to learn that so little mage had been done, and then informed Commodore rron that Captain Humphreys still insisted upon having men, and that he had received orders not to return ;hout them.

Commodore Barron, to avoid further trouble, mustered his w, the men were picked out and taken on board the Leop- l, then the British fleet unmoored and went to sea, bound Halifax.

Commodore Barron was tried by a Court-martial and nd guilty of gross mismanagement in not having his p ready for action. And also for hauling his colors vn, was suspended from the U. S. Naval service for a number of years, afterwards reinstated, and killed Comm- dore Decatur in a duel.

We now return to Halifax again.

"Down with the Yankees!" was the prevailing cry nc among men and boys. The fact of making a Yankee fri ate haul her colors down, and having her crew mustered l a British lieutenant, and three deserters taken out, w a "consummation devoutly to be wished for."

The independence of the U. S. was now to be forever a nihilated. The American Stars and Stripes would soon hanging among the trophies of St. Pauls, and the Yank rebels would ere long be made to receive their old shackl again. This was the bombastic grog-shop talk of Halifax

A gang of rowdy boys attacked me one morning on n return from market, and were determined to whip r because I was a Yankee. So I laid down my mark basket and looking them in the face, said, "whip aw my good fellows, I suppose you want another Chesapeake v tory, there are plenty of you to flog one, *only don't steal* ɿ *meat.*" They went off, doing nothing more than givi me a few hearty curses.

A Court-martial was immediately convened on board t Chichester, for the trial of the three deserters. The result which was, that Jenkin Ratford was to be hanged at t yard-arm, and the other two to be whipped through t fleet.

As we lay near the ships of war I had a good opportun of seeing both sentences carried into execution, those w were to be whipped were to receive 500 lashes each.

Kind reader, probably you have never seen a punishm of this kind inflicted, and I hope you never will. We r with horror, accounts that have come to us from the inqu tions of Europe. Our blood has fairly chilled in our vei when we have read of the rack, and of being broken on wheel, and the process of roasting over a slow fire. All t has been done through ignorance and superstition, and some inquisitorial dungeon, as though the dark hellish sce were too dreadful for the sun to look upon! But whippin man through the fleet throws that entirely in the shade;

EXECUTION OF RATFORD.

here, in open daylight, a human being is tied up, immovabl and lacerated to death.

It is not my purpose, at *this* time, to comment upon tl crimes, punishment, and discipline of seamen. This subject shall take up at another time.

I will now describe the *whipping through the fleet.* Tl poor wretch, after sentence has been passed upon him, is ke confined in double irons, under charge of a sentinel. Tl day of punishment is fixed by the commander-in-chief, aı at an early hour on that day the fleet are notified by sign

The punishment generally commences at nine A. M. launch, or large cutter is fitted with a platform from t stern sheets to the forward thwart; two spars are erect upon the platform about eight feet high, and another sp lashed across the top, from one to the other. Two hat gratings are now arranged, one for the prisoner to stand up and to which his feet are tied. The other is placed uprig between the spars, and to which also his knees are secur A piece of line called a seizen is fastened to each wrist, a both hands are tied up to the cross piece overhead.

Now, here he is, with feet and knees secured and bc hands lashed above his head. Before he is secured, howev he is stripped of everything but his trousers, his shirt is ca fully thrown over his back until the punishment commenc

In the boat there are the ship's surgeon, the lieutena and midshipmen appointed to see the sentence of the Cou martial executed.

A guard of marines with loaded muskets and fixed b onets, and every officer with his side-arms, and clad in f uniform.

The boat thus manned is towed to the admiral ship, wh the flogging commences. The number of lashes recei along-side each ship depends upon the number of ships the fleet. If they are many then, of course, the number stripes is lessened at each ship. The whole number as I h before stated, is generally from three to five hundred, an it is the opinion of the doctor that nature will not bear punishment at one time, the poor fellow is taken back to ship again, placed under the doctor's charge until he gets strong enough to receive the balance.

There have been cases however, where the victim has died under the punishment; nevertheless, the number of lashes must be given upon the back of the corpse! This, an old English man-of-wars-man assured me he had seen.

As soon as the boat containing the prisoner has arrived along-side the admiral's ship, all hands are called to witness punishment, which they do by manning the rigging and yards. The first lieutenant then goes down into the boat, and reads the sentence of the Court-marshal, also that clause in the articles of war relating to desertion; during the time of this reading, every head is uncovered and a death-like stillness prevails.

Previously, the boatswain of each ship has been directed to have his cats, (cat-o-nine tails) in readiness. The cat, is a whip, with a short handle about fourteen inches long, handsomely covered with cloth, to the end of which are nine pieces of small cord about the size of cod line, and about a yard long; at the end of each line are two or three knots, and every stroke with this whip, cuts through the skin quite into the flesh, and the boatswain's mate, who applies it, is commonly an athletic fellow, and is obliged to give his utmost strength at every blow, and generally a fresh boatswain's mate takes the cat at the end of each dozen.

As soon as the reading is over, the lieutenant gives a nod to the master-at-arms, who removes the shirt from the back of the prisoner; the boatswain's mate is then ordered to commence; and at the first blow, the master-at-arms, counts audibly, one, and so on, until the designated number is completed.

And if the smallest portion of pity is manifested by the boatswain's mate in slacking his hand in the least perceptible manner, he is sternly told, "Boatswain's mate, do your duty, Sir." At the first three or four blows the cries and entreaties of the poor wretch are heart-rending, crying out, *O God Almighty, save me! O Jesus Christ, have mercy upon me!* Many a time have I heard these piercing cries while the flesh upon the back was cut into strips.

The doctor has hold of his pulse and determines the condition for endurance. If the poor fellow faints, which is often the case, some brandy or cold water is given him, by means of which he is soon revived.

This is the mode of punishment in the navy; or rather it was until a few years since, when by the humane remonstrances of the people, punishment with the cat was abolished. These two men on whom this dreadful sentence was inflicted were carried to the Hospital in a state of insensibility. Although I was not near enough to see their backs myself, I was told by a man who had a good opportunity of seeing them, that they were a mass of coagulated blood from the shoulders tc the loins, as above the former and below the latter a blow must not be struck.

They were carried from the boat to the Hospital on a sor(of litter. Before we left Halifax I was told that one of them was able to sit up a few hours each day and pick oakum.

I refrain from saying anything more on this painful sub ject at present, as in the course of my narrative I shal have occasion to mention acts of cruelty in our own nav) that would put a savage to the blush.

Jenkin Ratford, one of the three deserters, who wa: sentenced to be hanged, was strung up to the foreyard-arn of the Jason, frigate, on the Monday morning subsequent t the whipping through the fleet. He was run up amid th smoke of the bow gun, over which the platform was erected His crime, though it was adjudged the most flagrant, ye his punishment was comparatively nothing as viewed wit that of the others; for the explosion of the gun instantl kills the victim and his death is easy.

As the reader may never have seen an execution o board a man-of-war, I will describe this melancholy scen by narrating the execution of Sam Jackson, a seaman, o board the U. S. Ship St. Mary's in the harbor of Vera Cru: Sept. 17, 1846. The account is given by the Rev. Fitch W Taylor, Chaplain in the U. S. Navy, and which I here tra scribe.

Jackson while in a state of intoxication had struck a

officer, the penalty for which is death, or some other punishment which a court-martial shall adjudge. He was found guilty, and the following sentence passed upon him, viz: that Samuel Jackson, seaman, of the U. S. Navy, be executed at such time and place as the commander-in-chief should direct; and that these proceedings, findings, and sentence having been approved by the commander-in chief, therefore, the commander-in-chief, directs that the said Samuel Jackson, seaman, be hanged by the neck, at the foreyard-arm of the U. S. ship, St. Mary's, on Thursday, 17th day of September, 1846, between the hours of ten A. M., and meridian.

The general order then continues. "In order that a suitable impression may be made on the minds of all persons in the squadron, and that there may be nothing to divert their thoughts from so melancholy a spectacle, and that they may be duly impressed with the awful consequences which must ever follow such violation of law, as were committed by this unhappy man, it is directed that no work be done on that day; that when the preparatory signal is made for execution by the Cumberland, a yellow flag shall be displayed from the foreroyal-mast head of the St. Mary's. The officers and crew of every vessel of the squadron present, shall be mustered on deck until the yellow flag on board the St. Mary's is hauled down. Commanders will direct that no boats nor persons be absent from the vessels of the squadron on that day, on any pretence whatever, without permission from the commander-in-chief." The fate of this unhappy man, it is hoped, will have a salutary influence, and impress the minds of all present, with the necessity of keeping a strict watch over their passions and tempers at all times and in all situations. The Rev. Chaplain goes on to state: "Yesterday, Sept. 13, being Sunday, I preached on board the St. Mary's. The preceding general order was read immediately after my leaving the ship for the Cumberland, having been received during the services, and to-day, Monday, I have visited the prisoner on board the St. Mary's; he had requested to be removed from the general gaze of the crew, and have a place assigned him where he might collect his mind and endeavor to prepare to meet the sudden summons to appear before his Maker. I had already been interested in the man, having heard a description of his proper demeanor before the Court — his being far superior to the general character of seamen, and his personal appearance at once pleaded much in his favor. His defense was brief, and it is said to have drawn tears to the eyes of several of the Court. He expressed to me much fear that God would not forgive his sins, therefore had but little hope. He continued, "it is a hard thing to die, but to die a violent death is harder still, and so short a time to prepare for it! I fear that my present desires and purposes of repentance and prayer to God, are but the result of the fear of meeting the judgment day; but a life of virtue and of piety looks to me far the most inviting, and had I to relieve my time, I trust I should pursue a different course and lead a religious life. But I fear again that even these feelings and impressions are but the result of my fearful apprehension as I cast my view into the other world. I have not got the brokenness of heart I wish to feel, and the peace of mind of which I have read that a sincere penitent experiences. I wish it — I have prayed for it — but do not feel it." Such was the drift of this man's own voluntary confession, made with great modesty and humility of demeanor. I spent considerable time with him — prayed with him — gave him marked passages in the different parts of the prayer book to be read, and left him; while he earnestly entreated that I would be with him as often as I could. I shall see him again to-morrow, early in the morning. Agreeably to my purpose, I went on board the St. Mary's this morning, 15th, to visit the prisoner, whose term of life seems in the opinion of most of the officers of the fleet, to be drawing to a close. I found Lieutenant P. with him, (the officer he had knocked down,) a young gentleman much to be commended for the course he had pursued towards this man. Lieutenant P. was now giving him christian counsel and endeavoring to further him to his preparation to leave the world. He too had already been to the commander-in-chief, to express his hope, if compatible with his view of sustaining the influence of the discipline in the navy, that this man might be pardoned. And the prisoner seemed not insensible to such kindness; and no one can be- iold it without approbation and commendation towards Lieu- enant P., and feel that it was an unkind blow indeed that should have been directed to such an officer. The young nan continued to weep, hopeless of having the time of his nortal life extended beyond "to-morrow," as he said, at this iour at which we were then conversing, "and might it be hat he himself could see the commodore, and plead himself efore him, in his own language, for his life — but it seemed t could not be, and I will think no more about it!" The iour, and more was passed! and the principle part of the nterview was spent in conversation on the topics that make ıp the plan of salvation, through Jesus Christ, who came to ave sinners. A boat having come for me, from the St. Mary's, n answer to a signal, made by the Cumberland, I went on oard the St. Mary's, this morning, Thursday, 17, a little fter 9 o'clock, as no indications were discoverable from any uarter, that the wretched man condemned to death would e pardoned or reprieved. There had been many conjectures nade as to the ulterior design of the commander-in-chief, nd various sentiments advanced as to the probability that he execution would take place. I believe it was quite a revalent impression throughout the squadron, though that entiment seemed to change at different hours, that this un- ortunate man at the last moment would be pardoned.

I had myself felt the influence of this impression, and I ad delayed until this morning, to make known to the cap- in a wish which the prisoner had expressed to me yesterday, iat I would be with him on the day of execution. It was sential for me to do this in view of the general order, That no boat should leave the ship on the day of execu- on." On application to Captain Forrest, a signal was made the St. Mary's for a boat for me.

Still did I hope there might be relief for this penitent an, and yet I take not upon me here to criticize the sen- nce of the court, its approval or its execution, while I yet lt in the yearnings of my heart, for the life of the young aman, that it might be his destiny yet to live, and yet to velop the better traits of a character that seemed to embrace much of native elegance and superior capacity; that he might evince in life the sincerity of a hopeful purpose of following a path of virtue and a course of penitential obedience to the precepts of the gospel of Christ.

I reached the St. Mary's after a short pull over th troubled sea, agitated by the north wind, which had throwi the usually more calm surface of the water between the tw ships, into a tumult which I now felt to be emblematical o the agitated bosom of the unfortunate man I was seeking t see. I went directly to the screen, behind which I found th prisoner sitting upon his cot, with Lieut. P. by his side, wh offered to leave us if either myself or the prisoner desired i Neither did, and the Lieuteuant remained a short time long er, and then left me alone to attend this unfortunate ma until the summons should be brought to announce that th hour of his execution had come.

"I wish it were a less bright day," said the prisoner, " a it would then be in nearer keeping with my clouded fate."

"I told him, on the contrary, I wish it might emblem fort the light of the countenance of a God of mercy in his cas who forgives the penitent sinner through Christ, who suffere and died that we might forever live and be happy."

"I have sometimes thought of death," he said, "and times of sudden death, but I never dreamed that I shou come to such a death as this. Oh, it is a dreadful hour me! Yes, 'tis a dreadful hour. But God at times is bett to us than our fears. I have often thought before now wi what feelings a man condemned to die must hear the me senger that came to tell him his hour had come and he mu prepare to die, but I never thought such a messenger wou come to me, but it will soon come!"

"Yes, and yet the Saviour's death was such in sorrow a in manner, that he can feel for a heart that gives itself him, though agitated at such a moment of near approach such a death as yours is to be."

"I know the Saviour suffered more than I shall suff and I would willingly suffer the whole day at the yard-a in agony of body, if it could but atone for my sins and sa my soul; but that would not save me. Oh, God, have m

:y on my spirit. I have been a great sinner; I see that the inner's course is a hard one, and I have brought myself vhere I never thought I should be, about to suffer a violent leath, and I see that virtue and religion are the desirable hings to be pursued to make a man happy in this life, and ad I my life to live over again, I trust my course would be lifferent, and my life too, a virtuous and religious one."

I now encouraged him to hope in God's mercy through Christ. "You see now you have been on the wrong tack, nd now you would change it, and we hope you have done it ertainly in your views."

"And in less than an hour more," continued the prisoner, I shall stand before the face of my God."

It was now near four bells, or ten o'clock, as the prisoner hus spoke. His execution was to take place betwen the ours of ten and twelve; in a moment more the ship's bell truck ten, and there was a stir through the ship that broke he stillness that had before prevailed.

"There it is," said the poor fellow, "the hour of my death as come! Oh, God, have mercy on me! Give me strength o meet my doom that is soon to attend me! Give me some ttle peace before the final moment comes!"

"I said to him, probably they will delay; a signal is to be ade from the Cumberland, before the preparation for the ast scene shall be made."

"Yes, they may delay it to the last moment, but I would ot care to have it delayed; and oh, let me not be detained ng on deck."

"You shall not be; your wish shall be gratified," I replied, "but repose yourself on Jesus; he knows what you re to suffer; he is now your only hope, your only stay for rength."

"Oh, yes, there is no help for me elsewhere; a poor sinər, who pleads no extenuation for his sins. But it is hard die so soon — a violent, a felon's death; *and I have ken no life.* It has occurred to me, as the captain said, who ame to see me this morning, that there is hope as long as ere is life, though he gave me none, and I have no reasonble hope to live but a few moments longer. No, no, my iend, none!"

"But 'tis right I should say to you, Jackson, to mitigat though not entirely to relieve one thought that your deatl though a violent one, will not be the same as *the murder on the gallows.* Yours is a punishment at the yard-arn according to the usages of the service at sea, and the charg on which your sentence was based will be known, as they ar a high crime indeed at sea, *but not murder.*"

"Yes, but I would rather be put on the forecastle, I thinl and be shot."

"But 'tis of no moment, now," I continued, "it will nc be to you, if redeemed; the agitation of this hour, and th fell dishonor of a death at the yard-arm, shall give you t estimate with a deeper gratitude the blessedness of tha calm of heaven that shall gather over the soul which was lo and is found, that was exposed to eternal danger and is no rescued to an unchanging safety. It shall be certainty, an no more doubt; honor, and no more disgrace; holiness, an no more sin."

"Had I been confined on shore, away from the noise c shipboard, I might perhaps have had a better opportunity c thinking of the soul, and preparing for death, in the spac given me, and could I have had a sister or a brother ther how it would have soothed these hours. But I have tried t do my best, and I fear it has been too little," and here th poor fellow paused a moment, and then added: "I think must kneel down and pray now," and accordingly rose fro the cot on which we were both seated, and desiring that would not move, fell on his own knees, and audibly commune with his God in a prayer so fit and accurately expressed, th no word was uncharged with the feelings of a man ready die and make his peace with God, and to commend his spir to His care. Would to God a world could have heard i would to God a slumbering world could wake to the feelin of this man, who viewed with the vision of his awaken spirit the relation of his responsible being to eternity. should have knelt with him at this time, but he requested n to retain my seat, from that generally inherent principle a sailor's difference for an officer, which before had caus him, as I prayed with him, to offer me his jacket to kne upon, lest the deck might be too dusty for a kneeling-place. Alas! I thought, as I refused it, and other articles proffered, there is no need of bunting, or a damask cushion here, to kneel upon, when the anxious soul would look to God for forgiveness and salvation in its need, and when but a few hours more should consign the spirit to eternity.

Six bells now struck, (eleven o'clock,) and yet the summons came not. Still there was a stir over the decks which eemed to indicate it might be on its way. The stir was in answer to the preparatory signal now made from the Cumberland to have all things in readiness for executing the entence of the court-martial. The prisoner knew not the ignal, but his quick ear detected the movement, and as the ignal of the Cumberland fell to her deck, the yellow flag on oard the St. Mary's ran up to the royal-mast head.

All necessary preparations had been early made on board he St. Mary's, for executing the sentence now so soon to be onsummated. A small platform had been arranged on the rboard side of the forecastle, a little above one of the guns, nd supported by a stanchion, one end of which rested on the uzzle of the gun. This gun was loaded, the clue line was sed as the whip rope by which the unfortunate man was to e run up to the larboard arm of the foreyard; and this line as so rove as to connect along the yard with a weight of und shot, that was to descend by the foremast, and rouse e prisoner to the yard-arm; and this weight, for the time ing, was held in its place near the maintop, by a line that d over the muzzle of the shotted gun. On firing the gun, e shot would cut the line, and the weight fall, hauling the or fellow up to the yard-arm. And around the St. Mary's, this beautiful sheet of water, lay the different ships and her vessels of the fleet, nine or ten in number, in full view the transaction, which was now so rapidly maturing to its nale. The yellow flag flying at the foreroyal mast head; l eyes from these different ships were gazing with interest r the succeeding signal from the Cumberland, the next sigl would order the execution of the sentence of the court.

But in the meantime how was it with the prisoner, still vaiting in the agitation and fulness of his feelings, the summons which the signal from the flag ship would soon lead to. A little before, he had put on his shoes, remarking that he would do it, though it was of little matter whether he did it or not. And again of his jacket, neatly folded upon his cot, he said he did not know that he should need it. The day was warm and bright, and the ship's crews were dressed in white. It was evident, however, that the hour was near at hand, and ere long, indeed, the sentry placed his hand upon the canvas and elevated one wing of the screen, as the first lieutenant of the St. Mary's entered, saying that he had come on the melancholy duty, (naming the prisoner,) to have him prepare for the execution of the sentence which had been pronounced upon him. The master-at-arms advanced, relieved the prisoner's wrists from the irons, when he immediately arose and allowed his arms to be tied at the elbows behind him; in deep anguish he now burst forth:

"Oh, my God, that I should ever have been brought to this!" calling upon his Maker and his Saviour to be with him, and to extend to him mercy and strength in such a needed hour, and to receive him with pardon to himself. It was soon over; and he preferred that his hands should be tied also, and that his slippers should be removed from his feet. He was now conducted to the main deck of the ship near the capstan.

All hands having been piped to witness punishment, and were now mustered on the upper deck; the officers in uniform on the quarter-deck. Capt. Saunders of the St. Mary's advanced near to the prisoner, and read the death warrant, a the authority by which he was now called upon to have th sentence of the court-martial carried into effect. It wa done with a voice that showed deep emotions, and the silenc of the assembled officers and crew, showed how deeply solem was the transaction now being in execution. As the captai ended the warrant, the prisoner, standing pale and hopeless which gave interest to his finely chiseled face, spoke in a respectful tone: "I am ready sir!" and then bursting int tears, he said:

"Shipmates! I warn you to take example from me, not t give way to your passions. By doing it, I have lost my li in this world, and I fear have lost my soul for eternity; yet I have prayed to God and Jesus Christ to have mercy on my soul. I offer no extenuation for my offence; I freely forgive any one who may at all have urged me on in the course of passion. I freely forgive the Court who have pronounced sentence of death against me; the Commodore who approved that sentence, and all who have had anything to do with it. I have but a few more moments to live, and I pray God to have mercy on my poor soul. I pray Jesus Christ to have mercy on me; and I ask you all to pray for me the few moments more that I have to live."

When the prisoner had ended his brief and unpremeditated ıdmonitions to his shipmates, he walked forward from the :apstan to the mainmast where he stood, myself at his side, :he master-at-arms attending him while the 1st Lieutenant ıdvanced to the forecastle, to see that all things were in 'eadiness for ending the fearful tragedy, and while he was ;one, the prisoner let his own thoughts commune with his ›wn soul and his God, making a single remark or two, and aying to me, with other expressions:

"I have a faint hope now that God will receive me, but it s a faint hope. And there! see, there!" directing my eye 'ather himself looking forward to the larboard foreyard-arm, nd seeing the preparations that had been made for the final cene, and on the forecastle beneath the yellow flag which was ow flying at the foreroyal mast head. But soon he turned is face to the mainmast, and knelt on a coil of rigging beide it as I placed my hand on his shoulder to support him, nd buried my own face in my handkerchief as I leaned on ıe bits, while this man offered up another prayer in an audile tone for his own soul. One condemned in a few moments) offer up his life as an atonement for the broken laws of is country. He offered nothing to extenuate his crime, he ıpplicated at this hour that God would give him a little rength for the few moments he had to stay on earth. The st Lieutenant soon returned. The prisoner had risen, and ıough a few moments had passed, this scene with the solemity of an eternity had occurred, and whoever this man may ;, his spirit at this moment was absorbed in its petition for it salvation. As the Lieutenant approached the prisoner, and was about to advance to the forecastle with him,

"Jackson, two men," mentioning their names, "wish to speak to you; will you allow them to do so?"

He assented, and near the forecastle they met him. The first said, as the tears stood in his eyes, for he was intimate with the prisoner, "Will you tell me if I have ever done anything to urge you on to any wrong course, that I should be selected as your executioner?"

"No, George, I don't remember anything; but I believe you have rather urged me to suppress my passions. And, George, *I charge you*, that if you meet any of my friends, that you never tell them a word of my end; never lisp it."

The second came forward and said, "Have I ever urged you on to any acts of insubordination whatever?" No tears were in the eyes of this man; he was older and of a different class of face. The prisoner paused, and then said, "I cannot conscientiously say that you *have not.* I do not accuse you, but if you think that you have in any way injurec me by your advice, I forgive you as I hope in Heaven to b forgiven!"

Here I interposed, and said that I could not consent tha the prisoner should be tormented by any further questions a such an hour. "*He forgives all and bids you good-by.*"

The Lieutenant repeated my objection and sustained it The prisoner immediately ascended to the forecastle deck As he approached the larboard side, his quick eye took in th scene, and he said to the 1st Lieutenant, "Mr. K., I thin this line should be overhauled a little more; there will no be drop enough to it."

"Yes there will be, Jackson," said the Lieutenant, "an besides, *the gun will kill you, Jackson!*"

As he moved across the forecastle, and his eye ranged wit a hurried glance down the larboard side of the ship, he sai as if catching the eyes of some, "Good-by, lads," and t the master-at-arms beside him, "Good-by, master-at-arms. He now stepped upon the platform.

I stood a moment beside him, though myself on the dec of the forecastle. The rope was placed over his head an fastened to his neck. Was there any hope? Could the scene have gone so far, and be ended without taking this man's life? No, I thought not. It was too late. He must, he will go into eternity in a moment more. I cast my eye to the flag ship. The fatal signal to execute the sentence of the Court was that instant run up. I turned away my face, and two or three times paced across the forecastle deck. The cap was now drawn over the face of the prisoner. As I drew near him, the words came from his lips in the earnestness of entreaty, "Oh, God, have mercy on my soul! Oh, Jesus, into thine hands I commit my spirit!" It was while one of the last two sentences were dwelling on the lips of this unfortunate man that the officer, leaning over the forecastle deck, said in rather a suppressed voice, "Fire!" At the same moment, the platform on which the prisoner stood, rose, the prisoner himself bounded a few feet in the air, as the loud report of the gun echoed over the waters, and as if no space had intervened, the now senseless, but one moment before praying man was hanging at the foreyard-arm of the St. Mary's. No muscle moved, no limb contracted, the concussion of the gun had indeed killed him; and there he hung, a spectacle for the fleet to look upon, as evidence that a broken law will have its penalty, and to what an end a man may be suddenly brought by the indulgence of *one ebullition of passion.*

I hope the reader will pardon this digression from my narrative, and also allow me a few remarks upon the discipline of the navy; not of the U. S. Navy alone, but of all the navies in the world. While there may be those who, entirely unacquainted with a ship of war, may condemn the severity of a law that consigns to death a man for merely striking an officer, when the same offense by the civil law would be only assault and battery, or an assault alone, what would be the condition of a man-of-war, if striking an officer was not made a capital crime. Subordination would be out of the question, and it would not be an uncommon thing to see officers walking the quarter-deck with black eyes and broken heads. We have gone over the scene of Jackson's last hours, and of his execution. He knew the penalty was death; he had heard the articles of war read probably once a week when practicable. The clause applicable to this crime reads: "*Whoever shall draw, or offer to draw upon a superior officer, shall suffer death, or such other punishment as a court-martial shall adjudge.*" Every man knows the penalty of striking an officer.

CHAPTER III.

Continuation of Sam Jackson,—Remarks,—Arrival home,—Embargo,—Study navigation,—Effort to obtain a midshipman's warrant on board the U. S. frigate Constitution,—Bound apprentice to a shipwright,—Remarks on my apprenticeship,—Ruinous effects of grog-drinking,—Violent tornado,—Sail-boat sunk,—Lives lost, Rescue five Swedes from drowning,—Gloomy times,—War between the U. S. and England,—Unprepared condition of the U. S.,—Capt. Allen's story,—Arrive at the age of twenty-one years,—Certificate of good behavior from my master,—Go to New York,—Employment on the steam-frigate,—Her description,—Remarks on Robert Fulton,—Speech of Ogden Hoffman,—Enter the navy,—Torpedo boat,—Experiments,—Necessity of a strict watch,—Fortifying the coast,—Orders to join the gunboats,—Remarks and occurrences,—Flying squadron.

WOULD the Commodore have been justified in pardoning Jackson? Humanity may answer yes, but stern Justice ays no. It is well known by all who are acquainted with he usages of a man-of-war, and the nature of many who ompose their crews, that were it not for this dreadful pen-.lty, as I have just observed, officers would be frequently truck, particularly by boats' crews, while on shore, where hey have an opportunity of getting intoxicating drink.

The author has seen a case where, had it not been for the resence of mind and immediate interference of the boat-nates, the midshipman of the boat would have been struck y a fine seaman when drunk, the penalty for which by the aw would have been death. The author has known an offi-er to be pushed down while endeavoring to prevent the men om leaving the boat, while on shore. This, by the law, ould also be considered as belonging to the death penalty. he officer being kind-hearted, and the boat's crew begging im to overlook it, he did so, otherwise the offender would have been tried by a court-martial, and would have suffered the punishment awarded him.

Suppose Jackson had been pardoned, what, in all probability, would have been the effect upon the other seamen in the navy? The trial and preparation for execution would have been looked upon as a farce, and many an old "Salt" would have rolled over his quid, hitched up his trousers, and with an arch look, quaintly remarked: "No more hanging now boys." The equanimity of discipline in the navy would be at an end. Intoxicated seamen sometimes are very abusive to their officers, and are put in double irons and not unfrequently gagged with an iron bolt, are placed under charge of a sentinel, and when the commanding officer sees fit, the offender is flogged at the gangway, and sometimes these offences are brought before a court-martial, but the penalty is not death.

I knew Commodore Conner when a midshipman, have sailed with, and always thought him an exemplary man, and no doubt there was a severe struggle in his mind between duty and inclination. His heart yearned over the unfortunate man as deeply as any other, and more so, no doubt, from the fact that the prerogative of life or death was with him. But duty predominated over feeling, and the man was executed. As we have gone through with the throbbing emotion of the unfortunate Jackson, his anxiety for the salvation of his soul, the kindness and sympathy of all around during the solomn interval, yet there is not the least doubt that if the St. Mary's had gone into action before the sad affair occurred for which he died, however perilous the fight might have been, Jackson would have fought at his gun without the smallest fear of death, or perhaps any solicitude about his future welfare; and had he been mortally wounded, he would have met death with a smile, as all brave sailors do. At least, this is my opinion; perhaps some philosopher can explain it better than I can.

I return to my narrative. All things relating to our capture being settled, we had permission to depart with the barque minus that portion of the cargo, which was given up by compromise, rather than carry the case to London which, as I have before stated, would have detained us several months and perhaps the loss of the vessel would have been the result. John Bull at this time cut a great swell on the ocean, and was very abusive to the American flag, and to American shipmasters in every port were they met.

We sailed from Halifax for Plymouth, where we arrived safe in seven days, the owner of the Barque, and the captain's 'amily, not having heard from us since leaving Rotterdam, hought we were lost. Captain H. treated me very kindy wishing me to remain with him during my apprenticehip. I preferred returning to Boston where I found one of ny uncles who had just returned from the coast of Sumatra, is ship had been cut off by the natives or Malays, and himelf severely wounded. He insisted on my studying navi-ation immediately, saying to me at the same time that if it 'as my determination to go to sea, I must be bound to some xperienced shipmaster as taut as parchment could bind ie.

I commenced the study of navigation, and got along quite ist. The Constitution frigate was then ready for sea ing off Long wharf bound for Tripoli. I was desirous getting a midshipman's warrant and entering the navy, it as that was rather difficult, being attended with a great al of ceremony, I gave it up, as there was a prospect a war with England or France, and our commerce uch cut up, I concluded to learn a trade.

One day, shortly after my return, I met my old schoolaster who flogged me so nicely, he was glad to see me and peared very affectionate, and asked how I liked going sea, and expressed much regret for the cause of our sepa-tion, saying, "you are a good scholar and I hope you will ike a good seaman." We parted with a mutual good ling.

A large portion of our merchant vessels were hauled up d all kinds of business prostrated. A non-intercourse act our government, put a stop to all commercial business, cept those who had obtained permission to go after propy that was considered in jeopardy. Then came the long bargo which put a stopper on American commerce, the carrying trade then fell into the hands of foreigners whicl made business for many.

Our political horizon now became very much obscured there were two parties in evident opposition, one called th war party, the other for peace on any terms, and had th latter succeeded, our glorious Stars and Stripes would hav decorated Westminster Abbey and these prosperous State would have been numbered with the Colonies, the shackle firmly clenched and the boasted liberty of this great Repul lic thrown back upon our children with taunts and insult

In April, 1808, I was bound apprentice to a shipwrigh and served my regular apprenticeship; I shall always ente: tain the highest respect for my master and mistress, thoug both are dead. The recollection of their kind treatment ı me will always be cherished with sentiments of profoun gratitude.

Many a time in after life have I in retrospect gone bac and reviewed my apprentice days, which were the happie in my life, with only those exceptions, where boys are eager looking forward to their maturity, and feeling the many r straints which apprentices must be subjected to, as rath irksome and "grievous to be borne."

But we seldom find a man who, after having arrived the meridian of life, that ever complained of a *too str: bringing up while an apprentice.*

When I look around me now, (1856) and enquire for aı of my fellows, or those who were apprentices contempora with myself, I can find but one, Mr. E. D., who has retain his integrity, prospered in his business, and reared a num ous and respectable family. I believe many of the rest we long ago into the drunkard's grave.

There were many customs in those days that were p nicious and destructive to the morals and habits of boys. allude particularly to that of supplying grog at eleven M., and at four P. M. This was the incipient training drunkenness, and I have known both masters and appr tices to have been inmates of the Alms House at the sa ı me.

And there is no doubt that their sensibilities were too .uch blunted for mutual recriminations.

Some that were my associates and quite respectable, who ere learning different trades, took their grog, frequented .e theatre, and other places where low and obscene jests id songs went round, and spent the Sabbath in boat-sailing riding.

Now, all this seemed perfectly harmless, the influence on future character was not thought of, neither did these ung men think, at the time, that the foundation they were ying would destroy every principle of integrity, and ultiately prove their ruin.

Three of these which I have just alluded to served out eir terms in the State Prison for thefts. And two of them ter being liberated ended their days in a most miserable anner, being frozen to death while in a state of intoxican. And I could record the sad end of many others, but e few that have been noticed, may suffice to show young prentices how easy it is to *imbibe* bad habits, and how hard escape the consequences.

Early habits fasten upon youth, and if good, they never se the salutary influence which result from them, but on other hand, if evil, they grow more and more obtuse, until y bring their victims to destruction.

At the period of which I am now speaking it was customy when an apprentice had attained the age of twenty-one his master to give him a freedom treat, or collation. If master was a generous man then it was ample, consisting all sorts of spirituous liquors, cold meats, &c. The young n went around the neighborhood and invited his friends, h young and old, to partake of the feast.

All this would be well enough, were it not for the result. On such days, many, both young and old, become intoxied, and the getting drunk at a freedom, was always looked n with some degree of excuse.

This custom and the serving grog to workmen has long e been discontinued. It may be asked, how my fellow rentice Mr. D. and myself escaped the general ruin. I wer, we pledged ourselves that we would not taste a drop of intoxicating liquor during our apprenticeship, and *ne* during our lives if we saw fit to extend the pledge thus f

My master and mistress were both strict observers of t Sabbath, and in no case would they allow an apprentice absent himself from Church except something very extra dinary prevented his going.

I remember one Sunday in August, about the time of t first bells ringing, that I took a walk up to the ship-ya before meeting time, and it was evident that a shower w at hand, as it had already begun to look very black. I s also, that a heavy squall was near by, and as it began rain I got under an old shed for shelter. Just as I l entered, a sharp peal of thunder broke near me, and t rain came down in torrents. At the same time a viol tornado swept along as if it would carry everything bef it.

Just before the tornado I saw a large sail-boat p up the channel near to the wharf where I was standing. S had lowered her mainsail, ready for the squall, th were three men on deck, and in an instant as soon as she the force of the wind she went over, filled, and went dow

Instantly springing to the dock, I found a man near called and told him what had happened.

We jumped into an old canoe half full of water, and pr identially found two oars near by. The man pushed canoe out, while I bailed the water with my Sunday hat.

When we got near the sunken boat her mast heads w about six feet out of water. The three men were then go ashore in the small boat.

We asked them if there were any more on board and derstood them to answer "no," it was blowing so hard, t we probably could not distinctly hear; while at the sa moment there were five souls in the cuddy. They had g in to keep out of the rain and had drawn the scuttle d over and fastened it.

Notwithstanding, had we known that there had been one below, I could have dived down and possibly might h saved them.

But we had hardly got up to this boat when we saw fu

ıarter of a mile from us another boat that had capsized ıd sunk, with five strapping Swedes holding on to the masts, ıd anything they could get hold of, neither of whom could 'im.

And when we reached the boat, encouraged them to hold ., and by no means to touch our canoe; for it was certain at if they got hold of our gunwale, they would capsize us, ıd then we should all struggle together.

We placed our boat so as to haul them in over the bow, e at a time, until all were in. They could not have held much longer.

Our boat leaked badly, and with these five clumsy fellows . board, brought her down to within six inches of her gunıle; but by keeping perfectly steady, and constantly bailing, reached the shore in safety.

These fellows were put upon the wharf, they turned ıout and went off without a thank or a single mark of gratıde.

By the time we had reached the dock, the large boat had en hauled in, the cuddy opened, and five bodies were taken t; two of which I recognized; a father and his son. fter all was over I met my master on the wharf, who re-.ked me severely, for being absent from church. Besides, vas dripping wet, my Sunday clothes and hat were spoiled. *But,*" he continued, "as you have saved these men I shall erlook it this time."

I was not allowed to be absent after ten at night without ecial permission. This I did not consider as a restriction, I had no desire to be out after nine, as my evenings were stly spent at school or with my relatives. I also had nty of books, so that on evenings when there was no ıool, I remained at home, and spent the time in reading.

In 1812, war was declared between the U. S. and Great itain; and if there ever was a justifiable war this most suredly could be called one.

No country had ever been more grossly insulted; and we re justified in applying the well known maxim, "tread on vorm, and it will turn," not that the worm has any means of defence, but it turns, to show you that it cannot rema motionless and passive under the insult.

When the war question came up in the British parlimei one noble Lord arose, and with an indignant frown demand why the house condescended to *discuss* the paltry subj- *A war with the U. S.* Pray, who and what are these madm with a few fir built frigates, with a patch of striped bunti at their mast heads, and no seamen to man them!

This noble lord fairly scouted at the idea. And su enough, what preparation had the U. S. for this formidal contest. Not a ship of war of any size fit for service un repaired.

The following list comprises the names of all the vess belonging to the United States Navy in 1812, before the la war with Great Britain. Those marked in italics were lo during the war. The *Boston*, burnt at Washington, was mere hulk, not worth repair, as was also the *New Yo* which escaped the flames.

	RATE.		RA'
Ship United States - -	44	Ship Hornet - - - -	
President - - -	44	*Wasp* - - - -	
Constitution - - -	44	Brig Adams - - - -	
Chesapeake - - -	36	Oneida - - - -	
Constellation - -	36	*Syren* - - - -	
Congress - - - -	36	*Argus* - - - -	
New York - - -	32	Enterprize - -	
Adams - - - -	42	*Rattlesnake* - -	
Boston - - - - -	32	*Nautilus* - - -	
Essex - - - - -	32	*Vixen* - - - -	
John Adams - - -	24	*Viper* - - - -	
Louisiana - - - -	18	Sch'r *Vixen* - - - -	

Besides gunboats, bombs, &c., and nothing larger than frigate. No navy yards of any magnitude, except at Wa ington, no money in the treasury, no materials for sh building at hand, no preparation on the frontiers, no facilit for transportation or carrying guns, and the necessary artic required in war, including provisions and the numer requirements for ship building, from the Atlantic States the Lakes.

No army, no horses, scarcely any copper, but a small amount of iron in the country, very little hemp or rigging, and a very small supply of duck fit for war-ships sails. Here we were, in this comparatively destitute condition, and more than all this, an important question arose how were we to get these articles in sufficient quantities for our present use. Our ports would of course be immediately blockaded; but we were now "*in for it*," war was declared, and all we have to do now is to go ahead. Here was another item on the catalogue of our troubles; very soon, in all probability, our coast would be lined with British men-of-war, and many of our harbors were without any protection whatever. And it would take some time before we could erect any sort of defence.

It would also require several weeks to repair, and equip our ships of war for actual sea service.

Before an efficient army could be recruited and properly drilled, the enemy would have landed upon our shores, many of her veterans from Europe, that had been cradled among battles; the heroes of Waterloo, and of other conquests; where the legions of Bonaparte had been put to flight. All these, with their well-trained officers, who had gained experience on the battle-ground, must be met and *repulsed* too.

But how can our raw recruits meet these well disciplined and hardy English, Scotch, and Irish regiments, who never retreat from the point of the bayonet or seldom turn their backs to the enemy except for stratagem.

Have we officers well enough versed in military tactics, to meet this formidable foe?

And then, our Lilliputian navy must go out upon the ocean and cope with the heroes of the Nile, Trafalgar and Copenhagen. This fearful odds we must contend with. WE DID, and history tells the sequel; our cause was a just one, the contest was for the honor of our country, and for our national rights. The God of armies was with us, and we can truly say, that "the *battle is not to the strong, nor the race to the swift.*

But we had among us, an enemy far more potent than the one we met.

The strong opposition party, who, I believe would at one time have given up the country to the enemy if it had been in their power.

But the patriotism of '75 preponderated! Ships were built on the lakes, harbors fortified, armies raised, roads cut around the frontier, naval depots, and cannon founderies established, the seaboard put in a state of defence, war-ships of every class were built, armed, equipped, and manned with noble fellows, and the result of our first naval battle is too well known to be repeated here.

I have dwelt longer on these details than I had intended at the commencement; but as they came along in the course of my aprenticeship, I felt as though they belonged to the story.

The enemy had now partially blockaded our eastern coast, or what amounts to the same thing, they had cruisers all along our eastern shore, for the purpose of destroying the lumber and fishing business.

There was an old veteran coasting-captain named Allen, with whom I was well acquainted, who owned an old sloop, and by skill and courage had managed to keep her running between Kennebunk and Boston, during the war. At one time, when she lay upon our graving ways for some slight repairs, I saw that the oakum was hanging out of her seams throughout the bottom, and asked him if he was not going to have her calked.

"Calked! no; I expect these British devils will take me, and then the calking bill will be a total loss. Besides, we *calculate* to pump the whole Atlantic through her every trip."

When he returned, he came round to tell us about his narrow escape, which I had already seen in the newspaper. Said he:

"I had just got out of the river, with a thundering deck load of boards and shingles. The wind was light, but blowing on shore, and it was rather thick; the sun had not yet burned up the fog, when, *by George!* the first thing I saw was the *Boxer*, not a musket shot from me. I up helm, eased off my main boom, and run back as fast as the old sloop would carry me. I run in round the point, let go my anchor, and lowered my mainsail. We had hardly got the sail stowed, when we saw a boat pulling in round the point. I knew it was the Boxer's boat, and that she was after me, and that there was no time to lose. I had four good men and a boy with me, and I had four good muskets. We got them up and loaded in a jiffy. We then piled up a tier of shingles on each side the quarter-deck. The four men lay down flat upon the boards, with their muskets pointed at the boat. There were six men and an officer in her, and when she had got near enough to hear me, I stood on the taffrail, and told them '*in the name of the Commonwealth to keep off.*' The officer sung out, 'Shut up, you —— old Jonathan.'

"I stepped down, told the boys to get good aim and *fire!* They fired and popped off three of them. We loaded again, stepped on to the shingles, pointed our guns at them. The officer sung out, 'We have surrendered.'

"I then ordered him to come along-side instantly, or I would shoot every one of them. They pulled up along-side. I ordered him to pass up his muskets, breech first, and then come aboard. When he got on deck, I said to him, 'What do you mean, you *puppy*, by calling me a —— Jonathan? if you wasn't a prisoner, I'd seize you up to the rigging, and take the dust out of your jacket. Come, unbuckle that sword; it is just what I want to cut brush with.'

"We hauled the dead bodies out of the boat, hove up our anchor, and went up the river. We had no hand-cuffs on board, so we tied the prisoners back to back, but treated them kindly. We expected the brig after us every minute, but we had got into a nook where she could not hurt us, and in the afternoon we buried the dead, and put the prisoners on board the revenue cutter, and the next news we heard was, that the Boxer had been taken by the U. S. brig Enterprize, after a sharp action of about thirty minutes. The Boxer had her colors nailed to the mast head, and when she was nearly cut to pieces by the shot from the Enterprize, they sung out for quarters, saying 'their *colors were nailed, and could not be hauled down.*'"

This story of Capt. Allen may be relied on as strictly true.

July 16, 1814, I was twenty-one years of age. My master, according to the custom, gave me a freedom collation, and endorsed my indentures, certifying that I had been an honest and faithful apprentice. This I found to be of much benefit in many positions in which I was subsequently placed. As there was not much business doing in Boston at this time, I concluded to try my luck in New York; and on arriving there was much surprised at the contrast between the two places.

While Boston was still and silent as the Sabbath, New York was all bustle and life. Privateers were fitting out from nearly all the principal wharves; recruiting parties drumming through the streets, and the whole city seemed to be one continuous scene of activity. I found employment immediately, on the steam frigate Fulton, at A. & N. Brown's yard, on Manhattan Island. She had just been raised, and was now nearly ready for planking. Robert Fulton, Esq., had made a contract with the U. S. government to construct and deliver the steam battery, at a given time, with a guaranty as to her speed and draught of water. Her length I think was 175 feet; breadth, 60; her form or side-line was oval; her bottom below the lower deck was in two parts, to admit the wheel amidships, in order that it might be protected from the enemy's shot. Her sides above water were five feet through, timbered and bolted in such a manner as to make her shot-proof. She had two masts 90 feet long, calculated for lateen-sails, the yards for which were 175 feet long, The guns, thirty in number, were to be columbiades, carrying a shot of 100 pounds; the carriage was to run on a slide, and they were the best constructed gun carriages I have ever seen. In consequence of both ends of the frigate being round, four guns from each end could be brought to bear on one object. Her machinery was protected by a wall of white oak four feet thick, and truly she was a formidable creature.

While this frigate was in process of construction, Mr. Robert Fulton, her projector, was at the ship-yard every day, and it was very evident that he labored under a doubt about her coming up to his guaranty, for by a close mathematical calculation it was ascertained to a certainty that she would draw more water than was at first expected.

Hence the opening amidships would be too low for the water to pass off from the wheel. These difficulties would materially affect the efficiency of the frigate. This caused Mr. Fulton a great deal of mental anxiety, which visibly wore upon him, and gave him quite a haggard look.*

Notwithstanding this, he was very agreeable and sociable with the workmen, and I thought him one of the finest men I had ever met with.

The old maxim of "one beat the bush, and another catch the bird," was fully applicable with Mr. Fulton, for all who ever knew or have read of this gentleman, cannot suppress a feeling of regret at the manner in which his persevering genius was requited; for after he had succeeded in getting a permanent steam communication between New York and Albany, wading through innumerable troubles and mortifications, and what was worse than all the rest, he was involved in lawsuits with those who, *world-like*, would deprive him of the honor due to him for his invaluable discovery, and by these ruinous litigations was stripped of his hard-earned property.

I well remember his first boat, and when she started on her experimental trip to Albany. He was looked upon as *certainly a crazy man.* Even the boys hooted at him, and around the wharf where the boat lay, it was so densely crowded that vehicles could scarcely pass. And when the wheels began to move, a tremendous shout went forth that made all ring again.

Mr. Fulton, in his coarse working dress, was busy at work and unmoved by the insulting epithets which he could not help hearing. As for instance, a great, swarthy looking fellow forced his way through the crowd, and when near the boat exclaimed, "Where is the —— fool?" Even this last insult did not disturb his equanimity, nor discompose him

* He did not live to see the completion of his contract; he died Feb. 15, 1815.

in the least. The world knows the result of this so-called *foolish*, incipient attempt at steam navigation.

In one of my school books I remember the following saying:

> "The evil that men do lives after them, but the
> Good is oft interred with their bones."

How very seldom do we hear the name of Robert Fulton, although it is registered among the great men of America. I know of no monument or cenotaph erected to his memory.* He gave to the world a system of communication which has brought the nations of the earth in close proximity. The advantages of steam over sail ships are beyond calculation, and this was accomplished through the indubitable and persevering, yet unremunerated energy of Robert Fulton.

In 1838, an attempt was made by his friends, (I believe in legislature of New York,) to obtain a grant as a compensation for services rendered the State. Ogden Hoffman, Esq., was employed as an advocate on behalf of the claimants. The following is an extract of his excellent plea in behalf of the object.

"This House, and the world, have been told that Robert Fulton was not the inventor of steam navigation.

"England asserts that it is to a Scotchman that the honor of this discovery is due, and that it was the Clyde and the Thames that first witnessed the triumphs of this wonderful invention. France, through her National Institute, declares that it was the Seine. Even Spain, degraded and enslaved, roused by the voice of emulation, has looked forth from her cloistered halls of superstition, and declared that in the age of Charles, in the presence of her court and nobles, the experiment was successfully tried.

"But America, proudly seated upon the enduring monument which Fulton has reared, smiles at these rival claims,

* One street, leading from Broadway to where his boats lay, was called Fulton street.

and secure in her own, looks down serenely upon the billows of strife which break at the base of her throne.

But it has been denied in this debate that any other credit than that of good luck, is due to Fulton for his invention. Gentlemen would have us to suppose that good luck is the parent of all we admire in science or in arms. If this be so, why, then, indeed, what a bubble is reputation! How vain, and how idle, days and sleepless nights devoted to the service of one's Country! Admit this argument and you strip from the brow of the scholar his bay, and from those of the statesman and soldier their laurel.

Why do you deck with chaplets the statue of the Father of his Country, if good, and good luck alone, be all that commends him our gratitude and love?

A member of this House retorts "bad luck would have made Washington a traitor." Aye, but in whose estimation? Did the great and holy principles which produced and governed our Revolution depend for their righteousness and truths upon success, or defeat? Would Washington, had he suffered as a rebel on the scaffold? Would Washington have been regarded as a traitor by women; and Hancock, and Green, and Hamilton, by the crowd of patriots who encompassed him, partners of his trial and sharers of his patriotism? Was it good luck that impelled Columbus through discouragement, conspiracy and poverty, to persevere in his path of danger until this western world blessed his sight, and rewarded his energy and daring? Does the Gentleman emulate the glory of the third king of Rome, Tullus Hostilius, and would he erect in our land a temple of fortune? It cannot be that he would seriously promulgate such views; that he would take from human renown all that gives it dignity and worth, by making it all depend less on the virtue of the individual than on his luck!" I believe an appropriation was voted to his family, but the amount I never learned.

As in all probability ship building would be dull, and everything about New York seemed to be of a warlike character, I concluded to enter the U. S. Navy for the steam frigate. It occurred to me, that I might sign the shipping papers, and at the same time get permission from the recruiting officer to work on her until she was launched. Thus I should be drawing pay from the yard and from the government at the same time, as it would probably take a month to get her ready for launching.

I went to the rendezvous, made my wishes known to the recruiting officer Mr. Edward Barnwell, who was much of a gentleman, and subsequently a good friend to me. He immediately complied with my request, and I entered as first carpenter's mate. He gave me two months advance, requiring no other security than the endorsement on my indentures; also a written permission to continue working on the frigate until my services should be required in the naval service.

Besides this monstrous steam battery, we constructed a torpedo boat for the purpose of destroying enemy's ships at anchor. She was ninety-six feet long, thirty feet beam, and six feet deep in the ocean. Her shape was very much like the bowls of two spoons put close together. At the smallest end a place was fixed on the outside for the torpedo or vessel containing the powder (about 200lb) and communicating with this vessel of powder were three common gun locks, with wires leading inside the boat and well covered with cloth to prevent water from coming inside.

At the other end was a submerged wheel about six feet in diameter, to which a crank was fixed and attached to a shaft seventy-five feet in length, and running along in the boat, about two feet from the bottom.

Holes, two inches in diameter, were bored through the shaft four feet apart, and through these were bars six feet long projecting three feet on each side; fifteen men were to be seated on each side the shaft and every man with a bar in his hand.

It was calculated that the horizontal movement of this shaft would propel the boat rapidly through the water. The submerging process was arranged by copper tubes and buoys upon the surface of the water calculated and arranged so as to admit a sufficient amount of pure air, and also to graduate the depth of the machine; as it was intended to be placed under a ship bottom at night in such a position as to explode the powder, and at the same time to make an immediate retreat.

This infernal machine was never wanted, peace having taken place before she was launched, and while speaking of Mr. Fulton, perhaps it may not be out of place here, to remark, that the "commencement of hostilities between the U. S. and Great Britain, gave new activity to Mr. Fulton's thoughts on sub-marine warfare. The *power* of his machines, the officers of the British navy had learned from what he had done in England, and it is certain that they approached our shores with no little caution. This was manifested by their solicitude to know where Fulton was, and what he was about, whenever they had an opportunity of making inquiries.

By the respectful distance at which they generally kept their ships from our shores, and the precautions they took whenever they approached them, evidently showed that they were afraid of Fulton.

On these accounts there was no opportunity of doing anything with the common torpedo. During the war, several partial, and ineffectual attempts were made upon the enemy's vessels, by different enterprizing individuals. It is very possible that the dread of what might be done by Mr. Fulton, who they knew was a resident of New York, and had there been trying experiments with sub-marine explosions, determined the British to direct their hostilities to other parts of the U. S., rather than to that port.

But Mr. Fulton's plan for sub-marine warfare, met with no countenance, (*with the exception of the torpedo-boat, built to accompany the steam frigates*) from the government. He had not been able to inspire the executive officers with any confidence in them.

The unfavorable opinion of some of our gallant naval commanders, was calculated to have great influence against any reliance on Mr. Fulton's machines. No system was arranged for preparing or employing them. Attempts, which were made, were conducted by persons who were entirely inexperienced in the use of torpedoes, and had none of the qualifications for such an enterprize but courage.

Under such circumstances, nothing but failures were to be expected. Had Mr. Fulton's proposition to organize a marine corps, to be practised and instructed in the use of torpedoes been adopted, the war might have afforded an opportunity of giving them such a trial as would have been decisive as to their utility.

But Mr. Fulton's thoughts on sub-marine warfare took another direction.

Having ascertained by the experiments he had made with his cable cutter, that powder might be discharged from a piece of ordnance under water with effect; he conceived the idea of forming sub-marine batteries.

With this view, he instituted a number of experiments, to try the practicability and effect of discharging cannon loaded with ball at different depths under water.

He made a number of calculations on this subject.

His desire to ascertain what resistance a ball of given dimensions, propelled with a certain velocity, would meet with in passing through a body of water, at a certain depth. The basis he took for these calculations, and the calculations themselves, mark his ingenuity and science.

He assumed, that a body passing through water, would meet with a resistance equal to the force of a column of the same diameter as the body moving with the given velocity. He then ascertained what head or height of water would be required to discharge a stream of water from an orifice at the foot of a perpendicular tube, with the same velocity with which the body was supposed to be propelled.

He then, by the well-known rule of hydraulics, found what force or power the ascertained head of water would give, and thence formed his estimate as to the resistance which a body projected in water would meet with.

In this instance, as in others, he was not satisfied with arriving at the information necessary for his particular purpose; but he established from his calculations, a rule which may, by a very brief and simple arithmetical process, afford all the information and accuracy generally necessary for practical purposes.

His first experiment was with a four pounder having the breech and as much of the gun as is usually within the sides of a vessel, in a water-tight box, and the muzzle stopped with a composition. The box and gun were then submerged three feet in the Hudson. The gun was fired by dropping a live coal thorugh a tin tube which penetrated the box immediately above the vent of the gun, and rose above the surface of the water. The ball was found to have struck the sand at the bottom of the river, at the distance of forty-one feet from the muzzle.

The gun was uninjured. This experiment satisfied him that guns might be placed in a ship, below her water-line with their breech on board, and their muzzle in the water, without any more danger of their bursting, than there is when they are fired in the air. This gave him the idea of arming ships with guns to be fired in this way.

He proposed that the muzzle of the gun made for the purpose, should recoil through the stuffing box, and be followed by a valve which should exclude the water when the gun is not protruded. An elegant model on this construction is now in possession of his family.

He next tried the same piece with a pound and a half of powder, and fired it by means of one of his water-tight locks, when it was entirely in the water, three feet below the surface.

The ball penetrated eleven and a half inches into a target of pine logs, which had been prepared for the purpose, and placed beneath the water at the distance of twelve feet from the piece.

His next experiment was with the Columbiade, carrying a hundred pound ball, fired at the target as in the last instance. All that we know is, that the ball tore the target to pieces, and that the cannon was uninjured. We have not information that will enable us to give any further details of this experiment, but we know that Mr. Fulton was entirely satisfied with the result.

He proposed to use cannon in this way, by suspending them, two for instance, from the bows of the vessel. A single shot, as he demonstrates, from a piece of large calibre, which should break through into the side of a ship, at any considerable depth beneath the water-line, must be fatal to her. And though the range of shot fired through the water, may be but a few feet, yet, conflicting vessels, whenever they engage yard-arm and yard-arm, with accounts of which our naval heroes have of late made us so familiar, must be so near as to give effect to sub-marine discharge.

Mr. Fulton did not propose that these guns should be always in the water; but that they should be suspended so as to be raised when the vessel was not in action. These plans for the sub-marine use of cannon, were submitted to one of our most distinguished naval commanders, who gave them his decided approbation.

He expressed a strong opinion that such an attack would be fatal to any vessel exposed to it, and that it would be extremely difficult for any enemy to evade an attempt, made with sufficient resolution, to destroy her by these means.

In 1818, Mr. Fulton took out a patent for several improvements in the art of maritime warfare, and means of injuring and destroying ships and vessels of war, by igniting gunpowder under water, or by igniting gunpowder on a line horizontal to the surface of the water; or so igniting gunpowder, that the explosion which causes injury to the vessel attatched, shall be under water.

This description, in the words of his patent, includes another idea he had, which was to plant batteries of submarine guns near the channels through which hostile vessels must pass to attack our seaports.

He communicated to Mr. Jefferson an account of his experiments on sub-marine firing, with drawings of his various plans. Mr. Jefferson expressed himself much pleased with this novel mode of maritime warfare, and assured Mr. Fulton that he would recommend it to the attention of government.

This curious project gave rise to the steam man-of-war. It having been suggested by the distinguished naval officer before alluded to, that in approaching an enemy so near as was necessary to give effect to sub-marine cannon, the vessel, if she were rigged in the ordinary way, would be liable to be entangled with her adversary.

To meet this objection, Mr. Fulton proposed to move the vessel by steam.

His reflections on this project, and what he saw of the performance of so large a vessel as the Fulton, her speed, and the facility with which she was managed, led him to conceive that a vessel of war might be constructed in which, to all the advantages possessed by those now in use, might be added the very important ones which she would derive from being propelled by steam, as well as by wind.

At the commencement of the year 1814, a number of the citizens of New York, alarmed at the exposed situation of their harbor, had assembled with a view to consider whether some measures might not be taken to aid the government in its protection.

This assembly had, in fact, been invited by some knowledge of Mr Fulton's plans for sub-marine attack, and of his contemplating other means of defence. They deputed a number of gentlemen to act for them, and they were called the Coast and Harbor Defence Committee. Mr. Fulton exhibited to this committee the model and plans for a vessel of war to be propelled by steam, capable of carrying a strong battery, with furnaces for red-hot shot, and which, he represented, would move at the rate of four miles an hour.

The confidence of the committee in this design, was confirmed by the opinions of many of our most distinguished naval commanders, which he had obtained in writing and exhibited to the committee.

In this document, which is signed by Com. Decatur, Capt. Jones, Capt. Evans, Capt. Biddle, Com. Perry, Capt. Warrington, and Capt. Lewis, these gallant and experienced seamen, enumerate the following advantages that such a vessel would possess: In a calm or light breeze she could make choice of position or distance. If she could move at the rate of four miles an hour, she could in our harbors, bays and rivers, be rendered more formidable than any kind of engine hitherto invented, and in such cases she would be equal to the destruction of one or more seventy-fours, or of compelling them to depart from our waters. They therefore gave it as their decided opinion that it was among the best interests of the

United States, to carry Mr. Fulton's plan into immediate execution.

It was contemplated that this vessel, besides carrying her proposed armament on deck, should also be furnished with sub-marine guns.

The committee without delay addressed a memorial to Congress, recommending the invention of Mr. Fulton, and praying that measures might be adopted for executing his plan.

With this memorial the committee addressed a letter to the Secretary of the Navy, soliciting in a very earnest manner his patronage and influence with the government. Without the skill and talents they say, of Mr. Fulton, the machine cannot be constructed. It was apprehended that there would be great difficulty about funds. On the one hand there was a great disinclination to make the project public by inducing a discussion on the subject in Congress; and, on the other, it was doubtful whether the executive was authorized to make the necessary appropriation, without a law for the purpose.

To obviate these difficulties, the committee offered in behalf of the association which they represented, to construct the vessel at their own expense, and risk of assurances were given that the government, which alone could give employment to her, would receive and pay for her after she was built, and her utility demonstrated.

It was estimated that she would cost about 320,000 dollars, nearly the sum requisite for a frigate of the first class.

This activity of private citizens for their own protection, this voluntary offer to risk their funds, first upon the success of the project, and then upon a bare assurance of the executive of the government, and this intimate intercourse between the rulers and the people, presents a view of a state of society of which it is believed there are few examples.

The projet was zealously embraced by the executive, and the national legislature in March, 1814, passed a law authorizing the President of the United States to cause to be built, equipped and employed, one or more floating batteries for the defence of the waters of the United States.

The building of the vessel was committed by the Coast and Harbor Defence Association at New York, to a sub-committee of five gentlemen.

They were Gen. Dearborn, Col. Henry Rutgers, Oliver Walcott, Sam. L. Mitchell, and Thomas Morris, Esqs., who were recognized by the government as their agents for this purpose. Mr. Fulton, whose soul indeed animated the whole enterprise, was appointed engineer.

On the 20th of June, 1814, the keel of this novel and mighty engine was laid; and in little more than four months, that is, on the 29th Oct. she was launched from the yard of Adam and Noah Brown, her able and active architects.

The scene exhibited on that occasion was magnificent.

It happened on one of our bright autumnal days, multitudes of spectators crowded the surrounding shores, and were seen upon the hills, which limited the beautiful prospect. The river and bay were filled with vessels of war, dressed in all their variety of colors, in compliment to the occasion.

In the midst of these was the enormous floating mass, whose bulk and unwieldly form seemed to render her as unfit for motion, as the land batteries which were saluting her. Through the fleet of vessels which occupied this part of the harbor, were seen gliding in every direction, several of the large steamboats of the burden of three and four hundred tons, these, with bands of music, and crowds of gay and joyous company, were winding through passages left by the anchored vessels as if they were moving by enchantment. The heart could not have been human that did not share in the general enthusiasm expressed by the loud shouts of the multitude.

He could not have been a worthy citizen what did not then say to himself with pride and exultation "this is my country," and when he looked on the man whose single genius had created the most interesting object of the scene "this is my countryman."

I have now gone over with what might be called a lengthy detail of Mr. Fulton, and some of the results of his remarkable genius. Also, the projecting building and launching of the steam frigate whose christened name was Fulton Demologes. And as I am about to leave her, will just add, that while she was on the stocks it was pretty well ascertained that boats from the British cruisers off New London, and that vicinity, had been seen in Hurlgate with muffled oars; and it was also well ascertained that British officers had actually been upon the spot where she was erected. And once during the time that we were at work on her, a fire was discovered in the lower part of the yard, at noonday, evidently the work of an incendiary.

This fire had no doubt been placed there with a view of its bursting out in the night and for the purpose of destroying the steam frigate.

A volunteer guard consisting of two companies of infantry were placed at different posts around the yard, with positive orders not to permit a boat to come along-side the wharf unless she had an American flag at the stern, and was commanded by an American naval officer.

No spectators or visitors were allowed in the yard except passed in by the officer of the day, and on no consideration could a visitor be allowed to remain in the yard after the workmen had knocked off.

Besides these precautions, two gunboats were stationed in the river, about 200 yards from the frigate's stern, and on the opposite shore, the workmen voluntered one Sunday and built a block-house, in which were placed four eighteen pounders and a sufficient number of men to handle them.

Another block-house was built on mill rock in Hurlgate which was also well armed and manned. And I think it would have required a pretty large quantity of British skill to have enabled them to do any mischief to the steam frigate.

Independent of all the precaution I have named, every one of the workmen had a loaded musket, placed where he could put his hand upon it at a moments warning. The frigate was to be commanded by Commodore David Porter who had just returned from Valparaiso, after the unfortunate capture of the Essex frigate, which he commanded, and so nobly defended.

The particulars of this battle I shall give in another chapter.

Several of Commodore Porter's surviving officers and a number of the crew came home with him, who were also ordered to the steam frigate.

A few days after the launch I received orders to report myself on board gunboat No. 98, (one of the guard-boats) for public duty.

Only one of the regularly appointed officers (Lieut. Odenheimer) had joined her; he had charge of gunboat 110, and was also commander-in-chief of all the flotilla, stationed round the frigate.

Commodore Porter, with his officers and crew, had been ordered to the River Potomac, to assist in preventing the British fleet from ascending the river for the purpose of destroying the City of Washington.

But notwithstanding the alacrity with which guns and men were collected, the British ships got the start and succeeded in reaching Washington City, and in a hurried manner set fire to the capitol. And after doing much damage to the buildings made a hasty retreat just in time to save themselves.

Before the return of Commodore Porter to New York, the Secretary of the navy had ordered a number of small fast sailing vessels to be purchased, and four to be built. These vessels were to be from three to four hundred tons, and were intended for Atlantic cruisers and were called the Flying Squadron, to be commanded by Commodore Porter.

According to my orders I went, bag and baggage, on board the gunboat, and thus commenced my life *on board a man-of-war.*

It was thought necessary to increase the number of gunboats, as the frigate was to lie in the river, probably two weeks longer, there being much work to be done preparatory to receiving her engine and machinery, which were to be taken in at Jersey City. And it was possible that the British might be foolish enough to make an attempt on her with their boats.

Accordingly, four additional gunboats were placed around

her, and on board of them were the seamen who had shipped for the U. S. Naval service. Each gunboat was commanded by a master's mate or passed midshipman, and as before stated, Lieut. Odenheimer had charge of all.

The officers, such as the sailing-master, midshipman, boatswain, gunner, carpenter, and sailmaker, had the cabins, and the petty officers and seamen the hold. The boats were soon crowded to overflowing, and if the infernal regions were raked over, a more villanous set of vagabonds could not be found than were among these fellows.

CHAPTER IV.

Hard living on board gunboat,—Drunken brawls,—Contrast in my life,—Riot and desertion from a gunboat,—Sent in chase of the fugitives,—Return without them,—The big nigger comes back of his own accord,—John, the cook, quarrels with his wife,—He jumps overboard,—Rescued with difficulty.—Wife sent on shore,—Frigate goes to Jersey City,—Came near falling from the mast head.—Went ashore without liberty,—Came near being flogged,—Much flogging going on,—Pompous sailing master,—Flying Squadron purchased,—Am sent from steam frigate to Navy Yard,—Put aboard old Alert,—Filth and misery,—Savage treatment,—Brutal inhumanity,—Miserable condition of sick and dying,—Deplorable effects of whiskey,—Came near being stabbed by an Irish sentinel,—Ordered to join the Firefly,—Poor opinion of some U. S. officers—Recruits daily coming on board the Alert,—History of Harris,—a cruise out of the yard, and difficulty in getting back,—Black cook confined for theft,—His feet frozen,—Our boat sunk,—Lucky escape,—Two young men cruelly whipped,—Become dissatisfied, and determine to desert,—Kind remonstrance of a friend,—Gave up the idea of deserting,—It returns again,—Made another attempt,—Was kindly admonished and gave it up,—Returned to the brig,—Was promoted,—Condition after,—Made a warrant officer,—On board the Firefly.—Fleet ready for sea,—Sent to Algiers,—Story of John Cribbs.

MANY of them having returned from the various prison ships in Europe, and others were old discharged privateers-men; here and there might be found a good and respectable sailor.

No. 98, the gunboat to which I was attached, was in a very filthy condition, and among her crew were some of the Essex's 16 men, who were very quarrelsome and overbearing; supposing themselves to be entitled to more privileges than any of the others. The officers of the boat were also from among the Essex's 16.

We often came short of our rations, especially of the fresh beef; one pound per diem was sent on board for each man

F

and boy; but the officers in the cabin usually kept two or three women, besides company from the shore to dine.

The cook was ordered to select the best pieces for the officers, and the remainder was given to the crew, which very often was quite insufficient; and for this, we had no remedy, as complaint was out of the question. A plentiful supply of rum was brought on board, without any restraint whatever; consequently the crew were continually drunk, and very quarrelsome.

The nights were hideous, both among officers and seamen. Scarcely a night passed without a fight.

I selected a berth near the cabin bulk-head, and close up in a corner, and as soon as I had taken my supper, crawled into it, to get out of the din. Among the men in the hold were several bad women, who usually mingled in the fights, of which they were often the cause, and scarcely ever were without a pair of splendid black eyes. Many a night have I lain in my snug hiding place, and looked out on the drunken tumult before me, and how bitterly did I lament the course I had taken, in entering the navy, as in all probability this was only a specimen of my two years life on board a *man-of-war.*

This sudden transition from a civilized life to a residence among brutes, was overwhelming to my feelings. I found that I had an important lesson before me, and that the earlier it was learned, the better, viz: to *make the best of everything,* and as the old adage says, "there is no use in crying for spilt milk;" mistakes that have already happened, cannot be prevented, although they may sometimes be rectified.

The mistakes and follies of the past may teach us to be more cautious for the future; but they should never be allowed to paralyze our energies, or surrender us to weak repining.

"I knew that I should not remain long on board a gun boat; my habits were good; I used no intoxicating drinks; never had played a game of cards, nor was I ever found in bad company; and I had another cheering thought, which was, that I might be promoted to the rank of carpenter, as I was now only carpenter's mate, and was resolved to do my duty faithfully, and leave the rest with God.

One night, about nine o'clock, we were alarmed by a terrible shouting from one of the other boats, who were hailing us, and at the same time, keeping up a brisk fire of musketry; we could just discern, through the darkness, a boat pulling rapidly towards the shore, and a gruff voice crying out, "*Blood for supper! Blood for supper!*" Lieut. Odenheimer hailed every gunboat, and ordered them to man their boats, and go in pursuit of the fugitives.

Our boat was instantly hauled alongside, and six men, of which I was one, and a midshipman, ordered into her; each man was armed with a loaded pistol and a cutlass.

We pulled directly for the runaway boat, that was now close under the Brooklyn shore; we followed them by their noise, and as soon as they saw that they were pursued, they struck off again for the New York side. It being very dark, we could just discern the boat a short distance ahead, but they succeeded in landing before we could get up with them. And now commenced the hunt.

Here were seven of us, that composed our boat's crew, and all armed to the teeth. We went directly to the "hook," the abode of infamy and wretchedness, where we supposed the deserters had gone; and here, in going from house to house, we were exposed to the insults of those who inhabited these dens. It was certain, that we should not find either sympathy or co-operation in the object of our pursuit, for deserters, thieves, murderers, and pickpockets all find an asylum in this pandemonium of wretchedness. The midshipman who had charge of our gang, was a blustering fellow, and I thought he would get us into a fight, which was, however, avoided.

We gave up the chase, and returned, unsuccessful, to our gunboat. We understood the next day, that the deserters were four in number, and among them was a great strapping nigger, who went by the name of Big Tom; and he *was*, sure enough, a powerful fellow. A row had occurred on board their gunboat, and the officers had attempted to put this big fellow in irons, when he swore that he would kill any man who laid a hand on him. He then, with the other three, started off as before stated.

At one time during our cruise at the "hook," we went into a house where he *was*; he being in the back room, we did not see him; and when he was told that there were armed men after him, he immediately seized a stick of hickory firewood, and swore death to any man that should approach him; and upon the whole, I think it was fortunate for us all that we did not see him.

A few days afterwards he came voluntarily on board and delivered himself up. He was confined for a few days and then set at liberty. The others were not taken.

The cook of our boat had his wife on board; she was a little red-haired thing, and a regular team. She went on shore nearly every day to pick up a little spending money and often came on board *not sober*. This sadly provoked John, who swore that she should not set foot on shore again unless he went with her. This injunction on her liberty was too much for Lizzie. She began to snuffle and cry, and vowed she would jump overboard. Now John unfortunately had but one arm. He had lost the other in the engagement on board the Essex.

Lizzie went to the bows and threatened to drown herself.

"Well, drown and be —— " says John; "you are too much of a coward to jump overboard." And as though suddenly inspired with an impulse that it was highly important that one or the other should die, he jumped overboard, and was borne along by the rapid tide; with a heavy pea-jacket on, and his head just above water, and with his one fin splashing away at a great rate.

She began screaming and wringing her hands, begging some one to get the boat and save her dear John. "*O, my dear John!*" John was fortunately saved, and brought on board half drowned. She clenched him round the neck and nearly smothered him with kisses. O, such a display of conjugal felicity. They both took a good horn of whiskey, and turned in.

The frigate being now ready to receive her machinery, was towed to Jersey City. One hundred men were selected to go with her, to assist in getting the boilers on board, to take in the masts, and also to rig her. I was one of the number, as there was much carpenter's work to do. And it was certainly a great relief to me to be clear of the miserable gunboats, and to have employment for both body and mind.

It was now December, and the weather extremely cold. We soon had the greater part of the machinery on board, and both masts in, and expected to have her ready for service by the following May.

But I came near meeting with an accident which would in all probability have stopped my career. I had a temporary stage rigged at the mast head for the purpose of putting in two heavy composition sheeves.

I was hoisted up to the stage in a girt line, and then the sheeves were sent up to me. The morning was very cold, and the north wind very piercing; the handling of the sheeves had so benumbed my hands, that they were nearly useless, in consequence of which I took a cant backward, but fortunately held on. A little more and I should have come down a distance of eighty feet, but my time had not yet come, so I lived on.

While lying at Jersey City, a new sailing master joined the frigate who had never been in the United States naval service before. And it appeared that he thought flogging was as much a sailor's due as his rations, for he kept the cat agoing on the most trifling occasion, although, according to the strict rules of punishment, as they then existed in the navy, a sailing master had no more right to seize a man up and flog him, than a midshipman had. But as he had sole charge of the frigate for the present, he was determined that every one should know the full measure of his authority.

I went over to New York one evening, to see a particular friend, and as the time slipped away rather imperceptibly, I concluded to remain over night and go on board the frigate early in the morning.

In consequence of there being much ice in the river, the ferry-boat did not go over as soon as usual; by this delay I could not get on board before the hands were turned to. Our brave sailing master called me to know where I had been.

I replied, "To New York, sir," When, drawing himself up, and putting on an important look says, "Remember, sir, this is the first time; now beware of the second." I fully appreciated his meaning which was, that if I went to New York again without asking his liberty, that he would flog me.

I was well aware that I had no right to absent myself from the ship without liberty. And I was also well aware that he had no authority to strike me, I being a petty officer, and none but a *commandant* or a *post captain* can flog a petty officer.

However, this all passed off, and during the time we were together all was well.

The small vessels which I have previously alluded to as comprising the Flying Squadron, were purchased and lying at the Brooklyn Navy Yard. And as they were to be fitted out with dispatch, we were shifted from the steam-frigate to the Navy Yard to man these vessels, as they were all to undergo more or less alterations, the crews could not live on board of them until after the repairs had been completed. Accordingly we were put on board the old prize ship Alert. She was the first prize taken by the frigate Essex, and as she was rather old, was converted into a receiving ship.

When I first went on board this filthy tub my heart sunk within me. I thought the gunboat was the filthiest thing that floated, but as the saying goes, she was not a circumstance to the old Alert.

As a general thing, order and discipline are seldom found to prevail to any extent on board of a receiving ship. In some cases they are commanded by some old worn-out or superannuated naval officer, whose energy, if he ever had any, has entirely gone out. Or, perhaps the command is given to some dissipated fellow who does not know how to treat men. And then, the seamen who are put on board these dismal abodes, are constantly shifting; some probably do not remain twenty-four hours. So there is but litttle opportunity for establishing any permanent rules and regulations on board a receiving ship, whatever may be the disposition of the commander.

These remarks are intended to apply only to the time of the late war with England. Since then I believe there has been much improvement in this class of ships. At the time I was on board the Alert she was commanded by a drunken tyrannical master's mate, and when I had reached the berth deck, with my bag and hammock, I walked aft to the place set apart for petty officers, and was just about laying them down when a fellow sung out to me:

"I say! look out for the lice there; there are some as big as cockroaches."

I thought if they were as large as that, I could easily catch them, so I left my dunnage and went on deck.

I had hardly stepped from the ladder, when close by me, this master's mate knocked a man down for not touching his hat as he passed him. Everything was in the utmost disorder; men were drunk and roaring about the deck, and away forward, in a hole which they called a sick bay, were some ten or a dozen miserable creatures. One was raving in a paroxysm of delirium tremens; there were ten in the last stage of consumption, and could not live many hours, and several with fever and diarrhœa. And such a smell!

I had now a fixed determination to harden myself to everything that came along, even to death itself; and in any shape.

There were about two hundred men and boys on board this ship, who had been recruited for the Flying Squadron.

The weather was very cold and stormy, and many of these poor fellows had sold every article of clothing except what they stood in, for rum. Hence they were unprotected from the weather. The ration of a half pint of raw whiskey, was served to each man at seven and a half o'clock in the morning, and scarcely a dozen out of the whole crew that had a blanket or a bed. The government furnished them with a hammock, and many kept themselves too drunk to hang them up, and would lie down and sleep upon the wet deck; then followed severe colds, which often terminated in consumption, fever and death. But the half pint of raw whiskey in the morning gave them new life for a short time, and then they were down again.

There was one young man of very fine appearance, who had been thoroughly educated and had studied for the ministry, and who, through the influence of bad company and dissipation, had been induced to enter as a landsman, at the naval rendezvous, for the sake of the miserable pittance of advanced wages which he would receive, and with which he might, while it lasted, feed that insatiable appetite for rum, which was soon to terminate his unhappy career. After he had taken his deadly potation, and during its exhilarating influence, he would mount an empty cask, and preach a fragment of a sermon, condemnatory of the very course which he was pursuing. And I must say, that in point of language and enunciation, there were few ministers then or even at the present day, that could excel him. But he died, and was put into a drunkard's hole.

One morning a dead man was found on the berth deck, near the main hatch. The poor fellow had died during the night, probably from exposure, as he possessed neither bed nor clothing. It appeared that there was no one on whom the duty of taking proper care of the corpse devolved, so it lie there all that day, frozen stiff.

I ate but little, for my stomach fairly loathed everything I saw in the shape of food. As the weather continued very stormy, we were kept on board, and I had as much as I could do to watch my clothes bag. We spent about a week in this miserable manner, when the weather became clear, and all that were able were sent on shore, and to be employed on board the several vessels of the squadron.

The commodore's flag was hoisted on board the brig Firefly, of four hundred and seventy tons burthen. She was a beautiful vessel, having been built for a privateer; but she needed much alteration to fit her for the armament intended for her, which was fourteen guns in the waist, and two long eighteens on pivots amidships. Lieut. Edw. Barnwell, my friend, of whom I have previously spoken, was 1st Lieutenant, and through him I was ordered to her as chief carpenter's mate. Com. Porter had committed the fitting of this brig to Mr. Barnwell. I had charge of several jobs, and I soon perceived that he put great confidence in me, and often gave his orders to *me* instead of the master-workman.

One morning, I had passed the sentinel at the gangway, on my way ashore from the Alert, an officer standing near to pass the men out. Just as I had got upon the wharf, it occurred to me that I had forgotten a list of spars which had been made out on the previous evening. I immediately returned on board, and as I passed the sentinel, said to him, that I had forgotten a paper, and should pass out again in half a minute, and in about that time was at the gangway again, and as I was passing out, *he*, quicker than a flash, put his bayonet at my breast and ordered me to stop, threatening that if I moved an inch he would put it through my body. I just stepped back and called an officer, who passed me out, and when upon the wharf, I turned round to get a look at this (as I then called him,) infernal scoundrel, and surely, he could not well be mistaken. He was a tall, gaunt, lantern-jawed Irishman, with but one eye, freckled and horribly scarred with the small-pox. I never saw him afterwards and probably it was well for both of us that I did not.

Perhaps the reader may think that in my description of the gunboat, and the receiving ship, Alert, that I have dealt altogether in superlatives, or that I have painted things in too high colors; but I assure you, that the half has not been told. I find myself at a loss for words and sentences, that will give an adequate idea of scenes that I have witnessed, while in the United States Navy; but more particularly, during the war with England. It may be, that I was more sensitive than I should have been, considering my place and position; and took more notice of things and circumstances, which appeared so unpleasant to me, and which, perhaps, to another would hardly have been noticed. I have also spoken, and shall have occasion again to speak, in what may be thought a disrespectful manner, of officers with whom I have come in contact during my service in the United States Navy.

It is well known to every one, at all acquainted with the United States or any other navy, that in the time of war, besides the regularly commissioned, and warrant officers, there are those, who enter the naval service, as subordinate officers. Such as masters, mates, and sometimes sailing masters, without either warrant or commission, and men of whom nothing is known of their previous habits; the only qualification required is seamanship.

It is of this class that I have had occasion to speak thus harshly.

But I regret to say, that before I get through with my naval life, I shall have occasion to state facts highly derogatory to the character and standing of both commissioned and warrant officers.

I return again to the old Alert, and to scenes in the Brooklyn navy yard.

Additions were daily made to the Alert's crew, by men that were shipped in New York, and also of exchanged prisoners, many of which had lately arrived in New York. One day there came on board, a boat load of men from the rendezvous; and among them was a man who, although intoxicated and in sailor's garb, I knew at once was not a sailor. But strongly suspected that he was a victim either of rum or some rascally land shark, and very probably of both; he was tumbled on board with the rest, like so many dead hogs. Neither of them had a rag of clothing or a cent of money. I kept the run of the man just alluded to, until he was sober, when I commenced a conversation, but I soon saw that his mind was not sufficiently composed to enter upon the subject I wished to broach.

Next day, I succeeded in catching him sober, and at leisure, said I to him, "you are not much of a sailor, I presume?"

"No," he answered with a deep sigh. "I am no sailor, nor do I ever expect to be."

"How long have you been shipped?"

"Yesterday morning."

"Did you get any advance wages?"

"No; the fellow that took me to the rendezvous became my security, and took the two months advance."

"Who was this fellow?"

"It was a landlord, that I had staid with a few days. I had been drinking freely, and he told me I must pay my board and liquor bill, and in order to do this, I had better ship for the navy as landsman; the pay is eight dollars a month. It was quite immaterial to me what I did, so I shipped, and he put me on board this recieving ship without any clothes, but what I stand in."

"You shiver very much, are you not cold?"

"Yes, I am very cold, and have been shaking all night; I don't feel very well neither."

It so happened that it was a stormy day, and we should not be sent on shore, which would give me a good opportunity of finding out my new acquaintance. I led him into my berth, where we were not likely to be interrupted, and then requested him to tell me his story, which he began as follows:

"My name is James Harris, and I have been a merchant in Boston for the last thirteen years. My place of business was in Market Square, — the firm was James Harris & Co. My partner resided in New York, he had married a lady of great wealth, from Albany. The brother of this lady was a very dissipated fellow, and had often enticed my partner into gambling houses where he had lost large sums. Still he was attentive to his business; we frequently had large consignments arriving at New York, the business of which was attended to with punctuality. About three years ago, 1811, I received a confidential note from a friend, advising me to come to New York, as my interest required it, and as I had not received my usual letters, I began to suspect that something was wrong. Accordingly I started for New York, went to our office in South street, and found all right apparently; except that Mr. P. had not been out for several days, being confined at home with rheumatism. Just as I had reached the door to go, the cashier stepped out, saying he wished to say a few words to me before seeing Mr. P. We went into a small lobby, and he then told me that probably my partner would not like to see me, as he had got into a difficulty where he had been obliged to use the name of the firm, for the present, 'and,' said the cashier, 'I have managed it thus far, and taken up all the paper as it came to maturity; but am not able to say how much more there is out with the firm's name, though it having nothing to do with the business of J. Harris & Co.' He also informed me that Mr. P's. brother had requested him to take up the drafts, and he would see it all made right."

Harris now paused a few moments. I readily saw that he was much agitated. He placed both hands to his face, resting his head on his knees. I waited patiently a few moments, when he again resumed, but seemed to forget where he had left off, and on my reminding him, he continued:

"O, yes! Well, I called on P., who was sitting in the parlor, and in close conversation with a gentleman, who immediately left without my being introduced. As what I had heard at the store, had troubled me very much, and P. evidently saw my agitation, I thought I would commence the business without delay. As soon as I began to enquire why the weekly letters had been discontinued, he burst into tears, and for ten minutes did not utter a word; at length he raised his head, saying, 'Harris, I am a ruined man, I have gambled away all my own property, and a great amount that belonged to my wife. O, those cursed cards! that damnable billiard table; and what makes it more distressing, my wife's brother has been my ruin; he has actually led me to, and remained with me all night in houses of ill fame, thus deceiving my wife, by telling her I was detained on business. I have been diseased for a month, and that alone has almost tempted me to commit suicide. Sherman has property, and has promised to see me out of the scrape. My wife knows all, and has forbidden her brother ever to enter the door again; the gentleman you saw when you came in, is a broker, who has engaged to raise what I need at present to keep the business of the firm straight.' "

Here Harris paused again, and said he should like a little whiskey, as he felt a gnawing at his stomach. It was now nearly eleven o'clock, and neither of us had taken any breakfast, and I was determined at first that he should not have anything to drink, at least, until I had got his story, that is if I could help it. But he insisted on going to his mess for the grog, which he drank, and of course rendered him unfit for further conversation at that time. When I conversed with him again, which was a few days after, he seemed to have forgotten me; but when I took his hand, and reverted to the conversation, the corner of his eye brightened up; he returned the squeeze of my hand, and said:

"O, yes! yes! you are my Boston friend."

"Yes, my dear fellow," said I. "if I can befriend you in any way, I will most cheerfully do it. Come now, and tell me the rest of that story." He agreed to it. I took him into a snug place, and reminded him where he left off, but I found his mind was too much agitated to proceed in a regular manner, so I began the conversation.

"Well, how did you come out with your partner?"

"Oh! he died soon after this."

"Well, how did your business matters turn out?"

"Oh, ruined! ruined! I lost everything in Boston, and then I gave myself up to intoxication. My wife died with grief. My oldest son supported me until a month ago. I came to New York, called on Sherman, my partner's brother-in-law, to see if he would give me some assistance, as he had been the cause of my ruin. He was much bloated, and looked badly. He ordered me out of his house. I told him I would not leave him until he had given me enough to buy a suit of clothes. He replied, 'I will give you some clothes; come with me.' So I followed him to a common sailor's clothing store; he ordered a suit of sailor's clothes, which he paid for and left me. I threw them into the street, the shop-man picked them up again, and persuaded me to put them on, which I consented to, and these are the clothes I now have."

I had no opportunity of conversing with this unfortunate man after this, though frequently saw him among the crowd, sometimes drunk, and sometimes sober.

One cold, drizzly morning, I heard the boatswain's whistle, and the call "all hands on the quarter-deck to muster! I soon ascertained that a draft was to be made from this receiving ship of seventy-five men for Lake Ontario as it was expected that Com. Chauncy would soon fight the decisive battle. When the men were all up, the purser sung out,

"All you, whose names are called, pass over to the starboard side." And among those selected, I saw poor Harris. He was a fine looking man, very much resembling Daniel Webster. Very soon these men were ordered to the boat along side, to be conveyed to the Albany packet. Harris had no pea-jacket, and was wet through before the boat left the ship's side. I saw no more of him, and think it probable that he died very soon after arriving at Sackets Harbor, as the dysentery was very prevalent, particularly among the intemperate, and but a few survived.

The old Alert was now so crowded with fresh recruits, that it became necessary to ship some of us on board the Corvette John Adams. I was among the draft selected for her; we went on board early in the morning. The purser's steward had not arranged for our rations, so we had nothing to eat that day, until just at night, when we got some fresh beef, which I ate raw. The John Adams, soon after we joined her, was ordered to be fitted as a cartel for Bermuda, to bring home the crew of the U. S. frigate President, which had been captured by a British squadron off New York, and carried into that place. We were now divided round among the gunboats; myself and twelve others were put on board a gunboat which had been used as a tender for the frigate President, while she lay in the harbor of New York. This gunboat had been hauled up in a cove, and was full of rats and old rigging. A negro was given us for a cook, and we were to live on board this craft, until the vessels composing the Flying Squadron were ready to receive their crews. We who were on board the Tender, were among those selected for the Firefly, and of course we belonged to the commodore. I had two companions, with whom I was more intimate than any of the others; although when drunk, they were furious, and would as soon kill me as they would a rat. Still they were excellent seamen, and men of good information, when sober; and as I did not use any kind of intoxicating drink, I frequently became the butt of their ridicule and sometimes of abuse. Their names were Jack Wilson and Jack Anderson; the latter was a Scotchman, and belonged to Aberdeen, and a man of excellent information; he had a wife in Brooklyn, near the Navy Yard, although not allowed to leave the yard, I have many a time assisted him in getting out at night, that he might visit his family, and frequently supplying him with money. His wife at one time was very sick, and notwithstanding my kindness towards him, he got drunk one night, and abused me shamefully. Next day, however, he felt quite ashamed. and asked my forgiveness. Wilson was in the battle of Lake Champlain, was wounded in the head, and a little grog would make him crazy.

As we had been pent up in the Navy Yard nearly ten months, we devised a scheme to get out and have a cruise; not a drunken one, however, but merely a look around, as we termed it, and in order to effect this without being stopped by a sentinel, we remained on board the Firefly, where we had been at work all day, until after sundown; it was bitter cold, but we were determined to have a cruise, at any rate. When all was still, we got out on the jib-boom, and dropped on to a fence, and then to the ground, and by climbing over two or three other fences, found ourselves in the street. We went along until we came to a church, lighted up for a lecture; went in and took seats near the organ. We enjoyed the meeting very much, particularly the closing part, which was an infant baptism.

When the water was put upon the little fellow's face, he commenced crying. Wilson spoke out, so that all who were near could hear him, "That's no sailor's child—afraid of water." We left the meeting-house, and walked round to keep ourselves warm, and as the night was very cold concluded to go back to the yard. But, sailor-like, we had not once thought about getting past the sentinels without the countersign.

After trying at the regular gates, and refused *entrance* by the sentinel, we made out to crawl in under an old fence, and we were now but little better off than we were when outside, and now had three sentinels to pass, before we could get to our sleeping place. And when we approached the first, were hailed, "Who comes there?" "Friends." "Advance, friends, and give the countersign." We *had* no countersign, and stood at the point of the bayonet, until the corporal of the guard came.

He demanded who we were, but would not allow us to pass. There was no other way to get to the gunboat, but by swimming across a dock two hundred feet wide; and then there was danger of being shot by the sentinels, if discovered, to say nothing about the risk of freezing, after we had left the water.

We went off a short distance, got into an old shed, and crawled in among some shavings, and there shivered it out until morning; it was truly a long night.

We went on board our craft, made up a rousing fire, and after taking some hot coffee, were all right again.

This affair rather cooled our devotion, so we went to no more evening meetings.

The weather continued very cold, and we could do but little work in the yard. Our black cook had been detected in stealing from an officer, and was sent on board the boat in double irons, and there confined, which of course deprived us of his services, and himself, the use of his limbs; for in consequence of his confinement both feet were frozen, and the groans of the poor fellow were really distressing.

He was removed to the hospital, but lost both feet; they were amputated soon after he entered the doctor's list. Truly "*The way of the transgressor is hard.*" In consequence of a trifling theft, this man is a cripple for life.

I have previously stated that our gunboat was full of rats. They were so thick that while we slept they would run over us in all directions. We were obliged to hang our provisions up to one of the beams, and place a man with a club, to watch the bag until morning. Our boat was also very leaky, and no one would take the trouble to pump her out. One night, just before we turned in, the water made its appearance over the platform, and when we come to examine the pump, it was found to be choked and entirely useless. We concluded, however, to stay on board that night, and on the morrow to apply to the captain of the yard for other quarters. About twelve o'clock, one fellow got out of his hammock and found himself knee deep in water. He gave the alarm, all hands roused up, and before we could get all our clothes and bedding on deck, she heeled over and sunk.

I made a jump and got on board another boat that lay along-side; and she was half full of water. The rest of the crew got off by means of the boat and some spars. In jumping on board the other boat, I fell on an iron belaying pin, and hurt myself severely. All this was in the night, it was quite dark and cold, but we made no noise.

By the sinking of this boat many lives were lost, as might be seen by the floating bodies around her next morning. And as the gunboat had been condemned before we went on board of her, we now considered her condemnation as fully Rat-ified. The repairs on board the Firefly were now so far advanced that we, poor sunken fellows, had permission to take our hammocks and bags on board of her, and our meals on board the Cyane.

As Commodore Porter had not yet assumed the command of the squadron formally, it devolved on Captain Wolcott Chauncey, brother of Commodore Isaac Chauncey,—he being the seignor captain among those of the Flying Squadron, and had come down from Lake Ontario to join the fleet. And he was a Tartar sure enough, as the following little incident will show. Two young men, who, I believe, were mechanics' apprentices, had shipped for the squadron, and had been at the Navy Yard but a few days, when, probably feeling a little homesick, took French leave one evening, and went over to the city. On the following morning, they were missed at muster, and their absence reported to Capt. Chauncey, who immediatately sent a midshipman to find them. They were both found together, having met with some of their companions, and who had all been on a frolic. These young men were brought on board an old bomb ketch, and confined with double irons two days, and on the morning of the third, at nine o'clock, all hands were called along-side the ketch, to witness punishment. This was an interesting sight, and reminded me of the whipping through the fleet at Halifax.

Here were about three hundred men, boys and marines, assembled round the old hulk to see these two young men nearly flayed alive, for going over to New York without leave. When all had assembled, the two prisoners were brought from their place of confinement, apparently more dead than alive. The first was stripped and seized up.

On these occasions, every man and officer stands with hats off, and perfectly silent, in order to show the *supremacy* of a law that cuts a man's flesh to pieces.

Capt. Chauncey, standing on a slight elevation, and with a stentorian voice, thus addressed the crowd: "*Men! what the law allows you, you shall have, but by the eternal —— if any one of you disobeys that law, I'll cut your back bone out.*" "Go on with him, boatswain's mate and do your duty, or by ——, you shall take his place."

The shrieks of the youngster were dreadful, calling upon God and all the holy angels to save him. After the first dozen, another boatswain's mate took the cat, and when he had received two dozen, he fainted, and hung by his wrists. The punishment was suspended for a few moments until he had revived sufficiently to stand on his feet; he then took four dozen more, making six in all, and when taken down he could not stand.

The other received seven dozen; he fainted however, before he had received the first, and received the greater portion of his punishment in that state. The flesh was fairly hanging in strips upon both backs; it was really a sickening sight.

The punishment being over, all went to their respective duties. The last I ever heard of this celebrated knight of the cat was, that he was employed at a very high salary in superintending the building and fitting out a frigate for the Greeks.

Notwithstanding my previous determination to make the best of everything, and to become hardened to whatever might come along, discontent seemed to return again with additional force. I began to give a gloomy look into the future. The idea of being captured, and then of lingering in a British prison, and this horrid flogging, and the companions that I must pass the remainder of my servitude with. These feelings seemed to work like an avalanche upon me; and there was a possibility that in my present position, I might be flogged at the gangway, too, as many a man has been, without knowing for what.

I was heartily disgusted with everything that belonged to a man-of-war; and after a night's deliberation, came to a fixed determination, that I would desert, and get into some foreign country, and there remain until I had accumulated something; and probably by that time I should be forgotten, and could then return to my native country.

Accordingly I took from my bag some letters and other small matters, and made known my intention to a particular friend, and gave my bag into his charge.

At sundown, a boat went to the city for the officers, who had been on liberty during the day.

I watched the opportunity, after the boat had been called away, to get into her and to stow myself forward, and as it was rather dark, I was not seen by the midshipman who had charge of the boat. As soon as she touched the wharf at New York, I jumped out, and just as I had got upon my feet, the midshipman sang out, "Who's that?" But I was soon among the crowd upon the wharf, and went up to the house of a friend, who was not then at home; but I communicated the whole matter to his wife, who was an excellent and kind lady, and who had always manifested much interest for my welfare. When I had got through with my story, she begged, with tears streaming from her eyes, that I would abandon this dreadful determination, and return to the brig. She could not endure the idea of my being a deserter from the United States Navy, and, if ever taken, would, in all probability, be subject to severe punishment. These arguments, and such visible demonstrations of regard for my future happiness, weighed heavily with me.

I could hardly refrain from tears myself, and very soon my friend came in, and when I made known the affair to him, he insisted on my immediate return.

I spent the night with this kind family, and on the following morning, went back, without having been missed. Still there was a fixed gloom that hung over me. This spell, or infatuation, or whatever it might be called, was like an incubus that bore me down. I was like one determined on self-destruction, and seeking a place and an opportunity for its consummation.

I kept busy at my work, and received the kindest treatment from Mr. Barnwell, as well as from every officer on board the brig. There was a rumor among the seamen that Mr. Barnwell was to be removed to another ship, which, although it caused me some little regret, was without foundation, at least, for the present. My mind still brooded over my unhappy condition, and again I was determined to leave the navy, and also to leave the country.

I obtained permission to go to New York, and managed to get my clothes bag on shore, and deposited it with Jack Anderson's wife. I crossed the ferry, and had no sooner stepped out of the ferry-boat, than a strong feeling of self-reproach came over me, which nearly staggered me in this foolish resolution. Mr. Barnwell had given me liberty to be absent twenty-four hours; his treatment to me had been like that of a kind father, and now to requite this good feeling by desertion, seemed to be the heighth of ingratitude. All this made me half determined to re-cross the ferry.

I thought if I could find a friend into whose ear I could pour my trouble, and obtain from him some consoling advice, even that would make me happy.

I went to the Bull's Head Inn, in the Bowery, the depot for wagons that plied between New York and Boston, (as the water communication was cut off by the British cruisers) and found that a wagon would start next morning by daylight. I saw the driver, and bargained with him to carry me to Boston, and for which I was to give him my pea-jacket.

I did not awake the next morning until after the hour at which the wagon was to start; so, of course, I lost my passage; but such a night as I passed cannot be described; what with horrid dreams and direful forebodings, I was nearly distracted. I spent the day in walking round the wharves, as no wagon started until the next day. I did not at this time go near my former friend, who so kindly dissuaded me before, but I called on another, an elderly gentleman, and to whom I told my story. He happened to be the friend I had been seeking, and he urged me by all means to abandon this rash alternative, and serve my time out honorably, and then I should have nothing to embitter my future life. He offered me any assistance that lay in his power, which offer I gratefully received, and at the same time assured him that I needed nothing but advice. I had plenty of money, and plenty of good clothing, and that all I wanted was to be reconciled to my unhappy condition. He urged upon me very forcibly his own opinion, backed up with his long experience, that all things came out right in the end, if our intentions were pure; and my conversation with this good old man caused me again to waver in my present intention.

On the afternoon of the second day of my absence from the brig, I met Wilson, who had just come over from the Navy Yard. Mr. Barnwell had enquired for me, and he had told him that I was sick, and at the house of a friend in New York. Mr. Barnwell sent him for me, with orders to have me brought over if I was able to stand.

Jack and I understood the whole affair, and I went with him to the Navy Yard, and quietly on board the brig, and resumed the job on which I had been at work, when I went ashore. Next morning, Mr. Barnwell came to me, and enquired about my health, to all of which I replied in a satisfactory manner.

In the afternoon, he called me on the quarter-deck, and said he, "I observe that you are a young man of good habits, and acquainted with your business; I have also observed that you are active and get quickly through any job you undertake, and shall appoint you carpenter of this brig; your official appointment I will hand you to-morrow; and that I feel a pleasure in doing this from what I have seen of you since your attachment to the Navy." He then gave me twenty dollars and liberty to go over to New York. All this seemed to me like a dream, and yet it was real; my trouble was over! I was now a warrant officer—out of the reach of the lash—had a comfortable state-room, and a boy to wait upon me. Truly, this was a metamorphosis.

Just as the Flying Squadron was well equipped, and all ready for sea, peace was proclaimed between England and the United States. This of course put a new phase upon everything, The voice of war was hushed, and all warlike preparations, such as fitting out privateers, enlisting soldiers, &c., now suddenly terminated. Business of another kind now sprung up, such as the repairing and fitting out merchant ships. The Sound was now clear, and all things began to wear a cheerful aspect. The Flying Squadron, with the Constellation, Macedonian, and Gueriere frigates, and Ontario, and Epervier sloops-of-war, were all anchored off the Battery.

For some years past, the Dey of Algiers had committed frequent depredations upon American merchantmen; had captured several Mediterranean traders, and still held their crews in slavery. These depredations were now to be punished in a summary manner, the United States having formally declared war against the regency of Algiers. We also had demands against the governments of Tripoli and Tunis, for permitting the capture of American vessels in their harbors by the British during the late war.

The fleet was placed under the command of Com. Decatur, was destined for Algiers, and to sail in a few days, or as soon as the diplomatic matters could be arranged at Washington. The fleet had left their moorings off the Battery, and had anchored near Sandy Hook.

One evening, while sitting in my state-room, a marine (sea soldier,) came to the door and asked if he could speak with me a few minutes. I answered yes, invited him in, and he then commenced the following story:

"You know, sir, that I go by the name of Cribbs, but that is not my true name. Now, sir, if you will allow me to tell my story, which you may rely upon as truth, you will soon learn how I came by the name of Cribbs. Last December I arrived at New York from Madras. We run by the blockading ships in the night, and took a pilot just outside the Hook. My native place is Saybrook, Connecticut. I had been absent fifteen months. I left a wife, but no children. After I had been paid off, I went on board a sloop bound to Saybrook, and agreed with the captain to work my passage home. In order to keep out of the way of the cruisers, he always started at night and kept close in shore, and used their sweeps or long oars, and I being a sailor, the skipper was glad to have me. After breakfast I took my chest on board, and meant to stay there myself. The captain said to me, that the strap of his throat halliard block was broken, and he wished to have it repaired before he sailed, and asked me to go up and send it down. I immediately went up for that purpose, and had just commenced unhooking the block, when I heard a talking on deck, and on looking down, saw that they were all looking up at me, and at the same time the captain hailed me, saying that there were two men that wished to see me.

"I came down, and one of them asked me 'if my name was John Cribbs?'

"I answered, 'no; my name is Jones.'

"'Well, we want you to go with us, as far as Market street.'

"'Go with you? who *are* you?'

"'We believe you are a deserter from the marine corps of the United States, and we wish you to go with us, and if you are not the man, then there will be no harm done.'

"The captain of the sloop said that I had better go, and show them that I was not the man they were in search of. I had then in my possession four treasury notes, of twenty dollars each, the amount of my wages, which I had tied up in a corner of my black handkerchief, that I wore about my neck, and in my pocket, about three dollars in pennies and small paper bills. I went with these fellows, they keeping one on each side of me. I was carried to the United States rendezvous for the marine corps, and put into a back room, which was locked upon me and a guard placed at the door.

"I sat down on the floor, wondering what all this meant. I had nothing to eat or drink all that day, nor a bed on which to sleep at night.

"Early next morning, a sergeant and two marines came in and told me I must go to the Navy Yard. I swore I would not go, and demanded an explanation. The sergeant told me that resistance was of no use, as he could call twenty men if necessary. I asked him what right they had to imprison me; I had never been in the United States service, and could prove where I had been during every year of my life. I was then told that I must go, and if I was peaceable should not be ironed, but if I attempted to escape I should be shot. I had eaten nothing since yesterday morning; I felt hungry and demanded food. They gave me part of a small loaf, a piece of cheese, and half a tumbler of gin. I then went with them over to the Navy Yard, and was there put in irons under charge of a sentinel. I asked for pen and paper, and was told that these things were not allowed to prisoners. I had hard work to persuade myself that I was not dreaming.

"I remained here in confinement until one morning the sergeant came in, knocked off my irons, and told me I was to go on board the frigate President. I was washed and shaved, and a suit of marine uniform given me, with orders to put it on and be ready for drill at eleven o'clock. All this I did, because I could not help myself; a musket was given me, and I was placed by the corporal in the ranks, and I solemnly swear that this was the first time in my life that I ever had on a soldier's dress, or ever handled a musket as a soldier.

"Myself and nineteen others were put on board the frigate President. She was bound on a cruise round Cape Horn, but on going out, you know we struck on the bar and injured our keel, which very much hindered our sailing. We fell in with the English Fleet, Pomone, Endymion and Majestic, and, after a hard-fought action, we were captured and carried to Bermuda. We were exchanged, and came to New York in the John Adams. I have been in the barracks ever since my return, have written once to Commodore Decatur, but have received no answer. I have now been ordered to this brig, and when I shall be liberated I know not.

I looked him full in the face, and said I to him: "Cribbs, do you tell the truth? Is what you have told me positively true?" "Yes, sir, on my oath," and then made a solemn appeal confirmatory of what he had told me. "And now, sir, what I wish you to do for me, if you please, and which I shall consider a great favor, is that you will state my case to some lawyer in New York before we sail on this cruise." I replied that I would give him the form of a letter to Mr. Emmet, probably one of the best lawyers in New York, and would prefer that the writing should be in his own hand. I gave him the use of my writing materials, and also assisted him in getting his letter to the city, which went up in the morning boat, and on that same evening after he had been relieved from his post, I called him into my room and asked him if he could, in any way, account for this strange affair. He said that he could only account for it in this way: " The day after I was paid off I went to a boarding-house, (I think in Water street) kept by a man named Sweeney, and while we were sitting in the bar-room, a good-looking man came in and asked if any one would like to enter the United States service, either as seaman, marine or landsman; and out of a joke, I asked what were the wages. He said seamen got twelve dollars a month and twenty dollars bounty; ordinary seamen and landsmen something less. 'And how much do marines get?' said I. 'Eight dollars and their clothing.' This fellow now went off, and after he had gone, Sweeney, the landlord, observed, "That fellow is a — pimp; his business is to go round and hunt up deserters, for which he gets a large reward.' Now, Sweeney knew that I was going home, and also *how* I was going; and whether it was not a contrived plan to entrap me I cannot say. I had been told that he was not the most honest man in the world, as many sailors could also testify. This is the only way that I can account for my imprisonment. I was pounced upon as a deserter, and it may be that this fellow obtained a reward for my pretended apprehension."

On the following morning a boat came from the Gueriere, with an order from Commodore Decatur for John Cribbs; he was put in double irons on board the Gueriere and this was the last I ever heard of John Cribbs. Mr. Emmet had, no doubt, written to Commodore Decatur about the man, and in order that the case might be properly investigated, the Commodore had sent for him for that purpose; but why he was ironed I cannot tell. We got under way on the next day and thus ends the story of John Cribbs.

I will only add, that if the statement which he gave me was true, and of which I have not the slightest doubt, it goes to show a most mysterious, but successful piece of villany, and for which, if justice be done him, he will have a claim against the United States for immense damages.

CHAPTER V.

Fleet sail,—Firefly dismasted in a gale,—Return to New York,—Receive a warrant as carpenter in the navy,—Refit,—Sail again,—Cruelty of a lieutenant,—Fall in with a strange sail in the night,—Passionate behavior of the captain,—Remarks,—Enter the Straits of Gibraltar,—Pass the Rock,—Arrive at Carthagena, Receive intelligence of the capture of an Algerine frigate by our squadron—Fleet appears off Algiers,—Treaty,—Consul established,—American captives delivered up,—Put on board the Epervier, and sail for home,—Their extreme joy at their deliverance,—They all perish at sea,—Fleet arrive at Carthagena,—Firefly ordered to Gibraltar,—Sickness of the crew,—Cause,—I have orders to obtain a spar from the dock-yard,—Meet a great personage, who gets cooled down,—Politeness of Mr. Sprague,—Explore the rock,—Remarks,—Arrival of the fleet,—Officers shifted,—I am ordered to the Ontario,—Ships,—Sail for home,—Sail for Tangier,—Return to Gibraltar,—Fleet sails for Port Mahon,—Receive intelligence that the Dey had broken the treaty,—Proceed to Algiers,—Make preparations to burn their fleet,—Betrayed by a Frenchman,—Apology by the Dey,—Treaty resumed,—Cowardly management of the Dutch,—Return to Port Mahon,—Obtain permission to refit our ships at the arsenal,—Assist in fitting out the Ferdinand,—Miserable condition of the Spanish Navy, and of naval officers,—Small pox breaks out on board the Ontario,—Filthy marines,—Lord Exmouth's Fleet,—Sail from Port Mahon,—Wreck of the Ferdinand in a severe levanter,—We arrive at Tarragona,—Vows of a Catholic lady passenger during the gale,—Its performance,—Arrive at Carthagena,—Examine the dock-yard,—Receive intelligence of the fate of seventy American seamen that were on board the Ferdinand,—They were carried to Algiers,—Sail from Carthagena to Algiers,—Account of the wreck of the Ferdinand,—American seamen taken off by the Erie.

While the Firefly was fitting at the Navy Yard, I had provided a large quantity of mast-fishes* and shot-plugs, and

* Mast-fishes are long pieces of oak, hollowed and fitted in such a manner that if a mast or spar of any kind is broken or injured, by a shot from an enemy's gun, the fish is bound with lashings round the injured spar, so that it may be strong enough to bear the sail. A fish is to a mast what a splint is to a broken limb.

one of our "*bully*" lieutenants, of whom I shall again have occasion to speak and to bring before the reader, whenever he had the morning watch, and while the decks were washing, would give a very emphatic order to "wash round that — lumber," and would begin to curse because the deck was lumbered up with so much "*useless trash.*" This was always intended for me to hear, as I had been blamed from the time it first came on board; but wait a little while and see what became of this *useless lumber.*

The Firefly was commanded by George Rodgers, Esq., brother of Commodore Rodgers. He was an excellent man, and subsequently showed his friendship for me. Our first lieutenant was David Geisinger, now one of our oldest commodores. Also an excellent man, and for whom I shall always have the highest esteem.

On the 10th of May, 1815, as I have already stated, the fleet got under way and stood to sea in regular order, with a fine westerly breeze, which continued until we reached the gulf, when we took a heavy S.E. gale, which commenced at about 10 P. M., and the next morning, about 2 o'clock, we were on the Eastern Edge, having run during the night and up to that time under close-reefed top-sails, and now it commenced blowing a perfect hurricane.

The brig, when in smooth water, was very low, her gun-deck being only about eighteen inches from the water's edge, our armament consisted of twelve 18 lb. cannonades, and two long eighteens amidships, and two long eighteens on pivots. She was also very heavily sparred, and, being built for a privateer, was not very strong. She was, however, a fast sailer and a good vessel.

The sea ran very high; the hurricane raged with unabated fury, attended with heavy thunder and lightning, and torrents of rain.

The brig labored very much, and was continually under water. At daylight I had gone below to shift my wet clothing, and had hardly got to my room when the boatswain's mate came running down, to tell me that the foremast was sprung. I jumped directly up, and, sure enough, the mast was broken in several places.

Captain Rodgers had gone below to get some rest, having been on deck all night. Mr. Geisinger, with every other officer, were doing their best. I reported to him the state of the foremast. "Well, sir," said he, "do the best you can with it." The top-gallant masts were already housed, but the top-masts were on end, the weight of which very much endangered the mast; but to get them down was out of the question.

Our rigging, which had been put over the mast heads in cold weather, had now now become so slack that it was very little support to the masts.

But it was no time now to reflect upon what *had* been done. Our business now was to do something for the preservation of our lives.

I called my carpenter's crew, four in number, around me, we knocked out the mast wedges, and in the meantime the boatswain's mates were clearing away the mast-fishes, this "*useless lumber*," and others, were passing the lashings around the masts, all ready for securing the fishes.

I requested the gunner to get up four of his largest gun tackles, two on each side, and haul them taut with jiggers; this was soon done although she was wallowing in the sea, at such a rate that it was almost impossible to hold on. The fishes were put in their places. I got into a bowline, and was hoisted high enough to fasten the heads with spikes; with a maul in one hand and spikes in the other, and contriving to hold on, so that, when I swung against the mast, I could hit the spike; but before they were fastened, my poor body was badly pounded against the broken stick.

In two hours we had it secure, or at least, we were not afraid of its going over the side. Our attention was now called to the mainmast, which was broken one-third off under the saddle. We unshipped the main boom, and got up two large tackles on each side, as we did with the foremast, and with much difficulty managed to set up two shrouds on each side, and fished it firmly, now with the fishes on both masts, well spiked and woolded, we felt that we could get short sail on both.

The gale now began to abate. None of the fleet had

been seen since the evening before, and the last ship we saw was the Macedonian frigate; she passed close by, and to leeward of us; and was under a close-reefed maintop-sail, and fore and mainstorm stay-sails. She had met with some damage to her main rigging, which they were repairing. And while lying in this apparently destitute condition, we fired minute guns for about four hours, but concluded that, in all probability there was nothing within hearing of our guns, so it was of no use to waste powder. Towards sunset it ceased blowing; and the clouds indicated fair weather.

On the morrow, we commenced getting sail on her, the bowsprit was broken nearly off at the knight heads; but it held on, and was of some service; we set a top-gallant-sail on each top-mast, and two close-reefed top-sails below, and turned her head for New York; and in fine weather, we could set small sails about in any direction where they would draw.

It was very fortunate for us that neither of the masts went over the side, for had that been the case we should have inevitably gone to the bottom; for the mast in falling would have cut through the side, and being under water as we were, nothing, but the All-powerful arm of Jehovah, could have saved us; and had it not been for the fishes, the masts could never have been kept on end. And much also depended on the promptness and the alacrity, with which all this was done.

On the second day, after we had got pretty well to rights again, Capt. Rodgers sent for me to come on the quarter-deck.

Said he to me, "Young man,* how long have you been in the United States service?"

"Since October, sir."

"What is your age?"

"Nearly twenty-two, sir."

"Well sir; allow me to say, you are one of the most active men I have ever met with, and it is to your exertions,

* Capt. Rodgers had joined the brig only a few days before we sailed, and had not yet become acquainted with but few of his officers, which was the reason of his addressing me as young man.

UNITED STATES BRIG, FIREFLY, IN A GALE, MAY 18th, 1815.

that we are indebted for the preservation of this brig, and I may also add of our *lives* too; and it shall be my first business, if we arrive safe in New York, to obtain for you a warrant from the President of the United States."

I thanked him, bowed, and retired.

I soon saw that this compliment caused some little jealousy or envy from my messmates, the gunner and boatswain, but it soon wore off, and we were on the best terms, and in sixteen days arrived safely in New York.

Now with regard to the compliment paid me by Captain Rodgers, and in justice to myself, and without assuming to be egotistical, had I not have taken right hold, and in one sense assumed the whole charge of securing the masts, they would have gone over as sure as the world.*

The first lieutenant's place was on the quarter-deck, and there was not a soul among the rest of the officers that knew anything about fishing a mast, or what to have done, in this emergency; for the very first step towards their security, was knocking out the wedges, in order that the mast might have longer play; and it will be seen in the course of my narrative, that this was not the only scene where "*useless lumber*" was the means of saving valuable lives.

We arrived at Brooklyn Navy Yard on the 1st of June. Capt. Rodgers wrote to Washington, and in six days my warrant came, which he presented me on the quarter-deck of the brig, with many compliments, and good wishes.

A Court of Inquiry was held at the navy yard, by officers sent from Washington for that purpose, to investigate the proceedings of Capt. Rodgers during, and subsequent to the gale. His conduct was highly approved, and a vote of approbation given in his favor.

On the 5th of July we were all right again, and the little brig looked beautifully. We sailed with a fine south-west

* I saw that I must take the most hazardous part in this affair, while the rest of the carpenters were making wedges and cleats for the lashings, which, considering the rolling of the vessel was of itself a difficult job. I hung, more than half an hour, thumping against the mast, and drove sixteen spikes while in this perilous position, for had the mast gone over while I was hanging in the bowline, in all probability, I should have been killed.

wind, for Carthagena, in Spain, the port fixed upon as the rendezvous, in case of separation. On the sixth day out, we fell in with another gale, though nothing like the other; even had it been so, we were now in a much better condition to meet it than we were before.

Then, our rigging was slack, and our masts were made of single sticks; but now, our rigging was newly fitted, and our masts were built, and in fact, everything was in much better order than before.

I told the reader that I meant to show up the "*useless lumber man*" again, and here he is. During the gale it was his watch from 8 to 12 in the morning. I was sitting on the forward pivot gun, and a man named Tom Burns, a fine fellow, and a good sailor, was sitting just under me. This *gallant* officer came puffing along, for he was quite fat, and says to Burns, "Go up and secure that staysail." It had blown out of the netting, and was getting loose. "Aye, aye, sir," said Burns. He went up and hauled it in as well as he could, and, as he thought, secured it.

In about half an hour afterwards, this noble lieutenant came forward again, and looking up, saw that a small corner of the sail had got out of the netting. He sung out, "You Burns, you —— scoundrel, didn't I send you up to stop that sail?" "Yes, sir." "Well, come here. Boatswain's mate." "Sir." "Come here. Take your jacket off sir," to Burns. The boatswain's mate then put a dozen into him. "Now go up and see if you can stow that sail in a proper manner." Burns, while going up the rigging, merely said, "I thought I did my best before." I heard what he said. "What's that you say? Grumbling again, are you? Come down here, sir. Boatswain's mate." "Sir." "Come here. Take off your jacket, sir," to Burns. The poor fellow took another dozen, and then went up and tried again; and when he came down, he sat in the same place on the gun carriage, which gave me an opportunity of looking down his back, which was covered with blood, and he was then giving vent to a copious flood of tears. This *was the useless lumber man.*

One night, when we were within a short distance of Cape Trafalgar, a sail was seen on our weather bow, apparently coming towards us. It was reported to the captain, who was almost instantly on deck; we beat to quarters, and, notwithstanding everything preparatory to action was going ahead with the utmost expedition, the captain was nearly frantic with anxiety, supposing the stranger to be an Algerine.

The two long guns in the waist, amidships, were usually run in and secured in a fore and aft position. The crews belonging to these guns were at work like good fellows, clearing away, and getting them round. But it seemed that the impatience of the captain knew no bounds; he seized hold of a long rammer, and being a powerful man, commenced banging away, right among them, as though he meant to break every bone in their bodies; and poor Burns, who happened to be one the crew of the larboard gun, got a blow on the loins which disabled him from further duty. The rammer was applied indiscriminately, and I came near being one the lucky ones, as my station at quarters was at the pumps, and right abreast of this gun; and as it was quite dark, and the captain being so blinded with rage, that he did not know who he hit.

But after all the fuss, the strange sail proved to be nothing more than a Portuguese polacca.

Notwithstanding the many good qualities which Capt. Rodgers possessed, he was a very passionate man; and being very powerful, it gave him frequent opportunities of displaying his great strength. One day, a very large Dutchman, whose grog had been stopped for some offence, went aft to ask the captain to please to let him have his grog again, stating his innocence of the crime for which it was stopped. The man told his story, when the captain up fist and hit him between the two eyes, and sent him his length flat upon deck. It appeared that the fellow was rather impudent in his address, using improper language.

I would further remark, that we never find perfection, either in man or woman, whatever may be the sphere of life in which they move. Neither do we often find perfect uniformity in conduct; the bravest men are sometimes timid; the most discreet and judicious sometimes make the most egregious blunders; and we seldom read an impartial description of any noted character, that does not seem to be almost a paradox. Over against a virtue will be set a prominent weakness, as in the lives of Chief Justice Hale, and Cotton Mather, both of whom assisted in the condemnation and execution of witches. Sir Isaac Newton was a believer in alchemy, and with his relative, Dr. Newton, set up furnaces, and were some months engaged in searching for the philosopher's stone. And yet no men, perhaps, ever lived, that possessed more brilliant ideas, than those whom I have just named.

Observation induces me to make these remarks, and I apply them more particularly to the navy.

Capt. Rodgers was, without doubt, a brave man; and, had there been an opportunity of testing his courage, I think he would have acquitted himself with honor to his country. But he was passionate, and in a paroxysm of rage, what might he not do? Even in the circumstance of the gun—here were two or three men rendered unfit for service, and one probably injured for life.

And if the strange sail had been an enemy, would these men have fought at their gun with the same animation, as they would have done had they not been thus beaten? I answer at once, No. That gun would have been useless!

But Capt. Rodgers was an amiable man, after all. He was a finished gentleman; courteous and kind to all, from the first lieutenant to the smallest waiting boy; and though now numbered with the dead, I shall always remember him with the highest emotions of esteem and respect; and not merely for his kindness to me, but for his general deportment as an officer of the United States Navy.

We passed Gibraltar on the 10th of August, and anchored at Carthagena on the 14th. Here we found an Algerine brig-of-war, which had been captured by our Squadron, and sent in here for the present. The American Consul came off to us as soon as we had anchored, and as we were quarantined, communicated the following intelligence while seated in his boat: "The fleet were hourly expected in this harbor; Commodore Decatur had concluded a treaty of peace with the government of Algiers, and had gone from thence to

Tunis and Tripoli, to settle matters with those governments." He then gave a short detail of the doings of the fleet after entering the Mediterranean. On their way from Gibraltar to Algiers, they fell in with an Algerine frigate, which they captured after a hard resistance on her part, and sent her into Carthagena. The fleet then appeared off Algiers on the 20th of June, 1815.

A flag of truce was hoisted on board the Gueriere, with the Swedish flag at the main. A boat soon came off with Mr. Norderling, Swedish consul, and the captain of the port, to whom we communicated the intelligence of the capture of the frigate and brig, which greatly surprised him; and he expressed to Mr. Norderling much anxiety for the other ships of their squadron, from whom nothing had been heard for some time.

The captain of the port was also informed that a very large addition to our fleet was daily expected, consisting of several line of battle ships, and four frigates. The captain of the port requested a statement of the conditions on which we would make peace, when the following letter was then handed him:

"*The American Commissioners to the Dey of Algiers:*

The undersigned have the honor to inform His Highness, the Dey of Algiers, that they have been appointed by the President of the United States of America, Commissioners Plenipotentiary to treat for peace with His Highness. And that pursuant to their instruction, they are ready to open a negotiation for the restoration of peace and harmony between the two countries, on terms just and honorable to both parties; and they feel it incumbent on them to state explicitly to His Highness, that they are instructed to treat upon no other principle than that of perfect equality, and on the terms of the most favored nations. No stipulation for paying any tribute to Algiers, under any form whatever, will be agreed to. The undersigned have the honor to transmit herewith a copy of the treaty, from the President of the United States of America, and avail themselves of this occasion to assure His Highness of their high consideration and profound respect."

The captain of the port then requested that hostilities should cease, pending the negotiation, and that persons authorized to treat should go on shore, he and Mr. Norderling both affirming that the minister of marines had pledged himself for their security and return to the ships, when they pleased. Both these propositions were rejected, and they were explicitly informed that the negotiations must be carried on on board the fleet, and that hostilities, as far as they respected vessels, could not cease. They returned on shore, and on the following day the same persons returned and informed us that they were commissioned by the Dey to treat with us on the proposed basis, and they appeared extremely anxious to conclude the peace immediately. The treaty was then brought forward, which the Commissioners declared would not be departed from in substance, at the same time declaring that although the United States would never stipulate for paying tribute under any form whatever; yet, that they were a magnanimous and generous nation, who would, upon the presentation of consuls, do what was customary with other great nations, in their friendly intercourse with Algiers.

The treaty was then examined, and they were of opinion that it would not be agreed to in its present form, and particularly requested that the article requiring the restitution of the property they had captured, and which had been distributed, might be expunged, alleging that such a demand had never before been made upon Algiers. To this it was answered that the claim was just, and would be adhered to. They then asked, whether, if the treaty should be signed by the Dey, we would engage to restore the captured vessels, which was refused. They then represented that it was not the present Dey, Omar Pacha, who had declared the war which they acknowledged, to be unjust, conceding that they were wholly in the wrong, and had no excuse, and requested us to take the case of the Dey into consideration, and upon his agreeing to terms with us more favorable than had ever before been made with any other nation, to restore the ships, which they stated would be of little or no value to us, but would be great of importance to him, as they would satisfy the people with the conditions of peace we were going to conclude with him.

The commissioners consulted upon this question, and determined that, considering the state of those vessels, the sums that would be required to fit them for a passage to the United States and the little probability of selling them in this part of the world, they would make a compliment of them to His Highness in the state they then were, the commodore engaging to furnish them with an escort to this port. This however would depend upon their signing the treaty as presented to them, and could not appear as an article of it, must be considered as a favor conferred on the Dey by the United States. They then requested a truce to deliberate upon the terms of the proposed treaty, which was refused. They then pleaded for three hours. The reply was:

"Not a minute; if your squadron appears in sight before the treaty is signed by the Dey, and the prisoners actually off, he should capture them."

It was finally agreed that hostilities should cease. They then went on shore, and in three hours we perceived their boat coming off with a white flag hoisted. The Swedish consul pledging his word not to hoist it unless the treaty was signed and the prisoners in the boat, they had returned to the shore, which was five miles distant, they came back with the treaty signed as it had been concluded, bringing also a part of the prisoners. While they were absent, a corvette with a large amount of money on board, hove in sight, which in one hour more would have been captured. The Dey was aware of this, and the fear of losing his fleet hastened him on to sign this treaty, which he violated in less than three months afterwards.

Mr. William Shaler was appointed United States Consul for the regency of Algiers, and established his residence on shore. The prisoners were all delivered up and put on board the sloop-of-war Epervier, with orders to proceed to the United States. She was never heard of afterwards, and these poor fellows, with my good friend Barnwell, went to the bottom. How mysterious are the ways of Divine Providence. These unfortunate men, who had endured the rigors and cruelties of Algerine slavery, some of them for more than two years; and when they were liberated and told they were going home, they cried for joy, believing it must be a dream; but they were not to see home. Many of them had wives and mothers, brothers and sisters; and some had families, I believe, in Massachusetts. Often did their hearts swell with gratitude to God for their deliverance from cruel bondage, and the prospect of soon embracing their loved ones. But it was not to be — the ocean was their grave. No headstones could tell their burial place, nor mound on which to place the passion flower, or shed the tear of affectionate memory. The howling blast their funeral dirge, and the briny wave their winding-sheet. Poor fellows, may you in the morning of the resurrection awake to a happy immortality, where there shall be no more prisons, no more shipwrecks. The fleet arrived at Carthagena a few days after we had obtained pratique. The Firefly was then ordered to Gibraltar, with despatches to our Consul; also, to order a new top-sail yard for the Independence, and to be ready on her arrival there.

Proceeding according to orders, we arrived there late in the evening, ran in, and anchored off the Ragged Staff, and very near the English frigate, *Undaunted.* She was light and high up. Our little brig looked like a boat under her stern, and while they were washing decks on board the frigate in the morning, an officer standing on the taffrail, looked down upon our deck, and by way of derision, says: "Hook our davit tackles on your little boat, and we'll hoist you out of water." An old fellow on our forecastle, who had been a Marblehead fisherman, just turned his eye up to this noble Briton, and dryly observed: "The Guerierre and Macedonian will be in to-day, sir, and you had better hook one of those on. The officer stepped down, and was seen no more upon the taffrail.

Early on the following morning, the officer of the watch sent our boat to the watering place for a few casks of water for present use. The scuttle butt was filled from these casks, and no other water was used.

At about eleven o'clock, A. M., several of the men were taken with a violent pain in the bowels, and it was not long before nearly all hands were down, many of them writhing in great agony. Then the officer of the deck was taken, and before twelve o'clock, nearly every soul on board the brig, myself included, were in the most excruciating agony.

The doctor, who also was slightly attacked, was flying round, administering doses, and doing all in his power to relieve their suffering. A boat's crew was mustered, and a message sent on shore, informing the captain of the affair. He came off immediately, and was much alarmed; but all were now fast recovering, and at four, P. M., all was right again.

It was subsequently ascertained that the water pipes at the landing place were of lead, and our boat was the first there. The officers of the boat did not know that it was necessary to let the pipes run a short time before receiving the water in the casks, so we thus drank what had been standing all night in the pipes, which being impregnated with lead, caused the difficulty among our crew.

On the next day after the disaster, I went on shore to get from the American Consul an order for a maintop-sail yard for the U. S. Ship Independence. The yard was to be ready against her arrival at Gibraltar, which would probably be in a few days. The consul gave me the necessary order accompanying it, with a note of introduction to the commandant of the royal dock-yard.

When I reached the yard, ascertaining that the commandant had gone to his residence, it being his dinner hour, I proceeded to his house, rang the bell, requested the servant to say to Mr. *Pownal* that I wished to see him directly. This great personage made his appearance; I handed him the order for the spar, also my note of introduction.

He then straightened himself up, and with an indignant scowl, demanded why I had come to his *house* on business of this nature. "Do you know, sir, that we don't make spars here?"

"I am well aware of that, sir, but my order from Commodore Bainbridge was to attend to this business immediately on my arrival at Gibraltar, as in all probability the ship will remain but a few hours in the Bay after her arrival."

"Well, sir, this is no place for such business," and turned to leave me in this abrupt manner. But I was determined not to stand such treatment, and advancing towards him, said:

"Look here, sir; you are but a man, after all. I am an officer of the United States Navy, and have been sent to you with an official order for a maintop-sail yard for the United States ship, Independence. I came to you in a respectable and polite manner, and *expected* to meet a gentleman; I have performed my errand, and now sir, leave the matter with you and the American Consul."

I put on my hat, and turned to leave. He then, assuming a different tone, requested me to remain in the parlor a few minutes, and he would go with me to the spar maker. In a few minutes he was ready, and walked to the dock-yard in the most sociable manner, paying us a very high compliment on our most favorable and expeditious treaty with Algiers. On arriving at the spar yard, it was decided that there was not a spar at the garrison large enough for the requisition. I parted with my stiff friend, with the utmost good feeling on both sides. Next day I went on shore quite early, for the purpose of rambling through the Rock, and availing myself of a polite invitation to dine with the Consul. I had read much of the Rock of Gibraltar, and had heard old sailors tell about guns being hung in chains, and about the old Moorish Castle, that millions had been offered for the privilege of opening it. All this created a desire to see for myself. So on landing, I got an intelligent soldier for a guide, and the necessary permit, and proceeded on my exploring tour. And without being very elaborate, I will give, although in the language of another, a pretty fair description of the Rock.

"Gibraltar is a high rock, projecting about three miles from north to south into the sea, and is the most southerly point of the Continent of Europe. It is connected with Spain by an isthmus of low land, the southern part of which belongs to the English, the northern to Spain, and the central to neither, being called the *neutral* ground. If convicts escape from Gibraltar, and succeed in crossing the neutral grounds, they are safe, as the Spanish authorities will not give them up. The muskets of the sentinels are, however, loaded with ball, and they must fire on any convict who is seen endeavoring to escape. English officers often cross the line into Spain to hunt and shoot, but are compelled to be well armed, as kidnapping is by no means uncommon."

There are many Jews in Gibraltar, and those of the most villainous sort; licentiousness also prevails to a great extent, especially among soldier's wives. The gates are shut at sundown, after which no one can get either in or out. I cannot see any great use in its occupation as a garrison. It is not as many suppose, the key to the Mediterranean, any more than whatever use might be made of the Bay as a rendezvous. It costs the British Government an enormous annual expenditure, and after all, it amounts to nothing.

The treaty of peace with Algiers, and the settlement of the demands against Tunis and Tripoli, enabled the greater part of the fleet to return home. And in designating those that were to stay, and those that were to return, caused much discontent among the officers, as there were many among those appointed to stay, that wished to go home. But the convenience and wishes of officers, are not generally consulted on these occasions. The whole matter was arranged by those high in authority, and the following ships were appointed to remain in the Mediterranean; some of which had arrived after the treaty of peace.

United States frigate U. S., 44, Com. Shaw; Washington, 74, Com. Chauncey; Java frigate, 44 Com. O. Perry; frigate Constellation, 38, Capt. Gordon; Erie, sloop-of-war, 22, Capt. Crane; Ontario, 22, Capt Downes.

I was removed from the Firefly to the Ontario, and of course among those that were to stay. This exchange and arrangement was made in Gibraltar Bay. After the homeward-bound fleet had sailed, the Ontario was sent over to Tangier for live stock, but the Moors would not sell us anything that had life, it being contrary to Mahometan law. We returned to Gibraltar, joined the fleet, and sailed for Port Mahon, Island of Minorca.

Scarcely had the homeward-bound ships left Gibraltar,

when Omar Pacha declared to our consul that he would not abide by the treaty; alleging as an excuse for this gross infraction of what we supposed to be an honorable treaty, that our fleet had come upon him unawares. When his fleet were out, and just at the moment of signing, it was announced to him, that a ship with a large amount of tribute money had just appeared, and he was afraid that if our ships had got possession of this valuable prize, they would have kept her, together with all the treasure on board, and that when he signed the treaty, we had him like a man upon his back with a razor to cut his throat.

Accordingly, they sailed out with their Corsairs, and captured an American brig. As soon as this intelligence had reached us, we sailed immediately for Algiers. The consul came off, and confirmed the report, stating also, that as soon as the fleet had left the Bay, the Dey began to be abusive, and complained loudly against his folly in signing the treaty so hastily, affirming that he could, with any one of his batteries, have blown our diminutive fleet out of water. The Algerine fleet were now in winter quarters, and secure inside the moles. Commodore Shaw was now determined on an attempt to burn the fleet. All the carpenters were set at work planing every piece of spare lumber into shavings, oakum and thacking, well tarred, and sprinkled with spirits of turpentine. These combustibles were put into empty barrels and secured ready for use; boats were selected, stout and able crews appointed for them, noble and daring officers were put in command of the expedition, and the night fixed upon for this hazardous undertaking. But it was a matter of regret to us all that a rascally Frenchman happened to call on board as a visitor just at this time. He saw these preparations going on, and suspecting that something hostile was in the wind, though pretending not to notice anything. Immediately on his getting on shore, he informed the captain of the port of what he saw, and in less than an hour the forts were crowded with men; the ships all manned, and every preparation made to repel any attempt that might be made to burn their ships. The difficulty was finally adjusted, the treaty resumed, and the brig which they had captured given up, and damages paid. I understood afterwards, by a gentleman who obtained his knowledge from one of the consuls at Algiers, that when the Dey was informed that the United States had just concluded a peace with England, and that during the war with this great nation, the United States had captured a great number of their ships, that he became alarmed, fearing that a large fleet would be sent against him, when he reconsidered his treacherous act, and apologized to the consul. It appeared to me very mysterious, that long before our fleet arrived off Algiers, the Dutch had been at war with them, and had several frigates cruising off their coast, and even while we lay there, these Dutchmen would run in within two gunshots, and fire away bravely. The Algerines seemed to care no more about them, than for the sea-gulls, that flew about the bay. And now, supposing all right, we sailed again for Port Mahon, which is a very extensive and commodious harbor for ships-of-war, formerly a rendezvous for the English fleet, but not a place of much commerce. It possessed a very fine dock-yard and arsenal, and in the days of Spain's prosperity, ships were built, and all the necessary equipments, such as making rigging, casting guns, &c., were done here. The Constellation and Ontario, needing some repairs, the commodore applied to the governor for permission to lay the ships at the navy yard wharf. The governor gave the permission, provided that we should assist with our seamen to fit out and get ready for sea the Ferdinand, of 120 guns. Her destination was Carthagena, in Spain. She was to be hove down, caulked, and coppered, and there were not half men enough in Mahon to do this work. Commodore Shaw readily assented; so we turned on our boys, and in fact, we performed the greatest portion of the work. For the whole posse, carpenters, caulkers, and sailors, were certainly the most miserable trash I had ever seen. And I never before, knew the meaning of the old saying, "as lazy as a Mahon soldier." While heaving the ships down, there were about a hundred of these wretches hold of the capstan bars; and actually they hung on and were dragged round instead of using any exertion to heave at the capstan. There were about three hundred of them at the arsenal, who were filthy and covered with vermin.

The admiral also was a great character. Indeed, his dress looked as though, if it ever was new, the time was so far back as to make it necessary to search the archives of Spain to determine the date. Then he was a very brave man. He wore a string of medals on his right breast, that looked like the bobtail to a kite. But the principal one, somewhat resembling the cover of a tin blacking-box, was for his gallant exploit of running away with his ship at the battle of Trafalgar.

While lying here, the Corvette, John Adams, and the Alert store ship came in with provisions and spars for the fleet. The Ferdinand was repaired and hauled off. We then took her berth at the wharf, repaired our ships, and were soon ready for sea. Unfortunately for us, the small-pox made its appearance on board, which very much reduced our crew. The disease came out in a very singular manner. There was a fellow among the marines who had been for some weeks on the doctor's list, but the doctor could not determine the nature of his complaint. The man was very filthy, and on close examination it was discovered that he was full of vermin. The first lieutenant ordered him to be taken on shore to a pond of fresh water, and there to be scrubbed and his hair cut off close to the skin. All this was done. He was brought on board, and complained of a pain in the back, and next morning he was broken out with the small-pox, which went through the ship; and on some it terminated fatally, but soon disappeared, after which our ship was very healthy.

Lord Exmouth's fleet, consisting of his flag-ship, the Boyne, 90, and five other ships of the line, had been lying with us several days, and were now ready for sea. The governor of Mahon requested Commodore Shaw to loan seventy-five American seamen to assist in carrying the Ferdinand to Carthagena, pledging himself for their security and safe return to their respective ships, unavoidable accidents excepted. Commodore Shaw, desirous to extend every courtesy to the Spanish government, and considering this request as a case of necessity, let him have the men, also an officer to see that they were well fed and well treated, besides a young Greek, as interpreter. All being ready for sea, we got under way, stood out of the harbor and then separated. The English fleet were bound to Algiers, our ship (Ontario) to Barcelona, and a cruise, the Ferdinand, to Carthagena, the United States, Commodore Shaw, to Gibraltar. The weather looked unsettled when we got under way and a very heavy sea outside. At night we took a strong levanter which increased in severity until it became a regular hurricane, which lasted six days. We left Mahon on Monday morning and on Tuesday afternoon saw the Ferdinand far off on our lee quarter: her mizzen-mast was gone and her colors were at half-mast. We were lying-to and had as much as we could do to take care of ourselves, could render her no assistance and saw no more of her after this.

We had on board, as passenger, a Lady Gavino, who had taken passage with us for Barcelona. She was much frightened during the gale, and being a Catholic, made a vow to her patron saint, that if she was spared to put her foot on the land again, she would go barefooted to the nearest church and return thanks for her preservation. We landed her at Tarragona and afterwards heard that she performed her vow like a good Christian, but took a severe cold which nearly cost her life.

We sailed for Carthagena to meet the commodore, who was to call there on his way from Gibraltar to receive his men, and we learned on our arrival at Carthagena that the Ferdinand had foundered at sea, near Bona, on the Barbary coast, that the crew had got safe on shore in their boats, and that on their reaching the shore, the Turks had made them all prisoners and treated them very badly. This intelligence came by a Greek Coaster.

Agreeably to our orders we were to wait here until the commodore arrived. While we lay here I had a good opportunity of examining the arsenal and capacious docks. This was once a strong naval depot for the Spaniards, an admirable harbor, and every convenience for building and equpiping their largest ships. The country around is beautiful and productive, but the inhabitants are abominably lazy.

At length the commodore arrived. He had heard the news about the Ferdinand, and we were sent to Algiers for our seamen. On arriving there, we ascertained that the sloop-of-war Erie had been there a few days since and taken them. I received the following account of the disaster from a young man on our arrival at Port Mahon. His story was as follows:

"Shortly after the gale commenced, we sprang a leak, and neither pumps nor pump gear were good for anything; so the pumps were entirely useless. And instead of bailing or hoisting the water up, as might have been done, until the gale abated, the officers and men were in groups all over the ship with their beads and St. Antonios, crying most hideously, without doing a hand's turn to save their lives. The sails were nearly all blown from the yards, no one willing to go aloft, except our men and four young Greeks. There were but four or five among the Spaniards that knew any seamanship or that could steer the ship. The mizzen-mast and fore and main top-mast went over the side. Her head was kept in shore as long as she was manageable, and on the following Wednesday she went down, head foremost. The land was on the lee bow, about ten miles distant. The Americans cleared away the boats and kept possession of three of the best. She was fortunately well supplied with boats, all of which were tight and strong.

CHAPTER VI.

Continuation of the loss of the Ferdinand,—Misunderstanding of the Spanish Government,—Attempt to retain our Stores at Mahon,—Find their mistake,—Promptness and energy of Com. Shaw,—Arrival of a wreck,—Superstitious observance of a vow,—Terrible row between the U. S. Seamen and the Spanish Soldiers,—A midshipman killed,—Funeral,—Affair at the burial ground,—Energy of Major Hall,—Sailed for Marseilles,—Arrival there,—Receive orders from the Captain of the Port to land the Powder,—Positively refuse to conform with the order,—Captain of the Port yields,—Curious idea of a French Custom officer,—Remarks on Marseilles,—Bonaparte excitement not over,—Sail for Malaga,—Arrive,—Arrival of U. S. Frigate,—Dreadful gale,—Get on to the rocks,—Frigate slips, and goes to sea,—Fortunate rescue,—Expectations of the Spaniards disappointed,—Visit to the Cathedral,—A good piece of advice from an invisible mouth,—Sail for Barcelona,—Death of a Sailor by a fall,—And of another by relapse,—A man overboard,—Stave the boats,—In consequence of which a boat's crew get overboard,—All rescued,—Miscellaneous character of our crew,—Story of a privateersman,—Boxing match between two men,—Arrive at Naples, Splendid view of an eruption of Vesuvius,—Visit to Herculaneum and Pompeii,—Description,—Visit through the grotto of Pausilippo, and other places of much interest,—A brief description of Naples,—Beggars, maimed and deformed,—Wretched condition of the population,—Sail for Messina,—Mount Stromboli,—Arrive at Messina,—Superstition of my Cicerone,—Account of an Earthquake,—Superstitious reverence.

HAD it been otherwise with our boats, probably every soul would have perished. Part of her hull remained above water, which was also a fortunate circumstance, enabling them to prepare the boats with everything necessary for the shore, as the sea was very high, and it was dangerous to attempt a landing in the surf. The Spaniards had now ceased to cry to St. Antonio, and began to make preparations to save their lives on their own hook, having no further confidence in their Saint. The Spanish captain and officers, began to fly round, but all discipline and control was at an end. Our seamen took possession of their boats and only awaited a favorable chance to shove off for the shore. It was very evident that the Spaniards depended on the American seamen as leaders, and after a great deal of confusion, the boats left the wreck. The ship was fast settling in the water, and would, in all probability, soon disappear. The boats in which were our men, went ahead, and at times were nearly filled with water. The Spaniards were far behind, and it was almost certain that they could not reach the land, as their boats were so badly managed. On approaching the shore, it was discovered that the breakers extended out some distance, and very heavy surf running on the beach. By this time the inhabitants had come to the sea-shore in large numbers, and were waving to the boats to keep further South, where at last they effected a landing."

I could not ascertain whether all had been saved. It was supposed that some were left on board when she went down.

"We had no sooner landed," continued the young man, "than we were all seized as prisoners, our clothes torn from us, then secured and placed in an old stone building. Our young Greek interpreter, who understood Arabic, told the Algerine soldiers. that there were seventy-five Americans among the crew; but they made no distinction, treating all as Spaniards, with whom they were at war.

When we asked for something to eat, the Turks pointed to the stones, saying, "They were good enough for Christian dogs." The Greek, by knowing their language, was permitted to go at liberty. He fell in with a fisherman that was going to Algiers, and with much difficulty procured materials, and wrote to the Consul; giving a brief statement of the wreck, and of our confinement, which as soon as the Consul had received it, employed means for the immediate liberation of the Americans, and their passage to Algiers; all which was promptly done. On their arrival at Algiers, were properly cared for, until the sloop-of-war, Erie, took them away."

When we left Port Mahon, the John Adams was stripping her rigging requiring to be fitted, and some of it to be replaced with new. The commodore had ordered her to be ready for sea against his return, as he intended to send her home with despatches. All the rigging, provisions and stores that came in the Alert, were put into a Government store, and when the account of the loss of the Ferdinand reached Spain, the Spanish Government were disposed to be suspicious, that there had been some foul play, and gave an order to the Governor of Mahon, not to allow any stores belonging to the United States, to be taken from the public store. In consequence of this order, the John Adams could not proceed in fitting for home. When the commodore arrived at Mahon, and found how matters stood, and feeling much vexed at not finding the John Adams ready for sea, he sent a polite note to the Governor, requesting the store key. The Governor had always been on good terms with the American officers; and the commodore knew that the detention of the stores was by an order from the Government, and not from the Governor of Mahon. The Frigate was hauled up abreast the store, the guns double shotted, our ship lay just astern with guns shotted. No key was received. The commodore sent another messenger, saying to the Governor, that if the store was not opened in one hour, he would open it with his guns. The people on shore became now much alarmed, knowing the determined character of Com. Shaw; but before the expiration of the hour, the store was opened, so ended this matter. The John Adams was fitted, and went home with despatches, and with the sick men of the fleet.

A few days after our arrival, a wreck came to the Harbor, that had struck on a reef out-side, she filled, but floated with her deck only out of water; the crew were all on the deck, and had been in that exposed condition, two days and nights, without food or water. They had promised old St. Antonio, that if he would bring them safe into port, they would walk on their bare knees to church, and return thanks, and on landing from the wreck, they made known their vow to the people, who immediately commenced sweeping a path for them. Several old women came with brooms, and continued sweeping before them; but notwithstanding the way was swept, before they had got half-way up the hill, their knees were in a dreadful condition, torn, and streaming with blood. At last they reached the church, which unfortunately for them was up a hill, and there performed their promised vows.

An unpleasant and fatal affair took place while we lay here, which cast a gloom throughout the fleet. The Frigate Constellation, Capt. Gordon, returned from a cruise, and on the following Sunday, fifty men from each of the frigates, and twenty-five from the Ontario, were permitted to go on shore on liberty. Now, all who know anything of the character of a man-of-war sailor, knows also that he heartily despises a soldier. There is but one general resort for seamen at Port Mahon, which is at the farther end of the town, near the barracks of the soldiers. The principal house, is well known by all who have ever been there, as the "Jackass tavern," where is an abundant supply of ruinous liquor. Around this place, are hundreds of "donkey boys," who keep these animals, to let to sailors, for a ride to Georgetown, about four miles from Mahon. These donkeys will not budge a step without a club, which must be constantly applied by the boys upon the rump of the brutes. And frequently they jam the half drunken sailor up against a stone wall, thus tearing his trousers, and bruising his limbs. The price of hire is about twenty cents; which is generally clear gain to the boys, as the sailor seldom, or never succeeds in making him go; and all the fun lies in seeing the sailor thrown off and sometimes much injured. On the Sunday that our men had liberty on shore, they of course went up to Jackass Tavern, and after partaking freely of miserable sour wine, they had got into the right trim for fun. Went out among the donkey boys where they went through all the usual evolutions of drunken sailors. During this time the soldiers had mingled with the crowd, which rather disconcerted the sailors, the latter supposing that all the ground and all the fun belonged to them. But the soldiers did not think so, and began to laugh and make fun of them. Inside the tavern were crowds of soldiers and sailors. At last the latter began to kick up a row with the soldiers, and drove them all out, and commenced flogging them. They retreated into the barracks, got their bayonets and came out ready for a fight. The sailors seeing this, drove them back again. By this time their officers had been apprised of the row, and attempted to interfere; but it was of no use, the fight had now become general. There were about one hundred and fifty American seamen and officers on shore, and about one hundred and twenty-five seamen engaged in the fight, with over three hundred Spanish soldiers. They were not what I have before called Mahon soldiers, they were a regiment sent from Old Spain, to protect the Island. The fight now became alarming; the sailors when they turned and faced the soldiers, the latter would retreat, but as soon as the sailors started again towards the town, these cowardly soldiers would throw the paving stones at them, and in some instances rush upon a half drunken sailor, plunge his bayonet into him, and then run. Many of these poor fellows received dreadful wounds from bayonets and large stones. This running fight was kept up for the distance of nearly a mile, and when they had got within a short distance of the Crown Hotel, the noise was heard by the American officers, who were there at the time; who rushed into the street, to see what the trouble was. Just as the mob had got abreast the door of the hotel, Midshipman Moore, of the Ontario, happened to be the first who got into the street. He had no sooner stepped upon the sidewalk, when a Spanish soldier officer, run him through the body with a small sword, killing him instantly. He fell into the gutter, and remained there until the mob had passed. He was then taken into the hotel and prepared for burial.— The mob had now approached the centre of the town. The American officers were in the midst of them with their side arms. Capt. Downes was also among them, like a brave one. The town authorities now took the matter up, and by sundown all was quiet, the sailors having been sent on board their respective ships. I came on shore again after dark, with a party well armed, to bring the body of the murdered officer on board the ship. We could never identify the murderer, although much exertion was made to find him out. The funeral was appointed for the following Tuesday. The body was placed in one of the cutters, spread around with American flags, and a large ensign for the pall. The pall bearers were officers, about the age of the deceased. The line of boats was very long, accompanied by many from the shore, filled with citizens of Mahon who deeply lamented this unfortunate affair. Accompanying the funeral procession which consisted principally of all the officers of the squadron who could be spared from duty, there were also a number of seamen from each ship handsomely dressed, and forty marines, headed by Major Hall. When the boats arrived at the landing place, the marines were drawn up to precede the body, which was borne on the shoulders of four seamen. The funeral procession was large and well conducted, and when it had arrived at the graveyard, the marines were drawn up for the purpose of fireing a volley over the grave, when the coffin was lowered into its resting place. The major gave the word, Fire! It was not what is generally called a good fire, there being some few seconds interval between some of the reports. At this the Spanish soldiers seemed inclined to laugh; as there was a large body of them near the grave. This insult, and coming too from these cowardly rascals, raised the ire of Major Hall, who instantly gave the order to "load with ball cartridges." The Spaniards, rather suspecting something, began to move off. The order now given, "right about face!" present, and if ever sheep-jumped quickly over a wall, these fellows cleared and went over the graveyard fence, as if old Jemmy was after them. The marines did not fire, but they ought to have done so, and shown these cowardly rascals who they had to deal with. Those who had attended the funeral, returned to their several ships, after having paid all due honor and respect to the memory of the unfortunate young midshipman.

The weather had now become fine, and we were getting ready for a summer cruise. About the middle of April we sailed for Marseilles, arrived safely there, and hauled into the mole. We were boarded by the health officer, and put into quarantine, in consequence of having a few cases of sickness on board. The captain of the port ordered the guns to be unloaded, and our powder landed. To this, Capt. Downes positively objected. He consented to unload the guns, considering this requirement no more than a proper precaution against fire. The authorities finally withdrew the order to land the powder, this being the first American man-of-war that ever entered the mole*. They were not posted up with regard to the way of getting along with Yankee Captains. They sent on board a "savage" looking Frenchman as a Custom house officer to remain on board while we were in quarantine. The first lieutenant ordered the purser's steward to serve this fellow his ration for the day, which was, 1-4 lb. of salt beef, 14 oz. bread, and 1-2 pint of whiskey. The Frenchman, when he understood that he must take his food with the men, became quite indignant, threw the beef and bread down, swearing horribly in French, his hands agoing like the paddle of a steamboat, saying, he "always had lived in the cabin with the Captain." It was some time before the fellow could be made to understand what kind of a ship he was on board of, and finally made an arrangement with some one on shore, to send him off some grass and a beef bone, with which he made himself a pot of soup, and became quite contented.

Marseilles had not yet recovered from the downfall of Bonaparte. They had always been bitterly opposed to him, and only three months previous to our arrival, there had been a massacre of three hundred men, women and children, for proclaiming their adhesion to him; and there was also a ship in the mole, and lying near us, with twenty-six French officers, adherents of Bonaparte, who were under sentence of death.

We remained here three weeks, and then sailed for Malaga. We had scarcely let our anchor go in Malaga roads, when we discovered the U. S. Frigate in the offing, bound in. She reached her anchorage about 4 o'clock in the morning. At noon, a gale from the S. E. commenced, which increased so rapidly, that we found it necessary to send down our top-gallant yards, house top-gallant masts, and lower the fore and main yards down to the rail. The gale increasing, Captain Downes made a signal for a pilot to take us inside the mole

* Marseilles is now, 1856, quite another place to what it was in 1816. Then, there was no harbor to the left of the tower; all that portion has been added, with many other improvements.

as there was danger where we lay, of foundering at our anchors; the sea making a clean sweep fore and aft the decks. The frigate could render us no assistance, and as no pilot came off, we accordingly made preparations for slipping our cables, and make an attempt to enter the mole. Our anchors and cables were buoyed, a spare anchor and cable got in readiness, when we watched our chance, let fall, and sheeted home, a close-reefed maintop-sail, slipped the chains at the same time, and put the helm up. She did not pay off as was expected, neither did she gather headway soon enough to round the molehead, but drifted on to the rocks. We let go the spare anchor just in the right time, and fortunately, it held on firmly, our stern only striking the ground. We hung now in a perilous position ; should our cable part, or our anchor come home, we must inevitably have swung round square upon the rocks, which would have made an end of the Ontario.

While we lay in this critical position, a well-manned boat came from the frigate with a large hawser and anchor. They made one end of the hawser fast to the mole, and brought the other end on board, which we took to the capstan, and hove it taut. A large well-manned boat also came to our assistance from the captain of the port.

All along the shore, the Spaniards had collected to see us go to pieces on the rocks, and were doubtless much surprised at seeing us use any exertion to extricate ourselves from our dangerous position. For had they been in our place, there would have been nothing done but praying to some saint for assistance, and making large promises to the Church. We succeeded in heaving the ship off into deep water, and then considered ourselves out of danger. The gale continued through the night; the frigate slipped her cables, and went to sea, but returned in two days. When the gale had abated, we ran up into the mole and anchored in a good berth, I had a good cruise on shore, and in company with another officer visited the Cathedral, and while looking about and walking round the gallery, we came across a very large book, the letters of which were two inches long. I observed to the gentleman with me, that these letters were large enough to be felt. Directly we heard a voice from the other side speaking to us in English, and in a gruff voice, "*A still tongue makes a wise head.*" We looked round, but saw nobody, when directly an old fellow raised his head and commenced scolding us for talking loud in church. I must confess I felt rather uneasy, as there were many ugly looking places in the building, and I began to think about inquisitions hot pincers, and roasting over a slow fire, which I did not care about enduring at present. So we left Malaga Cathedral unexplored, and walked down towards the Fort. As it was very warm, and the sun shining out very bright, there were lots of Spaniards with their shirts off, "lousing themselves." And of all the miserable wretches on the face of the earth, I think a Spaniard is the worst.

We hauled out and got our anchors, and from Malaga we sailed for Barcelona; remained there but a few days, and sailed for Naples. The day on which we left Barcelona, a Frenchman that had shipped at Marseilles fell from the mizzen-top, and was killed. We also lost a fine English lad, an active young sailor, named Williams. He was truly an amiable young man. He had nearly recovered from a dangerous fever. His appetite having rapidly increased, one of his messmates imprudently gave him a piece of duff, or sailor's pudding, which was as indigestible as a handspike. This produced a relapse, and on the next morning he was a corpse. One of his shipmates produced the following lines, which were very appropriate:

THE DYING SAILOR BOY.

Dark flew the scud along the wave,
  Repeated thunders rolled on high;
All hands aloft the storm to brave,
  At midnight was the boatswain's cry.

On deck sprang every soul apace;
  But *one*, bereft of human joy,
Within a hammock's narrow space
  Lay stretched—a hapless sailor boy.

Once when the boatswain's pipe would hail,
  The first was he of all the crew
On deck to spring, to trim the sail,
  To steer, to reef, to furl, or clew.

Now fell disease had seized a form,
  Which Nature cast in happiest mould;
The bell struck midnight through the storm,
  His last, his funeral knell it told.

"Oh! God," he cried, and dropped a tear,
  "Before my spirit mounts the skies,
Are there no friends, or messmates dear,
  To close in death my weary eyes?"

All hands aloft, loud blows the wind,
  Surrounding billows loudly roar;
He raised his head, he bowed resigned,
  Then backward sank to rise no more.

The morning sun in splendor rose,
  The gale was hush'd, and still'd the wave;
The sea-boy found his last repose,
  In ocean's deep and boundless grave.

But He who guards the sea-boy's head,
  He who can save, or can destroy,
Caught the pure spirit as it fled,
  And raised to heaven the sailor boy.

And on the same day a man also fell from the mizzen-top-gallant yard. He fell clear of everything into the sea, when a rush was made to clear away the starboard quarter boat. The boat's crew had got in, and all ready to lower away; the fellow who had hold of the bow tackle let it go all at once, and spilled the men out, together with the oars and everything that was in the boat. Here were now seven men overboard, when orders were given to lower away the captain's gig, that was hanging at the stern davits; and in the hurry, they managed to let her strike against the rudder, and stove her. The only thing now to be done was to clear away the second cutter, which was stowed in the first, and full of spare sails and rigging. We soon cleared her away, and at the same time the yard tackles were got up; the boat was successfully hoisted out, and every man picked up, although they had been overboard near a half hour. We passed through the Straits of Bonifacio between Corsica and Sardinia, as it very materially shortens the distance to Naples.

We had a fine crew, nearly all of which had served in government ships or privateersmen, and many of them had been in severe battles. There were some from the Essex frigate, some from the privateer, Gen. Armstrong, that so nobly defended herself at Fayal, and some that were on board the President when she was captured by the British fleet off New York. We had also a funny old salt, who was on board a schooner privateer out of New York, mounting one long twenty-four on a pivot, amidships, and eight nine-pounders on her deck. He told us the following story:

"One morning, we found ourselves close along-side an English frigate. There was a good breeze from the south-west, the schooner was hauled close on the wind, and the frigate commenced firing, the shot flying around, cutting away the rigging and riddling the schooner. We slewed our long gun round and gave the enemy several raking shot, which must have done much damage. The frigate was now fast gaining upon us, and our capture was certain, unless we could get away by superior sailing; so we threw all our guns and shot overboard, started the water, reserving only a small quantity for present use. We now began to drop the frigate, who kept up a continual fire from her bow guns, which fortunately did but little damage, and being anxious to get out of the reach of her shot, we threw over everything that could be spared, hoisted water aloft and wet the sails, and very soon, to our great joy, the enemy's shot fell short of us. He gave up the chase and tacked ship.

Here now was the privateer a thousand miles from New York, without guns, short of provisions, and in the track of English cruisers. A few days after, at about four o'clock P. M., the man at the mast head sung out:

"Sail, ho!"

"Where away?"

"About two points on the weather bow!"

"What does she look like?"

"She is a large ship, sir, standing to the eastward."

The first lieutenant took his glass and went upon the foretop-sail yard, and made her out to be a merchantman. And now what was to be done? We had no guns, and but one boat that would float, but Yankee ingenuity is always equal to any emergency, and we immediately turned to and took a spare top-mast, sawed it into eight pieces, blacked the ends, and stuck them out of the ports. We then took two empty beef barrels, placed them on the pivot carriage amidships, over which we threw a large tarpaulin. While all this was going on, we had kept along with our eye on the stranger, being rather cautious until her true character could be known, for resistance on the part of the schooner was out of the question.

About an hour before sunset, the captain of the schooner was resolved to run along-side and find out who and what the stranger was. She had two guns on each side run out, and on deck were twenty-five men who could be counted with the glass. We run along-side, keeping clear of his guns, and hailed, and now hoisted the American flag and ordered him to send his boat on board immediately, which he did not seem inclined to do. We could easily see several spy-glasses pointed at us from persons we supposed to be passengers. Our captain now stepped upon a gun carriage, and with his trumpet, gave the order:

"Clear away the midship gun! Stand by your guns in the waist!"

The sun had now set, and it would soon be dark, the ship had not yet shortened sail. Our captain then hailed him again:

"If you wish to avoid bloodshed, sir, back your maintopsail, and come immediately on board."

When to our great relief he backed his main yard, and prepared to lower his quarter boat. Our captain then gave a loud order:

"Secure your guns! *Call all hands, out boats, sir!*" *We had but one boat that would swim*, all the others were destroyed by the frigate's shot. As soon as we saw the boat shove off from the ship, a prize crew was selected, and our first lieutenant was the prize-master. He was a fine man, and belonged to New Bedford, (I have forgotten his name.) As soon as *his* boat struck our side, *our* boat shoved off with as many men as she could carry, and each with a pistol. The captain stepped on board and was hurried into the cabin. The crew were ordered out of the boat, and immediately sent below. Fifteen men were sent on board the prize, to assist in securing the command, and to get up some fresh water and what provisions could be spared. As the weather was fine, we lay by her until daylight next morning, when all things being arranged, we squared away for New York.

The prize was the Albion, of London, seven hundred tons, Capt. Edward Shields, from Rio Janeiro, with a cargo of coffee and sugar, and bound to London. But, says the narrator, the scene next morning was beyond description. When this poor fellow found how he had been deceived, he began to rave like a madman. He tore out his hair by the handful, saying he was ruined, for all he had in the world was in that cargo. Our captain assured him that his private adventure should be restored to him, which somewhat mitigated his distress. "But," says our captain, "suppose we get taken, and your ship retaken, what will you do with me?"

He jumped up, and with a half smile, said, "Upon my life, I should like no better fortune than I could make with you by showing you up in England as a live Yankee."

We arrived with the schooner in New York on the fourth of July, and got pretty well in for it, sold my prize ticket for sixty dollars, and shipped for the States service."

This is the sailor's story, with a little alteration in the language, and leaving out the usual interlading of a sailor's yarn. We had two fine looking fellows that belonged to the forecastle. One was a Boston boy, named Badger, the other, Jack Dixon, an Englishman; these men had not been on good terms for many days, and finally agreed to fight it out in fair play if they could obtain permission. They both came to the first lieutenant and made known to him their difficulty, and requested permission to settle the matter in an honorable manner, on deck, as fighting below was a punishable offence. The first lieutenant acquainted the captain of the request, when he immediately came on deck, had the two men sent aft, and asked them if they could not settle their difficulty without fighting; they answered in the negative. "Very well," says the captain, "get ready. Send the master-at-arms here, sir," to the officer of the deck; "each of you choose a friend," which they had already done.

A ring was now formed, the master-at-arms was placed to see fair play; officers and crew gathered round. They stripped and went at it, and it was a grand display of that species of science called "fisti-cuffs." Every blow was measured with mathematical precision. As soon as either was knocked down, he was immediately caught by his friends, his back rubbed, and placed upon his feet, ready for another drop. These men fought nearly two hours, and were both so much exhausted they could scarcely stand; the captain ordered them to desist. They separated, with an understanding that they should have another game on some other day, but that night, preliminaries of peace were ratified over a bottle of grog.

We arrived at Naples late in the afternoon, and anchored over against Portici. Were quarantined here six days, and one night while lying here, an eruption of Mount Vesuvius occurred, which was truly a beautiful sight. The lurid flame from the crater, and the streaming lava running down the sides of the mountain, with an occasional belching up of flame, as though old Vulcan was stirring up the fire, and then the whole bay was so beautifully illuminated that, take it altogether, it was a splendid panorama.

After we had obtained pratique, our ship was swarmed with every sort of beggars, in the shape of blind fiddlers, horribly distorted, deformed men, women and children; and lots of priests and friars, begging for their several communities. And the most deplorable sight of all was, mothers bringing off their daughters, urging them on the seamen for prostitution. And these same deluded beings, priestridden and oppressed in the vilest manner, carry about them a crucifix, with their beads and rosary, which they frequently resort to while engaged in the worst of crimes. And this they believe to be a propitiation.

The excavation at Pompeii was progressing moderately. I visited the Museum where the curiosities were deposited. There were many things here which were taken from the uncovered houses, such as bread, dough, cloth, thread, and many domestic articles that looked as though they were about to be used when the sad calamity occurred. I saw skeletons that had been pressed into the earth, and many human bones, and an immense quantity of broken pottery, and about seventeen hundred pictures on fresco. The excavation at that time had not developed much of the city, in fact, nothing compared to what can be seen at the present day.

"Naples is the chief city of the Two Sicilies, with a population of 400,000 souls. The environs cannot be surpassed for scenic beauty and delightful reminiscences. They are painted over Virgil's tomb, in the stupendous grotto of Pausilipo." The Grotto del Cani, in which you can perceive the mephitic gas, rising some fifteen inches from the ground. They threw a dog into the grotto while I stood in it; the dog was immediately seized with convulsions, but taken out and water thrown upon him, or he would soon have died. Then there are St. Germain's baths, warmed only by the heat arising from the ground. I noticed quite a number of ancient looking coaches, the horses, miserable looking affairs, and the harness made chiefly of pieces of rope, clumsily knotted, and one in particular, the driver who was in rusty livery, and the footman with a cocked hat, epaulets, and barefooted. The rider in this unique equipage was a beggar. I was told that these were poor noblemen, still clinging to the exterior show of nobility, and at the same time starving. The street beggars were so numerous that a stranger could hardly get along through the vast crowd that surrounded him. To give anything, however small, was to involve yourself in a much greater difficulty than before. The environs of Naples are very interesting to the classical traveller; such as Lake Avernus, Baia, Ischia, Procida, and Capri, Castellamare, and the ascent of Vesuvius. Some of the church festivals, particularly on the 8th of September, the Nativity of the Virgin, is quite amusing. The traveller can well spend three months in Naples without diminishing its interest.

We remained at Naples three weeks, and then sailed for Messina, in Sicily. Here, too, is another delightful spot for the traveller. In going from Naples to Messina, the voyage, though short, is highly interesting. You pass Mount Stromboli, the " most northern of the Lipari Islands. It is a volcano, which rises in a conical form to the height of 3000 feet; on the east side are three or four little craters, ranged near each other, nearly at two-thirds of its height. Notwithstanding its fires, it is inhabited, and produces a great deal of cotton. Of all the volcanoes recorded in history, Stromboli seems to be the only one that burns without ceasing, and it has long been looked upon as the great light-house of the Mediterranean, the flames being seen by night at a great distance." And on your left is the beautiful promontory of Calabria, the southern extremity of Italy. The Apennines, too, intersecting the whole territory, from north to south. This country abounds in excellent fruit, corn, wine, oil, silk, cotton, and wool. In 1783, a terrible earthquake destroyed a great portion of Calabria and Sicily. We now were at anchor in Messina, one of the safest harbors in the Mediterranean. Here also a great trade is carried on in silk, oil, corn, and excellent wine. This city suffered much by an earthquake, in 1683, when it was half destroyed; it was, however, rebuilt, and suffered again very severely in 1770. There are some handsome buildings, and beautiful promenades, but like all other Italian cities, full of priests and monks, of almost every order. I employed a Cicerone to show me round, and it was truly amusing to hear the fellow go on describing things and places. He spoke good English, as many do here, for prior to 1814, Messina was the head-quarters of the British army in Sicily. My guide took me up a hill to a convent, and near by to which was a pond of muddy water.

" Here," says he, " I wish to relate to you why this pond has its milky appearance. When the holy virgin was on earth, she made a visit to this city, and laid the foundation of that convent; and in order to show that she had been here, squeezed a drop of milk from her breast into the pond, which gave it this color which it has retained ever since."

" Indeed !" says I.

We passed on until we came to a long, broad street, when he stopped me, and commenced:

" You see this long street before us? Now in the last

earthquake, it opened in the middle through its whole length, and swallowed up many hundred people, and then closed again. My father says he saw a man that was caught with only his head above ground, when it closed upon him. He sung out like a good fellow, but he was finally dug out alive."

He next took me to an old and dilapidated stone fort. "Here," said he, "when the Saracens were on the Island, and had nearly got possession of Messina, an angel stood on that corner, (pointing to it,) and, waving his sword, preserved the fort from being taken." And while walking with me, he kept his hat in his hand a great part of the time. As he invariably bowed to every image we passed, and they were quite numerous, it was less trouble to walk bareheaded than to be constantly lifting his hat.

CHAPTER VII.

Get tired of my Cicerone.—Discharge him.—Sail to Syracuse.—Catania. —Arrive at Syracuse.—Description.—Singular customs of the priests. —Sail for Palermo.—Its description.—Also, description of Sicily.—Ignorance of a Sicilian broker.—Readiness to advance money.—Sail for Malta and Tripoli.—Not to communicate with Tripoli.—Politeness of the Pacha. — Death of Capt. Gordon at Messina.—Arrival of the fleet.—Sail for Tunis.—Mistake in the course.—Perilous condition.—Arrive at Tunis.—Anchor off Carthage.—Duel between two midshipmen. No blood shed.—Intelligence that Lord Exmouth had demolished Algiers by bombardment.—Sail for Algiers.—Cautioned not to approach within gunshot.—Explanation of the difficulty with the British Consul. —Indignation towards Lord Exmouth.—His visit to England.—Returns with an efficient fleet.—Bombardment of Algiers, and subjugation of the Dey.—Its final destruction by the French.

I BECAME tired of the fellow, paid him, and let him go. From Messina, we went to Syracuse, passing Catania, a beautiful city on the east coast of Sicily, a place of great antiquity, but has suffered greatly, as well by the eruptions of Mount Ætna, as by earthquakes. It was nearly overwhelmed with lava from the former, in 1698. An earthquake destroyed a great portion of the city, and buried 18,000 persons in its ruins. It has risen from these disasters with increasing splendor, and in 1825, ranked among the finest cities in Europe. It is situated at the foot of Mount Ætna on the south side, and contains about 50,000 inhabitants. In passing, it presents a beautiful appearance, rising gradually on the slope of Ætna. We arrived at Syracuse late in the evening, and could not see the city until the next morning. There is not much of any interest to be seen here, as the city has been much reduced by war, tyranny and earthquakes. Great stories are told about Dionysius and his cave. And I noticed while lying here, that a little after sundown there was a peculiar noise on shore near the church, and asked the boatman one day what this noise meant. He told me that the church was shut up every night, and that previous to locking the doors, the priests went round inside with long poles to beat the devil out; and this was the noise that we heard.

We sailed from Syracuse to Palermo, passing nearly round the Island, and arrived there in four days. Palermo is situated at the head of a bay of its own name, surrounded by high and rocky mountains. The country between the city and the mountains is one of the richest plains in the world. A visit to the Botanic Garden and the Catacombs, is well worth the attention of the traveller.

I should have mentioned that while at Syracuse, the commodore applied to a rich Jew banker for a loan on credit of the United States, as the officers needed money to replenish their wardrobe, and also to pay their little hotel bills on shore. The commodore and purser waited on the banker, who was entirely ignorant of what part of Europe the United States might be found, having a Map of the World before him at the same time. But when it was shown him who, and what, and where the United States was, he lifted up both hands, exclaiming: "Oh, yes! yes! You are the country that have just concluded a peace with the English. Yes, I have read of your war. You can have what money you wish." Bills on the United States were cashed, and the officers liberally supplied with the needful.

I should also have stated that the fleet, consisting of the Washington, 74, Commodore Chauncey; Java Frigate, Commodore Perry; and Peacock, Capt. G. W. Rodgers; frigate Constellation, and Erie, sloop-of-war, had arrived at Messina after we had left. The Ontario had received orders to proceed from Palermo to Malta, and from thence to Tripoli, but not to communicate with the shore until the arrival of all the ships. According to orders, we lay off Tripoli ten days. During this time, the Bashaw kindly sent off a bullock, some sheep and a large quantity of fruit, which was to us at this time, a very acceptable present. At length the squadron appeared in sight, and we soon learned that the cause of their delay was, that Capt. Charles Gordon, of the Constellation, had died at Messina.

He had been out of health for some time, which I believe was caused by having a bullet in his body, which he had received many years before, and which had not been extracted, and continued suppuration had very much reduced him. He was a brave officer and an accomplished gentleman. We remained off Tripoli two days, and then by signal from Commodore Chauncey, (who by seignority, superseded Commodore Shaw,) received orders to proceed to Tripoli in the line of order designated by signal. The course was given by signal also, but it was observed that Commodore Shaw kept two points to windward of the course given by the Commodore.

It had been blowing very fresh before we left Tripoli, and attended with a very heavy sea. While we were at Palermo, an old priest came off to the ship with a large bag, and a St. Antonio box, in which he kept the charity money which he from day to day could beg. This bag he intended to contain anything in the way of provisions that the charitable were disposed to give to his "poor monk brethren." He brought the bag to me, and with an imploring look, offered to sell us a fair wind for a small sum of money or a few biscuits. And as the purchasing of a fair wind did not exactly belong to me, I declined the offer, but was sorry afterwards that we did not accept the old man's bargain, as we had a head wind all the way to Tunis.

The second day after leaving Tripoli, in consequence of the previous and continued bad weather, the fleet had become scattered, and out of their regular order of sailing. It so happened, and very fortunately too, that the Erie, drawing less water than any other of the ships, had, by tacking, got ahead of the fleet; where, if the weather had been good, the commodore should have been.

About nine o'clock in the morning, all at once we saw a change in the color of the water, and immediately a signal was made from the Erie, of danger. The commodore gave the signal to tack, which we obeyed. He then, by signal, ordered each ship to run under his lee quarter, and as they did so, were ordered to make their best way to

Tunis. The dangerous place in which we found ourselves, whether by accident or carelessness, I shall not attempt to say, was the Gulf of Cabes, which may be recognized on the chart as a dangerous place; lying between Tripoli and Tunis. On our arrival at Tunis, we found the U. S. frigate, which had arrived the day before, she had made a straight course, avoiding the difficulty we had so providentially escaped, and anchored off Carthage. The officers visited this renowned spot, and also Tunis, as often as they wished.

A rather laughable, or what might might have been a serious affair, came off while we lay at Carthage. Two passed midshipmen, who had quarrelled some months before, and at the time of the quarrel, belonged to the same ship, but by the changing of officers and crews, these two belligerent gentleman had been separated; but had always, since the quarrel, been determined to settle the matter honorably, on the first opportunity that presented itself. Accordingly, the preliminaries for a duel were arranged, and a meeting had on the beach at Carthge with pistols. They had exchanged shots before, but neither had been lucky enough to hit his antagonist. They were now determined to fix the matter up, man fashion. So they measured their distance, and fired. But where the bullets went, no one could tell; it was certain, however, that neither of them did any harm. The *friends* (?) loaded up again, and one, two, three, fire! and no one either killed or wounded yet. They now concluded, at the suggestion of the seconds, to try small swords; when, after about twenty-five minutes, P—e received a scratch upon one of his ribs, which decided the battle in favor of the hero, who first drew blood. So ended this tragic affair.

There are some interesting remains of old Carthage still to be seen. Some very large broken columns still standing on the heights, and traces of the old walls are still visible. Hannibal's wells are shown, but now nearly filled up. The top of the hill presents a beautiful view; away toward the eastward is the Lybian desert, and near by the pretty and busy town of Tunis. At the goletta there are some guns left mounted, whose calibres are twenty-one inches in diameter; these were intended for stone shot. The short passage from Carthage to Tunis is through a lake of water so highly impregnated with salt, that the spray is ruinous to fine clothes.

News had just reached Tunis, that Lord Exmouth had completely demolished Algiers. This caused us to hasten there with all possible dispatch, fearing that our consul might be in danger. We ran down in two days, and entered the Bay. The commodore, being ahead with the signal flying at the mast head, "*prepare to anchor*;" but scarcely had the signal been run up, when a boat was discovered coming off with great speed, and a man standing up waving his hat. The signal for anchoring was annuled, and another to tack ship, hoisted in its stead. We all tacked and backed our main yards for the boat. She soon reached the commodore; and in the boat was Mr. Shaler, our consul, who told the commodore, as our ships were seen entering the Bay, he had received a message from the captain of the port, advising him to go himself, or send a messenger to prevent the ships from approaching within gunshot of the batteries, as the Dey had declared that he would fire upon them if they anchored within his limits. "For," said he, "I have been deceived once, and am determined not to be deceived again."

We stood out beyond gunshot range, and anchored. Exmouth's fleet had been gone only a few days, and everything was in great confusion on shore. The Dey alluded to the manner in which Lord Exmouth had brought his ships close into the mole, and commenced firing while the negotiation was pending. The particulars of this bombardment I was fortunate enough to obtain in England, and as it must be interesting, to any one, to learn that this abominable nest of Pirates have received from Lord Exmouth a severe chastisement, and also, of the subsequent total destruction of this Piratical government. It will be recollected, that a few months since, when we left Port Mahon, with the Ferdinand, that Lord Exmouth, with the Boyne, 90, and 5 ships of the line, sailed for Algiers. After our treaty had been accepted and signed by the Dey, the British consul represented to the

Dey, that the treaty with the Americans was on much more favorable terms than that with his Majesty's government, and earnestly requested that certain alterations might be made, that England might stand on as favorable terms as any other great nation. To this the Dey replied, that in the treaty with the United States, he had relinquished the gunpowder, which he much regretted, and considered it unjust in the American President, to insist on withholding the powder as one of the articles of the treaty; and he therefore could not relinquish it from the British treaty. The English consul told him that his Majesty's government had many more ships, and much larger, than those of the Americans, and could bring a strong force at any time against him. The Dey very indignantly turned away, saying, "very well, let them come; I am ready for them."

And when Lord Exmouth's fleet appeared in the offing, the consul waited upon the Dey, informing him of the arrival of his Lordship, who had come for the purpose of ransoming the Christian prisoners. The consul endeavored to draw his attention to the ships, as they could easily be seen from the castle, thinking, possibly, that their formidable appearance might have some effect in a renewal of the treaty. It was reported that some English officers while passing the Dey's palace, did not, as was customary with all who passed, lift their hats. The guard, on noticing this omission of respect, stepped out, and motioned to these gentlemen that they must touch their hats, which, on their refusing to do, a soldier raised his hand to lift the hat himself, the officer put out his arm to keep the Algerine off, when the latter with his cimeter made a blow at him, and cut off a part of his hand. This was a commencement of hostilities, which the English account, which I now give, will fully explain. It was also reported, that when Lord Exmouth arrived at Gibraltar only a few days after the above insult, the officers and English residents of the garrison, severely censured his lordship for not resenting the insult immediately, by firing upon the City; and on his arrival in England, much indignation was expressed towards him throughout the country, particularly by the admiralty, who ordered him to Portsmouth, and there to select what number of ships he wanted, and go immediately back, and retrieve his own, and the honor of his country. Here follows the English account, which commences from Gibraltar bay; the fleet having been fitted with unusual dispatch, and arriving at Gibraltar bay, Wednesday, 14th August, 1816.

"Wednesday, 14th, 1816. Lord Exmouth arrived at Gibraltar with the powerful fleet which the Lords of the Admiralty had placed at his command, for the purpose of either reducing Algiers, or of obliging the Dey to submit to a treaty which had been prepared; annulling many of the articles contained in the former, and inserting others which would place the English consul on an equal footing with the consul of the United States. Also, on a demand for the immediate release of all Christian prisoners, with reparation for insults offered to the British consul.

"His majesty's brig, Prometheus, had been dispatched to Algiers to bring away the consul's family in a private manner previous to the arrival of the fleet. But Capt. Dashwood succeeded only in bringing away the consul's family, the consul being detained under the following circumstances.

"The Dey, having heard of the expedition through the French papers, felt suspicious that something was going on when the Prometheus arrived there, and having discovered that the consul's wife and daughter had embarked, disguised in midshipmen's clothes, the discovery having been made through a female Jew servant who had been employed as nurse to her child, she felt it her duty to tell the Rabbi, who immediately through fear of bringing the Jews into trouble, apprised the Dey of what had happened. He would not permit the consul to leave, but instantly put him in irons to which was attached a heavy chain, and confined him in a small room in the ground floor of his house; and also detained two boats with eighteen men belonging to the Prometheus.

"Capt. Dashwood was obliged to sail without them as he expected the arrival of the fleet every moment.

"On the 26th August, Lord Exmouth arrived, ran in, anchored his ships in fine style abreast the batteries, to the utter astonishment and consternation of the Turks. A boat with a flag of truce was immediately dispatched toward the shore with an interpreter and a letter for the Dey. It was expected of course that a boat from the shore would meet them before they had approached near enough to be in danger, which however was the case. A long and prevaricating conference on the part of the Algerine government, determined Lord Exmouth to demand immediate decision, which they not only refused to do, but opened their batteries upon the fleet.

"No sooner was the smoke seen than his lordship gave the order, 'Fire, my good fellows!' and I am sure that before his lordship had finished those words, our broadside was given with cheering, which was three times within five or six minutes, and at the same instant the other ships did the same. This first fire was so terrible that they say more than five hundred persons were killed and wounded by it, and I believe this, because there was a great crowd of persons in every part, many of whom, after the first discharge, I saw running away under the walls like dogs, walking upon their feet and hands. After the attack took place on both sides in this horrible manner, immediately the sky was darkened by smoke, the sun completely eclipsed, and the horizon became dreary. Being exhausted by the heat of the powerful sun, to which I was exposed during the whole day, my ears being deafened by the noise of the guns, and finding myself in this dreadful danger of such a terrible engagement, in which I had never been before, I was quite at a loss, and like an astonished and stupid man, and knew not where I was. At last, his lordship, having perceived my situation, said, 'You have done your duty; now go below.' Upon which I began to descend from the quarter-deck, quite confounded and terrified, and not certain that I should reach the cockpit alive, for it was terrible to hear the whizzing of the shot, to see the wounded men brought from one part and the killed from another; and especially, at such a time, to be found among the English seamen! To witness their manners, their activity, their courage, and their cheerfulness during the battle! It is really overpowering and beyond imagination. On this subject I wish to make one remark. While I was going below, I was stopped near the hatchway by a crowd of seamen who were carrying two wounded men to the cockpit, and I had leisure to observe the management of those heavy guns on the lower deck. I saw the crews of the two guns nearest the hatchways; they were out of wads and sung out for them, and not being immediately supplied, two of them, with an oath, took out their knives and cut the breasts of their jackets off and rammed them into the guns for wads.

"At last I reached the cockpit, when Mr. Dewar, the surgeon, Mr. Frowd, the chaplain, and Mr. Somerville, the purser, with some friends, met me and began to congratulate me on my safe return, for they never expected I should escape. They gave me some refreshment, but I could eat nothing, I only drank a little wine and water. Now I wished to assure myself if I was out of danger or not. I asked how much we were above water. They told me we were pretty safe, because the cockpit was about two or three feet below the water line, and that I had nothing to fear. as I was now out of the greatest danger. Hearing this, relieved me, but having heard that several shots had passed through our ship between wind and water, and that the carpenter had stopped the holes, I then lost the idea of perfect safety, and walked fearfully into the cockpit.

"Observing that the action was going on without any appearance of ceasing, I began to encourage myself by thinking that every living being is uncertain of his existence, and that, through life, we are continually exposed to the mercy of circumstances, and thus I commenced assisting those poor men after their wounds were dressed, for humanity and natural sensibility at such a dreadful time, call upón everybody to pity and help the unfortunate. Some of them could not walk, others were deprived of their sight, and some were to be carried from one place to another. It was, indeed, a most pitiable sight; but I think the most shocking sight was the amputation of limbs, in preference to beholding which, if I were a military man, I should certainly prefer being on deck than with the doctor in the cockpit.

"From curiosity I wished to observe the doctor's operations.

But while observing the first operation, which was the amputation of an arm, I could not bear it, and began to faint, especially when the doctor commenced sawing the bone. I then went away. At this time I saw Lieutenant John Frederick Johnstone come down the cockpit, wounded in his cheek. After the wound had been dressed, he remained a short time, laughing. He asked me to assist him to put on his coat, and went to the hatchway, wishing to go on deck again. I then held him by the shoulders to hinder him, and said, 'Where are you going? you are wounded.' In reply, he said, 'I am very well now, and must go immediately.' After two hour's time I saw him, poor fellow, brought down to the cock-pit again by four seamen, with his left arm nearly taken from his shoulder, and when I met him in that state, he could not bear to be carried, but wished to lie down where he was, and began to call 'Doctor! Doctor!' when we all took care of him, and the Doctor came and amputated his arm quite from the joint to the shoulder. I saw that the side of his breast was terribly torn. After the wound was dressed, we laid him on a sofa with great care, and were all very sorry, and did not expect he would live.

"After he had been a week between life and death, the doctor began to give us some hope; and so by degrees, we saw him almost out of danger, and shook hands with him; when, some days after, he wrote a letter to his friends in England, and we were all happy in seeing him getting better; (although the doctor still feared he would bleed again) and Lord Exmouth took him to his own cabin, and conferred upon him the greatest care in every possible manner.

"Better indeed would it have been for us to have endured the grief of his death all at once, when he was first wounded, than to have him with us thirty-six days after the battle, and then to bury him before his own home.

"This melancholy event gave us double sorrow. This brave and unfortunate young officer was about 25 years old. He was wounded on the 27th of August, and continued to get better until the 27th of September. On the 28th, his wound bled again, when the doctor was obliged to cut the flesh and take up that vein, in order to stop the blood. But poor Johnstone, being very thin and weak, survived the operation five days only, and at 6 o'clock on the evening of the 3d of October, departed this life. At 12 next day, he was buried in the sea, when we had arrived opposite Plymouth, with great honor and ceremeny. Minute guns were fired; the Royal standard was waved over his coffin, and the flags of all the ships were hoisted at half-mast, and his Lordship and all the other officers were at his funeral. But to continue.

"About this time I was sorry to see my friend Mr. Grimes (his Lordship's secretary) conducted below; he had received several wounds from splinters, and was obliged to quit the deck from loss of blood, having seen that the battle was going on favorably; and the Algerines, after fighting extremely well for about five hours, began to slacken their firing.

"And after that, our seamen, every time an Algerine frigate took fire, or any of the batteries were destroyed, gave a loud cheer. I began to have more courage, and jumped up now and then, to the lower deck, to see what was going on; so, for the rest of the action, employed myself in passing the empty powder boxes to the magazine; because I found it more agreeable than watching the doctor.

"I observed with much astonishment, that during all the time of the battle, not one seaman appeared fatigued, nor lamented the dreadful continuation of the fight; but on the contrary, the longer it lasted, the more cheerful and pleasant they were.

"Notwithstanding, during the greater part of the battle, the firing was most tremendous on our side, particularly from this ship, the firing of which was kept up with equal fury, which did not cease, though his Lordship in several instances wished to cease firing for a short time, in order to make his observations; and it was with great difficulty he could make the seamen stop for a few minutes.

"Several of the guns were so hot that they could not use them again; some of them being heated to such a degree, that when fired, they recoiled with their carriages with such force, that the trucks ploughed into the deck, and some were dismounted and rendered useless.

"At eleven o'clock, P. M., his Lordship having observed the destruction of the whole Algerine navy, and the strongest parts of their batteries, with the city, made a signal to the fleet to move out of the line of the batteries; and thus with a favorable breeze we cut our cables, and as well as the whole squadron, made sail. Our firing ceased at about half past eleven, when the action was over. Mr. Stair, (the gunner,) came out from the magazine and said that he was about seventy years old, and that in his life he had been in more than twenty actions; but that he never knew or heard of any action that had consumed so great a quantity of powder as this.

"After the ships had hauled out without any danger, (although the Algerines began to throw shells from the higher castles,) I went on to the poop to see his Lordship, and to observe the effect of our shot on the enemy's batteries, and to behold the destruction of their navy, which, at this time, with the storehouse within the mole, was burning very rapidly. The blaze illuminated all the bay. The town, with the environs, were almost as clear as in daytime; the view of which was awful and beautiful. Nine frigates, with a great number of gunboats, with other vessels, being all in flames, and carried by the wind to different directions in the bay.

"I observed with great surprise, how, in these nine hour's time, our shot had effected such horrible destruction in their batteries. Instead of walls, I saw nothing but heaps of rubbish, and a number of people dragging the dead bodies out. When I met his Lordship on the poop, his voice was quite hoarse, and he had two slight wounds; one on his cheek and the other on the leg.

"On the morning after the battle, Wednesday, 28th August Admiral Lord Exmouth wrote the following letter to the Dey:—

To His Highness, the Dey of Algiers:

SIR,—For your atrocities at Bona on defenceless Christians,

and your unbecoming disregard to the demand I made yesterday, in the name of the Prince Regent of England, the fleet, under my orders has given you a signal chastisement, by the total destruction of your navy, storehouses and arsenal, with half your batteries. As England does not war for the destruction of cities, I am unwilling to visit your personal cruelties upon the inoffensive inhabitants of the country; and I therefore offer you the same terms of peace, which I conveyed to you yesterday, in my sovereign's name. Without the acceptance of these terms you can have no peace with England. If you receive this offer as you ought, you will fire three guns; and I shall consider your not making this signal as a refusal, and I shall renew my operation at my own convenience. I offer you the above terms, provided neither the British Consul nor the officers and men so wickedly seized by you, from the boats of a British ship-of-war, have met with any cruel treatment, or any of the Christian slaves in your power; and I repeat my demand, that the Consul, officers and men, may be sent off to me, conformably to ancient treaties.

(Signed,) EXMOUTH.

Queen Charlotte, Algiers Bay, August 28, 1816.

"After I had translated this letter, his Lordship gave it to me, and ordered me to accompany Lieutenant Burgess on shore again, to deliver it, and to wait for an answer as yesterday, and at the same time gave orders to the bombs to take their position, and to be in readiness for renewing the bombardment.

"My companion, Mr. Burgess, and myself got into the boat with one flag of truce, and rowed towards the city. I was not so much afraid as yesterday, in consequence of the destruction of their batteries; yet, when we got rather too near the mole they fired two or three shots at us, from a castle at the south end of their fortifications, but fortunately these shot fell a few yards short of our boat. Upon this, we stopped and began to think seriously. However, after some time, we saw a boat coming out of the mole at about eleven o'clock, nevertheless, we were in great doubt whether they were coming to meet us civilly, or whether they would seize us, as was their usual practice.

"When the boat had reached us, I found she had on board a person by the name of Omar Capitan, who was commander of one of the frigates that was burnt the day before. He asked how the great Admiral was. In reply, I asked how the Dey was, and gave him the letter, and told him it was for the Dey, and that we should wait three hours, as yesterday, for an answer; and in case he did not come in that time we were instructed to return on board, and that the Dey would never have peace with England on any other terms. In answer, he said:

"'How? Yesterday our letters were ready with the Dey's answer, but you would not wait to receive them, and your fleet took its position so suddenly that we had not time to look about us, and immediately you began firing.'

"'You must excuse me,' said I. 'What you say is not true, because yesterday we waited more than three hours for an answer, notwithstanding two were stated by your captain of the port to be sufficient, and it was not our fleet that began the fire but your batteries; and, as a proof of your implacability, you see now those shots that have been fired upon us from that castle, when we are under a flag of truce, without arms, exposing ourselves, for your peace and tranquillity.'

"Then finding himself convicted, he said: 'Everything happened by God's decree, and now let us forget the past and be greater friends than ever.'

"'This must depend,' I answered, 'on the answer which your Dey gives to Lord Exmouth's letter, and if the Dey wishes to send anybody to treat with our admiral we shall receive him with pleasure.'

"He replied: 'I hope it will be so;' and added; 'You must not mind those shots, for they were fired without the Dey's order, and he has already sent orders to all the fortifications not to fire one gun.'

"I told him I was sure of that—that those shots were fired without any order—because I know your people's character, and am certain that when they saw our boat they began to say, 'There are the infidels coming; come, let us kill some of these, to revenge our dead people;' and they thought by killing two or three people without considering the consequences, they should have a general revenge."

"He then laughed and said, 'How do you know that?'

"I said, 'Because I was in your country for some time.'

"In reply, he said, 'Once you knew our manners; you must not, therefore, consider this as a fault, since we are now friends.'

"I replied, 'On the contrary, just because we are on the point of reconciliation, I must consider it as an extraordinary fault."

"He then said, "You Europeans are very religious people, and we are not able to debate with you.' And then he went away, saying, 'I hope to be back again directly with a good answer from the Dey, and then,' he added, 'you may come near to the city, because you are too far off with your boat now; you must be afraid of nothing.' He rowed his boat towards the mole, to behold more distinctly the effect of our action. From his conversation and manner I understood that they were very glad to make an end of the business. He went in, and we stopped outside the mole, waiting for the Dey's answer.

"During this time, I was indeed quite surprised to see the horrible state of the batteries and the mole since the preceding day. I could not now distinguish how it was erected, nor where the batteries had stood, as well as many fine houses which I had seen in the city the day previous; and I observed too, that they had not more than four or five guns mounted on the carriages. Besides, the bay was full of hulks of their navy, smoking in every direction, and the water inside and out of the mole was black, and covered with charcoal and half burnt pieces of wood. But the most shocking and dreadful sight was the number of dead bodies which were floating on the surface of the water. Among the bodies we saw a white one, which afterwards, on finding it was one of our seamen, we took it with us on board, and waited there for about one hour and a half. And at half past one we saw three guns fired from the shore, and at the same time a boat coming out of the mole. Then I understood that the

Dey was prepared for his own and for the Algerines happiness, to accept our demands; and I began to thank Almighty God for this glorious success.

"When the boat came near to ours I saw the captain of the port, with the Swedish Consul on board. The former paid his compliments, and asked to go on board with us to meet his Lordship, with the Swedish Consul, who was sent by the Dey to speak with him. Meantime the consul said: "I am authorized by the Dey to have a consultation with Lord Exmouth, relative to the arrangement of the treaty. There were many points in the treaty which the Dey demurred at most bitterly; — such as giving up the three hundred thousand dollars which he had recently received for the ransom of the Sardinian prisoners; the relinquishing his annual tribute of powder, and of being forced to sign a treaty dictated under such humiliating circumstances.

"He knew there was no alternative—he must either accept the treaty or his destruction was sure; and not only must he receive the English treaty, but that of the Dutch also, who, by the way, were solely indebted to Lord Exmouth for the termination of their war, which had already lasted nearly three years, and in all probability would have continued until the destruction of Algiers by the French, in 1827.

"At length matters were so far advanced, that officers from both the English and Dutch fleets visited the shore for the purpose of consummating this important business. The narrator goes on to say: 'When we entered the consul's house, it was full of rubbish, and we counted thirty shots of various sizes, collected there by the servants. We walked through the house, and observed one small room of ten feet square. In this room, Mr. Mc. Donnell, our consul, wished to remain when the Dey arrested him, but it was too good a room for their malicious disposition, so they refused to let him stay there, and confined him in a dark room below, which, fortunately, was the cause of his safety, as will soon appear.

"We ascertained that nine shots had passed through the very room where the consul had wished to remain. We went on to the top of the house to observe the whole city, although it is ordered that no Christian shall appear there, as throughout the whole coast of Barbary it is prohibited for a Christian to appear on the top of his house, and if any one should violate this order, he would be immediately shot, because they believe that the Christians come there to see their women.

"The next business to be attended to after the ratification of the treaty and re-establishing the consul in his diplomatic position, was to see that the prisoners were all brought in from the country, ready to embark when the appointed ship should be ready to receive them. The cruel treatment of these poor slaves being in an excessive degree barbarous, my feelings do not permit me to describe it in detail. I only wish to present a small idea of it by mentioning the following points. When the Algerines or any of the Barbary pirates capture an European or an American vessel, they seize their goods, and every species of property they can get hold of (they do not touch the money the prisoners have in their pockets) and put them immediately in chains. There are three classes of chains, viz: of one hundred, of sixty, and of thirty pounds weight. The one hundred pounds are for strong men; the sixty for old men, and the thirty for young persons. These heavy chains are placed around the body as a sash, with a long piece of chain hung on the right leg, and joined by a heavy ring, to be placed upon the foot. All these chains are shut by a lock, and never can be taken off. Thus, these poor fellows must walk any distance whatever, and work, sleep and live always with these chains; the marks of which I have seen round their bodies and their legs in very deep furrows eaten into their flesh, which becomes black and as hard as bone, the sight of which is truly distressing. After these poor creatures are put in chains, they make them work at the hardest work; as cutting stone from the mountains, felling trees, carrying sand and stones for building, moving guns from one place to another, and such kinds of laborious work. They have no machines to facilitate the workmen; all must be done by the strength of these poor people. Every ten slaves are bound together, and followed by a guard with a whip in his hand; and if any one of them has occasion to perform any natural evacuation, they went all together, whether by night or day. They sleep all together on the ground, in a large stable, with a mat under them. If any of them have money then they can make themselves rather more comfortable.

"The government allows to each person for every day of the week, (except Friday,) a loaf of eight or ten ounces of a very black kind of bread, made of barley and beans, one handful of peas, and a small measure not larger than a thimble of oil; that is the whole of their food; and on Friday nothing at all.

"An Aga of the Janizaries of Algiers, observing the miserable state of the prisoners, and the inhumanity with which they were treated, was induced by his feelings to allow them a portion of meat and wheat bread for every Friday, on which day they would have had nothing. This allowance was continued for several years; but for their misfortune this good man died of about a middle age; and nobody, after him, was so humane as to follow his benevolent example. And thus these unfortunate creatures were again deprived of assistance and continued to pass their lives as before till the Divine Providence released them through the medium, and through the exalted and merciful government of Great Britain.

"The troops seeing several ships coming near the town to receive the slaves, and to take away our anchors from the environs of the mole, thought that they were agoing to renew the attack, or to do some improper thing; and they rushed into the mole with their arms. Some of them, when our boats shoved off with the slaves, were so brutish as to fire several musket shots, which fortunately passed over the boats. On my arrival on board, I reported this conduct to his Lordship, who ordered me to claim redress for it, from the Dey. On the next day, after all the slaves were embarked on board the two transports, and anchored near the Queen Charlotte, they all came on deck, on the shrouds, and on the yards, exclaiming and shouting in the same words as before; and giving cheers and plaudits to every ship; so that it was a most joyful noise on both sides. Lord Exmouth then gave orders to have them counted. We took a list of people of each nation, and they amounted to one thousand and eighty-three in the whole. Then his Lordship ordered them to be embarked on board several ships to convey them to their respective countries, which was done according to the following table:

Neapolitans, - - -	471	Sicilians, - - -	236
Romans, - - - -	173	Tuscans, - - -	6
Spaniards, - - - -	161	Portuguese, - -	1
Greeks, - - - - -	7	Dutch, - - - -	28

"The Wasp was ordered to call and receive such slaves as might be at Bona; and the Mutine proceeded to Oran for the same purpose. Five Spaniards were afterwards brought by the Mutine, from Oran to Gibraltar; and fifty slaves had been sent from Oran to Algiers, previously to the Mutine's arrival, to be conveyed to their respective homes, through the medium of the British Consul. All the slaves therefore amounted to eleven hundred and thirty-eight, besides those of Constantina, and Bona, who were seventy-three in number; making in the whole, twelve hundred and eleven slaves. Besides these, there were released by Lord Exmouth on his first visit to Algiers, Tunis and Tripoli, seventeen hundred and ninety-two slaves; making a grand total of thirty hundred and three helpless victims restored from slavish durance, to liberty.

"This was the number of slaves we knew of; and if in process of time, we or our consul come to understand that any other slave is detained in any part of the kingdom of Algiers, the Dey is obliged to produce him, and give him up to the British Consul.

"Saturday, 31st. In the morning, a Neapolitan slave came on board the Queen Charlotte, and told me that his son, a little boy eight years old, was detained by a lady, in the city of Algiers, and that she had made him a Mahometan. I directly reported this to his Lordship, who had also received in telligence that the Dey had detained still in chains two Spaniards: one of whom was the Vice Consul at Oran, named Don Hequira, and the other a merchant, named Don Sebastina Padrone; — both had been unjustly arrested, put in chains, and doomed to hard work from the time of the revolution at Oran, in the year 1813, against the former Dey of Algiers.*

"His Lordship then directed Capt. Brisbane to go with me on shore to claim the little boy and the two Spaniards from the Dey. At noon I went on shore with Capt. Brisbane, for the receipts of the money; and it was the first business which we had to do with the Dey previous to any contest respecting the Neapolitan boy, and the two Spaniards. Capt. Brisbane remained at the consul's house, and I went to the Dey's palace, where I found all the sum put up ready in the court yard of the palace. I met the treasurer, who asked me in what manner I intended to receive it? He wished to deliver it to me while I was in the palace, and that I would take care of it until it should be embarked. But I refused, and told him I would count one thousand dollars, replace it in the bag, and put it into a balance, and by that means should receive all the sum by weight, that afterwards he must send the money by his own people down to the mole where our officers would receive it, by counting and putting it into their boats. After considerable controversy, and much shuffling on the part of the Dey, the money was conveyed to the boats by his own men, and duly received by the officer appointed for this particular department.

"Capt. Brisbane notified the Dey that on the morrow at an early hour, boats would be sent for those prisoners that were in town. Also, a request that those in the country should be brought in without delay. The hypocritical scoundrel then said to Capt. Brisbane, that some of them were many miles in the interior, and that a hasty march would fatigue them

* In the year 1813, the Dey of Oran rebelled against the former Dey of Algiers, (Hagi Ali Pashaw, of which I shall give a full account in another part of my narrative.) and after having been killed by order of said Dey, two of his sons escaped with their money and some jewels of their own, and went to Malaga; upon which the Dey put the said Spanish vice consul in irons, and made him become responsible for the return of the fugitives, but as he (the Dey,) had received no satisfactory answer from the Spanish government, he availed himself of an occasion over the other Spanish merchant in consequence of a law suit on some mercantile business to put him in chains too, (according to his idea of justice,) and treated them worse than slaves.

very much! He was very humane all at once, fearing now that the march would fatigue them, but when he had them in chains, (some of whom had worn them thirty years,) and made them perform the most laborious and servile work, with miserable food and barbarous treatment, now afraid that their joyful march to emancipation would fatigue them.

"When our boats came inside the mole, I wished to receive the slaves from the captain of the port by numbers, but could not, because they began directly to push and throw themselves into the boats by crowds of ten or twenty together, so that it was impossible to count them. Then I told him that we should make an exact list of them in order to know their amount. It was indeed a most glorious and ever-memorable and merciful act, for England all over Europe to see these poor slaves, when our boats were shoving off from the shore, all at once to take off their hats and exclaim in Italian,

"'Viva il Re'd 'Inglitera, Il Padre eterno! e'l ammiraglio Inglese che ci ha liberato da questo secundo inferno!'

"[Long live the king of England, the Eternal Father! and the English Admiral who delivered us from this second hell.]

"And afterwards they began to prove what they had suffered by beating their breasts and loudly swearing at the Algerines. I spoke with some of these unfortunate people who had been thirty-five years in slavery, and had become so inured to hardship and the most servile slavery, that when told they were free, could scarcely comprehend the term; but soon their hearts began to expand, as the blood of freedom circulated through them. They were all well received on board their ship, comfortably provided for, and carried to their respective countries. All things now being duly arranged between the several governments, the ships got under way to return to England.

"Thus ended one of the most sanguinary bombardments that England had ever been engaged in. The Dey, villain as he was, fought like a hero, cheering his men at the different batteries, and worked hard himself, he being a brave man, encouraging his men to repel the infidels. When I went with the dispatches on the first day of the attack, I saw his own flag hoisted on the tight horse battery. This particular flag is carried with him, always to be hoisted when he takes his station. It is of red, white, and yellow stripes. But the strongest proof of his being in the batteries is, that when I met him on the second day of the battle, I saw that all the folds of his turban and dress were full of dust and smoke of powder, as well as his face and beard. The number of killed and wounded on board the British ships was eight hundred and fifty-two; in the Dutch squadron, killed and wounded sixty-five. The loss of the Algerines is not even known to themselves, because they do not take care of their people as we do. They have no surgeons to dress the wounded men directly. They never perform the operation of amputating limbs to save the life of a person, but on the contrary, put all their wounded men into a large stable till the day after the battle, by which many who might have been saved by the immediate amputation of an arm or leg, were left to perish. Of their killed and wounded I had several reports; some said the number was about eight thousand, some six thousand, some five thousand, and some four thousand. I am sure, however, that their loss must have been very great, because they said that if the Dey had not ordered the gates of the city to be opened during the battle, to let the rest of the inhabitants run away, (though a great part of them had left the town ten days previous to the fleet's arrival,) numbers more would have been killed; nevertheless many were killed by the explosion of our shells and by the rockets in the city, and while they were going out of town, whose bodies were afterwards found. The Mahometans in burying their dead are followed by a great number of men and women crying and howling, as well as a great number of men, who are continually rushing forward to carry the coffin, confidently certain that each person by supporting the weight of the coffins for a few minutes, will assume a portion of the dead men's sins, and that the great number of people who carry the coffin will diminish the sins of the decased, so that he may go to heaven pure, or without any grievous offence on his shoulders. All these customs, while we were at Algiers, were prohibited by the Dey, and he gave orders to bury the dead privately, without making any noise or abusing any ceremony. This proves that the Dey wished not to let the number of the dead be known to us. But I learned by many reports that there were three large houses full of dead bodies, and that the people were employed to bury them every night during the week of our stay there.

"They buried them in a ground separated from the other cemetery, because according to Mahometan doctrine, they consider every person killed in battle, a martyr, and as the attack happened to take place on the fourth of their holidays of Ramadan, previous to which they had passed thirty days of fasting, they were fully persuaded that the whole of those who fell were the purest of martyrs. At first they thought that our rockets were a kind of signal rockets; but, when some of them had burst among the troops and killed a great number, then they changed their opinion, especially when several of the rockets fell on board their navy and some of the houses. They wished to put the fire out by water, but found that the more water they had, the more ardent the flame became. The materials of the composition, they said, stuck to the wood and penetrated like oil, the effect of which filled them with horror.

"The quantities of powder and shot spent in this tremendous action are really so surprising that I thought the following detail worthy of insertion. Two hundred and sixteen thousand six hundred and fifty-eight pounds powder, forty-one thousand two hundred and eight round shot, nine hundred and sixty shells, thirteen and sixteen inches. This is the British squadron. On board the Dutch fleet, forty-six thousand one hundred and nineteen pounds of powder, ten thousand one hundred and forty-eight round shot, making in all, two hundred and sixty-two thousand seven hundred and seventy-seven pounds of powder, fifty-one thousand three hundred and fifty-six round shot. These incredible quantities of powder and shot, which are nearly one hundred and eighteen tons of the former, and five hundred tons of the latter, were spent in the course of about nine hours. And I think the Algerines very justly observed: that,

"'Hell had opened its mouth against them through the English ships.'

"Previous to our arrival at Algiers, they heard that the British fleet consisted of fifty sail, and then they said, 'Let them come! What can they do with their fifty sail? The Spaniards once came here with four hundred sail and forty thousand men, and could not succeed against us.' They were on this account fully persuaded that their country was unconquerable.

"The whole of the Algerine damage, in my humble judgment, after many reports and information, may be computed about a million sterling. Many of the inhabitants of Algiers, and nearly all the people of the interior, were quite glad at our success, as they expected we were going to take possession of the kingdom and release them from the tyranny of the Turks; for being very badly treated they are dissatisfied with that government, and if they could free themselves from the slavery which they suffer under the Turks, they would do it with the greatest pleasure.

"The Kingdom of Algiers extends about sixteen hundred miles in circumference; is very fertile, producing much corn and many species of vegetables, indigo and wool. They have many cattle, sheep, fowls, and on this coast a famous coral fishery. This fertile and beautiful coast has been for many centuries in the hands of pirates, the fear and dread of every nation under heaven, and gladly paying to them annually, immense tributes, quality and quantity dictated by their haughty Dey. The peasantry have always been oppressed, not daring to call their crops their own, most exorbitantly taxed, and so sorely, that they placed very little value on their lives, and often for the most trifling offence their heads were cut off; and quite in desperation, parties of the country people rush upon the Turkish tax-gatherers, and put them to death.

"The government of Algiers is made up of the most consummate villains throughout Turkey. All the murderers, thieves and vagabonds from Constantinople come here, and enlist under the banners of the Dey of Algiers, and notwithstanding that these piratical rascals would not hesitate to kill a Christian, any more than they would a dog, yet when our purser purchased a quantity of live stock consisting chiefly of sheep and fowls, the soldier at the gate would not allow them to pass without an order from the captain of the port, as they do not allow the Christians to have live animals, because they say that we strangle them, and do not kill them as we should by cutting their throats. The Mahometans in general, when they wish to kill any kind of animal, prepare always a very sharp knife; and previously to cutting its throat, use the following words:

"'May God give thee endurance to bear what is predestined thee in the name of Almighty God.'

"And immediately they pass the knife twice round the throat of the animal, and hold it till it discharges all the blood. On this account, they say that the animals suffer a great deal under our hands by our style of killing them, and they are allowed to eat in case of necessity, any meat killed by the Jews, and not that killed by the Christians, because they consider our meat as stifled.

"The Dey with whom the treaty with the English, American and Dutch was made, was named Omar Pashaw. He was between forty-five and fifty years of age, of a short make, and about five feet six inches in height, and well shaped; but his appearance was altogether savage, and his malevolent and violent spirit, marked by an exterior coldness and apathy. He could neither read nor write; was a native of Mytilene in the Archipelago, and came from thence to Algiers as a common soldier, but being a brave one, was promoted to Bulook-Bashlike, to Beeng Bashlike the former captain of a company. The latter, captain of a thousand, afterwards, in the year 1813, at the revolution at Oran, he was created by his predecessor, Hagi *Ali* Pashaw, Aga, or chief of the Janizaries, in consequence of having distinguished himself by his bloody and ferocious cruelty, (which was not less than that of his said predecessor, of whose horrid acts we give a full account,) in the execution of the Bey of Oran, under the following shocking circumstances:

"The Bey of Oran was born there, of a Turk man and an Algerine woman. Being of rather a good character, he was elected by the inhabitants to be their governor. After some time the former Dey, Hagi Ali Pashaw, came to the throne;

and being of a very bloody disposition, had committed many shocking crimes, such as beheading people without any reason, seizing property, plundering and taking away other men's wives and daughters, &c., &c., and his troops had followed the same example. At last all the inhabitants of the kingdom became tired of these horrid acts. In the year eighteen hundred and thirteen, the Bey of Oran being very popular, and having observed the misconduct of the Dey, consulted with his uncle, (his mother's brother, who afterwards betrayed him,) to declare himself with the people against Hagi Ali Pashaw, and to drive all the Turks from the kingdom and to make their government free and hereditary like those of Tunis and Tripoli.

After his uncle had agreed with him, he wrote to the Tunisians to come to his assistance, and promised them that he would annul the annual tribute, (paid by the Tunisian government to that of Algiers,) and would then remain a friend to them forever. These proposals were accepted by the Tunisians, who were very glad to drive the Turks out of the Barbary coast. They made their preparations, and marched from one part, and the Bey of Oran from another, towards the city of Algiers. Hagi Ali Pashaw, on hearing of this conspiracy, began to make his preparations, but being too late, had not time to oppose both armies, and was obliged to call off his troops, and to keep himself within the city, notwithstanding he and his people had lost every hope. Observing his dangerous situation, he thought of sending a letter to the uncle of the Bey of Oran, promising him great things if he would put an end to this rebellion. The Bey unfortunately succeeded in introducing himself among the army of Oran without being discovered, and delivered the letter to the treacherous uncle, who believed the false promises of the Dey, and began to manage his nephew, (who wholly relied on him.) And instead of bringing the army of his nephew to unite with the Tunisians at the opposite place, he changed the route so as to keep one body apart from the other, and sent a private message to Hagi Ali Pashaw to come to such a place, (where he intended to remain, together with the army all night,) and seize them in the early part of the morning. The Bey of Oran, at the same time having suspected something of his uncle's perfidious management, deemed it proper to turn back towards Oran again, and secure his uncle, who was on his guard, and fled to Algiers.

"After the Bey of Oran had returned to his residence, as well as the Tunisians, without having met each other, the Dey of Algiers sent the Aga of the Janizaries, our present Dey, with the uncle of the Bey of Oran, to blockade the city of Oran, and to bring him the head of the unfortunate Bey.

"This expedition, by the instigation of the traitor's uncle, (who was afterwards beheaded,) was successful. The town was surrendered without fighting, and the Aga of the Janizaries took possession of it, when the Bey could not escape, but was arrested with all his family, except two of his sons who were out of town, and were lucky enough to escape to Malaga, in consequence of which the Spanish Vice Consul and the merchant before mentioned, were unjustly arrested, one after the other, as has already been explained. After the Aga had settled himself at Oran, he sent a message to Hagi Ali, apprising him of his success, and that he had in his power the Bey and family, except the two eldest sons. The Dey's answer was that he might decapitate the Bey and his uncle too, and send both heads to him. He immediately arrested the treacherous uncle, who well deserved his fate, and beheaded him; and now, willing to show his bloody and barbarous nature, and with horrid cruelty, perpetrated the following shocking deeds in the execution of the poor Bey. At first, he brought out the Bey with his three infant children, and in his presence, opened their bellies, took out their hearts, roasted them, and made the unhappy father eat them, and placed their bodies before him, (the father.)

"Secondly, he brought the two black slaves, who were constantly with the Bey, and obliged their master to impale them himself. And after the stakes were raised up and fixed in the ground, with the two slaves upon them, he made the Bey sit down on a red-hot iron waiter and fastened each hand to one of the stakes; afterwards he took a hot iron pot and put it on his head; when this became cold he ordered him to be scalped, and gave him a pipe to smoke, and at last opened his side and took out his heart and all his intestines. And so the poor unfortunate Bey expired. He afterwards took off the whole skin of the Bey's head, filled it with straw, and sent it to the Dey.

"This was once a custom among the Turks; but thank Heaven, it is now done away. All these horrible executions took place before the house where the wife of the unhappy Bey was. Any one who possesses human feelings, can judge what was the bitterness of such a dreadful impression on the senses of this inconsolable wife. There are no terms in which to express a proper sense of horror at the atrocities of this monster in human form, and as a reward for which, he was promoted to the agalik of Janizaries, and afterwards raised to the throne.

"Then I wish to relate, as they were told to me, some of the horrid acts of Hagi Ali Pashaw, to show how both characters, the Dey and that of his Aga, agreed one with the other. At the palace, the government residence in the city of Algiers, the Dey is not allowed to keep any wife. The harem, or Dey's wives, are always kept in a separate palace out of town, where he visits them every Friday evening only. But Hagi Ali Pashaw had two women brought privately into the Government palace, and he had besides five Greek boys and four black slaves. After some time, when the two unfortunate women became pregnant, he took the first, opened her belly, took out the child, filled the poor mother with salt, and when she was dead, he took the body and cut it in pieces, salted it well, and put it into a jar. He took the other, and suspended her by the hair to the top of a room. He wounded her body with small wounds, and put a basin under it to receive the blood; and so the poor woman was kept bleeding by drops, shut up in the room. He visited her at intervals, increasing the wounds till she was dead. He took her body, salted it, and preserved it in the same way as he did the first. After these unfortunate ladies were dispatched in this brutal manner, he took the poor Greek boys, one after the other, filled their mouths and noses with cotton, put them under some heavy mattresses, adding a great weight over them, till they were suffocated. He then cut their bodies in pieces, and put them into the private place. He turned with the same horrid design towards the black slaves, one of whom was his confidant and assistant in all his horrid transactions. Having observed that his master had already killed two of his black brothers, perceived that his turn would come at last, and when his master went into the bath of the palace, he, (the slave,) was prepared to shut him up in the inner room, which is always kept extremely warm, and made a much greater fire than ordinary, until he was suffocated. On the next day, the perpetrator came and apprised the Aga of the Janizaries, (the present Dey,) saying 'that he was sure his master would have killed him, and even now was not sure of his life. But if they killed him, he should die with a full satisfaction of having obtained the revenge of his brothers, and of those innocent women and boys; and at the same time he had done a great service to the poor people of Algiers by killing such a bloody and atrocious tyrant as Hagi Ali Pashaw;' and began to show the salted bodies of the two women, and gave a full account of all the horrible and barbarous deeds of his master. This poor fellow was put to death by the present Dey.

"These are some of the cruel and inhuman acts of the former Dey under whose order Omar Pashaw was an Aga of the Janizaries. There are still more charges of a villanous character against Omar Pashaw since he ascended the throne. While he was Bulook, and Beeng-Bashi, he was acquainted with two European families who lived at Algiers, as merchants, and frequently dined and drank at their houses, and professed great friendship for them, but did not prove it by facts. However, they never expected anything from him, but merely wished to keep him a good friend, for fear of his villanous character, he being known to be a most rapacious and wicked plunderer.

"After becoming Dey, he sent a message to these two friends that they must leave the kingdom. Although they were surprised at the news, they went and requested him to give them time, till they could settle their affairs with the people. He then agreed to allow them six months; but some days after that, he called them, and beheaded them in his palace, and sent a message to their unhappy families to quit Algiers immediately.

"What is now to be said to this atrocity? Is this his gratitude for the hospitality which he had experienced from those families? or the reward and acknowledgment of their friendship towards him? Notwithstanding, there are many other horrid facts committed by him, which are too horrid to relate. One more however, we will narrate.

"Since Hagi Ali's time, a young Algerine, of a rich family, was confined in prison for a debt of about one hundred thousand dollars, owed to several persons, who, after the death of said Dey, having observed that the young man had been so long time in prison, and that his father had died without leaving him anything to pay his debts, thought proper to set him at liberty to take care of his father's property without requiring anything from him, until he should become able to pay his debts. But when Omar Pashaw came to the throne, he refused to free the young man from prison; put him in chains, and made him work as one of his slaves. The creditors said, 'we do not wish to receive one dollar from him, we wish to set him free, to take care of the family, and property, &c.' The Dey's answer was, 'you do not wish to receive the one hundred thousand dollars from this young man, I wish to receive them myself, and shall not set him at liberty until he has paid the sum.'

"The unfortunate man was still in chains when Lord Exmouth made the treaty of peace, but of course could not demand his release, not being a Christian.

"To this brief and sickening account of that horrid den, I would just say, what Lord Exmouth left undone in entirely destroying that abominable hell, which he certainly should have done, the French accomplished in 1830."

Lord Exmouth doubtless went as far as his instructions from his government required, and which has been named in the treaty. But even after he had obtained the slaves, and the ransom money back, should the Dey have been compelled to pay a remuneration to these unfortunate men to their years of servitude and suffering? This demand should have been made and enforced too. And after the treaty had been signed by that inhuman monster, Omar Pashaw, and all the business apparently adjusted, and all the ships had left the bay, still there was the same perfidious wretch upon the throne, whose evident intention it was, after he had collected another fleet, to make reprisals on any merchantmen he could find, whose governments did not possess the means of resistance by a strong naval force.

Had Lord Exmouth completely annihilated the place, so far from having any imputation of injustice cast at him, he would have received plaudits of approbation from every Christian nation on earth. But this, with the taking of the Malakoff and Redan, were reserved for the French.

The account of the bombardment of Algiers by Lord Exmouth, which has just been given, was written (by permission of the Admiralty,) by an Arab, who was engaged by the British government as an interpreter for the squadron, during the expedition. His account is very correct and minute. I had frequent opportunities during my stay in the Mediterranean, of conversing with those who were well acquainted with all the particulars of the battle. But there is one item in the Arab's narrative which I do not wholly agree to, which was the great destruction done to the batteries.

We were there only a few days after Lord Exmouth had gone, and with our glasses could see but very little alteration in anything bordering on the water, although there was no sort of doubt that the destruction in the city was immense. It was with much difficulty that I obtained the account of the bombardment in its detailed form. I made several enquiries for it while in England, and finally obtained it from a library in Liverpool.

It is very mysterious, that, during the conversation with the Dey, particularly on matters of the treaty, and also of the slaves, that no mention was made of the United States, who, but a few months before, had forced the Dey into a treaty, which placed the American Consul on a more favorable footing than that of any other consul at the Algerine court, independent of the elements of the treaty, which also were more favorable than those of any other nation.

Whether this was carefully concealed by the Dey, or by the English officers, I am unable to say. But there is one thing very certain, and it cannot be denied, that the very favorable treaty made between Omar Pashaw and the government of the United States, and under such circumstances too:—*three frigates, two sloops-of-war, two little gun brigs, and two schooners,* were a terror to the Dey, for the safety of his fleet—a frigate and a brig having within a few days been captured by Commodore Decatur, while in search of his other ships, before he appeared off Algiers.

When, notwithstanding the fear manifested by the Dey for the safety of his six frigates, who were out on a cruise, six Dutch frigates, and two or three smaller vessels had been cruising before Algiers for two years, and had never dared to approach within gunshot of the batteries; yet for these the Dey felt no alarm, the Dutchmen always taking good care to keep out of the way of the Algerine frigates.

Again, by the treaty with the United States, the ammunition tribute was stopped, and the United States Consul was permitted to be seated while in conference with the Dey, a privilege denied all others. All these things were hard to be "swallowed" by the English Consul, who remonstrated with the Dey on the unfairness of not placing the representatives of his Majesty's government on as favorable a footing as that of the United States. To all of which the Dey turned a deaf ear; and it was certain that Lord Exmouth's visit to Algiers, only a few months previous to the bombardment, was for the purpose of exhibiting his fleet before the castle, to try if it would have some effect in inducing the Dey to accede to the consul's demand. His fleet then consisted of his, the flag-ship, Boyne 98, and five other line-of-battle ships, which were all lying with us at Port Mahon; and, as it has already been stated, the English officers of the Boyne had the temerity to take the responsibility of showing disrespect to the officers of the palace which led to the issue already narrated.

DESTRUCTION OF ALGIERS BY THE FRENCH.

After the European peace of 1815, M. Duval was named Consul-General at Algiers. He was born in the East, and understood the Oriental languages, and the manners and customs of the inhabitants; but his policy was marked by great weakness, and he inspired none with confidence or respect. He consented, without making any objections, that the annual tribute paid by the African Company, established by treaty for the purposes of trade, should be raised from £24,000 to £80,000—and he also agreed that France should raise no forts or batteries around her factories, a privilege she had always reserved in her ancient treaties.

Hussein Dey succeeded to the government in 1819; and was so emboldened by the repeated concessions of the French Consul-General, that he openly announced his intention, when a favorable opportunity occurred, of abolishing the African Company, and destroying its establishments. His conduct soon brought about a very hostile feeling on the part of the French government towards his own, which was much increased by a dispute relative to a debt due from France to the house of Bacri aud Busnach, of Algiers, which house was itself a debtor to the government of the Regency. The final rupture however, took place in 1827, when the Consul-General went to congratulate the Dey on the eve of the Bayram. A discussion having arisen, Hussein struck the consul with his fan. The news of this outrage was received with the greatest indignation in Paris, and on the fifth of June, 1827, the Moniteur announced that a squadron had sailed from Toulon to demand satisfaction for the insult offered to the Representative of France. This squadron was composed of a ship-of-the-line, five frigates, two brigs, and some smaller craft, in all thirteen sail. On the arrival of this force, the consul and all French subjects embarked, and through the medium of the Sardinian Consul-General, the following demand was made by the commodore.

1. The chief officers of the Regency, with the exception of

the Dey, will proceed on board the flag-ship, and make apologies for that Prince to the French Consul.

2. At a given signal, the French flag will be hoisted at the Casbah, and at the surrounding forts, and saluted with one hundred and one guns.

3. The property of French subjects embarked on board an enemy's ship, is not to be seized.

4. No vessels hoisting the French flag, are to be visited by the Algerine Corsairs.

5. The Dey, by a special treaty, will execute, as far as his dominions are concerned, all conventions concluded between France and the Sublime Porte.

6. The subjects of the following States are to be treated as French, viz:—Tuscany, Lucca, and the Papal States.

The Dey would not listen to these terms, and in his answer alluded to various violations of treaty on the part of France. A blockade then commenced, and the squadron was reinforced by three vessels of the line, and an Admiral appointed to the command. This state of things lasted till July, 1829, when an incident occurred which sealed the conquest of the Regency.

The "Provence" ship of the line, and the brig "Alerte," hoisted signals demanding a parley, and anchored in the harbor of Algiers. The Admiral, accompanied by his secretary, an interpreter, some officers, and a guard of honor went on shore and made arrangements with the Minister of marine and foreign affairs, for being presented to the Dey the following morning. Two interviews took place, and no satisfactory arrangements were concluded. In a few days they embarked, and sailed out of the harbor, (the flags denoting a parley still flying, consequently forbidding a resumption of hostilities) during which time they were repeatedly fired at by the town and fort batteries. This event decided the French government to more energetic measures than had hithorto been adopted, and Charles X., at this time becoming from day to day more unstable on his throne, welcomed heartily this unsettled state of Algerine affairs, and desired through that channel, to turn the minds of his people from political questions at home, to schemes of conquest abroad. The mass of the nation however, doubted the policy of the expedition; with the army alone it was popular.

Early in the year 1830, the principal dock-yards of France equipped eleven sail of the line, twenty-four frigates, seven corvettes, twenty-seven brigs, seven steamers; in all about one hundred sail, which fleet was destined to carry over 37,000 men to the shores of Africa, besides which, many merchant ships were chartered to carry over military stores. The army was commanded by General de Bourmont, and the fleet by Admiral Buperre. The troops disembarked at Sidi Feruch, about thirteen miles west of Algiers, and after a hard fought battle at Strucli, and the capture of the forts around the town, Algiers unconditionally surrendered. Thu-terminated the reign of Hussein, and the Turkish dominastion in Algeria. A war of nearly twenty year's duration, has left France almost the undisputed master of the country; for since the surrender of Abd-el-Kader, the war against the natives has been confined to small expeditions for the punishment of a few refractory tribes.

That extraordinary chief who surrendered himself to France in 1847, was born in an encampment near Mascara, in the year 1806. His father took him to Mecca at the early age of eight, and showing great quickness of perception during his youth, much pains were bestowed on his education. Mohhy-ed Din, his father, it appears, conceived the possibility of establishing an Arabian dynasty in Algeria, and such ideas were installed into the mind of the young Abd-el-Kader. Their discourses however, on this subject, acquired too much publicity, and awakened the suspicions of the Bey of Oran, who arrested both father and son; but they were soon set at liberty on condition of quitting the country. They returned to Mecca, proceeded by land to Tunis, and from thence by sea to Alexandria. From Mecca they visited Bagdad, and in 1828 they returned home, to which step no opposition was made.

They apparently renounced politics, leading a most austere and moral life, and gaining the respect of all. The state of anarchy amongst the Arabs, which followed the conquest of Algiers, afforded an opportunity for the gratification of Abd-el Kader's ambition; he rallied around him the tribes of his immediate neighborhood, placed himself at their head, and excited them by his poems, in the name of the Prophet, to resist the invaders; he was stimulated in his efforts by promises of aid from the Emperor of Morocco."

"His descent from Mahomet, and a pretended vision, in which he represented himself as sitting on a splendid throne, giving judgment amongst the Arabs, tended in no small degree to strengthen his influence. At length, having collected considerable forces, he attacked the garrison of Oran, and for some time compelled the French to remain within their defences. Treaties of peace were at different times, concluded with him; but the restlessness of the Arabs, and the encroaching spirit of the French, soon caused them to be broken; places which, after the dissolution of the government of the Regency, acquired an independence of their own under the authority of the Emir, fell one by one, into the hands of the French; such was the case with Tlemcen, Mascara, Mostaganem, and some others.

"He was at last considerably harassed, and was continually obliged to take refuge in the desert—he was accompanied by a numerous force of cavalry, and inflicted great loss on the French, by appearing where he was least expected, and cutting off supplies. He continued, however, to harass the French till the end of 1847, when, finding his resources entirely exhausted, he offered to surrender himself to General de Samoriciere, on condition of being allowed to reside at Mecca, or Alexandria. Abd-el-Kader performed his part of the contract, but the French government detained this brave man a close prisoner till 1852, when he was released by the Prince, President of the Republic, and Broussa was agreed upon as his future residence.

"Since his surrender, no opposition of any importance has been made to the French, and their territory may now be defined as composed of the four ancient provinces of the Regency—Algiers, Tituri, Constantine, and Oran; that of Tituri has now been united to Algiers." (*Broussa was destroyed by an earthquake, while I was in Turkey. Abd-el Kader just escaped with his life, besides wasting nearly all his property. The French Emperor gave him permission to reside in Beyroot, in Syria, until a future residence should be fixed upon. He arrived at Beyroot some weeks previous to my leaving that place for Alexandria.*)

I hope I shall not fatigue the reader by dwelling so long on Algiers, but having been so many times there, and witnessed the cruelties of the Algerines, and then too, when we consider the incredible number of captives that have pined away in miserable bondage among these wretches, probably during a space of five hundred years. And, who knows, how many missing vessels that have been given up as foundered, or otherwise destroyed at sea, have been taken by Algerine Corsairs, and their crews sent into the country heavily chained, and slaves for life! Lasting honors are due to the French, for the final destruction of this once abominable place.

CHAPTER VIII.

Sentence of court-martial carried into effect at Algiers, — Visited by Algerine officials,—Sail from Algiers,—Cruise on the Barbary Coast,—Death of Lieut. Elliot,—Return to Mahon,—Christmas at Mahon,—Double allowance of grog,—Fighting,—Remarkable English boxer,—Trouble on the berth deck,—Careless accident,—Narrow escape,—Orders to prepare for home,—Ship ready,—Good men taken out,—Convicts and hospital rangers in their stead,—Leave Port Mahon for Malaga,—Sail for Gibraltar and Cadiz,—Sail from Cadiz for Annapolis,—First part of the passage pleasant,—Latter part continued gales,—Poor crew,—Arrive on the coast,—Fall in with wrecks,—Make Cape Henry,—Take a Pilot,—Get lost,—Go back to Cape Henry,—Take a new departure.—Arrive at Annapolis,—Came near killing a nigger,—Was very sorry,—Made it all up with him,—Sailed for Norfolk, and for New York,—Arrive at the Navy Yard,—Villanous Landlords,—Foolish sailors,—Deprived of their money,—Ludicrous scene on the birth deck,—Cruelty to Tom Smith,—Sailors in jail for debt,—Scheme of a midshipman to obtain leave of absence,—Obtain leave of absence,—Return to Boston,—Receive orders to join my ship again,—Not liking her destination apply for orders to Charlestown,—Wishes complied with,—Dissatisfied,—Obtain a furlough for a voyage to India,—Join my ship, and prepare for the voyage,—Missionary passengers,—Sail for Bombay,—Man overboard,—Was saved—Turned out to be a great rascal,—Commence calking the deck,—Ship rotten, — Repair her, — Trouble with the Missionaries,—Villany of the captain,—Cruel treatment of a female passenger,—Make Ceylon,—Natives come off to the ship,—Pleasant sailing up the coast of Malabar,—Visit of the natives,—Speak a ship with dogs.

WHILE our fleet were at Algiers, the sentence of a court-martial was carried into effect upon a man who was convicted of cowardice and desertion, and exciting others to follow his example. The following are the particulars of the charges, and of the transactions:

It appeared that while the Washington, 74, was lying at Marseilles, that she took fire in the hold from the accidental dropping of a candle from a lantern. The alarm spread through the ship that she was on fire below! It also appeared in evidence, that upon the alarm spreading among the seamen, and when the firemen were called, that this man sprung forward upon the forecastle, singing out, "now is your time boys, get ashore before she blows up," and jumped overboard, but was caught before he reached the shore. This was the ground of the charges against him. The court adjudged the following sentence, viz: that he should receive a certain number of lashes at the gangway of the Washington; and be shown through the fleet, in a suitable boat. in which there should be erected a gallows; with a halter around his neck and a white cap on his head, on which should appear, in large letters, the word *Coward.* According to sentence he was carried along-side each ship, the crews of which had previously been called to witness punishment. After this he was turned out of the ship, and sent on board the Constellation Frigate. I saw this young man several times afterwards, and he appeared to be a very clever fellow, having had no bad intentions, but was evidently frightened.

We left Algiers and sailed for Mahon, and after fixing up a little, sailed again on a cruise, first visiting Algiers. This time we ran in very close to the batteries, and being a single ship, of course the Dey could not be afraid of us. Our consul came off, attended by several Algerine officials who had expressed a wish to see the inside of an American ship-of-war. We were very politely treated, and our consul had also been well treated since we were there last. We found it neccessary to vist these chaps pretty often, well knowing their perfidious and treacherous character.

During this cruise, we were called to mourn the loss and perform the last duties towards a worthy and meritorious officer, Lieutenant William Elliot. He was sick but a few days, and left us for another and I hope, a better world, and with appropriate ceremony we committed his body to the deep.

Perhaps the reader may never have witnessed a burial at sea, and as I have alway looked upon it as solemn and impressive. The ceremony differs somewhat between that of a merchant ship, and a man-of-war. On board the former the ceremony is quite simple, seldom having any formality, but in all cases the body is properly sewed up in canvas, and a sufficient weight attached to sink it. When a death occurs on board a man-of-war, the body is brought from the sick bay and laid in some convenient place on the after-part of the gun deck, and over which is placed the national flag. At nine o'clock the boatswain and his mates pipe all hands to bury the dead. A broad plank which is usually kept for the purpose, is brought to the lee gangway; one end resting on the gunwale, the other raised upon a shot box. The body having been previously sewed up in his hammock by the sail-maker, and three or four shot sewed in at the feet, is brought up and laid upon the plank, with the feet towards the water. The burial service is now commenced by the Parson, who reads the service at sea All heads are uncovered, and every officer and man are at the burial, and the most solemn stillness prevails, and when he comes to the part, "We commit his body to the deep," the inner end of the plank is lifted sufficiently high to let the body slide off, when the solemn plunge echoes back, *gone*, to be seen no more until the sea is commanded to yield up its dead.

While sailing over the Mediterranean one cannot but be impressed with the fact that he is passing over buried nations, millions on millions, whose bones now lie at the bottom probably in a state of complete preservation. Antediluvian bodies, that at the receding of the waters were washed into the Mediterranean, Sidonians, Tyrians, Phœnecian, Roman fleets, besides the myriads of modern nations that have perished here. And who knows but it is owing to the decomposition of such a vast amount of animal matter, that this sea exhibits that luminous phosphorescent appearance at night.

After finishing our cruise on the Barbary Coast we returned to Mahon. Winter had now commenced, and we were ordered to fit the ship for home, to be ready to sail early in the Spring. We spent our Christmas in Mahon, which is always an exciting time on board a man-of-war. According to the old custom, a double allowance of grog was served out, and also according to custom the day given to the men as a holyday. Man-of-wars men generally on these occasions save a great portion of their grog until evening, when they calculate to have a good time. About sundown however, Mr. whiskey began to get rather noisy, and somewhat quarrelsome withal. While we lay at Barcelona a few months before, there came off to the ship a short, chunky, good looking fellow, representing himself as a shipwrecked sailor, who had travelled all the way from Malaga to Barcelona, he wished to ship with us, and was accordingly shipped. He had no clothes except what he stood in; and upon his head an old Scotch cap. He gave his name as John Williams. For some time after he came on board, he appeared much reserved, wishing to avoid everybody, and would sit for hours on a shot box with his arms folded, as though involved in deep thought. He was a firstrate sailor, and in a few weeks gradually became more familiar; still there appeared something very mysterious about him, which gave room for much conjecture among those who noticed him. On the Christmas day which I have just alluded to, he appeared more cheerful than usual, but kept perfectly sober, or rather, he showed no appearance of having drank more than his allowance. Soon after the hammocks were piped down, I noticed a fight just under the top-gallant forecastle; I went forward, and found it was Williams, engaged with one of the forecastle men, who was much heavier than himself, and the way he put the licks into this big fellow was a caution to all boxers. The latter, though he had drank enough to make him quarrelsome, yet, was by no means drunk. Williams, by a well directed blow between the eyes, would drop him as fast as he could get up, and when he was down, the other would lift up both hands, saying, "*I am clear of you*," meaning, I don't strike you while down. And when he had given this man enough, declared himself ready for another. At this stage of the proceedings I went below to my room, which was right under the battle ground. But had hardly got seated before I heard a shuffling on deck, which I knew was another fight. I just stepped up, and sure enough, Williams was at it again with a fellow as large as the other, whom he also handsomely flogged.

The effect of the whiskey by this time was manifest throughout the berth deck. Half-drunken songs, fighting, yelling; the master mate of the berth deck, singing out for the master-at-arms, to put some crazy fellows in irons; but this functionary was drunk too. "You, Tom Wilson, if you don't make less noise there, I'll ram a grape-shot down your throat." "Ship's corporal, put out those lights there immediately." "The ship's corporal is gone ashore, sir, in an iron pot."

Right along-side of my room was an old fellow, that had a favorite song which he sung only when about two-thirds sprung. The chorus of which was:

"What can't be cu—red,
Must be endu—red."

And I have often thought of, and had to apply this drunken chorus many times during my pilgrimage.

At about eleven o'clock, I turned in, but had not been in my bed half an hour when my messmate, the gunner, came down.

"Well," said he, "Williams has flogged every man on the forecastle, and he is not used up yet."

Next morning at daylight, when all hands were called, and the hammocks piped up, there was a rich subject for a painter, more than half were too drunk the night before to hang their hammocks up; they had strewed themselves all about the deck, vomiting, &c., where they lie, and many of them yet too drunk to find their hammocks, and the master's mate flying round among them with a rattan. The officer of the deck repeatedly singing out, "Mr. Stevens, hurry up those hammocks, sir." "Boatswain's mate, go down there, sir, and start those fellows up." So the whole day after Christmas was one of wild confusion.

The Winter passed off pleasantly, although one incident occurred which came very near causing much distress, and probably of fatal results among the inhabitants. The frigate United States, was getting ready for painting, and the gunner had been ordered to draw the shot from the guns, as it was the commodore's intention to discharge them. But through the neglect, or carelessness of the quarter gunner, who had charge of the main deck divisions, a shot was left in the gun. The ship lay with her broad side towards Georgetown, and when the gun containing the shot was fired, it was instantly known that it had contained a shot. We heard it whistling along the shore until it got among the houses. The excitement on board may be easily imagined; a 24lb. shot whizzing through a village containing 2000 inhabitants. A boat was immediately dispatched from the frigate, following along the shore to Georgetown, in order to ascertain the the result. But to the inexpressible joy of every one in the fleet, not a soul was injured. This certainly was one of the most remarkable interpositions of Divine Providence that had ever come within my knowledge. The shot, just before entering the village, had struck the pavement, and thus, taking a ricochet, passed entirely over the houses, and buried itself in the sand beyond.

By the first of March we were ready for sea. The commodore had taken nearly all the good men from our ship whose times had not expired. For many of them had re-entered, and gave us in their stead, a parcel of old worn-out fogies, whose times of servitude had expired, and who were not considered worth re-shipping, and besides these, we had the incurables from every sick bay in the fleet, although it was known we were to arrive on our coast in one of the worst months of the year, still our crew was thus disabled.

We left Mahon early in march 1817, for Malaga, remaining there a few days, and next sailed for Cadiz; awaiting dispatches from Madrid, which having received, sailed for Annapolis, in Chesapeake bay. After leaving Cape Trafalgar, we ran to the south, for the purpose of a southern passage, and for ten days had beautiful weather, had made half the passage, when we took a hard, grinding north-wester. And now commenced our troubles, in consequence of breaking up our crew, and putting on board so many strangers, many of whom were entirely useless. Almost always, under such circumstances, discipline and subordination is at an end; for the first thing an officer hears, when an order is given any way peremptorily, is either a grumble, or, "*my time is out*," and the officers too, often being strangers, there seems to be a general carelessness predominating through the ship. With

U. S. SLOOP OF WAR ONTARIO, JOHN DOWNES, ESQ., COMMANDER RETURNING FROM THE MEDITERRANEAN.

us, we had all these difficulties, besides many more to contend with. When the bad weather commenced, many of these miserable fellows shammed sick. And in a very short time nearly half the berth deck was filled with those who were upon the doctor's list, and it was with much difficulty that able men could be found sufficient for reefing the fore and main-top sails at once. Had it not been for the extra energy and watchfulness of the old Ontario's, both of officers and men, I am not able to say what would have been our fate. After having been out thirty days, our provisions began to give out and we were put on a short allowance of water; and still nothing but hard gales. At length we reached the Western edge of the gulf, having been for a few days favored with a warm, south-east wind and much rain. Suddenly it shifted round into the old corner again, and whistled away with vengeance. We soon got among the "lame ducks." The first we fell in with was a sloop forty days from Newbern, N. C., bound to New York, and in a starving condition. It was in the night, blowing very heavy, and very dark. She had been thrown on her beam ends, but was now partially righted.—The crew did not wish to be taken off, but only to be supplied with provisions. This we succeeded in doing, although it very much reduced our scanty supply. We next fell in with a vessel bottom up, but saw nothing of the crew. And on the thirty-fifth day we made Cape Henry, ran in and took a pilot. Soon after the pilot had come on board, it came up quite thick, we kept along however all that day and the following night, under the sweet expectation of soon having something to eat. But in this we were disappointed. Early on the morning of the second day, the pilot seemed to be in much perplexity, running from side to side, enquiring the soundings, as we had kept the lead agoing on both sides. All at once he says to the officer of the deck:

"We must tack ship, sir; we are out of the channel, and I don't know which side of us it is. It has been so thick that I have not been able to see anything, to tell me where I am."

So we tacked and went all the way back to Cape Henry, and took a fresh departure, which kept us starving three days longer. At last we arrived at Annapolis, and had scarcely let our anchor go, when the wind shifted into the N. W., and blew a hurricane. So of course no boats could come off to us at present. Towards night it lulled so that a boat load of oysters came to our relief, which were quickly bought up and devoured.

Early on the next morning, the fresh beef and vegetables came off, which was immediately served out. Our fuel had been used up some days before our arrival, and none had yet been sent from the shore. But I was determined on having a beef steak; so I sawed up a boat oar, and sent my boy to the galley to cook the steak. I went below to my room, and began to sharpen up my teeth, and get my mouth in good shape, for a breakfast, which I had not had for a fortnight. Directly, the boy came down, and told me that black Williams, the captain's cook, had driven him away from the galley, it being jammed full of cooks. I sprung up, and in an instant was among them, and caught up a piece of the oar, about ten feet long, and "dropped the nigger." He soon picked himself up again. I saw that the wool began to grow red, and I began to grow sorry. I told Sam to cook his steak, which he did; or rather warmed it through, and I ate it like a cannibal. I now began to repent of my rashness, went to the poor fellow, and told him that I was sorry, that I was in a great passion, driven to it by hunger.

"*O, never mind, sir; I knowed you did'nt mean nothing, I only got a little bump on my head.*"

And sure enough, there was a lump on one side of his cocoanut, as big as my fist. So I made the matter up with him in good shape, and in material form, and thought after all that I was the worst nigger of the two. I met him in Boston, seven years after the affair, when we had a good laugh over the beef steak, and the knock down.

From Annapolis, we came to Hampton-roads; and from thence to New York, where we arrived on the 27th of May, 1817.

Scarcely had our anchor gone from the bow, before the ship was surrounded by land sharks and bad women; the latter, however, were not permitted to come on board; and only a few of the former. They obtained permission only by urgently desiring to see some particular friend. As none of the crew were allowed to go on shore, the landlords went off, but soon returned with any quantity of good things, such as pies, puddings, roast beef, chickens, and had also contrived to smuggle on board an ample supply of good stuff, to wash down the savory viands, notwithstanding, they were strictly forbidden against bringing any intoxicating liquor on board, the master at arms was placed in the gangway, with orders to search everything, and everybody, and "*the Maine liquor law in full force,*" there were bottles of brandy, gin, rum, and wine enough to supply a regular bachanalian feast. Tailors and watch venders came along-side; and all, knowing that the boys had between three and four hundred dollars a piece, coming to them; were very willing to trust them with any amount. Nothing pleases this sort of sailors so much, as to show a willingness to trust them; and what was very remarkable, nearly every one of those skulking lubbers, that had been in the sick bay during all the bad-weather, and were so sick that they could not be turned over in their hammocks without a crowbar, were the most lively and vociferous among the whole crew; and with the rest, were all blind drunk before morning. Many of these fellows had bought nice long-tailed coats, pantaloons, new hats, watches, and dandy boots; and everything, to constitute a fine go-a-shore-rig; for which, as it subsequently appeared, they were charged one hundred dollars, and some of them put on their new rig, to see how they would look. One fellow would try to haul a pair of dandy pantaloons over a thick pair of blanket drawers, and a great brawny leg, which would tear them, of course, and then off they go, and he must have another pair, which, with considerable trouble, and with the assistance of the tailor he managed to get on; then his legs looked like well stuffed sausages. Another would try to get a narrow backed coat, over a pair of broad shoulders, when, away goes the back, and another twenty dollars out of the fool's pocket, and in this way these land pirates contrived to rob this crew.

The next morning, these fellows who had tried on their

toggery the night before, and who thought it was not worth while to take it off again, as they would in all probability go ashore next morning, exhibited a ludicrous appearance, their fine clothes were covered with vomit and sand from lying on deck; their new beavers jammed up into the shape of a cocked hat, and many quite sick from their night's debauch, and all over the birth deck, there were strewn the remains of puddings, half-gnawed chicken bones, broken bottles, and all kinds of filth.

The ship hauled into the wharf, in the afternoon, and all whose *times* were out, were allowed to go where they chose. As the money for paying off the ship had not been provided, nearly all went ashore leaving only about a dozen, who had a few weeks longer to serve; and among those was an old fellow named Tom Smith. A lieutenant ordered him to do something, and Smith being a little corned, refused, saying, "my time is out." The lieutenant knocked him down, and then kicked him on the head; and at one kick, the toe of his boot struck under his ear, tearing it from his head. I saw this noble act, and know the gentleman that performed it. Not a week after these fellows left the ship, I was passing the jail, which then stood near the park, and heard some one call to me from the balcony. I looked up, and there were three of our boys in limbo for debt, and each of these were paid off, with nearly four hundred dollars. Such was the manner in which man-of-war sailors were plundered in those days, before saving banks, and sailor's homes were instituted.

I obtained leave of absence to visit my friends in Boston, and had not been home more than two weeks, when I received orders to join the ship again. On arriving at New York, I ascertained that the Ontario was to be fitted for a cruise to Columbia river; and was to be commanded by Capt. Biddle. Capt. Downes having been ordered to the Independence, at Charlestown.

Not willing to go the cruise, I applied for orders to another ship; and instead of which, was ordered to the navy yard, at Charlestown, and there to report myself to Commodore Hull.

Before I left the Ontario for Boston, one of our midshipmen had applied to the commader of the yard, for leave of absence, to visit his friends who resided in Charleston, S. C. The old gentleman gruffly answered: "No sir, your services are required in the yard."

As the midshipman was passing down to his ship, venting his disappointment audibly, in rather unmeasured terms, he met Mr. P——, first lieutenant of the yard, to whom he told his trouble.

"Ah!" Said Mr. P——, "you don't know how to approach the commodore, I'll teach you how to do it, and if you follow my directions you will surely accomplish your purpose. Just wait a day or two, say — day after tomorrow morning; and then watch when he enters his office, and in a few minutes go in, make a very low bow, — *Good morning Commodore;* how is your health this morning? you look charmingly; I have never seen you look better in my life! does your lady enjoy her usual health? Then pop the question about your leave."

Accordingly, P——y, followed out the suggestion, and on the morning appointed, watched the old gentleman as he entered his office, and in a few minutes knocked at the door, and was admitted. He made a very handsome bow, and in the most polite manner, commenced:

Good morning, Commodore; how is your health this morning, sir? I think I never saw you look so well in my life."

C. Exceedingly well; thank you sir.

P. And your lady? does she enjoy her usual health?

C. "Excellent, excellent. I am obliged to you, sir."

P. "Commodore, I should feel extremely grateful for a few days leave to visit my friends."

C. Certainly, sir. How much time do you wish?"

P. "About three weeks, sir.

C, "O take six sir, with my best wishes. Will you dine with me to-day, sir, at 3 o'clock?"

P. Thank you, sir. I shall be happy to do myself the honor."

So much for knowing how to approach a "great man."

According to my orders, I reported myself to Commodore Hull, for duty in the Navy Yard at Charlestown. Had not been here long, before I was convinced that it was no place for me; everything was solitary and dismal. There were no public stores except those on the right as you enter the yard. No mechanic establishments, except a small blacksmith's shop, and a boat shed. It appeared to me more like a graveyard, than a public naval depot. There were two or three master mechanics who had got on the right side of the commodore, and were feathering their nests out of Uncle Sam pretty successfully.

There were many very singular transactions carried on during my stay here, to which I shall not refer at present. There were several officers attached to the yard, and about in the same order as on board a ship-of-the-line, viz: commodore, captain, senior and junior lieutenants, sailing master, midshipmen, master's mates and warrant officers, such as gunner, boatswain, carpenter and sail-maker. My hanging-up place was on board the Java frigate.

Commodore Hull was an excellent seaman, and as all the world knows, a brave naval officer; yet he was evidently lacking in one point, and that was, a proper respect for his officers. The three years that I had then spent in the navy, were sufficient to show me conclusively, that a naval officer, no matter what his rank may be, must keep within his sphere; to go out of it, he degrades himself; and in no condition of life is a strict observance of rank more indispensably necessary than on board a man-of-war. Courtesy and good breeding demand a return of politeness even toward a slave; remembering at the same time, that familiarity begets contempt.

I noticed very soon after I had joined the yard, the boatswain and gunner with one of the master's mates, were often busy about the commodore's house, and frequently about the kitchen; and at one time I saw the boatswain go over to Boston with a wheelbarrow, and bring home the commodore's marketing, which was derogatory to their rank.

I had received orders to take the carpenters who were attached to the yard, and have all the boats repaired, and painted. I always appeared during the day in the uniform appointed for a warrant officer, and several times when passing the commodore, noticed that he looked rather closely at me, the meaning of which I well understood, from several hints which I had received from the boatswain. There was another officer attached to the yard, as a supernumerary—the gunner of the Java, who was a fine fellow, and much of a gentleman. The commodore had hinted to him several times that he must go to work, without ordering him to do it, however. He knew his place, and positively refused to touch his *hand* to anything; but was ready and willing to superintend or direct any work in his department which the commodore might place him over.

I was told that I was not one of the *old man's* disciples, and this I well knew before. So I was determined to leave the yard, at any rate. Not far from the Navy Yard there was a fine looking ship fitting out for India. I went alongside of her and was introduced to the captain, and asked him if he had engaged his carpenter. He replied that he had not, but was looking for one. I told him who and what I was, and that if I could get a furlough in season, would like to go the voyage with him. He seemed much pleased, and wished me to go about the furlough as quick as possible, as he would sail in four days. I knew that four days were not sufficient to get an answer from the Secretary of the Navy; made the matter known to Mr. Macomber, first lieutenant of the yard, who was a very austere man, but quite friendly toward me; always manifesting the greatest kindness. He told me that Mr. Crowninshield was not at Washington, but at his residence in Salem; that it was very doubtful whether he would attend to any official business, while absent from the seat of government. "But," he continued, "notwithstanding I am sorry to have you leave the yard, you have my permission to go to Salem, and see what you can do with the Secretary." As there were no railroads then, a journey to Salem and back used nearly a whole day.

I started off immediately, and found Mr. Crowninshield at home. Told him my errand, and the reason I had called upon him. After making some few enquiries, he gave me the furlough, at the same time wishing me a pleasant voyage. On my return to Boston, I notified the captain of the merchant ship, that I was all right, and would be on board ready for duty on the next day. My next business was to acquaint Commodore Hull about the furlough and the India voyage, and when I first named it to him, he was quite astonished at my not having first applied to him. Of course I knew better than to have done that. He seemed to regret my leaving the yard. I told him it was too inactive a life for me, and preferred a voyage to India, rather than the navy yard.

Next morning I went on board my new ship, and reported myself to the chief mate, ready to select the lumber and other stores required in the carpenter's department for the voyage. The captain directed me to go to the ship yard, and get what I wanted. Accordingly, with these unlimited orders, and not knowing what might happen, I selected six large white oak plank three inches thick, also some short pieces of various thicknesses, and six three inch deck plank, and four very wide two inch pine plank, with some pine and oak boards—besides some small pieces of oak stuff, which I threw into the cart. I took four bundles of oakum (200 pounds), a large pitch pot, a barrel of pitch, and one of tar, and a large lot of bolts, assorted spikes, nails, augers, and a good grindstone; when all this stuff was dropped along-side the ship, the mate swore that I was either crazy, or else had an idea that I was fitting out a line-of-battle-ship. To take all that stuff on board was out of the question—but after a great deal of talking, it was taken on board and stowed away very snugly on each side of the long boat; and I must say, that when I saw what a pile it made along-side, I began to think I had overstrained the matter. But never mind, it is all on board now—it may come in play and it may not.

Our ship was bound to Bombay, and perhaps to Calcutta. There were five Missionary passengers who were going to Bombay, Mr. and Mrs. Nickols, Mr. and Mrs. Graves, and a young lady, (Miss Philomela Thurston) who was to become the wife of Rev. Mr. Newell, husband of the late, and celebrated Harriet Newell. A large collection of stores and comforts had been provided for the Missionaries by their friends in Boston, and put on board the ship, and marked *Missionary stores.* As the ship was to sail on Sunday morning, I went on board on Saturday evening, Oct. 3, 1817, and on the morrow, as soon as the crew could be got on board, we weighed anchor and started. For the first two or three days, our passengers were quite sick ; the captain was very attentive to them but especially to Miss Thurston. He hung on to her with all the tenderness of a father. As soon as we were well off the coast, the captain wished me to commence calking the deck, as on account of so much bad weather, while lying at Charlestown, it could not have been done there. I soon discovered that the deck was rotten, and as fast as I found a rotten plank, took it out, and replaced it with a new one. Before I had reached the windlass, a large portion of my deck plank were used up. I just gave the mate a hint about his reluctance to take them on board. The deck was now finished as far forward as the fore hatchway. From what indications I saw forward round the bows, thought there might be some rot there, so I took an auger and bored into several places, and sure enough, the whole bow on both sides, was entirely rotten. I began now to set my wits to work for some plan to repair the ship ; but before commencing, to be sure that we had all the materials necessary for such an undertaking, as both bows were to be ripped down to below the deck and as far aft as the afterpart of the fore rigging—and on overhauling my stock in trade, I found I had just about enough of everything, and if we lacked anything it would be spikes. The captain was very much alarmed about it, and at first was afraid he would have to return and repair the ship.

I should before have related, that when three days out, we took a strong south-east gale, attended with a heavy sea. At 4 o'clock, P. M., I went into the cabin to secure the dead-lights, and had hardly commenced lashing the first one, when I heard an unusual rustling on deck, and it immediately occurred to me that a man was overboard. I jumped on deck in a moment, and saw it was what I supposed. Very near the companion-way, lay a large hood, or cover for a skylight. I caught hold of it, and it being very heavy, said to a man near by, "take hold here John," which he did, and we threw it overboard. All this was done in less than a minute. The captain then commenced upon me a volley of curses, calling me by every dreadful name he could think of, for throwing the hood overboard. I heeded not his curses, but sprang into the stern-boat with three other men. She was immediately lowered away, and when in the water, and tackles unhooked, we discovered that the plug was out and could not be found. Neither were there any thole-pins. Here we were in a boat with the plug out, and no means of rowing, a gale of wind with a heavy sea, and going to seek a drowning man. However, it was no time to ponder over our hasty imprudence. The boys put out their oars, holding on with one hand, and pulling with the other. I put my thumb in the plug-hole until I could tear off something to stop the water, which I succeeded in doing. We were pulling off in the direction of the man, as he was seen from the mizzen-rigging, they pointing to us in that direction; but we could make but little headway in consequence of our want of thole-pins, much water in the boat, drifting fast to leeward, and night near at hand. Under these circumstances we concluded to make our way back to the ship, and come within a trifle of staving the boat along-side. I jumped on board, and in a few minutes made some pins. Another crew jumped in the boat, started off, and brought the man on board. He was sitting in the hood very comfortably, but said he (after we had got on board the ship) when the boat turned back, I thought I was to be left, and opened my knife which I had slung around my neck, and if I had seen the ship make sail, it was my determinatiou to have cut my throat, and thus end my misery at once.

During all this time, the captain was raving about like a madman, cursing everybody and everything. He behaved in a most disgusting manner. This man, whom we had just rescued, and whose name was Smith, proved to be a consummate villain, which fact I shall have occasion to refer to at another time.

As I was observing about our rotten ship, — it was true that the ship was in no immediate danger by this discovery; although it might materially affect the voyage; if it was thought necessary to go back or even to wait long enough in a foreign port for the required repairs. I saw at once that much devolved on me, and must confess that, although I did not like the captain, yet wished to show him that notwithstanding his abuse, I had sufficient pride to let him see that I was somebody, and told him that if I could have the two boys that I should select, and as we were now in the S. E. trades, and in all probability should have good weather, that with the oak plank, and other materials of which we had plenty on board, I could repair the ship on the passage. With this he seemed much pleased, and told me to take as many men as I required, and Mr. Leach, or Mr. Lee (second mate,) would assist in any way they could. I requested Mr. Leach to get the larboard anchor aft out of my way, and the first thing to be done by me was to fit up a steam box, as the plank must all be bent. This I had no difficulty in doing, as there were pine plank enough among my load of lumber, that were just suitable. My pitch pot made an excellent steam kettle. The steam box was rigged across the windlass, and well secured, all things belonging to the steam department were fixed up in good shape. Next morning we turned to, took up the cathead, (beginning on the larboard side,) with the bow rail, and commenced ripping down; and sure enough, it was a bed of rot. My boys wrought like good fellows; we had no ten hour system, but kept at it from daylight until dark. We had plenty of old spars for timbers, and luckily plenty of tools, as I had taken my own tool chest on board. Our greatest trouble was in working on the outside stage, both on account of losing tools overboard, and of holding on when the ship rolled. All these apparent difficulties were overcome, and in eleven days the larboard bow was repaired in a thorough manner, as far aft as the fore part of the fore rigging, inside and out. We then commenced upon the other bow, which required a few more days' work, as there was rather more rot than on the other side. And when we had completed these repairs, there was not oak plank enough left to make a cleet, nor spikes enough to fasten it on. Oakum, pitch, and in fact, all that was put on board was used up. I suffered much from thirst as we were very foolishly on allowance of water, when we had the between-decks entirely empty, and could have carried an abundant supply. I have lain nearly all night on a water cask with the bung out, and with a horn cup and a string, vainly trying to satisfy my thirst; thus depriving myself of sleep to satisfy a burning drought, as I was not allowed any more water than the others, notwithstanding my work was harder. I met my two boys in after years and at different times; they were both shipmasters, and enterprising men, were very glad to see the old carpenter, and remembered the advice he gave them when boys.

A very unpleasant affair commenced between the passengers and the captain, shortly after we left Boston, which entirely destroyed the harmony of the cabin during the passage to Bombay. While the Missionaries were in Boston, previous to their going on board the ship, their friends had procured for their comfort many things, more particularly designed for the ladies, such as sweetmeats, and preserves of various kinds, tea of an extra quality, and many small articles which probably would not be included in the common bill of fare. These were in addition to the articles which have been named before. At the commencement of the voyage, the captain suggested to them that as their stores were many of them of a perishable nature, that they had better be used in common and when they were used up, then he would commence on his own. To this they cheerfully consented of course, supposing his judgment to be superior to their own. So their chickens and ducks were killed, and their vegetables eaten, and everything went on first rate. The unmarried young lady (Miss Thurston,) was rather handsome, and very prepossessing in her general deportment, and it was said that the captain had, previous to our sailing, made some indecent allusions to certain intentions during the voyage. We had not been long at sea before it was apparent that all was not right in the cabin. One of the gentlemen with whom I was on intimate terms, in conversation one evening, while leaning over the weather rail amidships, intimated to me in a very low voice, that their situation was rendered extremely unhappy through the counduct of the captain, but he hoped that strength would be given them to endure it until they reached their destination. I asked him what the trouble was.. He then told me that the captain had insulted Miss Thurston, and confined her to her state-room, and that at some better opportunity he would tell me more about it, as the captain was now watching us, evidently suspecting the nature of our conversation. The captain had prohibited service being held on deck upon the Sabbath. They seldom left their rooms during the day, but would come up in the evening, and take a seat on the lee side of the quarter-deck, avoiding the captain as they would a rattlesnake. I bade Mr. N——o, good night.

After we had separated, "the old man" called me aft, and says:

"What do you think of these fellows that we have on board?"

"What fellows, sir?"

"Why, these Missionary devils."

"Well, sir, from what I have seen of them, I think them to be very good people."

"You do, hey?"

"Yes sir."

"Well, they are a set of —— scoundrels, and that little strumpet, (Miss Thurston,) I mean to turn her down among the men."

I was thunderstruck. "Why, Capt. ——, what do you mean, sir?"

"I mean what I say." He then turned round and walked aft.

The steward had previously told me that the captain had forbidden him giving them anything but salt beef and bread; also, had ordered the molasses to be removed where they could not get it. They generally took their meals by themselves; sometimes the mate would dine with them, but very seldom, although they were on friendly terms. Notwithstanding, he was accused by the captain of going into Miss Thurston's room during his watch at night. The captain had his meals served at another hour.

I asked the steward how it was that *they* were obliged to live on salt beef, when they were so amply supplied by their friends previous to sailing. The steward's reply was, "that at the commencement of the voyage, the captain suggested that it would be better to have all as one common stock while it lasted, and then he would supply the table from his own; so all the chickens were used up, while his remained in the coop. And now they were not allowed anything but what I have before stated. I had often noticed that *after the* passengers had dined, the captain's dinner, consisting of chicken and a nice pudding, would be sent to the cabin. Both mates dined at the table d' hote with the passengers. The origin of the trouble, I found out in the following manner:

One very warm night, W. G——d, the third mate, after the watch had been called at eight o'clock, it being his watch below, got into the stern boat under the tarpaulin to sleep there, rather than go below, as it was very warm. Shortly after he had got into the boat, W. and Mrs. Graves, the two eldest of the Missionaries, accompanied by Miss Thurston, took their seat on the taffrail, very close to where W. G——d was, and where he could distinctly hear all they said. Mrs. Graves commenced the conversation as follows: "Now Philomela, as we have a good opportunity to converse by ourselves, I wish to open my heart to you. We have observed, with much pain, the familiarities and liberties the captain frequently takes with you. Now we do not accuse you, my dear, of encouraging these improprieties, but we do not think you are prompt enough in repelling them. Allow me to repeat again, my dear sister, we do not attribute these liberties to any forwardness on your part, but we do attribute it to your want of experience; and as you are, if your life is spared, soon to become the wife of an excellent minister of Christ, the requirement that you should be circumspect in your life and conversation, is incumbent on you now."

Philomela had been weeping audibly for some moments. She now ceased weeping, and began her defence, which was, that after her recovery from sea-sickness, the captain would, in a fatherly manner, take her arm and walk with her until she was tired. She would then go below and rest herself. The captain would usually follow and take his seat beside her, and at times he had put his arm round her neck, which she of course, immediately removed. "And yet," she continued, "I looked upon it as a parental freedom; not for a moment did I suppose he had any improper intentions, but the next time he shows any freedom towards me, I shall most assuredly resent it." The conversation ended here, as it was necessary to get a pull of the spanker sheet, which disturbed the conference.

And it now came out that the captain one afternoon, when smoking below, while Miss Thurston was engaged in sewing, advanced towards her, and blew the smoke in her face. She reproached him for his impudence, not not only for this ungentlemanly act, but also, of former attempts of freedom, quite unbecoming a captain of a passenger ship, and also of a married man. This the captain construed into insult, and ordered her into her state-room, and not to come out without his permission. She had been shut up for some time in this suffocating weather, and begged that some means might be adopted by which she could get fresh air. The captain asked me if an air port could be cut through the ship-side without injury to the ship. I answered yes; and was ordered to do it. I hung a stage over the quarter, and cut a hole through. And as it was the windward side, when the breeze found its way into the state room, she put her head close to the port, and exclaimed, "Oh, how refreshing."

I spoke a few words to her through the opening. The captain, hearing the conversation, leaned over the rail above, and says:

"Well, carpenter, how do you and Miss Thurston make it out?"

"First rate, sir," said I.

"Well, let us have less talk there."

I looked up at him with an indignant scowl. "I shall talk as much as I please, and you may help yourself the best way you can."

He went off without replying a word, I kept about my duty, and finished my job, and if ever there was a man that I heartily despised, it was this one. My duty was faithfully discharged, and my deportment such as not to come within the reach of censure. We drew near our destined port, made the island of Ceylon on the first of February, and Cape Comorin on the fifth. Our Sultan evidently began to repent his villanous treatment to these defenceless people, or else he hypocritically feigned it in order to escape that punishment he so richly deserved. He liberated Miss Thurston, saying it was done in a fit of rashness, and he had misconstrued her conduct. He also apologized to the others, who, not wishing to injure him, freely forgave all that had taken place. He was now as fawning as he was tyrannical before, and nothing was good enough for these "ladies and gentlemen."

We were ten days beating up the coast of Malabar, and fell in with a ship from London, with a deck load of bloodhounds. The crew had been on a short allowance of water for thirty days, and in consequence of not having plenty of water for the dogs, some of them would become frantic, run about the deck, frothing at the mouth — the crew escaping to the rigging until the dogs become quiet.

From Cape Comorin to Bombay, the coast, (Malabar,) is lined with pretty villages; and ships beating up, are generally close in with the land in the morning, standing off with the land breeze during the day, and running in with the sea breeze at night. The air from the shore is really refreshing after being four or five months at sea. The natives are all ready to board the ships when near enough to the shore, with a full supply of chickens, eggs, cocoanuts, and all sorts of tropical fruit, besides excellent fish.

CHAPTER IX.

Arrival at Bombay,—Intelligence reaches the Mission House,—Mr. Newell comes on board,—Artful design of the captain,—Imprudence of Miss Thurston,—Disappointment of Mr. Newell,—He is made acquainted with the proceedings of the voyage,—Excitement on shore,—Indignation of Mr. Newell,—Captain is despised,—Miserable death,—Subsequent visit to the Mission,—Bomb boat men visit the ship,—Orders of the captain,—No notice taken of it,—Poisonous liquor,—Its effects.—Visit of other crews,—Insulting language to the mates,—Mutiny,—Fearful results,—Mutiny quelled,—Grossly insulted,—Indignation of the captain,—Villany of Smith,—Remarks on the subsequent career of the crew,—Visit to the Elephanta,—Row between the bomb boat men and captain,—Sail from Bombay,—Meet a pirate,—Men's accounts made out,—They refuse to sign them,—Mate ordered to whip them into the cabin,—Pompous third mate,—Difficulty on the passage out.—Remarks on the dignity of an officer,—Quarrel with the third mate,—Fight,—Interference of the captain,—Strikes the mate,—All right again,—Arrive on the coast,—Take a vineyard pilot,—He gets drunk,—Does not know where the ship is,—We take a Boston pilot,—Arrive safe,—Macedonian frigate ready for sea,—Our ship boarded by the first lieutenant,—Interview,—Call on board the frigate,—Interview with Capt. Downes,—Consent to go the cruise,—Our ship hauls in to the wharf,—The mate flogs the captain,—Prepare for a three year's cruise,—Lay in plenty of stores,—Found fault with,—Meet Com. Hull,—Sail for N. W. C.,—Appearance of a gale,—Gale,—I was thrown down and injured,—Man knocked overboard,—Dreadful hurricane,—Mainmast sprung,—Our ship laboring heavily,—We fish it,—Main yard comes down,—Breaks off,—Injures no one,—Volunteers called to go up and cut away the topmasts,—Foremast is sprung,—It is fished,—Foreyard comes down,—Injures no one,—Mizzen mast goes by the board,—Boats blown away,—Dreadful night,—Gale abates towards morning,—Prepare for getting up jury masts,—Clear the wreck,—Make sail,—Think the ship is hailed,—Lay to for a brig,—Obstinacy of her captain,—Threaten to fire into her,—Arrive at Norfolk,—Anchor off Gosport, and prepare for refitting,—Ready for sea in eleven days,—Scientific corps leave us,—Anecdote during the gales,—Double Cape Horn,—Arrive at Valparaiso,—Lose a man overboard,—Warlike appearance of Chili,—Transports,—Chilian men of war,—Fatal duel.

ON THE 17th of February we arrived at Bombay. The intelligence of our arrival soon reached the Mission house. Mr. Newell came on board and made arrangements for the journey to the mission station, as soon as permission could be obtained for landing, which would probably be on the following day, and as the distance was only a few miles, Mr. Newell went home and was to return next day, with a carriage to carry them to their future residence. The permit for landing came off at nine o'clock A. M. The captain went on shore, and in an hour returned, saying to Miss Thurston that as he had specie for the Mission house, he must go immediately up, and engaged a horse and buggy, and should be happy to have her accompany him, as in all probability the carriage which would be sent for them would be crowded. To this proposal all seemed to acquiesce, so Philomela, dressed in her go-ashore attire, stepped into the boat, and no doubt the poor girl leaped for joy at the idea of once more stepping foot on the land, and of being liberated from what must have been to her a dreadful prison. But little did she think that in complying with this apparently very polite invitation, that she was adding to the weight of calumny that would naturally reach the ears of Mr. Newell. This wily and designing man, instead of driving directly to the mission house, which could have been reached in less than two hours, and thus giving Mr. Newell an opportunity of a private interview with his intended bride, drove around through the jungle, a solitary road through the woods, making a circuit of many miles, and taking up the greater part of the day. In the mean time Mr. Newell had come to the landing-place with a carriage, went on board the ship, and to his surprise learned that Miss Thurston had been gone two hours with the captain; he also expressed much surprise at not meeting them on the road, and appeared much disappointed. The sailors now began to make remarks very freely, and of course the transactions of the voyage soon became known on shore, and as a matter of course reached the ear of Mr. Newell, from a quarter which gave him much uneasiness. I afterwards learned that the whole matter was investigated, and that Miss Thurston was fully exonerated from any impropriety, or the smallest deviation from the character so indispensably necessary for one shortly to become the wife of a Missionary of so exalted a character as that of the Rev. Mr. Newell.

This affair created much excitement among the well-disposed at Bombay, while at the same time it caused some merriment among the low and vulgar. The captain was generally despised by every one, and we believe was entirely without associates. Mr. Newell was highly indignant at the treatment of Miss Thurston; but what could he do? A law suit would involve him in much perplexity and expense, so he gave it up, and let the fellow run. Had the passengers been any other than non-resistant missionaries, he would not have dared these cowardly insults. But he got his reward, for on his next voyage he died of a loathsome disease, unattended, unlamented and unmourned.

Mr. Lee (second mate,) and myself went up to the Mission house, and were well received by our friends, and passed a very agreeable afternoon together. Miss Thurston was to be married in a few days, and everything appeared pleasant.

On the second night after our arrival, we came very near having a fearful tragedy enacted upon our deck. Before we had come to an anchor, the ship was surrounded with boats, filled with numerous characters offering their services in any capacity, and among them several bomb boats, each man having a bundle of certificates from the last ship, testifying to his honesty and fidelity, and at the same time the greatest scoundrel on earth. The fellow that gets on board first claims the ship. The successful candidate for our custom was Franjee-Nabob, a Parsee, "with all ting to sell to the seamen." The captain called him aft, and in the most peremptory manner forbade him selling the men any intoxicating liquors, or of trusting them one pice, (a cent,) as he should not advance them a farthing. Old Franjee understood the matter, having had such interdictions before; he made his salaam, and very meekly responded:

"No, sir."

As soon as the captain had gone over the side into his boat the old Parsee bomb boat man went forward among the men, and told them what orders he had received. "But," said he, "*no much matter for dat. I trust you just how much you want. 'Spose you want 'rack,* (rum.) *I give you much you want I got plenty in my boat now. I bring 'em up.*"

This was good news for Jack. They soon had a fine treat out of all the good things that the shore afforded, availing themselves of this unlimited bill of credit. There were then lying in the harbor with us, three American vessels, two ships and a brig. The crews of these vessels, or rather the number that could be spared, came on board our ship, on what was no doubt intended as a friendly visit, and it would have been such, and ended well, if it had not been for that accursed crazy liquor called arack, made from the cocoa-nut, more maddening in its influence than any other intoxicating drink on earth. Our crew had been apprised of the intended visit, and had provided large quantities of grog for the occasion.

At about 9 o'clock P. M., they had become very noisy. Here were our own crew, eighteen, and twenty-four of the others, making in all forty-two, trying to sing, and bellowing out in a most frightful manner. Mr. Leach went forward and sung out to them below that it was time for them to go on board their ships. He was answered by a most insolent and indecent reply from one of our own crew. Mr. L. was a kind hearted and gentlemanly officer, and such an answer from one of our own men, who had always received good treatment and kind words from him, deserved severe punishment. Mr. L. came aft; there were the three mates, boatswain and myself, on the quarter-deck. Mr. Lee, the second mate, was a tall, raw-boned fellow, and very powerful. He wished Mr. Leach to let him go forward and order them to go on board their ships. Mr. L. thought he would wait a little longer, when probably they would go of their own accord. I had been hard at work during the day, and went below to my hammock, which was in the steerage, and hardly fallen asleep, when a voice from the deck called out:

"Jump up, carpenter, and knock the arm chest open."

I sprung out and ran upon deck, which I had scarcely reached before a handspike came, end over end, whizzing by me. There was a man standing on the arm chest, swearing by horrid oaths, "the arm chest should not be opened." Mr. Lee caught up a capstan bar, and with one blow dropped the fellow from off the chest, and then broke it open. During this time, the mob were rushing aft, throwing all sorts of missiles, crying out:

"Drive the —— rascals overboard!" meaning myself and the three mates. I dodged for a moment into the galley until I could get the hang of the mutiny.

By this time the two mates had got a loaded blunderbuss each, and held them cocked, swearing if they came any farther aft, they would fire.

"Fire, and be ——," said Smith, (*the fellow we saved from drowning at the commencement of the voyage.*)

They now closed upon us, and we sung out, "*Mutiny!*"

There was a French ship lying near us, who had heard the row, and were preparing to come to our assistance. We saw the lanterns running fore and aft, and their men getting into their boats. We were now clear aft on the spar across the boat's davits, ready for a jump overboard.

Just as the mates were about pulling the triggers, which would have sent death among them, each blunderbuss having fifteen musket balls, the Frenchmen sung out they were coming. The mutineers then began to move forward, hauled up their boats, and went over the side, uttering the most blasphemous imprecations upon us all; and when in their boats, they gave three cheers, singing out, "This is the first time the Yankee flag has been disgraced by calling a Frenchman to abuse American seamen.

Our crew in a most mutinous manner answered their cheers, and they went off. Thus ended this serious affair, and if the Frenchmen had not started just as they did, the blunderbusses would certainly have been fired, and who can tell the result? We thanked our French neighbors for coming so well prepared to our assistance.

When the captain came on board next morning, and heard the story, he fairly abused the mates for not firing into them, and ordered the crew to prepare for going before the authorities on shore, where he insisted they should go and be tried for mutiny.

On going ashore, he was told by his merchants that the proceeding would subject him to much expense and delay, and if the crew were convicted of mutiny, there would be a long tail to it, and it would be impossible to get another crew; so he relinquished the procedure until our arrival in the United States. They went about their duty, but were rather sulky, every one feeling a deep conviction that he had done wrong; and that villain, Smith, was the ringleader of the whole concern. And notwithstanding the mutinous conduct of these men, they were probably as intelligent a set as were ever together as a crew. Ten out of the eighteen became ship-masters, and I remember conversing with one, and as he is now dead, will call him by name, John Schofield, one of the leading mutineers of the night at Bombay, and also a quarrelsome man, and very impudent to his officers.

This man commanded the ship Arab, of Boston, about five years after our return from that voyage. One day I spoke to him about the affair on board the Saco, and as I was repairing the Arab, we had frequent opportunities of talking over old matters. And I ought to observe, however, that at the time he commanded the Arab, he was of course another man, quite gentlemanly, and seemed much ashamed of his conduct on board the Saco, and was unwilling to talk about it, attributing it solely to the effect of rum. Another, John Ward, a Boston boy. He afterwards commanded the ship London Packet, of Boston, and was finally killed by the pirates. Another commanded the fine ship Horatio, of New York, thus showing that bad men may become respectable and good men by forsaking intoxicating drinks and evil company. But to return to our voyage.

One Sunday, Mr. Lee, second mate, Mr. Goddard, third mate, myself and John Peverally, hired a native boat and went over to the famous island of "Elephanta," called by the Hindoos, Gharipoon. It is about 5 miles from Bombay. It contains one of the most celebrated temples of the Hindoos. The figure of an elephant of the natural size, but coarsely in stone, appears on the landing place, near the foot of a mountain. An easy slope then leads to a subterranean temple hewn out of the solid rock, eighty feet long, and forty feet broad; the roof supported by pillars, of which there are several rows ten feet high. At the farther end are gigantic figures of the three Hindoo deities, Brahma, Vishna, and Seva, which were mutilated by the zeal of the Portuguese, when this island was in their possession.

Elephanta was ceded to the English by the Mahrattas." John Peverally was a good player on the clarionet, and had an excellent one which he took with him, and the effect of these sweet notes, reverberating through these caverns, was delightful. There was a large pool of exceedingly cold water, and of sweet taste. I got into the boat from the ship without my shoes, for which act of carelessness I was well paid, by having to walk barefooted nearly two miles through briars and thorns; but notwithstanding this, we had a fine time.

About the middle of May, 1818, we were ready for sea. Our crew had, in consequence of old Franjee's willingness to give them credit, run up tremendous bills; some had bought boxes of tea; others had purchased beautiful India shawls, and Canton crapes, and had lived on the luxuries of the shore, besides a plenty of *wild fire.* I believe that they had an impression that the bomb boat man could not recover anything from them, in consequence of his being forbidden by the captain to trust them. But in this they were much mistaken. On the day previous to sailing, the old Parsee made out a general bill of all the items furnished to each man, and taking his brother with him as a witness in case of an assault, went to the captain's house, and presented his bill, somewhat over a thousand rupees. The captain, on reading the amount of the bill, caught up a chair and was going to strike the fellow over the head; but he lifted his hand in defence, saying:

"*No, captain! spose you strike me, your ship no go.*"

"*Begone, you —— scoundrel! How dare you bring that bill to me? Did I not forbid you trusting my men?*"

"*Me merchant. Me sell anyting to anybody dat buy. You no pay me, your ship no go.*"

This the captain soon found out, that he could not clear his ship with any debts due to natives, unpaid. There was no alternative now but to pay the bill, for which he was obliged to draw on his merchant. When he came on board, he seemed ready to burst with rage, but said nothing to the men until after we had sailed.

On coming down the Coast of Malabar, one day, while at dinner, a suspicious looking craft came off from the shore; she was about two hundred tons, lateen rigged, and full of men; they were rowing with all their might, and we could see with the spy-glass that they were all armed, and nearly naked. They seemed bound to catch us, but what they wanted we could not tell. So we cleared away two of our six pounders, and gave them a few iron pills, which soon made them alter their minds, and they went, with the Scotchman, "*bock* again."

After we were clear of the land, the first thing to be done was to fix up the Bombay matter. Each man's account was made out, and fifty per cent charged against him for the money, and they were called to sign their accounts, which they refused to do. The clerk reported to the captain how the matter stood; this raised him again to boiling heat; he ordered the mates to take a rope's end, and begin at the first, and flog him into the cabin. John Ward was the sea lawyer; he recommended resistance, but the rope seemed to alter his mind. The mates were glad of an opportunity to put the licks into these fellows, especially when the responsibility devolved upon the captain. Ward went down and signed his account, and the rest followed; so that their India purchases did not turn out so cheap, after all.

Our third mate G——d, was a very pompous, disagreeable fellow. His connexions were rich. He was a Boston boy, and had been several voyages to Europe. We messed together, but were never on very good terms. He had been well educated, and thus supposed himself superior to all around him. On the outward passage, he began to domineer over me, supposing of course that as he was third mate of an Indiaman, his rank was superior to that of carpenter, although he, the boatswain and myself, lived together in the steerage. I had taken my own tools on board the ship, and would not allow any one to use them as they were kept in good order, and always ready for use. The ship had a tool-chest under the stern of the long-boat on deck. My work-bench was between decks, near the fore-hatch. G——d came down one day, and says :—

" *Carpenter, I want a chisel to take up a mast-coat.*"

" *Well, you'll find one in the tool-chest on deck.*"

He took up one of my sharp chisels, saying:

"*I'll take this.*"

"No you don't take that chisel to rip up a mast-coat. Just lay it down."

He gave me a savage look, saying:

" *Who are you talking to?* "

"I am talking to you." and at the same moment I caught up an axe, and told him " to lay the chisel down instantly, or I would split him down."

Mr. Leach hearing the quarrel, came down to know what the trouble was. I told him.

He then turned to G——d, saying:

" You have nothing to do with the carpenter or his tools, there is the ship's tool-chest on deck."

G——d went off, rather "down in the mouth," evidently mortified.

I have mentioned this, apparently trifling circumstance, to show the necessity of maintaining our position, whatever it may be. It is a natural propensity in men, and more particularly in sea-faring men, to assume authority that does not belong to them, and also to abuse the *little brief authority,* with which their *position invests* them. I am aware, that on board a merchant-ship, a carpenter is hardly a remove above a sailor, and is often at the beck and call of a green mate, that hardly knows the stem from the stern; but in most cases, it is his own fault. If he is an intemperate man, he cannot look for respect. If, on the other hand, he undervalues his profession at first, by mingling with the crew, and by showing an obsequiousness to the officers, which a proper and becoming respect for them does not call for, he cannot look for anything more than common seaman's treatment.

I suppose that my coming so suddenly from a man-of-war to a merchant-man, caused me to feel the contrast more sensibly: for while in the navy, I had always received from my superiors the highest respect due me, and when I went on board the Saco, was determined to conduct myself in such a manner as to *command* respect. I drank no ardent spirits, used no tobacco, nor profane language. On the passage home, G——d would frequently boast of his pedigree, and of his brilliant prospects. This would generally take place at dinner. While in Bombay, I built a house on the quarter-deck in which the third mate, myself, boatswain and sail-maker lived. Our table was directly over the cabin skylight. One day while at dinner, G——d commenced his usual bombastic nonsense, at which I made a remark that he did not at all relish. He sat opposite me, and we were dining on bean-soup—he called me by a name too disgusting to mention here, so I took my plate of bean-soup and threw it in his face. We both rose and went at it in good fashion, and although he was all of thirty pounds heavier than myself, I knocked him down behind the door, and took him again as he arose, and was "pegging it into him," when the captain, who was below, hearing the difficulty overhead, came up, and seeing the fight, drew off and hit G——d a blow in the eye, saying at the same moment, "you —— scoundrel, you have been quarrelling all the voyage—that is a peaceable man, and quarrels with no one," alluding to myself. G——d did not feel satisfied at the termination of the fight, and wanted to have it finished in fair play. "Very well," says I, "my good fellow come on," but the mate (Mr. L.) interfered, and here the matter ended. We made up the difficulty, and were good friends the remainder of the voyage.

On the 4th of September, we took a Boston pilot, having been for the three previous days enveloped in fog. We saw a Vineyard fishing boat early one morning very near us. The captain hailed him and inquired how Cape Cod bore. "*Do you want a pilot?*" "*No, please tell me how Cape Cod bears.*" "*If you want a pilot, we will give you one.*" Finding the fellow was determined to make something out of our necessity, the captain asked him how much he would take the ship to Boston for. "*A hundred dollars*," was the answer. "I will give you seventy-five." "Very well," says the pilot, "we'll come along-side." The boat came and threw on board some fine codfish, and the fellow jumped on deck, and in a pompous manner stepped upon the round-house and cast a sort of knowing eye aloft, saying, "*give her the muslin—let her wear it.*" We loosed the top-gallant sails, and royals, and hauled on board the main tack. He gave the course, and then asked the steward for a glass of brandy. The decanter was brought to him, from which he helped himself very freely, and was soon stowed away behind the wheel-house drunk. He came to himself again towards night, urging as an excuse for getting drunk, that he had been suffering from a severe pain in his bowels, and a very little overcame him. The captain forbid the steward's giving him any more grog. He was on deck all night continually altering the course from three to four points, and in the morning freely owned that he did not know where we were, although we knew ourselves by the soundings, to be near Boston Bay. At 3 P. M. saw the pilot-boat ahead, and the old veteran Wilson came on board. Now we were all right. Our quondam Vineyard pilot now skulked behind the round-house, and did not show himself until the ship had anchored. Whether he was paid or not I don't know.

The pilot told me that the Macedonian frigate was lying in the harbor, fitted for a cruise to the North-West Coast of America. She was commanded by Captain Downes, my former captain, was nearly ready for sea, and would sail in a few days. As we were passing her, running slow, and being very near, I heard the boatswain's mate call away the second cutter, and saw my old friend Lieut. Maury, (our first officer on board the sloop-of-war Ontario) get into the boat. I knew in a moment what all this meant. It was known that we were expected every hour, and my furlough being out, this was to be my next ship. The boat came along-side, and Mr. Maury was received at the gangway by Mr. Leach. Mr. M. asked for me, and when he had shaken hands, said he had come on board at the request of captain Downes, who wished me to get ready as soon as possible and join the ship.

He also invited me to call on board and see him before I went on shore, which I did; had a very pleasant interview, and then went on shore to my friends.

Next morning our ship hauled into the wharf at Charlestown. I went on board for my luggage. G——d came down shortly after, rigged as a nabob. The captain had just gone into the cabin, when G——d went aft. Looking down and seeing no one there but the captain, he stepped on to the cabin-stairs, shut the doors and went below, took off his coat and turned to upon the old fellow and gave him a sound beating. There said he, "*You struck me on the passage home, when I could not help myself, and now I have paid you off.*" He put on his coat and went on shore.

My next business was to prepare for a three-year's cruise. Captain Downes wished me to come on board as early as possible to see about the stores belonging to the carpenter's department, as that had not yet been attended to. In two days I reported myself ready for duty, and was ordered by the first lieutenant to go with the launch to the Navy Yard, and select some oak and pine lumber for the cruise, and as we were shoving off, he says, "*Select only what you think will be necessary until we arrive on the coast; then we can get plenty. I do not wish to have the ship too much lumbered up.*" "Aye, Aye, sir, said I," and went off. On arriving at the Navy Yard, I met Commodore Hull who appeared glad to see me, and gave orders to the store-keeper to deliver what I wanted. My first selection was twelve white-oak mast-fishes suitable for fishing a frigate's mast, four gun-carriage pieces, six inches thick, seven feet long, and eighteen wide; also a number of pine plank, and some short pieces of oak of various thicknesses. When I got along-side, as I had previously expected, got a blowing up, for bringing off so much **useless lumber*, The second lieutenant, (now one of the oldest and most respectable post-captains in the Navy), refused to take it on board, without first consulting Mr. Maury. It was finally hoisted on board, and snugly stowed on the booms. I fitted up my store-room with

* The same term used by the officers of the Firefly.

every necessary article for a three years' cruise, and on the 20th of Sept. 1818, we sailed from Boston with a fine westerly breeze. Our frigate was rather deep in the water, but looked beautifully, as she glided "majestically slow before the breeze."

We had a fine run off the coast, and across the Gulf. On the morning of the 26th, it looked very much like a blow. Thick, black clouds were rolling up all around. Mr. Maury gave me orders to examine every thing aloft, and report to him. I visited each masthead, and found all things right. Very soon all hands were called to send down top-gallant-yards, which had hardly been done, when they were again called to shorten sail. The mainsail was hauled up, and top-sails close-reefed; then top-gallant masts housed. The gale had been increasing, and now it blew a hurricane. Every square sail was furled, and the fore and main storm stay-sails were set. Scarcely had the fore storm stay-sail haliards been belayed, when the sail blew away like a kite. The sea ran fearfully high, and although only 4 o'clock, P. M., it was so dark we could hardy discern the ship's length ahead. Still the hurricane raged with unabated fury; the hammocks were piped down, and a young man, (William Wilkins) while getting his hammock, was knocked overboard. The hatches on both decks were secured, and tarpaulins put over them. The ship was rolling and laboring very much, although she did not make much water. At 6 P. M., I went forward to my store-room hatch, and ordered the yeoman to pass up all the axes, thinking that possibly we might want them before morning. I had hardly given the order, when a heavy sea struck us, and threw the ship nearly over on her beam-ends. I was pitched headlong to leeward, and struck against a bolt in the side of the ship, which nearly deprived me of my breath. I lay there in the water until taken up and carried to my state-room. The doctor came and ascertained that no bones were broken, he bathed my head and back. I then lay down, as I felt faint, but had not been on my bed an hour, when I heard the grating of the after-hatch lifted, and a voice, which I knew to be the captain, giving directions to a midshipman, saying: "tell him if he is able to stand, I

U. S. FRIGATE MACEDONIAN AT THE COMMENCEMENT OF THE GALE.

wish to see him on deck." I knew this meant me, and that something had happened. I sprang up, and when the midshipman had reached the door, was ready to go on deck; he delivered his message and appeared much frightened, saying, the mainmast was sprung. My pain had left me and I felt quite able for duty. As I stepped upon deck, I saw a collection of officers holding on around the mainmast. The ship was rolling so violently, that it was impossible to stand without holding on. I went directly to the captain, who was very near, who said to me, "Our mainmast is sprung, sir! and if you are able I wish you to examine it." The howling of the wind was such as to make it almost impossible to understand a word or an order. I saw the trouble at once, and could see that the mast was dangerously sprung, gaping open in seven places, two-thirds the way up. As I had been through the operation before, understood something about it. I had all my carpenter's crew called, knocked up the wedges on the gun-deck, so that the mast might have room to play, set the boatswain's mates to clearing away the mast-fishes, and, rousing them out, suggested to the captain the necessity of cutting away the maintop-mast rigging, that the top-mast and top-sail yard might go over the side in order to save the mainmast.

Volunteers were now called that would go up on the tottering mast, and cut the weather laniards. Midshipman R. S. Pickney, with two others, undertook the hazardous duty; for had the mainmast gone over the side while they were aloft, there would have been an end of them. They succeeded in reaching a suitable position, with hatchets strung at their backs, and chopped off the rigging. They came safely down, and after a few lurches, all above the main cap went over the side. But before the top-mast went over, it was almost certain that the mainmast would go, as it was broken off in several places. At one time the captain ordered me to cut away the mast. I made a few blows, when, by the falling of the top-mast, the lower mast was much relieved. Some were now busily employed in clearing away the fallen spars, and others in assisting me in getting the fishes in their place. The incessant rolling of the ship made this a difficult

MACEDONIAN AT MIDNIGHT.

job; they were however securely spiked and plenty of good lashings packed round them, after which, we considered the mast secure. While we were engaged about this job, the slings of the mainyard broke, and it came down among us, and although there were twenty men at work on the mast under it, not one was injured. The yard broke off in the middle, and while hauling it out of the way, we heard the report that the foremast was sprung. This was apalling news, especially just at this time. Capt. Downes wished me to go forward and examine it, which I did, and sure enough, it was broken off just above the deck, and in several places higher up. I left the mainmast now in the hands of the sailors, who were securing the lashings, and took my crew forward, cleared away the wedges, and with much difficulty, we succeeded in getting the fishes in their places, and spiking the ends, as we had done with the mainmast. The top-mast and top-sail yard had already gone over, together with the jib-boom. The lashings were passed and secured in a workman-like manner. We got up two large tackles on each side, to assist in supporting the mast, as the fore-rigging was somewhat slack. This was done while we were securing the fishes, and we now considered the mast safe. And strange as it may appear, the foreyard came down in about the same manner as did the main, and without any damage to those at work under it.

The gale had not abated, but came on in sudden and fearful gusts that lasted from fifteen to twenty minutes, and during these squalls it seemed as if the heavens and earth were coming together. Our quarter boats were blown away as though they had been made of paper, and as though the tempest had marked us for a plaything, and before we had got through with securing the mainmast, crash went the mizzenmast over the side. It broke short off about four feet above deck. All hands were called to clear the wreck. A piece of the mast had got under the stern, and was thumping against the bottom, and would have soon made a hole in the ship if not speedily removed. All the axes, hatchets, and every sort of an instrument having an edge, were employed in cutting away the rigging. I took my position on

GALE SUBSIDED.

the weather quarter, and with an adze cut away whatever belonged to the mizzen-mast; and although busily employed, holding on with one hand, and cutting away with the other, I could not help pausing occasionally, when the full moon would shine forth at short intervals between the rapid scuds, and there, all around upon the white crest of the mountain waves, were the dark fragments of our shattered spars and broken boats. And then the black heavy clouds would shut out the light again, as if it was a favor too great for us. At length the morning dawned. It was the Sabbath. The Almighty had said "*Peace, be still!*" The raging billows, obedient to the Divine command, had drooped their proud heads, and now all was still. Here we lay like a rolling log upon the ocean, and all around the decks were groups of exhausted seamen, catching a few moments sleep. Here we see Nature acting in direct contrast. Only a few hours before, the elements seemed as if *soon to melt with fervent heat, and the heavens to be rolled together as a scroll.* Now all is hushed; a lighted taper may be carried fore and aft without being extinguished. The glorious sun emerges from the water, shooting his rays over the glassy ocean, as though nothing had happened. There is poor Jack perhaps, at this moment, in happy converse with some loved one on shore, but his dream must soon be disturbed, and changed into the reality of clearing the wreck, and getting up jury masts.

As we had taken no food for twenty-four hours, there was a hollow place in each stomach that required to be filled. Provisions were served out, and we all had a good warm breakfast. I knew well what part of the play devolved on me, and after consulting with the first lieutenant, went to work with my crew. My first job was to get up a jury mizzen-mast. This we did by cutting off the stump of the mizzen-mast close to the deck, then cut a mortice in it, took the longest part of the broken main-yard, cut a tenon in the end, and shipped it into the stump of the mizzen-mast. Mr. Percival, (now Capt. Percival,) had the management of the rigging department. We also got up a top-gallant mast on the fore, and another on the mainmast, next fixed up the waist that had been stove in by a heavy sea, got a top sail yard on each mast on which we could carry a whole top-sail in good weather, and top-gallant sails over them. Our jib-boom went with the foretop-mast, and the bow-sprit was sprung so that all that we could do forward was to set a flying jib, and in two or three days we were quite snug. When we turned the ship's head for home, we were one thousand miles east of Norfolk, and for which place we steered. Our rig was a curious one.

One day on our return, we saw a brig coming down with a fair wind across our bow.

We backed our sails and lay by for her, as the captain wished to speak her. He ran down quite near us, showing no colors. Capt. Downes hailed him, to which he returned no answer, evidently intending to run by us.

"Round to, sir," said Capt. Downes.

He paid no attention to this order, neither had he shown any colors.

"*Clear away the bow gun, and give him a shot across the bow, sir,*" which was no sooner said than done.

This brought him to his bearings; he came round under our quarter, and yet showed no colors. We had none hoisted ourselves, because we had no place yet prepared for them.

"*Why don't you hoist your colors?*" said Capt. Downes.

"Why don't you hoist yours?" said the stranger.

"*You —— scoundrel, if you don't show your colors, I'll give you a shot.*"

He then caught up his ensign, and gave it a shake, (it was English,) and then threw it down.

"*Hoist your flag at your peak, sir.*"

By this time he was close under our stern. The Englishman looked up, and said: "I don't know who and what you are; such a devil of a rig," and at the same time run his colors up to his peak. Capt. Downes told him of our disaster, and wished him to report us on his arrival, which he promised to do, and appeared to be a clever fellow, after all.

An incident occurred the night after the gale, which I should have mentioned before. At about 10 o'clock, a man on the forecastle sung out, "Some one is hailing the ship, sir!" I happened to be on deck at the time. The officer

UNDER JURY MASTS BOUND TO NORFOLK.

of the deck came forward and ordered silence. Not a breath was heard from any one, when directly we heard, from apparently a short distance on the weather bow, "Hoa! hoa!" We fired a gun, and hove the ship to; sent men aloft to look about in every direction, and lay by all night. As soon as day dawned, the captain, and every officer with spy-glasses, distributed about the ship, commenced searching for what we supposed to be a boat, with the survivors of some unfortunate vessel; but we could see nothing, nor did we ever know anything more about it. Many suppositions and opinions were given, but here the matter ended. There can be no doubt but that in this dreadful gale, some poor fellows found a watery grave.

In sixteen days we arrived at Norfolk, which I think was about the 17th of October; anchored off Gosport, near the Navy Yard. I had previously prepared a list of spars, with their dimensions, and as soon as our anchors were down, by order of Capt. Downes, went on shore to the Navy Yard; found Mr. Grice, naval architect, gave him the list of spars, and fortunately there were three masts, already put together, and only required hooping; they were of the right dimensions.

Preparations were now made for hoisting out the broken masts. I took the fishes off, determined to keep them for the good they had done; the mainmast hardly held together long enough to be hoisted out; and when they were lowering it over the side, it fell to pieces. Carpenters and calkers went to work on the ship, and the spars all commenced upon, and in eleven days our pretty frigate was all ready for bending sails, (which had also been made since our arrival,) and on the 1st of November, we were ready for sea.

When we sailed from Boston, there were several gentlemen that joined the ship as botanists, and naturalists, and scienceists; and as they had got their bellies full of sea, concluded not to try it again. During the night of the gale, two of these half-and-half fellows were drowned out of the cockpit, where they lived, and crawled up to the gun-deck. They were hanging on to a stanchion with the parson, a tall slab of a fellow. I had several old salts assisting me in getting the wedges clear of the mainmast. Occasionally they would rip out an oath, which completely shocked these poor useless beings. "Oh," said one, "don't use profanity at this time." There they were, hanging like a sick monkey to a lee-backstay; of no more use to the ship than a spare pump. Such chaps as these are of but little use anywhere, more especially in a gale of wind.

All the officers deserved much credit for their energy and promptness in refitting the ship. We dropped down to Hampton-roads, and from thence went to sea, with everything above deck new and strong, and the frigate throughout in firstrate order. I looked out again for plenty of stock in my line of business. My old friends, the mast-fishes, were snugly stowed away with some small additions from the Navy Yard at Norfolk. I have another story to tell about the fishes by and by, notwithstanding there was so much trouble about taking them on board at Boston.

We had a fine crew, generally; there were about forty, however, that were turbulent fellows. They had been on board of English men-of war, and found much fault with the discipline of the Macedonian. But Mr. Percival was a terror to these evil doers, and they soon became suppled down.

We doubled Cape Horn about the 1st of January, 1819, and arrived at Valparaiso in seventy-nine days from Norfolk. Two days before arriving at Valparaiso, we lost a fine fellow overboard; he was on the bridle port drawing water for washing deck. The lanyard broke, and he fell into the water, and although he swam nearly as fast as the ship was going, yet before the boat reached him, he went down.

Valparaiso presented a scene of warlike activity. Chili had declared themselves a Republic, and were at war with Peru. Lord Cochran was commander-in-chief of the Chillian navy, consisting of two or three frigates, a corvette, and some smaller vessels. A number of merchant ships were employed as transports to carry their troops to the head-quarters, near Lima.

I have now another tragical affair to relate, the result of cherished hatred, arising from the most trifling circumstance, of what is too often erroneously construed into wounded honor, and for which nothing can atone but blood! Two midshipmen, A——e and G——n, had quarrelled some six weeks before our arrival. It originated from a very trivial circumstance about relieving each other, as they were in different watches. Some sharp words passed, when one, in a hasty manner, gave the other the lie. These two young gentlemen had been, up to the time of the quarrel, like brothers. I have frequently seen them sitting with their arms around each other's necks, and reading from the same book.

CHAPTER X.

Frailty of human friendship,—Further particulars of the duel,—Unfeeling conduct of the murderer,—Land our provisions,—Prepare for going down the coast,—Chillian fleet,—Lord Cochran requests Captain Downes to defer his visit to Callao,—His Lordship visits the Macedonian,—Description of his person,—Foster, the thief,—He deserts,—Efforts to arrest him,—Seen on board the Rose,—While at work on board a whaler,—Wrote a note to Mr. Maury,—Rose searched,—Foster found,—Carried on board the frigate,—Put in irons,—The Rose swings near the whaler,—My life threatened,—No danger,—Threaten to kill me if caught on shore,—Mr. Lewis, sail-maker, waylaid by the Spaniard, stripped and buried in the sand, as dead,—Crawled into a shanty,—Messenger sent to the frigate,—Boat sent for him,—Specimen of the Rose's crew,—Capt. Downes becomes acquainted with a German baron,—I am requested to fit up Lady Cochran's palace,—Sail for Coquimbo,–Protection of the brig Warrior,—Accident to Mr. Brock,—Sail for Arica,—Receive on board a large amount of specie,—Smuggling,—Sail for Callao,—Requested by Cochran not to enter,—A good deal about the bazzar,—Arrival at Panama,—Suspicion,—Barron leaves,—Meet the Rose,—Prepare for action,—Search her,—Her imminent danger if she had fired,—Sail for Puna,—Arrival,—Send a boat up to Guyaquil,—Boat seized, men imprisoned,—Suspicion,—Gunboats sent down to take the Macedonian,—Another boat sent up,—Explanation,—Friendly terms,—Handsome present of fruit,—Beautiful sight,—Fight between swordfish, thresher and whale,—Sail for San Blas,—Our business,—Destruction of a fine ship through superstition,—Dreadful tornado, attended with heavy thunder and lightning,—Ship Two Catherines struck,—Mainmast shattered,—Her Capt. in much trouble,—No assistance from the shore,–Gets assistance from the frigate,–I make him a mast,—She is ready for sea in four days,—Foster, the thief and deserter, punished,—Description of his punishment,—Another duel under way,—It is prevented,—Contrast between the combatants,—Remonstrance, and remarks,—Not necessary to go to Columbia river,—Explanation,—Difficulty among whaling seamen,—Exchange,—Remarks,—Fears of becoming short of provisions,—Ration reduced,—Whiskey gives out, —Choice of the men,—Promises of pay for short rations,—Stops at Acapulco,—Procure a few miserable bullocks,—Boats worm-eaten,—Repair them,—Sail for Tumbez,—Anchored off the mouth of a river,—Boat sent on shore, to explore,—Discover an Indian canoe,—They make their escape,—Overtake the boat,—Only a woman left,—Quiet her fears,—Return to the ship,—Fit out an expedition for wooding, and ship timber,—Lieut. Percival goes to Tumbez river in a whale boat,—Returns without being able to obtain provisions,—Find some oysters,—Go up the river on an exploring tour.—Discover an immense bed of oysters,—Half the ship's company go on shore one day,—Treat out of oysters,—Next day the other half goes,—Remarks on the difference in the condition of the men since the whiskey was out,—Melancholy history of a young man,—Distress for provisions,—Water gives out,—I am taken down with fever,—Nauseous Medicine,—Several deaths,—Convalescence,—Cure myself by exertion,—Arrive at Valparaiso.—Whiskey,—Its effects,—Condition of the crew,—I obtain a good meal.

BUT alas! how futile and uncertain is worldly friendship; the most trifling incident, apparently, and may be positively without the slightest intention of insult or even of wounding feelings, is immediately caught up, and by officious *friends*, magnified into an affair of honor, that cannot be settled in any other way, than with the pistol, at ten paces.

On the morning after our arrival, they, with their two *friends?* and one of the doctor's mates, obtained permission to go on shore; no one in the ship, except their messmates, knew anything of the challenge, or of their intention to fight when they went on shore. On landing, they went behind a ridge of land, which screened them from the frigate, arranged their distance, and fired. A——e, fell dead. The bullet passed through his lungs, came out on the other side, and lodged in the arm near the elbow. When the ball struck him, he jumped up, exclaiming, "Oh my God!" and fell dead! A crowd of Spaniards soon gathered around them, and the corpse was brought to the beach; a boat sent from the frigate, and it was brought on board, and placed in a coffin for burial. When this unfortunate young man was stepping out of the boat on shore, he requested Ch——d, his second, to write to his father, in Philadelphia, and say to him, "that he was sorry that he could not fall in a better cause," as though the dreadful presentment of death was before him, and when the body lay in the coffin, there was scarcely any appearance of death upon his face. The two red spots were still remaining upon his cheeks, and the expression calm and unruffled. He was buried on the beach, near the ship, as the Spaniards would not allow him an interment in their grounds.

Thus perished this young man. He died like a fool, and was buried like a dog; without a mourner or a sympathetic tear, far away from home. The news of his untimely death was soon wending its way to his beloved parents,* friends, and the large circle of acquaintances among which he had passed his boyhood. His aged parents were hourly expecting the news of his safe arrival at Valparaiso. They had written to him while at Norfolk, congratulating him for his deliverance from the storm, and safe arrival in port. But the letter that was soon to rend their hearts, was near at hand, and when it was received, although I was not there to witness the scene, yet can well imagine it.

The victor in this tragic affair, or the murderer, whichever you may please to call him, came on board apparently undisturbed, and as I thought, with a sort of exulting look. He was placed under arrest for a few days, and then liberated, as duelling was not considered a punishable crime in the navy. Therefore there was no law against it.

As our rigging required overhauling, the ship to be painted, which we had no opportunity of doing at Norfolk, it was expected that we should remain some time at Valparaiso. There was also another circumstance that would probably detain us somewhat longer. It was the intention of Capt. Downes to visit Callao on our way down the Coast. Lord Cochrane was apprised of this, and requested Capt. D. to delay his visit until he had made his contemplated attack upon the place. To this Capt. D. courteously consented. The transport ships were receiving the soldiers; the ships-of-war, and store ships were all ready for sea; and, taking the whole together, it was a formidable affair. Lord Cochrane had given the Chilians assurance that he would soon reduce the port of Callao, and Gen. San Martin with his vast army, encamped near the walls of Lima, gave encouragement that

* He was a son of the Rev. Dr. Abercrombie, of Philadelphia, and a young gentleman highly esteemed by all who knew him.

he should enter the city triumphantly, and thus carry all Peru.

I had never seen a more beautiful sight than this fleet presented when they sailed from Valparaiso. Lord Cochrane had managed to brush up the ships-of-war, and they certainly appeared well; his flag ship, the O. Higgins, was a 44 gun frigate, and I believe a prize from the Peruvians. He had managed to get a crew for her, by shipping every runaway sailor from whalers or merchant-men of almost every nation. The Chilian government, placing implicit confidence in him, sanctioned whatever he did. They had a fine corvette built ship, which they purchased in New York. She was called Indepentia, mounting 22 guns. The ships had all left the harbor except one, that was being fitted for guns, which was the ship in which Lord Cochrane, lady and suite had come from France.

The reader probably may not be aware that Lord Cochran was once a bold and daring admiral in the British navy, and in consequence of some misunderstanding with the British government, went over to France with his family. And, on hearing of the revolution in Chili, purchased the Rose, proceeded to Valparaiso, offered his services as an admiral, was cordially received, and placed immediately in command of the Chilian squadron.

His Lordship honored us with a visit just previous to his sailing. He probably wanted to see what we were made of, as the sequel will show that he considered us very much in his way. He was received by Capt. Downes with much politeness and attention, and as he was conducted round the ship, he noticed our guns with much scrutiny. They were of English manufacture, and all with the initials "G. R.," near the breech. He no doubt made up his mind on the spot, that we could lick any of his ships, *any how*, although he had one, the *Lotaro*, that mounted fifty guns. He was a tall, fine looking man, with red hair, and very small black eyes, that were not shut while on board our frigate. He passed a high compliment on our good looking crew, and also spoke of having been on board the Macedonian, when under another flag. The reader is probably aware that she was taken by the U. S. frigate, United States, Commodore Decatur, during our late war with England. His Lordship with much politeness left the Macedonian, and on the next day sailed for Callao.

The Chilians bought the Rose, which is the one now fitting for guns. We had a man on board the frigate that was a notorious thief, who belonged to the third cutter, his name was Foster.

This fellow made a practice of stealing frocks, trowsers, jackets, and also of robbing bags whenever he could get access to them. And when the boat was called away would run below, get his stolen goods, shove them under his jacket, and while the boat was on shore would sell them for aquadiente, (rum), which he managed to carry on board in a bladder, or skin, as sailors call it. Men frequently missed their clothes, not being able to account for them to the officers of their division, to whom they must account every month for every piece of clothing, and failing to do this, are either flogged or punished in some other way.

Foster was finally detected in his villany. The midshipman of the boat caught him in the act of selling his plunder, and rather than suffer the penalty of theft, he ran from the boat, and fled into the mountains. Officers in disguise went in search of him, but without success. He was given up as not worth looking after.

One day, some time after he had deserted, I was on board the Archimedes, a Nantucket whaler, Capt. Folger, under French colors. I had some carpenters at work on board of her. She was moored near the Rose, and when we swung, both ships came so near together, that it was an easy matter to jump from one to the other; and while in this close proximity, one of my carpenters says to me, in a low voice, "There's Foster!" I looked, and sure enough, there was his head plainly to be seen through the stern port. I immediately went into the whaler's cabin, and wrote the following note to the first lieutenant:

"*Mr. Maury, Sir: Foster, the deserter, is on board the Rose; I think if Mr. Percival goes on board, he will succeed in getting him.* *Respectfully,* *S. F. Holbrook.*

I hailed one of our boats that was just passing, and requested the midshipman to give the note to the first lieutenant as quick as possible. It was now 4 o'clock, P. M., and it would probably take the remainder of the afternoon to get him. Very soon after our boat reached the frigate, I saw two boats leave the ship, Mr. Percival and two midshipmen in one, and one midshipman in the other. Mr. Percival went along-side the Rose, and all went on board. The other boat proceeded to the shore with a written request from Capt. Downes to the Governor, for permission to search the Rose for a deserter, which permission was immediately given in writing, and taken on board the Rose, to Mr. Percival, who now, having authority, commenced the search, the officers persisting that no such man was on board. She was searched from stem to stern, every sail opened, not a hole but was probed with a sword, and when just about giving up the search, Mr. Percival stepped into his boat and came along-side the whaler, and asked me if I was positive that I saw him? My reply was, "Yes, sir, and he is now on board that ship." As he went into the boat to continue the search, he observed to me, "I should relinquish the search, had I not the greatest confidence in your eye." I must confess I felt rather unpleasant, as probably he might have been slyly put into a boat, or stowed away in some place where he could not be discovered; in which case, doubt might have existed whether I had seen him, notwithstanding I was so certain about it. The sundown boat had now come for us; myself and carpenters returned to the frigate. It was now dark; Mr. Maury observed to me that if I was sure I had seen him, he was also sure he was there. In less than half an hour, the boat approached the ship: she was hailed, and asked, "Have you got him?" "Yes," was the answer. This of course relieved my anxiety, and the doubts of others. He was discovered in a singular manner, and in a singular place. They had, after commencing the second time, examined every hole large enough for a cat to crawl through, and were about giving it up, when accidentally looking down between some barrels of bread, they saw what appeared to be a platform of loose plank. Mr. Percival run his sword down through every joint, and although he felt it go through what he supposed to be old rigging, paid no attention to it; but just as they were about leaving, a young chap crouched down and looked under the plank, and sung out, "Here he is!" The bread barrels were soon roused off, and the gentleman hauled out; and although he was a large and powerful man, he had stowed himself away in a place hardly big enough for a man half his size. He was bleeding profusely, as the sword had gone through his thigh. The captain ordered him in double irons, and to be placed under the sentinel's charge until the measure of his punishment should be determined.

Next day, I went on board the Archimedes with my carpenters, to finish the repairs on her deck; and when the two ships came near each other, a gang of these desperate piratical villains rushed aft, with an intention of jumping on board the whaleship, to take my life; and as the distance was rather too great for a jump, they did not attempt it, but shook their fists and knives at me, calling me by every horrid name they could think of, swearing with tremendous oaths, that if they could get near me, they would have my heart's blood. Adding also, "If we don't get on board that ship, we will have your life on the beach." They knew that I had given information of the discovery of Foster. Notwithstanding these threats, I was not in the least alarmed. The mate of the Archimedes, a fine, stalwart fellow, something over six feet in height, assured me that with himself and fifteen Nantucket whalemen with whale spades and lances, and myself with a good broad axe, and my three carpenters also well armed, we could put every man to death that would dare to put his foot on our deck. And had they made the attempt, there would not only have been a scene of bloodshed, but the world would have been rid of some of the greatest villains that it ever bore; and it would not have ended here. Our frigate would have hauled along-side and blown her to atoms. In all probability, had not Foster been just what I knew him to be, a consummate villain, I should not have exposed him, even at the risk of not doing my duty as an officer.

Valparaiso at this time was infested with a set of runaway

Botany Bay convicts, and it was dangerous to be on shore after sundown. Mr. Lewis, our sail-maker, in company with the gunner, had been out on a walk towards Ville de Mar, one Sunday afternoon; they had walked too far to get back before sundown. Night overtook them two miles from the landing. All at once they were assailed by a gang of these fellows, and were both knocked down. Lewis was stripped of all his clothes, stabbed, and as they thought, killed; he feigned dead, which saved his life. They dug a hole in the sand and buried him, and as he was nigh smothering, ventured to raise himself up. The robbers were now at some distance; he, however, ventured to crawl out of his grave, and though weak from the loss of blood, and much bruised, succeeded in reaching the shanty of a Spaniard, who took him in and covered him with mats. He urged the Spaniard to get on board the frigate in some way, and report his condition.

The gunner had succeeded in getting on board with the loss of his coat and hat. He was a very large and powerful man, and was successful in fighting his way to the beach, where there were plenty of boat's crews to assist him. When he got on board, he reported Mr. Lewis killed. A short time after, the Spaniard came off; telling the story of Lewis' rescue, a boat was immediately sent for him: he was brought on board, his wounds dressed, and soon recovered. These fellows were a sample of the Rose's crew.

During the time we were refitting the ship, Capt. Downes was often at the Capital, *Santiago*, where he was introduced to, and became intimately acqnainted with a German Baron, apparently of high respectability, who was making a tour through South America, but unfortunately, while at Santiago, was taken quite ill, and at the time of his introduction to Captain Downes, so far convalescent as to walk out. He accompanied our captain to Valparaiso, was invited on board the ship, and treated with much attention. He suggested that he thought a trip at sea would be extremely beneficial to his health. Captain Downes, with his usual courtesy, offered him a part of his cabin, and it was now arranged that the Baron was to be the captain's guest during our cruise down the coast. Some small alterations were made in the cabin, and the idea of having so great a personage as the Baron, for a companion, as he would doubtless be, among the ward-room officers, was quite pleasing.

The Chilian government had given Lord Cochrane the large building, formerly occupied as the Custom House, for his residence. Lady Cochrane, who was the belle of Valparaiso, requested Captain Downes, with whom she was on most intimate terms, to allow me to make some alterations in this building, before she could consider it as her palace. Capt. Downes readily assented, and I took on shore three of my best joiners, and fitted her ladyship out in good style, and for which she paid me handsomely. We were now about ready for sea, everything on board, Baron and all.

Mr. Rolla Weems, midshipman, an excellent young gentleman, was left on shore too ill to go the cruise. About the 10th of February, we sailed for Coquimbo, a short distance north of Valparaiso. Our business here was to liberate the brig Warrior, of New York. She had been seized for some pretended infraction of Chilian law, but as she was a very rakish looking brig, and would doubtless add to their small navy, it would be very convenient to seize and confiscate her. But they soon found that they had to deal with somebody else. We remained here but a few days and sailed again.

On entering the Bay of Coquimbo, we found the whale ship Factor, of Nantucket; the chief mate, Mr. Brock, had been cut down with the fluke of a whale, and barely escaped with his life. Our next stopping place was Arica, the most southern port of Peru. Much produce is brought here and shipped, and much however is smuggled. Previous to sailing, an arrangement was made at Valparaiso between Capt. Downes, and an English house, who had a brig trading at Arica, but was obliged to smuggle the money off at night. The arrangement with Capt. Downes was, that he should lay too off the port, during the night, and in the morning the brig would stand out to sea. We should then come together and receive the bars and plates of gold or silver, which she had received during the night, as there was some danger that she might be captured, as it was an enemy's port.

We lay off and on here, six days and nights, and received

on board, the proceeds of the brig's cargo, for which Captain Downes was handsomely remunerated. We sailed for Callao, but when close in with the island of St. Lorenzo, were boarded by the Gulverine, a gun brig belonging to Cochrane's squadron. This brig had been kept out here on the look out for us, and with a request from his Lordship to Captain Downes, that he would not enter the port of Callao for the present, as he should attack the ships that night. Capt. Downes, although anxious to go in, as he had official business, consented to this request. We then continued on our way to Panama. That night at about eleven o'clock, it being quite dark, a sail was discovered on our weather bow, close on board of us. We kept off a few points, beat to quarters, hung up the battle lanterns, masked* fore and aft; then hauled up and hailed the stranger, "*What ship is that?*" no answer for nearly two minutes, when we were right abreast of him. We were hailed, "*What ship is that?*" "This is the U. S. frigate Macedonian," and at the same moment giving the order, "unmask your lantern on the gun-deck." We were now within pistol shot of him, with our gun-deck illuminated and lighted matches. He now gave the name of the ship—it was the Rose, her Spanish name I have forgotten. Capt. Downes ordered him to lay to, for he wished to board him, suspecting he had some of our deserters on board. Lieut. Percival boarded her, and after an hour's detention, returned without finding any one. She had been fitted for twenty-two guns, and had a crew of one hundred and forty men. Her object was, without doubt, to capture any thing she could master, and if during our controversy there had been a flash seen on board of her, she would have been destroyed in fifteen minutes, for she actually was a pirate with a commission. We then sailed for Panama, where we arrived a few days afterwards.

There was evidently some jealousy here, about who we were. Although we showed the American flag, yet they believed us to be Chilians, and were no ways sociable, until they were convinced of our real character, and then the Governor

* A mask, or a lantern, is a canvas bag pulled over the lantern so as to entirely hide the light until the very moment it is wanted.

became very polite. Capt. D. and the Baron were his guests. The Baron became quite enamored with his only daughter, who was remarkably handsome and highly accomplished. There was something said about marriage, the particulars of which I did not learn. The Baron had now entirely recovered his health, had grown quite fleshy, and was really a good looking man. He had a full wardrobe of military dresses. Sometimes he would appear on deck with a green coat handsomely trimmed with silver lace, two splendid gold epaulets, and a long string of medals of honor, which he had gained at different battles. Another time he would appear in a white uniform of the Austrian style, handsomely trimmed with gold lace, thus showing off in fine display. He now intimated his intention of crossing the Isthmus, and making a tour through the United States, and to accomplish this, it was necessary that he should have a good lot of money. Captain Downes cashed his draft on Rio Janeiro, for several thousand dollars. The purser also advanced a large sum. Many of the officers solicited from him the favor of taking some valuable curiosities in charge, and to deliver them to their friends, to whom he was furnished with ample letters of introduction. He had about ten thousand dollars in money and valuables, and with any quantity of letters to all the great folks at home. He was to stay with the Governor of Panama a few days, until a suitable escort could be got ready for crossing the Isthmus. His luggage went on shore, and the Governor gave a ball on the occasion. I shall have something more to say about our Baron at another time.

Our next move was to the Island of Puna, at the month of Guayaquil river. On our arrival there, a boat was sent up to Guayaquil to apprize the Governor of the arrival of an American frigate in his waters. The boat was commanded by Midshipman W. T. Rogers, who was one of the most promising young officers in the Navy, and it is to be regretted that he has since left the United States naval service.

The boat had no sooner reached the pier at Guayaquil, than she was seized by the soldiers, and the crew put in prison. Mr. Rogers was allowed to remain on parole within the limits of the city. In the mean time, two large gunboats were fitted out, and sent down to take possession of the frigate, for they were sure we were Chilians, as no American frigate would ever presume to go such a distance from home. The gunboats anchored very near us, and rather seemed to hesitate about how they should go to work to take us. After waiting a whole day they pulled up their anchors and went up river again without the frigate; for we understood that they had positive orders to bring her up and moor her off the town, after securing the crew. Capt. Downes now thought it necessary to send another boat to ascertain what had become of the first. The second cutter was fitted out in charge of Mr. Percival, who went up to Guayaquil with an order from Capt. Downes for the immediate release of the first boat, with a suitable apology for imprisoning American seamen. The Governor being convinced of his mistake, not only released the men, but sent down a large quantity of fruit, with the required apology.

While laying at Puna, we witnessed a beautiful scene, which was an attack of a swordfish and thresher upon a whale. While these two allies were attacking their ponderous enemy, one upon his back and the other beneath, the poor fellow would throw himself entirely out of the water, with these two deathly foes still hanging on to him, when in less than an hour the monster gave up and lay quietly upon the surface.

We weighed anchor, and sailed for San Blas, a Mexican port on the south side of the Gulf of California, and at the entrance of the River Santiago. Our business here was to ascertain the particulars of the capture of an American brig at St. Joseph, at the head of the Gulf of California, and ascertained that she had been previously liberated. On entering the harbor of San Blas, we were particularly struck by seeing a new and beautiful corvette pierced for twenty-two guns, lying aground, and so badly hogged that she was not worth getting off. The masts and spars were all standing, the guns had fallen to leeward, and there she lay, a lamentable monument of bigotry and superstition.

The history of the affair was as follows, which we learned

from a gentleman on shore. The ship was built up the Gulf and came down to San Blas, preparatory to proceeding on a cruise. On entering the harbor the pilot was mistaken about the tide, and ran on to the flat; and instead of immediately throwing over the guns, and letting the anchors go from the bows, these jackasses all got upon their knees and began to cry to some saint, and all this time the tide was ebbing, and she being quite sharp, heeled very rank, and being much strained, on the next tide water flowed freely into her, and she never righted again. Poor deluded creatures! We found the ship Two Catherines, of Providence, Capt. Wyat, lying here. The captain had sold the greater part of his cargo, and intended going to another port. One night there come up a tremendous thunder shower, with very sharp lightning; one flash struck the Two Catherines, commencing at the main-royal-mast head, and taking everything clean as it came down, leaving nothing standing but a shivered piece of the mainmast, about ten feet above deck. Capt. Wyat came on board the frigate early next morning to consult with Capt. Downes, who advised him to apply to the governor for assistance. He did so, and the governor told him it would require five weeks to get a spar from the country suitable for a mast; also that he had no engineers—meaning carpenters.

It was the intention of Capt. Downes to have sailed the morning after the tornado, but was willing to remain if he could be of any service to Capt. Wyat. Now here was a dilemma; the ship without a mainmast, and no means of procuring one. Capt. Downes wished me to go on board and take a look and see what could be done. I went on board and began to plan. That part of the mast below deck about four feet above was perfectly sound; then there was a shattered part, about ten feet long above that. The mainyard could be repaired, but the rest must be new. There were spare spars on board the Two Catherines, and we had some on board the frigate that could be used, and then there were also our twelve mast-fishes, if the captain would be willing to part with them, and run the risk of wanting them ourselves.

I made my report to Mr. Maury, who asked me if, with

the materials within our reach, a mast could be made so that she could go to sea? My reply to him was: "that if Mr. Percival would go on board, with a gang of our men, and take out the stump of the mainmast, I could take my carpenters and make a mast and what other spars she wanted." This he reported to Capt. Downes, who acceded to the arrangements, and accordingly, next morning, myself and six others turned to on board the Two Catherines. The stump was hoisted out, and by much contrivance we succeeded in making a substantial mast. I set our blacksmith at work on the hoops, as fortunately we had plenty of bar iron on board, the hoops were made as soon as required, and in three days, the mainmast was ready for stepping, and as good and strong a mast as could be made anywhere. The other spars and maintop were soon made, and on the fourth day she was ready for sea. But very few of us eat idle bread during these four days.

Foster, the deserter, was now brought up to receive what he richly deserved. He had been kept in irons since he was taken, a condition often attended with much suffering. All hands were called to witness punishment. He was seized up, and six dozen were put upon him in good fashion. He then had a yoke placed around his neck, with "*thief*" printed upon it. The yoke consisted of two pieces of oak board, each three feet long and five inches wide, the two pieces were fastened together with two bolts, with a hole in the middle of the yoke for the neck, which is not to be taken off during the punishment. And in addition to this, he was placed in "the head," a most degrading position, and must mess alone, being considered as unworthy to associate with his former messmates. Certainly, "the way of the transgressor is hard."

While at San Blas, we came near having another duel, and I believe had it not been for my exertion, (please pardon the egotism,) we should have been under the painful necessity of recording another untimely death. Two midshipmen had quarrelled about some trifling affair, which of course resulted in a challenge. One of the parties, an amiable young gentleman, and with whom I was on very friendly terms, came frequently into my state-room for the purpose of arranging for this probably fatal climax. He had often conversed with me, and talked over his happy boyish days, and about his kind parents, his lovely sisters, and his extensive circle of friends. But now he was sad and downcast; the chance of an inglorious death, and the impossibility of avoiding it without the loss of what was dearer than life, particularly among naval officers, *honor*. He had accepted the challenge, and of course could not back out without disgrace. The gentleman he was to fight with was exactly his opposite, both in character and disposition. He was from Virginia, very intemperate, quarrelsome, and what is called by this class an *excellent shot*, and was very mean and unofficerlike in his deportment. This was the man before whom my highly esteemed young friend from New York was to stand, at a distance of ten paces, and ten chances to one receive the death bullet. And then to be buried like a dog, unlamented and unmourned, for he who falls in a duel seldom receives the sympathy that is shed for those that meet an honorable death. And as I before observed, then took the matter in hand, by laying before my young friend the dreadful consequences of being killed like a brute, representing to him the mistaken notions of honor, and the dreadful alternative he was about to resort to, in order to sustain that in which the very act of preserving it, was its complete annihilation. The young man shedding tears, said "that he well knew the result, and was not unmindful of what must follow.

"If I am killed, oh! what will become of my dear mother? My father may bear up under it, but it will kill my mother! And you know I cannot back out now; and suppose I should kill P——, I should be miserable forever after, and if I don't fight, I shall be a disgrace to my mess."

It being his watch he went out, and I went about the plan I had in view to end this unpleasant affair, and in conjunction with two others, not necessary to be named, it was talked over and arranged that a meeting should take place and one shot only exchanged, after which the matter should end, and the hand of friendship mutually given. It was also mutually understood that the shot was to do no harm. It may be asked why it was necessary to meet, if a settlement was contemplated. I would answer that in cases where duels are not consummated, apologies are made from one of the parties; this generally leaves a sort of stigma upon him who makes the apology, and he is sometimes accused of being a coward. But when the parties meet and *honorably* (?) exchange a shot, then both of them are considered of the right stuff. I would just add that the young gentleman whom I have named as my friend in this matter, arrived to the highest position in the navy, and is now one of our most accomplished and gallant post captains.

I mentioned at the commencement of this cruise that we were bound to Columbia river, on the north-west coast, but on our arrival at Valparaiso we learned that the difficulty which had required our presence at Oregon was now adjusted, hence there was no necessity of our going there. We left San Blas and stood out four or five days to the westward, where we fell in with several whale ships, some of which had been very successful. We saw dead whales whifed* all around them. There was Capt. Chase, and Capt. Folger, and Capt. Putnam, and many other old worthies whose very names were a terror to whales, and it often happened that on meeting with a whaler, that there was some difficulty with the men, who were dissatisfied with whaling, and wanted to leave their ships. These matters were generally arranged between the two captains, as it always happened that we had a gang of turbulent fellows, continually making mischief which we were very glad to get rid of, so whenever an exchange was to be made, the word was passed fore and aft,

"*All you that want to go on board the whaler, lay aft on the quarter-deck.*"

There was never any lack of candidates for a new ship, particularly among the class I have described, for two very important considerations weighed heavily in their favor. The first, there was no "*cat*," nor boatswain's mate, on board a whaler; second, they were discharged from the naval service, and last, though by no means least, they were settled with and

* WHIFED.—When more whales are killed than can be taken care of at the present time, a short staff with a flag upon it is stuck into the back of the whale so that they may be seen.

had their cash; and if the kind whale-catching captain would give them a day's liberty on shore where any grog was to be had, he was pretty sure not to see them again until their money was gone. When the volunteers had all arranged themselves on the quarter-deck, our first lieutenant, Mr. Maury, who had a keen eye, knew well *who could be spared*, and from these were selected the "whalers," and when the discontented men from the other ship had been received and their names on the ship's books, then the others went on board their new ship. I hardly ever knew a case where either party were much the gainers by the exchange.

On our first arrival at Valparaiso, we put our beef and pork on shore, reserving it for the passage home, and taking on board in its stead, the salted meat of the country, which does not receive salt well, and but small quantities are taken on board at a time. Also, calculating to get fresh meat at every stopping place, and it being now very evident that our cruise would be much longer than was at first anticipated, we were under the necessity of having the usual allowance reduced, as almost every article of provision was likely to fall short. The whiskey gave out first, of which the purser reported to the captain that there was but one week's full allowance on board, as some mistake had been made as to quantity before leaving Valparaiso.

The captain ordered all hands to be called to muster, and then stated the case with regard to provisions, adding that whatever the privation might be before reaching Valparaiso, he hoped it would be borne patiently, and that each man should receive his money for short rations. "And now for the whiskey, my lads; will you have the full allowance while it lasts, or half allowance that it may hold out the longer?" They gave three cheers and chose the full allowance, and were then piped down.

We now steered for Acapulco, but could not procure any provisions except a few skeleton bullocks. Our boats had become much worm-eaten, and we were obliged to remain here a week in order to re-plank them, after which we sailed for Tumbez river, where the Spaniards first landed under Pizarro. In running in for the land, finding the water grew shallow, we anchored off the mouth of a wide river. The shore was well wooded, and a boat was sent to explore a short distance up. I was one of the party. As soon as we had entered the river, we discovered an Indian canoe about a mile from us. We gave chase, and as we were well armed, felt determined to find out something about it, as it was not definitely laid down on any of our charts.

After a long chase we came up with the Indians. They had run their canoe ashore among some bushes, had all jumped out except one old squaw, who was so frightened that she trembled as though shivering with the cold, and by signs convinced her that we were friendly. We gave her some biscuits, and some meat; the men had all run off and probably would not return while we were there. We ascertained from her that the name of the river was *Chippeowee*, and that it ran a great distance into the interior, and that there was a large city far up. On our return we stopped at the entrance on the south side, and found some excellent timber, only it was very hard. We returned to the ship and reported the result of our cruise. Orders were now given to fit out a party of wood-cutters. I had orders also to cut *lumber* for ship's use, and *timber* for a new *launch*, which I was to build at Valparaiso. A gang of fifty men and officers went on shore next morning, fitted out with axes, saws, muskets, ammunition, and a scanty supply of provisions. We soon made the forest ring with the sound of the "woodman's axe;" it was fine sport for the boys. In the mean time Mr. Percival had been dispatched to find Tumbez river, and to ascertain if any supplies could be obtained there; we were also admonished that our fresh water was coming short. We finished our wood chopping in four days, and on the morning of the fifth, I took a cruise along the beach some way up the river, and in some places was obliged to wade out very far to clear the bushes, and while thus wading, with the water up to my hips, I felt occasionally something that appeared to be an oyster. On reaching down for it, sure enough it was an oyster, nearly nine inches long, and on going a few rods farther, came on to an oyster bed, took off my trowsers, tied up the ends and filled both legs full of as fine oysters as ever were seen. Returned to our encampment, when other parties started off and soon returned richly laden. Some of the boys had in their rambles through the woods, discovered an extensive salt pond, which was certainly the whitest and best granulated salt that I had ever seen. The pond was nearly a mile in circumference. Next morning we went on shore to gather up, and while they were doing so, I took a boat with four men, and went up the river, and ran on to a point of land on the other side, of which was an opening. We shoved the boat in round the point and there before us, was a large basin over a mile in diameter, surrounded, or walled in with piles of sea-shells whale's ribs and vertebra. We soon ascertained that the tide was ebbing, and as it began to leave the beach, discovered that it was one vast oyster bed, and in less than two hours the tide had all gone out, and the sight was beyond description. Here were oysters eight and nine inches long, and millions of bushels of them. We gathered a quantity in the boat, and when the water would permit, returned to the ship, with the news of our discovery. Next day, half the ship's company and officers had a picnic on this immense oyster bed. Large fires were kindled all over the place, and roasted oysters were the order of the day, and on the *following* day the other half went on shore: so we all had a good tuck out of oysters. Mr. Percival had succeeded in finding Tumbez, but could not obtain anything eatable except oranges. He arrived however, rather too late for the great oyster supper.

We sailed from this place for Payta, but could get neither provisions nor water there, so we sailed again for Valparaiso, as there was no prospect of getting supplies until we reached there. After the whiskey was gone, our ship appeared like a heaven, compared to what she had usually been before. There were always some poor fellows in the brig,* and the cause of their confinement in almost every case was whiskey, and as often as twice a week all hands were called to witness punishment, at which time the prisoners were brought up,

* The place of confinement near the galley and under the charge of a sentinel.

and received, according to the nature of the crime, as many lashes as the captain thought proper to inflict. But now all is hushed, no quarrelling on the berth deck after the hammocks are piped down, not a man flogged for missing his muster, the lion had become the lamb. No insolence to officers, the metamorphosis was complete. It needed to be witnessed in order to be appreciated, and the effect of this accidental, though fortunate privation, was more visibly manifested in one unfortunate young man, than upon any other that came immediately under my notice. He was the eldest son of a highly respectable clergyman, who had preached for many years in a town near Boston. William N——n had been educated at college and had studied for the ministry; he became addicted to ardent spirits, and it grew upon him so rapidly that he was soon known as a drunkard.

His repeated intoxication truly brought the gray hairs of his too indulgent father, with sorrow to the grave. William, now an abandoned inebriate, went off, entered the United States service, as a mariner, (sea soldier) and commenced his first term of service on board the Macedonian. It happened that he hung his hammock, or his number was near my state-room door, on the berth deck. I had not been long on board the ship, before I became acquainted with his history, and was somewhat acquainted with his venerable father, and his younger brother. Many a time have I sat by his side, while he was raving drunk, and even when his brains were fairly soaked in whiskey, his language was beautiful; and when he had become sober, would bitterly lament his thirst for rum. He would sob and cry like a child. I have seen an officer, as a punishment, turn down the throat of this poor fellow, a half pint of lamp oil. He had been whipped at the gangway, kicked and knocked about like a dog, but all to no purpose. Whiskey had usurped the intellectual empire, and what *might* have been a brilliant mind, was doomed to be a blank.

William N——n was now clothed and in his right mind; his conversation showed deep contrition. But alas! it was only for a short time. The evil spirit had truly left him walking through dry places, seeking *rest*, and finding none. His mind had become swept and garnished, only for a brief interval. Very soon seven other spirits more wicked than the first, were to enter, and the last state of this man, may be worse than the first. I employed every argument in my power, to dissuade him from drinking any more whiskey when it should again be served as a ration—but he was too far gone to give it up now; he had been disgraced, publicly whipped, and now what had he to live for. Poor young man! Reader, this is no fiction, and if you are a grog drinker, your end may be like his. There were many more individual cases, where men who were before quarrelsome and insolent, now became really amiable, and I do not believe a more wonderful change was ever made among the same number of men in so short a time, as was wrought among the crew of the Macedonian, for the ninety-two days in which there was no whiskey. And in addition to this, we were on a short allowance of beef, pork, and bread. The latter had become wormy and scarcely fit for food; the peas, flour, and rice, were all expended, our water was short, and we were on an allowance of five pints for twenty-four hours.

We were fortunate enough one day during a heavy thunder storm, to catch a quantity of rain-water, from which we all had a good drink, and then filled up our breakers. While I was at work on board the Two Catherines, at San Blas, it rained in showers every day, but not minding it, as I was anxious to finish the mast, and as the weather was warm, had no fear of being injured by it, so kept wet throughout the day. At the wooding place, I exposed myself very imprudently wading about in the water, in assisting to get my timber on board. The day after leaving Payta, I was taken quite ill, and reported myself to the doctor, who gave me a dose of something, which was to be taken in a quart of warm water. I had hardly swallowed this nauseous draught, when I became delirious, and entirely prostrated, raving like a madman, but my messmates were by me, and kindly administered to my wants. My delirium finally abated, and was succeeded by a high fever that in a few days terminated in severe ague-fits, or fever and ague. The disease soon reduced me very low; I suffered much for want of water;

what I drank was so warm that it would not remain upon my stomach. The disease had so reduced me that it became necessary to have a man at my side, night and day. I was removed to the gun-deck, where there was a greater circulation of air. Near by me was a man who was taken down about as I was. He lingered a few days, and then died. Mr. Johnson, lieutenant of marines, also died with fever; he came to see me only a few days before he expired. Next our chaplain, Mr. Wilson, was taken down and died; likewise several seamen were taken off by this epidemic.

When a seaman died at night in the sick bay, early in the morning he was brought out and laid upon a grating, nearly under my hammock, so that frequently the first thing when I awoke, was to look under my hammock to see if there was a dead body there. I began slowly to recover but was so much reduced, it was some time, before I had gained sufficient strength to walk. During my convalescence I had a craving appetite, and nothing to satisfy it with, and when I had recovered sufficient strength, went about preparing to build the large boat before alluded to, as I was aware that our stay would be short at Valparaiso, and that the boat must be built during the time we remained there, whether it be long or short. I did everything in my power to regain my health, used much exercise, rubbing myself freely, either with a brush, or piece of canvas, bathing every morning, which by so doing, I gained strength very fast, and before we arrived at Valparaiso, had nearly recovered.

We had been absent about eight months, when our anchor was let go again abreast the old fort at Valparaiso. Our happy ship was now to be turned into a hell. The anchor was hardly down, before the purser was on shore making arrangements for provisioning the ship. Whiskey was the first article sent on board; then came beef, vegetables, and bread. The whiskey rations of half a pint to a man, was immediately served out; this, together with what was bought from the bomb boats by the men, occasioned a scene at night that is beyond description. I was aware of all this before we arrived, and tried to caution those that I knew would sway away again as soon as they could get it. Among these was my friend, the marine, William N——n, who, before eight o'clock, P. M., was blind drunk, and stowed away among the bags. Yelling and fighting was now the order of the night, as there was scarcely a sober man in the ship. The old master-at-arms was drunk among the rest, and before morning, twenty-three were in double irons for fighting, and insolence to officers. I made out in the tumult, to get a good supper, and think I ate as much at that meal, as would ordinarily serve me for three.

CHAPTER XI.

Plenty of news,—False report concerning Capt. Downes,—Refit the ship,—I build a launch,—Trouble with my men,—They get drunk,—Mystery how they obtain their liquor,—Discovery,—Strange milk fron a girl,—She is forbidden to come again,—Affair between Weems and an American captain,—Cowskinning,—Affair between an English captain and one of our lieutenants,—Duel,—Broken arm,—Arrival of part of the Essex,—Whaler's crew,—Dreadful condition,—Boat nearly finished,—Unfeeling conduct of the midshipman who shot Abercrombie,—All ready for sea,—Sail for Callao,—Arrive off San Lorenzo,—Indepentia discovered,—Cochrane's fleet under way,—Beat to quarters all ready,—Ship standing for us—Back out,—Maintop-sail,—Boarded,—Communication from his lordship,—Fill away,—Along-side the Admiral,—Mutual courtesy,—Pass on,—Excitement at Callao,—Anchor,—Esmaralda and gun boats,—Rejoicing among the American ships,—Declaration of Cochrane,—Noble conduct of Capt. Downes,—Receive a letter of censure from Cochrane,—Capt. Downe's reply,—Our ship's position,—Accident to myself,—Confined to my cot,—Danger of bleeding to death,—Wound heals,—Suspicious movement of the blockading squadron,—They approach towards the forts, who open fire upon them,—We prepare for an emergency,—Capt. Downes at Lima,—Attack on the Esmaralda,—Our position,—Exposed to the fire of all the batteries,—Success of Cochrane,—Esmaralda cut out,—Great loss of life,—Melancholy murder of our boat's crew, by the soldiers,—Escape of one man with the boat.

We had an abundance of news to hear, and a large amount of work to do. The first item of news that required attention was, that it was currently reported at Valparaiso, the reason that the Macedonian did not go into Callao on her cruise down the Coast was, that Lord Cochrane had forbidden her entering past the blockade. When this report reached the ear of Capt. Downes, as a matter of course, he felt quite indignant at such a base fabrication. But now the Macedonian was bound to go into Callao, *anyhow*. My boat timber was sent on shore, together with the armorer's forge, and the two blacksmiths. I took four carpenters with me, as they were the only men in the carpenter's crew that could handle tools well enough to work on a boat. I commenced right away in good earnest, as I was told that I could have but eighteen days in which to build her. She was thirty-three feet long and eight feet broad. We had a tent erected, and everything on shore that was wanted. The frigate lay very near us, so that going and coming occupied but little time. The first two or three days we got along very well. One day after dinner I found both the armorer, and his mate, drunk, under the forge. Where they got their rum from, I could not imagine. I roused them out, and gave the armorer a blowing up, as he is considered a petty officer and had no right to get drunk. He promised not to do it again if I would say nothing about it on board the ship.

Soon after I began to suspect the carpenters. I was under very strong apprehensions that they had some method of getting liquor unknown to me. They were sometimes stupid before nine o'clock A. M., and several times quite drunk in the afternoon, and often went on board the ship in that condition at sundown. I assured Mr. Maury, that I was unable to tell how they could get anything to get drunk on, as they were not out of my sight a moment through the day, neither did any one converse with them. Now, here was a mystery, and a very unpleasant one for me, as I was obliged to work like a slave, to get the boat off in time; and if they got drunk, it would of course throw more work upon me. The mystery however was soon solved, much to my relief.

Since we had been at work on shore, we left the ship soon after daylight, and took bread and milk for breakfast. The milk was brought by a very pretty Spanish girl, who came to the corner of the fort, and put her face out, and in a shrill, musical voice cried out, "Leche," "Leche," (milk, milk.) The sea was high up against the wall of the fort, so that she could not advance any nearer. One of the men would take two tin pots, and go for the milk. And surely there could not be rum in the milk, for I drank of it myself. But the dear little creature, apparently so innocent, was up to a thing or two. Now for the denouement—a midshipman on board the frigate who happened to have a spy-glass in his hand, was looking towards the place where the milk girl came, he saw her turn out the milk, and then take from her bosom two parcels which he thought were bladders of rum, this was good news for me. He related it soon after I came on board. As soon as I got on shore next morning, I told the men of the discovery; that I should forbid the girl coming any more with milk, particularly of that kind that came from her bosom. She came as usual at eight o'clock, "Leche." *O, you little jade*," said I, as soon as I was near enough to be heard by her. I had taken the pots for the milk, and when she had turned it out, I reached my hand for the bladders which she took out and handed me, each contained a pint of agua diente. I returned them, and forbade her coming with anything more for these men. I gave them the pots, telling them this was to be their last milk breakfast while they were at work on the boat. They were very sulky all that day, but went on board the ship sober, and continued so until we left the beach.

I observed, that on our arrival, we had much matter in the shape of news to listen to, so we will leave the boat and hear the gossip. You know we left Midshipman Weems at Valparaiso, upon the sick list, when we sailed from there about eight months since. He very soon recovered his health, and grew quite stout, and was a fine looking young man, and very gentlemanly in his deportment. Some six weeks before our arrival, the Boston ship P—t arrived from China. The Capt. H—l, being a very proud man, had but few associates besides those with whom he had business. A social ball was given by the American residents to which Capt. H—l and Weems were invited; the ball was well attended, the governor and many of the first families in town being present. Mr. Weems and Capt. H—l, were quite intimate during the evening, conversing freely about the Macedonian, and the result of her entering Callao through the blockade, and on other topics of this nature. Next day, while Weems was walking out in undress uniform, having on a white jacket and white pantaloons, making a very neat appearance however, he met Capt. H—l.

"Good morning, sir," said Weems, the other appearing

not to recognize him. Weems very modestly observed, "I had the pleasure of an introduction to you last evening, at Madam Blanco's."

"I don't know you, sir," and passed along.

This was too much for Weems. To be cut in this disrespectful and unceremonious manner was more than his proud spirit could bear. So he just observed, with some considerable emphasis, (I omit the oath,) "You *shall* know me," so turning immediately back and following hard after the captain, stepped into a store and purchased a Spanish cowhide; walking briskly, soon overtook Capt. H—l, who had then reached the busiest part of the town. He stepped up to him:

"You don't know me, sir, do you? My name is Rolla Weems, of the United States Navy," and fetching him several cuts across the shoulders, at the same time remarked: "I think you *will* know me after this." Capt. H—l attempted to clench Weems, but did not succeed. The people gathered round enjoying the fun, as cowhiding is generally a funny affair. H—l made but little resistance, although much mortified, and evidently much humbled. Weems was well known, and much respected, and when the matter was explained, the general sentiment was, that H—l had received no more than he deserved.

Weems then made an honorable proposition to him, that he stood ready for any alternative that he might choose, whether by a mutual apology or with any kind of weapon, it was quite immaterial to him. By the interposition of friends, this affair was mutually adjusted and both were subsequently on good terms.

Sometimes it is necessary to bring John Bull up all standing. One of our lieutenants, an active and intelligent young officer, stepped into a hotel one very warm afternoon, and called for an ice lemonade, went into an adjoining room and sat down. The drink was brought to him, but before he had tasted it, he heard loud words between the bar keeper and another. He overheard expressions which he thought applied to himself, and somewhat of a derogatory character. He went into the room to ascertain the nature of the difficulty, when he was grossly insulted by a tall, raw-boned Englishman, who it subsequently appeared was captain of an English whaler. He accused Lieut. T— of requiring the bar keeper to wait upon him first, thus claiming the precedence on the score of his being a naval officer. Lieut. T— in a very mild and gentlemanly manner, assured him that he labored under a mistake, as he only *ordered* his lemonade, and immediately retired to the next room. The bar keeper alone was responsible for the supposed mistake. This explanation was not at all satisfactory to Mr. Bull, who commenced another volley of vituperation, ending with this most insulting remark: "It's that swab upon your shoulder that protects you."

This was more than Lieut. T— could stand. And however unofficerlike and imprudent the act was, and moved by an irresistible impulse, he threw off his coat, and demanded of the landlord a pair of horse pistols that lie on the shelf, and that were loaded with balls.

"And now, sir," turning to the Englishman, "the obstacle is removed, and if you are a gentleman, take one of these pistols, choose your friend, and come with me to the beach."

By this time several persons had collected, and hearing the altercation remained as spectators. The Englishman finding that he could not well back out, with evident reluctance accepted the challenge, took his companion, and T— took an acquaintance who happened to come in, all of whom proceeded to the beach, about two hundred yards distant. Arrangements were soon made, and the English captain had the first fire and missed. T— deliberately raised his pistol and fired, the ball struck the captain's right arm just above the elbow, and broke the bone short off. The parties then returned to the hotel. A surgeon was called and the difficulty amicably settled. The "broken-winged captain," subsequently made several visits on board the frigate, as a guest of Lieut. T—.

While lying at Valparaiso this time, a ship arrived that had picked up one of the boats of the ill-fated whale ship, Essex, that had been struck by a whale, her bows stove in when she almost instantly sunk. The crew at the time were all off in their boats, busily at work among a school of sperm whales, leaving only the ship keeper on board. The crews in the several boats, had but a small portion of provision, with some fresh water in their boats. I believe subsequent accounts stated that the remains of dead bodies had been found on an uninhabited and desolate island, which were thought to be part of the Essex's crew.

The boat that was picked up, I think, had three living men having protracted their miserable existence by eating the dead bodies of their companions, who died in the boat. I saw them after they had landed, and truly they presented a shocking appearance. They were well taken care of and drew much sympathy from the benevolent people of Valparaiso.

As we have now told you all the news, we return to our boat again. We have but one week longer in which to finish our job. The frigate is nearly ready, having her provisions and water on board, and very little to do to the ship. I cannot help noticing a circumstance, though trifling as it may appear, yet goes to show how thoroughly a heart may be steeled against the smallest feeling of humanity, and wholly void of any restraining principle.

G—n who shot A—e, only a few months since, and whose grave is near by where we are at work, frequently comes to this place, practising with his pistol, at a target placed almost directly over the grave of his murdered victim. The target being the size of a man, and he aiming at the heart. I think I have never seen a human being that I more heartily despised and for whom I had a greater contempt, than this man. He was neither a seaman nor a navigator, and yet he pretended to excel in both these branches. I had occasion to tell him one evening, that he knew nothing. He began to "bristle up," but soon found that he had hold of the wrong customer.

Our sailing day came, we had everything on board, weighed our anchor, and were now to let Lord Cochrane know that the Macedonian must enter Callao, *blockade, or no blockade.*

In getting our anchor we had some little delay in consequence of breaking and rendering useless our spar-deck capstan.

On arriving off St. Lorenzo, we soon saw that in all probability there would be an attempt made by Cochrane to stop us. A ship was now standing out under full sail, evidently having been sent by the admiral to forbid our proceeding any further. The whole blockading fleet were now under way and they also were coming towards us.

We beat to quarters, had all bulk heads down, deck sanded, guns double shotted, and matches lit; the first ship was now up with us. the captain stepped into the gangway to hail us, and as we had considerable way on the ship, Capt. Downes, very politely backed his maintop-sail to give the other an opportunity of making any communication from his Lordship that he desired. He also backed his mainyard, lowered a boat and sent an officer on board our ship, with a verbal request from Lord Cochrane that Capt. Downes would not persist in violating the blockade. When this officer got upon our deck and saw this preparation, he actually turned pale. Our captain's reply was, "Please communicate to his Lordship that it is my intention to anchor in Callao harbor before sundown at all hazards; and if his Lordship has any further communications to make, he must be quick about it. Fill away the maintop-sail, sir."

The Chilian officer went into his boat, his ship, (Indepentia, 22 guns,) was now quite near us, so that we could easily perceive that they kept their guns trained upon us, and we, of course, kept ours upon them. I am sure that we could have blown them out of water in a very few minutes.

We were now going ahead at a pretty good rate, and very soon were surrounded by the whole squadron. The O'Higgins,* Cochrane's ship, was close along-side of us, within half pistol shot. Lord Cochrane came to the gangway, and in a pompous tone, hailed:

"What ship is that?"

"This is the U. S. Frigate, Macedonian."

"How does Capt. Downes do?"

"Quite well, I thank you. How is your Lordship?"

We had now passed the O'Higgins, and were nearly alongside the Lotaro, a 50 gun ship, under the command of Capt. Guise, he however said nothing to us. We perceived the spy-glasses on board Cochrane's ship were busily employed in

*A 44 gun frigate taken from the Peruvians in the early part of the war.

reconnoitering us ; we really expected a brush, and so did the inhabitants and soldiers at Callao ; for as we approached the town, we discerned that the forts and house tops were lined and crowded with people. Had Cochrane opposed our entrance, it is very certain that with the excited feelings of our crew, we should have persisted in the attempt, while there remained a man to load a gun. Our arrival was a matter of rejoicing among the merchant ships; Cochrane had publicly declared that not a ship should leave Callao with a Spanish dollar on board; and there were many ships, both English and American, lying here, and all of which had large sums on board, and felt much anxiety on account of Cochrane's threat.

Cap. Downes received much credit and many compliments for his determination and perseverance in running through the blockade, and safely effecting an anchorage at Callao. Lord Cochrane, well knowing the determined character of Capt. Downes, and the efficiency of the Macedonian and her crew, (for he had been on board at Valparaiso) that notwithstanding the great superiority in number of ships and men, an action with her might, and most certainly would, retard his contemplated attack on the Esmaralda, besides the deserved retribution that would fall upon him, as soon as the attack should be made known in the United States.

All these things he very probably took into consideration, and did not resist us. Early on the morning after our anchorage, Capt. Downes received rather a tart note from his Lordship, severely censuring him for violating a regular constituted blockade. Capt. Downes, in reply, assured his Lordship that he should remain at Callao until all the American merchant ships had sailed ; he also should protect them until out of danger, and should keep the Macedonian in a continued state of preparation, to repel any undue attack* which might be made upon her, and declined any further communication, as it might have a tendency to vitiate his neutrality, and compromise the United States.

Our ship was moored close in with the shore, and abreast

* There had been a report among the ships at Callao, that Lord Cochrane had declared it as his determination to destroy the Macedonian, should she attempt to violate the blockade.

of a hot shot battery, a short distance astern the Peruvian frigate Esmaralda, of 44 guns, who was taking specie on board for the mother country. Between our ship and the Esmaralda were two Spanish gunboats, well manned and armed, as a protection against any attack which might be made on the Esmaralda.

I must here record an accident that befel me, and that came near using me up. While we were beating to quarters, previous to entering Callao, I had occasion to make a cleat for the security of one of the boats. I was amidships, on the gun-deck, and was working with a carpenter's adze; had just made a blow, when the man who was loading the gun near to me, hit my arm with the sponge, which caused me to receive the blow on my instep, severing the cords leading to the toes, besides making a fearful gash. I had the presence of mind to grasp my leg just above the wound, and thus prevent the blood from flowing so rapidly, as it otherwise would have done. I was taken below and laid upon the table, which was already prepared for cutting off legs and arms, should Cochrane have resisted us. I suffered the most excruciating pain while the doctors were getting the ends of the cords together, and tying them up; they were afraid that I should bleed to death while under the operation, and the way I sung out was a caution to doctors. The wound was dressed, I was put into a cot, and lay there eleven days and nights, in much suffering. During this time, the wound broke out afresh, and it was with much difficulty that the doctor succeeded in stopping it, and assured me that if it broke out again, he feared that it would be impossible to save my life; the nature of the wound being such as to make it extremely difficult to stop the arteries. But through the goodness of God, it healed, and I was not, as I feared I should be, deprived of the free action of my foot.

While sitting on deck, one Sunday, I think on the 4th of November, I observed the blockading squadron get under way from under St. Lorenzo, where they usually lay, and come towards the anchorage at Callao. When they had approached to nearly within gunshot of the forts, the latter began to blaze away at the ships, which was a foolish move on the part of the Spaniards, for it gave Cochrane an excellent opportunity of measuring his distance, which was to be as near the Esmaralda as possible, and at the same time be clear of the shot from the forts. The ships anchored in a safe position, but did not furl their sails.

I was now fully assured, in my own mind, that there was something in the wind, and some decisive step soon to be taken. Was it the capture of the Macedonian for running the blockade? Or the merchant ships, on board of which were large sums in dollars and in virgin silver? The forts were thronged with men, and bayonets glistening in the sun, the hot shot batteries along the beach all manned. We also adopted precautionary steps, in case anything should happen, which was to place the launch under the bow, with a stream anchor and cable, in case we should have to slip our chains. Capt. Downes was at Lima, and several of our officers on shore; the latter, however, came on board at sundown. Two of the lieutenants of the Esmaralda had dined on board our ship, and at 9 P. M., just as I had turned in to my hammock, which hung over the pumps on the gun-deck, heard them bid good night, and go on board their own ship.

I soon fell asleep, and think in less than half an hour was awoke by a tremendous noise. I jumped from my hammock as well as I could with my lame foot, noticing that our ship was in great commotion.

I looked out of the gun-deck ports, and saw the Esmaralda, apparently on fire, caused by an incessant blaze of musketry. She was very near us; we could distinctly hear every order that was given. "Cut away anything but sheets and halliards." "Let fall the top-sails, bear a hand there aloft, Britons. Here's a half a dozen Spaniards in the tops, sir, what will we do with 'em?" "Heave the —— rascals overboard," says some one on deck. "Hurrah, my hearties! she is ours. Jump into the boats, Britons! Get out a towline." During this time, we could see the fight on the gun-deck, while Cochrane had charge of the spar-deck, and it was he that cut the chain cables.

The forts were pouring their shot all around us, and many of them red-hot. There was a hot shot battery right abreast

CUTTING OUT OF THE ESMARALDA.

of our ship, on the beach. *Casas-Matas*, a tremendous castle, with over three hundred and sixty guns, were blazing away. The shot flew round us like hail, cutting away our cross-jack yard, and much of our rigging. Many of the red-hot shot struck very near us, and it was astonishing how far they could be seen while sinking. The firing during this time, was tremendous, like one continued peal of thunder, The musketry did us but little harm, the bullets just striking the side, and falling harmless in the water. There was not a breath of wind, and here we were, having slipped our chains, but dare not attempt to run out our stream anchor, for the very moment we should attempt to do this, our boat would be cut to pieces with the shot from the shore, for they were under the impression all this time, that we were assisting Cochrane.

In the meantime, they had towed the Esmaralda out clear of the shot. They then threw over the dead bodies, and hauled her along-side the O'Higgins, sent all the wounded ashore in their own boats, in charge of their own officers.

I shall never forget the impressions of the dawning morning, as the sailors call it. A cloud of powder and smoke lay all around like a dense fog; through it we could just discern the fleet with their valuable prize, and midway between them and the shore, were two gun-boats adrift, every soul belonging to them had been killed.

Here we lay, having drifted a half a mile from our anchors, and now hanging by a stream anchor. The English frigate Hyperion, that came in a few days before, lay quietly at anchor, having been, during the time out of reach of the shot, and as the sun rose, everything had a blood-like appearance; the sun himself looked like a huge ball of rayless fire.

Captain Downes at this time was at Lima; we were ignorant of his fate.

We had hitherto depended upon the shore for provisions, and a consultation of the officers was held to consider the expediency of sending the market boat to the landing, for our beef and vegetables; and it was their unanimous opinion, that there would be no impropriety in doing so. Accordingly a boat was called away, and the purser's steward, steerage and wardroom stewards, with a midshipman and ten men, composing the crew, went into the boat, but with downcast looks.

Mr. Smull, the purser's steward, observed when going into the boat, "*Well, I am now going to my grave!*" and, poor fellow, it was too true. When they had taken their seats and had shoved off, they looked as if a dreadful foreboding of their approaching death hung over them. Not a word was spoken; they pulled slowly along as though going to their own funeral, until they had reached within the boat's length of the steps. The bowman had tossed his oar, and almost instantly all but four were shot dead. The soldiers, seeing them coming kept hidden behind a wall, until they were near enough for good aim, and then fired. The purser's steward being only wounded, jumped overboard, when a soldier immediately got into the boat and drove a bayonet through his body, while he hung on to the boat's stern, asking for mercy. Mr. Marshall, the midshipman, in order to escape the bayonet of a soldier, jumped overboard also, and tried to drown himself by keeping under the bottom of the boat; not being able to remain there, came up, and was struck on the head with the but-end of a musket, but was rescued from death by a Spanish officer, who took him in charge and conveyed him to the hospital. Another man was shot through the body, but was not killed, he also, was taken to the hospital.

The only survivor who remained in bottom of the boat, as if dead, after she had drifted off some distance, arose, and with an oar, got off from the shore and was picked up by a boat from the Hyperion, who took our boat in tow, and brought her along-side our frigate; and what a sight did this boat present! Blood and brains scattered round upon the inside as though a bullock had been killed in her. The bodies had been taken out by the Spaniards, probably for the purpose of getting their clothes.

CHAPTER XII.

Boat rescued by a boat from the Hyperion,—Is brought along-side the frigate,—Horrid sight,—Some taken to the hospital,—Their danger of being murdered,—Erroneous impression,—Manner of their rescue,—Fugitives escape to our ship,—Their dreadful narrative,—Danger of Capt. Downes,—Reward offered for his head,—Secreted by the Viceroy,—Our unpleasant and unsafe position,—Awful suspense respecting our captain and the midshipman on shore,—Sinking the schooner Rampart, of Baltimore,—Escape of captain and crew,—Big Dick,—Send a flag of truce,—Result,—Conversation,—Midshipman Marshall and the wounded men,—Brought off,—Mistake regretted,—Permission to visit the shore,—Obtain necessaries,—Permission to haul the ship back to the old position,—Intelligence of the captain by an Indian,—Boats fitted,—Proceed to Chorillias,—Captain returns in safety,—Is cheered,—Receives the congratulations of the Americans,—A general regret among the Peruvians,—Ascertain that there are a number of Americans prisoners at Casas-Matas,—Capt. Downes demands them,—Permission to visit them,—Their miserable condition,—Contribution made for them,—Supplied with every comfort,—Promised their liberty in 90 days,—Removed to more comfortable quarters,—Had endured much suffering,—Joy at the prospect of being once more at liberty,—Fears of the Viceroy,—Large amount of specie on board the merchant ships,—Method of getting money on board merchant ships,—An American ship captured by Cochrane,—Came in to Guamas,—Fleet get ready to sail,—Cochrane's threats,—Order of sailing,—Ordered not to admit a boat along-side,—Arrangement of the English frigate Hyperion,—Beat to quarters,—Fleet sail,—Attempt to stop the ships,—Get out safe, and return to Guamas,—Account of the capture of the Esmaralda.

THOSE that were taken to the hospital, were in danger of being murdered while in their beds. There were many of the crew of the Esmaralda here, that were wounded in the fight, and were sent on shore by Cochrane, the morning after the capture. These desperate wretches, full of the impression that our ship was accessory to the capture, fairly gnashed their teeth with rage against our poor fellows that were so fortunately rescued from death; and made several unsuccessful attempts to get at them, in order to murder them.

I should have stated that Mr. Marshall, and the other man

who was shot through the body, were rescued from the hands of the infuriated soldiers, by a kind-hearted Spanish officer, who, with much difficulty succeeded in getting them to the hospital.

Our ship was now thronged with fugitives from the shore, who were principally Englishmen, but there were some Americans among them, all of whom gave a horrid account of the slaughter on the night of the battle.

Gangs of armed and desperate soldiers perambulated the town, shooting down every foreigner they could find. One man told us of his narrow escape, as follows:

"Himself and his shipmate were sitting in a grogshop, and when the soldiers passed by, they looked in, and seeing these men, were about to shoot them, but the landlord forbade them firing in his premises, and told the men they must run for their lives, which they did. We both made a rush through them, and ran for the landing-place. I turned short round, and got among some old casks, and crawled into an empty hogshead. My poor shipmate was overtaken, and I saw them cut his throat from ear to ear. I now began to shiver in the wind, for I expected they would look for me, which, had they done, would certainly have found me, and would soon have dispatched old 'Jim Carrol.'"

It was well known on shore that Capt. Downes was at Lima; parties were sent to search for him; a reward was offered for his head. Capt. Downes was soon made acquainted with these facts, and immediately sought the protection of the Viceroy, as he did not think himself safe at the house of the American minister.

The Viceroy was fully convinced that the Macedonian had no sort of participation in the Esmaralda affair; and knowing the excited state of feeling that prevailed, particularly among the lower class, and fearing that if it should be known that Capt. Downes was in the palace, a mob might collect, and thus create a tumult which nothing but the spilling of blood could allay. He therefore had him secretly conveyed to the mint, where he was comfortably provided for.

The Macedonian lay some distance from her former moorings, and was not in a safe place, if it should come on to blow. Here we were, without provisions, and in a state of the utmost anxiety with regard to our captain, and the midshipman and two men that were on shore. We dared not yet venture to communicate with the shore, for only a few hours since, an American schooner, Rampart, of Baltimore, that had been chartered by a Spanish house, at Lima, attempted to enter the mole in order to receive her cargo. The American ensign was flying at her mast-head, and just as she was rounding the pier-head, the batteries opened upon her, shot away the head of her foremast, and sunk her.

The crew had barely time to escape with their lives, and among them was the celebrated "Big Dick," a gigantic and most powerful negro, who reached the frigate in a very small boat. This was done in the short space of an hour.

Big Dick had a narrow chance for his life; for just as he had stepped into the boat, with his hand still upon the schooner's rail, a shot cut off the piece where his hand was, passed within a few inches of his head, and nearly knocked the breath out of him.

In this state of uncertainty, our first lieutenant concluded to try what efficacy there might be in a flag of truce. Accordingly, on the fourth day, a boat was prepared with an American flag at the stern, a white flag forward; a lieutenant and a midshipman, and the boats crew all neatly dressed. The officer of the boat had received orders to proceed towards the captain of the port's office, and to lie on his oars, out of the reach of a musket shot, and there remain one hour. And if, in that time no official notice was taken of the flag, to return to the frigate; but, should the captain of the port, or master of marine, or any one having authority to communicate, come off, then put the following interrogatories, (which were in writing,) and note the answers with your pencil:

"Do you know any thing of Capt. Downes?"

"What is the condition of our wounded men, who were taken to the hospital?"

"Can we obtain our provisions from the shore?"

"Can we haul up to our old moorings?"

According to orders, the boat proceeded to her peace, and

had hardly hauled in their oars, when a boat was seen coming off to them, with a huge Spanish ensign at the stern.

When within talking distance, an officer who was in a rich uniform, arose, and in a very polite manner, took off his chapeau, and enquired what was wanting, through the interpreter. The interrogatories were put in the order in which they were written. The answer to the first was as follows:

"I believe Capt. Downes is at Lima. We do not know that any harm has been done to him."

To the second, — "I do not know anything about them, but presume that they are well taken care of."

To the third, — "I cannot imagine any difficulty in obtaining what you wish from the shore."

And to the fourth, — "I will proceed to the office of the intendent and ascertain, and if you please to accompany me, you can have all the particulars very soon."

The officer declined doing this, as it would be contrary to his orders; but replied to the Spanish officer that he would return to the Macedonian, and report what had already passed and would probably be at the same place to-morrow at nine o'clock, A. M. Accordingly, on the morrow, the boat with the same officers and crew proceeded to the place, but with additional orders that the permits should be given in writing, as nothing verbal would be considered official.

When our boat had arrived at the appointed place, the captain of the port came immediately off, bringing Mr. Marshall, and Jacob Bull, the seaman who had been shot through the body. The captain of the port very much regretted the unfortunate mistake, as all were now fully satisfied that the Macedonian was perfectly neutral in the affair of the Esmaralda. The port admiral had instructed him to say, that the Macedonian had full permission to return to her former mooring, and also declared with much vehemence, that the officers of the Macedonian could visit the shore without the slightest fear of molestation, and that our market boat could also come to the landing-place in perfect safety.

The officer of our boat very politely acknowledged the courtesy of the captain of the port, and replied to him, that as this would in all probability become a government matter, he was instructed by the first lieutenant of the Macedonian, in absence of the captain, to request a written and official permit for what he had just stated to be so generously conceded by the port admiral; adding, that he would wait until the required document could be furnished.

The captain of the port assented, went directly ashore, and in two hours returned with a paper containing all that was required. Mr. Marshall was much bruised about the head and shoulders, and told us of the attempts that were made by the Spaniards to get into their wards to kill them. Bull was not dangerously wounded, as the ball had struck the ribs without touching any vital part.

On this same afternoon a small Indian canoe came alongside with a note from Capt. Downes, dated at Chorillias, a small place just south of Lima. Capt. Downes had fled there, and was still in his hiding-place, not knowing but that the feeling towards him was still hostile. He requested Mr. Maury to fit out the pinnace with a gun in the bow, and have her well armed with muskets, with a good boat's crew; also to arm and man his gig, and send both boats under guidance of the Indian, to a place which the Indian would designate. This was truly good news for every soul on board. The prevailing gloom and uncertainty respecting his fate, so visibly depicted in every countenance, was now entirely removed. Things now began to assume a cheerful aspect, although there was a general sentiment of sympathy and regret, for the cruel death of our shipmates, which was felt by every one, yet as in all cases of affliction, time soon fills the chasm, and it is highly proper that it should be so; for if we kept continually mourning over events that have passed, and against which we could have had no control, while we followed what might have appeared to us the most judicious course, we should be entirely unfitted for subsequent duty.

The boats being all ready the night before, started early next morning just after daylight. The Indian said he thought they would be back early in the afternoon. Our market boat had been ashore. We now had a good supply of fruit and fresh beef, and a good dinner for the captain.

At about two o'clock the quarter-master reported the boats in sight. Every eye was now eagerly directed towards the boats; every spy-glass was in requisition, and so earnest was every one to get a sight, that they fairly pulled the glasses out of each other's hand. Directly one says:

"The captain is not there!" which for a few moments was a damper; then again:

"Yes he is!"

Up went the mercury again.

"No, sir; that's not Capt. Downes."

"Yes it is; and there is some one beside him."

By this time the boats had approached near enough to ascertain for a certainty that Capt. Downes was in the boat, (pinnace,) and another with him, and it was also ascertained that he had disguised himself by shaving off his whiskers, and wearing a citizen's black coat.

The boats now being within a hundred yards, orders were given to cheer ships. Accordingly the rigging and yards were manned, and all eagerly watched for the signal. As soon as his foot touched the deck, there went up three as hearty cheers as ever came from the lungs of men, and a more hearty and sincere welcome no man ever witnessed. He was accompanied by an English captain and his lady, who solicited the favor of a passage, rather than to risk a journey by land during the excited state of feeling that pervaded the country. The account Capt. Downes gave of what took place with regard to himself in Lima, I have stated in a previous page. The merchant captains came to make their congratulations, for, had any accident happened to Capt. Downes, the event would have seriously affected their interests. The death of our men had a serious effect upon him, and very much diminished the joy he felt for his own escape. The frigate was hauled back into her old place, and was soon put to rights again. Many of the merchant ships had received damages by the shot from the shore, all of which, however, were soon repaired. The hasty and inconsiderate massacre of our men was deeply regretted by the authorities both at Callao and Lima. The Viceroy in his communication with the American minister, manifested the deepest sorrow, and as we are told that good frequently comes of evil, the saying was manifestly true in this case.

We had ascertained, shortly after our arrival at Callao, that there were a number of Americans who had been taken by the Peruvians, on board Chilian vessels of war, and who had been nearly two years in close confinement in the castle. On enquiry, Capt. Downes found it to be so, and immediately demanded their release as American citizens. Permission was obtained from the governor for the officers of the Macedonian to visit these prisoners, and to do anything for them for their comfort and convenience, that we thought proper, consistent with the rules of the prison.

A lieutenant and four midshipmen visited the prison and found thirty-five Americans, and about as many Englishmen, some of whom, as the report had stated, had been confined there nearly two years; during which time they had not seen daylight. Their cells were lighted by dim lamps, they were much emaciated, and several of their unfortunate companions had died of starvation. They were heavily chained, and scarcely able to crawl, and such were their emotions on seeing these friends, that they cried like children, taking hold of the officer's hands, and nearly devouring them with kisses. There were some who had not been so long in confinement, who were young men, on whom the hardships of a Spanish prison had not such a visible effect; there were about twenty of the latter, and to whom our officers communicated the object of their visit.

They were all assured that relief, if not liberty, was at hand. This was a happy day with these poor wretches, who, in all probability, would never again have seen the light of the sun, had it not been for this accidental discovery.

On the return of the officers to the ship, a contribution was immediately set on foot, and about three hundred dollars in money was raised, besides clothing of every sort, books, paper, pens, slates, and a quantity of beds, blankets, provisions; in fact everything that could be thought of that would contribute to their comfort. No distinction was made between English and American, all were claimed as Americans, and received the same protection.

When these things were carried to them, their joy knew no bounds. It was necessary to appoint six of the most healthy among the younger, to take charge of the articles, and to see that nothing was wasted. Capt. Downes made a business of waiting on the Viceroy, in order to effect the release of these unfortunate men.

The Viceroy evidently felt that the massacre of the Macedonian's men would be a subject of claim by the United States government, and that by conceding to the demand of Capt. Downes, in delivering up these prisoners, it might in some measure, ameliorate the affair; so he promised Capt. Downes that he would liberate them on our return to Callao, which would probably be in about three months; in the meantime, they should be removed to a more comfortable part of the prison, should be allowed the open air during the day.

These glad tidings put new life in the poor fellows, and when they were told that they would be liberated in three months from our departure, they really felt anxious for us to sail, notwithstanding our visits gave them such joy. And who, that dives into the mystery of human nature, can help seeing a full development of that innate desire for happiness which in many instances, appears a mass of contradictions. As in the case of these poor prisoners; their eyes glistened with joy at the sight of their benefactors, yet they wished them to go, that the time for their emancipation might the sooner come.

I have already mentioned that the merchant ships generally had large amounts of specie on board, and were waiting to be convoyed out by the Macedonian. Specie was prohibited from being taken out of the country, and it required much skill and some risk to get it on board the ships. The manner in which this was done, is as follows:

A merchant on shore, wishing to put money on board a ship, notifies a waterman, (who generally has two or more boats in his employ,) that he wishes to put a quantity of dollars, or virgin silver, on board such a ship. The Custom House boats are constantly prowling about for the purpose of making seizures.

These watermen, well understand these fellows, and with few exceptions, generally elude them. The waterman agrees to put the money on board for a stipulated premium, he is taken on board the ship and introduced to the captain and mate who are always to be in readiness to receive the money the instant it comes along-side. The waterman now obtains from somewhere three, four, or five thousand dollars, which he carries safely to the ship, where it is counted, and for which he takes a receipt signed by the captain and mate. He takes this receipt to the merchant and receives the amount and premium. This he also carries safely on board, and brings back his receipt, and so on. In this manner no one runs any risk but the boatmen, who often make five thousand dollars on one ship. Sometimes however, there happens fearful fights between these watermen and the Custom House soldiers, but as the former are much more numerous than the latter and always hang together and assist each other, it very seldom happens that they lose anything; although there have been instances where they have met with heavy losses.

One morning at about sunrise, a few days before we sailed, we saw a ship coming into the bay, under American colors, and evidently with the intention of running the blockade, but very soon we saw the Lotaro under way, she being the weathermost ship, and nearest the merchantman. There was a good breeze and it was certain that the Lotaro would head her off, and thus she would become a prize, which was the case. We saw them take possession of her, and both she, and the Lotaro went round to Guamas, a harbor a few miles north of St. Lorenzo, and in possession of the Chilians, and it is here that communication is had with Gen. San. Martin's army, who are encamped near the walls of Lima.

In the course of the day we learned, but from what source I cannot tell, that the captured ship was an American, and had on board for cargo, muskets, pistols, powder, and all sorts of warlike stores. This made Capt. Downes anxious to get away for he had determined on her rescue.

The fleet were notified of our time of sailing, which was on the morning of the second day from the notice. Every ship must be ready for getting under way at daylight, so as to have the advantage of the land breeze. The order of sailing was as follows:

The merchant ships to form two lines, and to proceed ahead of the frigates, and all who were armed with cannon or small arms, to have them loaded in order to prevent any boats from boarding them, also to pay no attention to any hailing from the blockading ships, and to put all the sail on which could be prudently carried. The English frigate Hyperion, not being ready for sea, sent two cutters well manned and armed for the protection of the English merchantman. We also had two cutters, well provided with small arms, and sufficiently manned, to prevent any of our ships from being boarded.

On the morning appointed, the ships were all ready, and the dropping of our fore top-sail was the signal for them to get under way, which they did in good style. The Boston ship, Panther, Capt. Austin, took the lead: as soon as it was discovered by the blockading fleet, that we were under way, they unmoored, and were quickly under sail. His Lordship was at this time confined to his bed in consequence of a gun-shot wound in the thigh, which he received on the deck of the Esmaralda. The Lotaro had gone, so there remained only the O'Higgins, Independentia, several small vessels, and one other ship, the name of which I have forgotten.

We thought it possible, that Cochrane might have the impudence or temerity to stop some of the ships, and possibly, he might have it in contemplation, to give us battle, thinking that he might get a better haul now, than when we went in. But we were at quarters all ready for him; running along under our three top-sails.

Cochrane's ship was now abreast of us, within pistol shot, and, although he was wounded, yet he evidently directed every movement of his ship. We kept perfect silence our guns trained upon him. We saw a boat from the O'Higgins, going towards the Panther, she was not allowed to come along-side, and retired with a flea in their ear. The merchant ships were now outside of St. Lorenzo, with everything on which they could wear. We now made sail, and were soon up with them. Our kind neighbors very prudently tacked ship, and sneaked back again to their den. We continued with our charge until the land was out of sight, and then stood back for Guamas.

The following is the English account of the capture of the Esmaralda:

"While the liberating army under San Martin were removing to Anson, Lord Cochrane, with part of his squadron, anchored in the outer roads of Callao, the seaport of Lima. The inner harbor was guarded by an extensive system of batteries, admirably constructed, and bearing the name of the Castle of Callao.

"The merchant ships, as well as the men-of-war, consisting at the time, of the Esmaralda, a large 40 gun frigate, and two sloops-of-war, were moored under the guns of the castle, within a semi-circle of fourteen gunboats and a boom made of spars chained together. Lord Cochrane, having previously reconnoitered the formidable defence in person, undertook, on the 5th of November, the desperate enterprise of cutting out the Spanish frigate, although she was known to be fully prepared for an attack. His Lordship proceeded in fourteen boats, containing 240 men, all volunteers from the different ships of the squadron, in two divisions, one under the immediate orders of Capt. Crosbie, the other under Capt. Guise, both officers commanding ships of the Chilian squadron. At midnight, the boats having forced their way across the boom, Lord Cochrane, who was leading, rowed along-side the first gunboat, and taking the officer by surprise, proposed to him, with a pistol at his head, the alternative of silence or death. No reply was made, the boats pushed on unobserved, and Lord Cochrane, mounting the Esmaralda's side, was the first to give the alarm. The sentinel on the gangway, levelled his piece and fired, but was instantly cut down by the coxswain, and his Lordship, though wounded in the thigh, at the same moment stepped on deck. The frigate being boarded with no less gallantry on the other side by Capt. Guise, who met Lord Cochrane midway on the quarter-deck, and also by Capt. Crosbie, the after part of the ship was soon carried, sword in hand. The Spaniards rallied on the forecastle, where they made a desperate resistance, until overpowered by a fresh party of seamen and mariners, headed by Lord Cochrane. A gallant stand was again made after a short time on the main deck, but before 1 o'clock, the ship was captured, her cables cut, and she was steered triumphantly out of the harbor, under the fire of the whole of the north force of the castle.

"The Hyperion, an English, and the Macedonian, an American frigate, which were at anchor close to the scene of action, got under way, when the attack commenced, and in order to prevent their being mistaken by the batteries for the Esmaralda, showed distinguishing signals. But Lord Cochrane, who had foreseen and provided even for this minute circumstance, hoisted the same lights as the English and American frigates, and thus rendered it impossible for the batteries to discriminate between the three ships. The Esmaralda was in consequence, very little injured by the shot.

"The Spaniards had upwards of 120 men killed and wounded; the Chilians 11 killed and 30 wounded. This loss was a death blow to the Spanish naval force in that quarter of the world; for although there were still two Spanish frigates and some smaller vessels in the Pacific, they never afterwards ventured to show themselves, but left Lord Cochrane undisputed master of the coast. The skill and gallantry displayed by Lord Cochrane, both in planning and conducting this astonishing enterprise, so peculiarly his own, and so much in character with the great deeds of his early life, that a copy of his instructions for the action, and his subsequent dispatch, will be read with much interest."

Copy of Lord Cochrane's preparatory memorandum to the Chilian squadron, dated on board the Chilian States ship, O'Higgins, 1st November, 1820.

"The boats will proceed, towing the launches, in two lines parallel to each other, which are to be at the distance of three boat's length asunder. The second line will be under the charge of Capt. Guise. Each boat will be under the charge of a volunteer commissioned officer, so far as circumstances permit, and the whole under the immediate command of the admiral. The officers and men are all to be dressed in white jackets, frocks, or shirts, and armed with pistols, sabres, knives, tomahawks or pikes. Two boat-keepers are to be appointed to each boat, who, on no pretence whatever, shall quit their respective boats, but are to remain therein, and take care that the boats do not get adrift. Each boat is to be provided with one or more axes, or sharp hatchets, which are to be kept swung to the girdle of the boat-keepers.

"The frigate Esmaralda being the chief object of the expedition, the whole force is first to attack that ship, which, when carried, is not to be cut adrift, but is to remain in possession of the patriotic seamen, to ensure the capture of the rest.

"In securing the frigate, the Chilian seamen and mariners are not to cheer as if they were Chilians; but in order to deceive the enemy, and give time for completing the work, are to cheer 'Vive el Roi!'

"The two brigs-of-war are to be fired on by the musketry from the Esmaralda, and are to be taken possession of by Lieutenants Esmond and Morgall, in the boats they command, which being done, they are to be cut adrift, run out, and anchor in the offing as quick as possible.

"The boats of the Independentia are to busy themselves in turning adrift all the outward Spanish merchant ships. And the boats of the O'Higgins and Lotaro under Lieutenants Bell and Robertson, are to set fire to one or more of the headmost hulks; but these are not to be cut adrift, so as to fall down upon the rest.

"The watchword, or parole and countersign, should the white dress not be sufficient distinction in the dark, are 'Gloria,' to be answered by 'Victoria.'

(Signed,) COCHRANE.

Whether Lord Cochrane really expected to extend his operations beyond the capture of the frigate, or whether he merely wished to inspire his people with courage by making the main object appear only a part of the enterprise, is uncertain; but in either case, the effect could not fail to be valuable.

The foregoing memorandum being addressed to Englishmen and North Americans, was written in English. The following letter I have never seen, except in the original Spanish translation of Admiral Lord Cochrane's dispatch to General San Martin, commander-in-chief of the liberating army of Peru:

"On board the Chilian States ship O'Higgins, before Callao, Nov. 14, 1820.—Most excellent Sir: The efforts of his Excellency, the Supreme Director, and the sacrifices of the patriots of the South to acquire the dominion of the Pacific, have hitherto been frustrated chiefly by the enormous strength of the batteries of Callao, (which being superior to those of Algiers or Gibraltar) rendered every attack against the naval force of the enemy impracticable with any class or number of ships-of-war. Nevertheless, being desirous of advancing the cause of national liberty and political independence, which is the great object your Excellency has in view, and to promote the happiness of mankind, I was anxious to dispel the charm which heretofore has paralyzed our naval efforts. With this intention, I carefully examined the batteries, the ships-of-war and the gunboats in this port, and being satisfied that the frigate Esmaralda would be cut out by men resolved to do their duty, I immediately gave orders to the captains of the Independentia and Lotaro to prepare their boats, and acquainted them that the value of that frigate, together with the reward offered in Lima for the capture of any of the ships of Chili would be the recompense of those who should volunteer to take part in this enterprise.

"On the following day, a number of volunteers, including captains Foster, Guise and Crosbie, with other officers, offered their services, the whole amounting to a force sufficient for the execution of the project. Everything being prepared, the boats were exercised in the dark, in the evening of the 4th inst., and the night of the 5th of November was chosen for the attack. Capt. Crosbie had charge of the first division, consisting of the boats of the O'Higgins, and Capt. Guise of the second, which was formed of those of the other ships. At half-past ten, we rowed in two lines towards the enemy's anchorage, and at twelve, forced the line of gunboats guarding the entrance.

"The whole of our force boarded the Esmaralda at the

same moment, and drove the enemy from the deck, after an obstinate resistance. All the officers employed in this service have conducted themselves in the most gallant manner. To them, and also to the seamen and mariners, I feel under deep obligations for their activity and zeal in boarding the Esmaralda. I was sorry that the necessity of leaving at least one captain in charge of the ships, prevented my acceding to the wishes of the captain of the Independentia, who accordingly remained with the squadron.

"I have also to lament the loss we sustained. That of the Esmaralda cannot be exactly ascertained, on account of the wounded and others who leaped overboard; but we know that out of 330 individuals originally on board, only 204 have been found alive, including officers and wounded men.

"The Esmaralda mounts 40 guns, and is not in a bad state as was represented, but on the contrary, very well found, and perfectly equipped. She has on board three month's provision, besides a supply of cordage and other articles for two years. A gunboat of four guns which lay directly in the passage of our boats, was boarded and towed out on the following morning.

"I hope the capture of the flag-ship Esmaralda, secured in booms, batteries and gunboats, in a situation always before deemed impregnable, and in sight of the capital, where the fact cannot be concealed, will produce a moral effect greater than might be expected under other circumstances.

"I have great satisfaction in sending you the flag of Admiral Vacaro, that you may be pleased to present it to his Excellency, the Supreme Director of the Republic of Chili."

(Signed,) COCHRANE.

CHAPTER XIII.

Arrive at Guamas,—Prize safely moored,—Plan contemplated for cutting her out,—Movements suspected,—Caution,—Preliminary movements,—Plan fixed,—Previous arrangements,—This daring plan successfully executed,—Consternation of Guise,—Gets under way for a chase,—Tacks ship and goes back,—Merchant ship goes to the Marquesas,—Frigate goes North,—Report of an American ship in trouble,—Enter a small port,—We are fired on,—No notice taken of it,—Negro's story,—Sail for Panama,—Anchorage,—Rather Suspicious,—Depredations of Cochrane,—Land at Toboga,—Natives alarmed,—Become reconciled,—Description of the island,—Remarks,—Rescue a fugitive prisoner,—An old acquaintance,—His history,—Story of his escape,—Manner of living,—Made purser's steward of the frigate,—Rescue a young Irish prisoner,—Water-filled,—Sail for San Blas,—Small-pox,—Its ravages,—Arrive,—Catch a monstrous shark, —Remarkable tenacity of life,—Contents of his stomach,—Midshipman Wilson leaves the ship,—Goes to Manilla,—Is murdered,—Cut into seventy pieces,—Cause of the general massacre,—Leave San Blas for Moliendo,—Its description,—Singular method of fishing,—Boys playing in the surf,—School for Children,—Jesuit.

Our entry into Guamas very much alarmed Capt. Guise of the Lotaro; but it was a matter of rejoicing to the American captain, (whose name I have lost.) His ship lay moored near the Lotaro, and just as she came from sea. Capt. Downes had some fears, that they would strip her; which, if they had done, would have prevented any attempt on our part to have cut her out. We ran in and anchored within about two cables length of the Lotaro, and in a good position for getting under way. The prize lay inshore of the Lotaro, leaving just room enough for both ships to swing clear of each other. There were several transport ships and two American whalers lying there. We had hardly come to an anchor, when the captain of the prize came on board; and both he and Capt. Downes went into the cabin to talk over matters and things.

Now, our sole purpose in coming here, was to rescue this ship; and I must say, to judge from the position of the prize and that of the Lotaro, an attempt to get this ship clear, would, to say the least, be extremely hazardous, if not wholly impossible. To attempt, and make a failure, would not only be very mortifying but in all probability the means of much bloodshed. Capt. Guise could not help feeling some intimation that Capt. Downes would endeavor, in some way, to liberate the ship, as he well knew his bold and determined character. And yet it seemed a matter of impossibility, that the ship could be taken from under his broadside. Capt. Downes, in order to lull any suspicion of an attempt of this kind, had an interview with Capt. Guise, as to what he thought of a proposition to ransom the ship. In the meantime, the captain had spread abroad a rumor, that through Capt. Downes, his ship would be ransomed, and in a few days he would be off. Now there was no time to be lost, as there remained but one alternative, and that a desperate one, the sooner it was carried into effect, the better. Ransoming or compromising, was entirely out of the question, as neither Capt. Downes nor himself had any authority for entering into a business of this kind. Besides, the ship was a valuable prize, if she could be legally condemned, and in all probability a great sum would be required for her. The plan was kept as private as possible; for, if the boats' crews got wind of it, there would be a danger of its leaking out on shore, and then the jig would be up.

The following plan was then agreed on, which the sequel will show proved successful. The crew, ten in number, were all on shore, and in order that they might be on hand, were persuaded to stay on board the frigate. At first they hesitated; as there was strong inducements held out to them to enter on board Cochrane's ship; such as good wages, plenty of prize money, and what was more alluring than all, plenty of grog, and no flogging. And, as they all had a considerable amount of wages due them, were holding on, to await the issue of the trial. But they finally consented to come on board. It was highly important to secure these men, as we could not well spare a crew from our ship. It was also necessary that they should be let into the secret, and in the event of success they were to have a handsome present.

This matter being arranged, the next thing was, to know how to get clear of the officer, and the twelve marines, or soldiers, who were constantly on guard during the night, as well as on the lookout during the day. All this must be effected by stratagem, and in the following manner. It was well known by the officer on board the prize, or rather he had heard, that through the official interference of Capt. Downes, the ship would be liberated by compromise. Notwithstanding all this, Capt Guise had given him orders not to admit any one on board, except the captain, who still held his state-room, and slept on board; and the mate was also retained for the purpose of taking care of sails and rigging, and to lookout for cables and anchors in case of a blow. Neither of them were allowed to have any fire-arms or powder in their possession. Capt. Guise seldom left his ship, as though he feared that something might happen.

A crew of seventy-five men were selected from among our best seamen, who were all to be armed, with a pair of pistols and a cutlass each. The night was fixed upon, and it was necessary and important that the ship should be clear before two o'clock in the morning; as up to that time there was generally a good breeze blowing off shore, and this breeze, brought the prize in a more favorable position for getting under way.

On the afternoon previous to the night when the attempt was to be made, the captain went on board his ship apparently in high glee, exhibiting a roll of paper, and saying to the officer, "well I am clear; you will have your orders to quit by to-morrow morning." He had brought off a demijohn of brandy, and a box of champagne to treat his friends on this happy occasion, after he had obtained his liberty.

A bottle of brandy was placed upon the table; and a large tin pot full privately given to the marines. The effects of the brandy were soon visible among the marines, who, by eight o'clock, were all drunk. The prize officer also felt rather sleepy, and took a snooze on the cabin sofa. And now was the time for the captain and mate to work, as all depended on the promptness with which everything was done. One of the cables, (hemp,) was sawed off on the windlass, and just stopped to keep it from running out.

A sharp axe was laid near the other, ready for use; the mate then went aloft very silently, cast off the gaskets from the top-sail yards, and stopped the sails with rope yarns; and did the same with the top-gallant-sails. He then loosed the jib and fore top-mast staysail, but kept them on the boom, then saw the sheets and halliards clear. During this time there were two soldiers walking the gangway; but had too much brandy on board, to suspect anything wrong; and at intervals sung out "All's well." It was not thought expedient to make any signal from the frigate, that might be seen by the Lotaro; so it was arranged that when six bells (eleven o'clock) struck on board the frigate, the boat would leave with the men selected for the occasion.

As this enterprise had been carefully planned, (for as I stated before, a failure would have been disastrous) it was indispensable that a line should be run from the merchant ship to a projecting rock, about three times her length, from where she lay, in order to give her headway, and to get her from the range of the Lotaro's guns as quick as possible. This was accomplished in the following manner: Two coils of rope were put into our boat that was to carry the men to the ship, and when the boat left the frigate, the men, all except the two who were to row with muffled oars, were to lie down so as they might not be seen. The boat was to creep along inshore close to the land; cross the entrance of the harbor to the rock; make the line fast, and take the end to the prize. The mate, who being on the lookout in the head, was to haul the end on board. They were then to board the ship over the bow, and knock down the sentinels. The captain was to secure the cabin doors, to prevent the officer from coming up. The cable was then to be cut, the line manned, and the ship hauled out. All this was done with admirable precision. As soon as the blow was struck upon the cable, it was heard on board the Lotaro, and directly all was commotion on board that ship. Capt. Guise was up in an instant, and hailed the prize: "What are you about there, sir." The ship was now ranging ahead, when Guise immediately hailed: "Let go your spare anchor, sir, immediately, or I will fire into you." "Aye, aye, sir," says the mate. "Clear away your guns; all hands unmoor ship," were the mixed and confused orders on board the Lotaro, "*Sheet home your top-sails!*" says the captain, in a long, bold, and authoritative manner, so as to be distinctly heard by all on board the Lotaro. "Run up your jib and fore top-mast staysail." And now she was clear!

Before the boat had left the frigate, we had hove short, and hoisted our top-sail yards without loosing the sails, or making the least noise. The wind was right aft for us, but on the starboard quarter for the prize. We were soon up with her, and both ships were ahead of the Lotaro, who had cracked on every thing she could wear. But it was of no use now for Capt. Guise to think of a re-capture. We beat to quarters, and were all ready for him in case he should fire; but he very prudently *did not.* We kept close to our prize, and both, making all sail, soon dropped the Lotaro, who tacked and went back. Both ships now hove to, shifted our men, and put the prize officer, and his twelve soldiers on board his boat, gave them two bottles of brandy, a keg of water, some bread, and salt fish, and sent them on their way rejoicing. They reached the shore in safety, as we shall afterwards see. Thus ended this well planned and successful scheme, and the brilliancy of the achievement is equal, if not superior, to the cutting out of the Esmaralda.

In the former case, there was not a single life lost, and here was a prize taken from under the guns of a fifty gun ship, who might easily, had they known enough, have manned four or five boats, and boarded her, when of course there would have been a fight, which would have caused a detention, and in all probability, her re-capture. We separated, and proceeded down the coast and our quondam consort stood over to the Marquesas.

While we were at Guamas, a captain of a whale ship told Capt. Downes, that there was an American ship in some difficulty at a small port about thirty leagues north of Callao. We followed the coast down, and entered what was supposed by description, to be the place alluded to. We found plenty of water, and sufficient room to work ship. At the entrance, there was what appeared to be a fort, and when abreast of it we were saluted with a shot from a nine pounder! which came whistling over us. No notice was taken of it, as it was not repeated. We could count, I think eight men in the fort, and but one mounted gun. We ran up just far enough to ascertain that there was no ship there; then tacked and stood out again. We could easily see that our entering the harbor, had caused much consternation and alarm among the inhabitants. It was a pretty little town with a fine large church standing on an eminence. We had a negro on board, who had run away from the Lotaro, and had got on board our ship at Guamas. He had formerly belonged to Cochrane's ship. He told us "that about three months before, Cochrane had taken a cruise down the coast, with his ship only, and that they had landed and plundered many small places along the coast, and had taken many valuable things from the churches, which he invariably robbed wherever he went.

He said that at this place he went in, let go his anchor, sent three armed boats with sixty men, took the fort, which, however, was a very easy matter, for on the approach of the boats the soldiers ran away. They landed at a short distance from the fort, entered it and capsized the guns overboard. They then proceeded to the town. The terrified inhabitants were seen fleeing in all directions; the sight of the frigate had so alarmed them that they made no resistance. The marauding party proceeded first to the church and took away a great amount of silver, among which was a number of massive silver candlesticks. They knocked the valuable eyes out of the Virgin Mary, and stole the golden crown from her head, and the rich slippers from her feet, which were studded with precious stones, and in order to get the jeweled rings from her fingers, these sacrilegious scamps actually broke the hands off at the wrists, but showing no further indignities, left this so-called queen of Heaven, without hands or eyes, crownless and barefooted. They then proceeded to the stores and dwelling-houses, and as an expeditious method of opening chests and boxes, they applied a loaded pistol to the keyhole, which did away with the necessity of a key, taking however only valuable articles and money. Before they had got quite through with their plunder, they were attacked by the inhabitants and what soldiers could be mustered, and a severe fight ensued, but they all reached their boats with the exception of ten, who had laid siege to a grog shop, and were wholly unable to fight. These were marched off to prison, and came very near being killed by the infuriated populace. Many of those who made their escape to the boats were severely wounded, besides the boat-keepers who had been attacked by the soldiers for the purpose of getting back their stolen property. When the boats had returned to the frigate with the plunder, and it was reported to Cochrane that there were ten men made prisoners on shore, he sent a message saying, if their men were not immediately given up, he would lay the place in ashes. As any resistance on the part of the people was out of the question, the drunken sailors were given up, and when our ship made her appearance, although with a different flag, they supposed her to be the same one, come again to finish up what they had left undone of their previous depredations. We sailed from this port for Panama, where we stopped to fill up our fresh water, as it was inconvenient to do it at Callao.

The watering-place was at Toboga, an island in the Bay of Panama. We anchored about ten miles distant from it, so that we could easily communicate with Panama at the same time. The entrance into the city from the water, was by one gate only, and that strongly guarded by soldiers, as in most Spanish towns the guard house is near the gates. It was, at a former visit, rather difficult for any of the officers of the frigate to enter the town, as they were rather suspicious of us, not knowing our true character. Cochrane had anchored there only a few months before under English colors, but they soon became suspicious, and would not allow him to land, and finally ordered him off.

They then went down to Toboga, destroyed a fort and robbed a poor family (the only one on the island,) of their fowls and pigs; and when our boat landed they were terribly frightened, but we succeeded in assuring them that we were friends and Americans, and not as they at first supposed, Chilians. The place where we obtained our water was one of the most lovely groves I had ever seen. Oranges, lemons, pineapples, growing spontaneously, and all around us birds of beautiful plumage and of the sweetest notes warbling on every tree throughout this Paradise. These kind and hospitable semi-Indian islanders, treated us to roasted plantains, and delicious bananas in which the island abounded. Plainly showing that the milk of human kindness is indigenous to the soil of our natures, and does not always require civilization for its development. In my travels through the world how much have I learned from the half-civilized and untutored, and from the savage too. The Fejee and Tongataboo cannibals kill, roast and eat their victims, not because their hearts are more prone to wickedness and cruelty than was that of Napoleon Bonaparte, Nicholas of Russia, and many others whose deeds of cruelty have almost given the lie to any pretensions of an advancement towards civilization or of humanity. The former, act from an impulse springing from what they suppose and actually believe to be lawful and justifiable revenge for injuries. And there is not a doubt in my mind, and if this were a proper place, I think I could demonstrate it fully, that these and all the Oceanic islanders are the descendants of the lost tribes of Israel, evidently retaining that innate vindictive law, "an eye for an eye, and a tooth for tooth," and also of the indiscriminate slaughter of their enemies.

And even among these, there is in their hearts a small reservoir of uncontaminated benevolence kept there to show that they came from God! One day on returning to the ship from the watering-place, on passing an island near. Toboga, and being close in, we saw something that looked like a large seal on a projecting rock, but soon ascertained that it was a man. He jumped into the water and swam to our boat; we took him in. He was nearly naked; his hair was long and matted; his beard very black and bushy; taking him altogether, he was a frightful looking fellow.

He told us that he and several others were taken in a

Chilian privateer, by a Spanish frigate, brought to Panama, and imprisoned; being heavily chained, and put in dungeons. Such being the fate of all privateersmen sentenced to death. They had been in prison about sixty days, when he and two others, in a most remarkable manner, made their escape. As these three were confined in one cell, they had during the day contrived to wrench off their chains, and at night to remove heavy stones and get away almost under the very nose and eyes of the sentinels. They were obliged to drop some distance into the sea, and fortunately for them, it was then high water. If, however, the tide had been out they must have dropped on the rocks, and run the risk of breaking their limbs, or of dashing out their brains. I have stood over the place many a time, and the very look of it is enough to frighten one. They swam round the fort, got upon the beach and made their way into a mass of thick under brush, burrowed into the ground, burying themselves completely up, and there they lie; the day was just beginning to dawn.

Hardly had it become light, when they heard the cry of the soldiers in search of them. It so happened, that there were no traces left of their entrance into this brushwood, or in all probability, they would have been discovered. On the following night, when all was still, they very cautiously crawled out, weak and nearly famished for want of water. They concluded to separate and each to do the best he could for himself. He made his way to the water side, having taken neither food nor water for ten days, and was so weak that he could scarcely crawl. He came to a hut, where was an old Spanish woman, and from her he obtained water and some plantains, with which he was much revived. It was dangerous to remain here; for if her husband should come home, and find him, he would in all probability inform against him for the sake of the reward, which is always paid for the apprehension of prisoners who have deserted. He started off, continuing his course along the beach; but it occured to him, that if his track was discovered, they would surely be after him. So he went aside into the bushes, and shortly came across the trunk of a tree that was very dry and light, and about ten feet long. As soon as it was dark, he contrived to get it into the water; and got upon it and committed himself into the hands of his Maker. The wind was off shore, and by paddling with his hands, and keeping very steady, by daylight he found himself near the island. He said that during the whole night the sharks were around him in all directions; he expected every moment to be dragged off and devoured. But God protected him, and he reached the island in safety, and at first was unable to stand. But after lying a few hours, his strength returned, and he began to look around, and to his great joy he found that the rocks were covered with periwinkles, and other kinds of shell-fish, and a short way up the hill was a running spring of excellent water.

He now felt secure, as the island was uninhabited, and he could hide himself away in a hundred caverns where no mortal man could find him, and if the spring held out, he could live there many years. But he felt sure that Divine Providence would open the way for his escape in his own time and in his own way. "When I saw your ship come to an anchor, and the boat come this way, I felt that my trouble was over."

By this time we had reached the frigate. We took the man to the first lieutenant, related how we had found him, and left him to tell his own story. He was taken below, shaved, washed, and clothed, and when he appeared on deck again, I immediately recognized him as an old acquaintance in Gibraltar. His name was John Laird, a Scotchman by birth, and had been a merchant in Gibraltar, dealing principally in hardware, and it was from his store that the United States ships were supplied with articles in that department. He had been unsuccessful in Gibraltar, and took passage for Valparaiso to try his fortune in Chili. On his arrival there he found a Chilian privateer fitting, which held out great inducements for adventurers "*to make a great deal of money in a very short time.*" His story however, was the sequel of his adventure.

As he was well educated, he was appointed purser's steward of the frigate; performed his duty faithfully, proved himself a gentleman, and remained on board the ship until she was paid off in Boston. One day while the midshipmen were walking through a street in Panama, and just as they were passing an apothecary shop, they were addressed in English, by a young man who appeared to be the shopkeeper. They went in, and as there was no one there but himself, he told them that he was a prisoner, and had been taken in a Chilian ship-of-war, by a Spanish frigate, and that the old Spaniard who owned the establishment had hired his services from the government, and was also responsible for his safe keeping. He was a fine, likely looking young man, and immediately engaged the sympathy of the midshipmen in his favor, and they at once hit upon a plan for his escape, which was, that they were to come on shore the next day, with an extra suit of midshipman's uniform, which just before sunset he was to put on, and pass out of the gate with them, as an American midshipman.

The plan was successful, and he found himself safely on board an American frigate, although he was an Irishman. He had received a college education in Ireland, and was an excellent surgeon. Having filled up our water, we sailed for San Blas. Very soon after leaving Panama, the small-pox broke out, and spread rapidly through the ship; although but few died, yet the ship was a complete hospital. Two tiers of hammocks were hung along on each side of the gun-deck. Fortunately the weather was good, and by the unremitting attention and skill of Dr. Edgar, with Dr. Ticknor, the disease was stayed, and the ship's company restored to perfect health again.

This second visit to San Blas, was through the solicitation of several merchants, who had been largely engaged in business at Guadalaxara, and other places in the interior of Mexico, and in consequence of the unsettled state of the country, felt that their property was unsafe, and wished tohave it removed to the United States. On our former visit to this plaec, Capt. Downes had given them encouragement that he would return again in the course of a few months, which would give them time to collect their specie ready for shipping.

While lying here we caught the largest shark I had ever

seen. He had been several hours playing round the ship; and it seemed as though he wanted to be taken; so we baited a good strong shark hook, and hung it over the bow; and it had hardly reached the water, when he came up, rolled over, opened his tremendous jaws, and swallowed the hook. I could not refrain from thinking how many well baited shark hooks, there are set to catch unwary young men, who are in the habit of lurking round places of danger; when it too often happens, that if they once get hooked they are gone. Possibly it may be with them, as it is sometimes with the shark, they escape with a broken hook in their mouth, which must be to them a source of pain and misery the remainder of their lives. Young reader, think of this! But to return to our shark. We tried to drown the monster and thought we had succeeded. We then got a good rope with a bowline over him, and a tackle on the fish davit, and roused him up, but he had no notion of dying, and appeared as lively as ever. We ran boarding pikes down his throat; that also had but little effect upon him. We then turned boiling water down his gullet, this stilled him for a few minutes, but he soon revived again and began to thrash round in a terrible manner. We then tried what efficacy there would be in red-hot firebrands, which were jammed down his throat; and the tenacity with which this fellow hung on to life, was truly astonishing. We finally hoisted him on board, and as soon as he touched the deck, he commenced again, and fairly took possession of the forecastle. One fellow shoved a white oak capstan bar into his mouth, which he ground up like a biscuit.

Next, we ripped him open, and took from his maw, a whole bullock's head, the entire hide, and a full bushel of fish. Even when his entrails were taken out, he would snap at a piece of wood, and hold it so firm that a man could scarcely get it away. He measured sixteen feet in length, and about eight feet nine inches round the body; he could have swallowed a good sized man whole, and there still would have been room for a bushel or two of fish for dunnage.

This, although a fish story, I assure the reader is true, as I was an eye-witness to the whole transaction. We had been accompanied from Callao, by a beautiful little hermaphrodite brig called the Macedonian. It was said that Cochrane had robbed this brig once, of two hundred thousand dollars, but I believe it was proved that the property belonged to a Spanish house, which if true, the property was a lawful prize. This brig was bound to Manilla. A young midshipman, (a very excellent young gentleman) obtained permission from Capt. Downes, to return to the United States, via Manilla, and accordingly took passage in the brig. We afterwards heard that he had been brutally murdered at Manilla, and the report stated that he had been cut up into seventy pieces.

It appeared that just about the time that he arrived there, from some unknown cause, the water was thought to be poisoned, but the Spaniards would have it that it had been done by foreigners. They accordingly sallied from their houses, crying, "death to the foreigners," and immediately fell upon every one they met, when a general massacre was the consequence, and poor Wilson, was among the victims.

As it happened the Fourth of July occurred while we lay here, the following is a sketch of the manner in which it was passed.

It always has been customary in our navy to give the men a double allowance of grog on the Fourth of July, when in port; this old custom was now to be observed. Everything is generally pretty still during the fore part of the day, excepting the usual firing of salutes, displaying of flags, &c. If it happens that the ship is in a port where there are but few or no Americans, the festival is then confined to the officers and crews. The former of which, however, always contrive to have a good dinner, if it can be procured from the shore, and plenty of something good to wash it down with. It happened that all these things could be obtained here. The wardroom officers invited the captain to dine with them. The midshipmen were also well provided with everything for having a good time.

Dinner hour in the wardroom was at 4 o'clock P. M. Capt. Downes left the table at 5, and retired to his cabin, as he drank no wines or any kind of spirituous liquors, probably concluding from what preparations he saw, that there was to be a considerable business done in that line; and fearing that his presence might possibly retard the "flow of soul," very generously retired; and thus leaving no obstacle to this convivial celebration of the glorious 4th.

At about sunset, the wine began to do its work; loud "hip, hip, hurrah's" were frequent and husky. The midshipmen too, were going it in grand style. Fragments of songs, mutilated toasts, loud calling from one side of the steerage to the other, gave full evidence of the patriotism that pervaded this all-important class of naval officers, and there were some fine fellows among them too.

The seamen were not idle neither, and although they had not dined on roast beef and plum pudding, yet the plentiful supply of good old rye whiskey, which they had stored up for the occasion, was fully adequate for raising a powerful pressure of steam, which for the present was only let off in small quantities, through the upper valve, by songs and cheers. By nine o'clock at night, I verily believe that there were but few sober souls in the ship. The captain was one, and your humble servant was another. He was a regular teetotaller, using no intoxicating drinks, and on such an occasion we must overlook any little improprieties among officers which at any other time would be highly reprehensible, and perhaps might result in serious consequences.

One midshipman came up with his coat off, squaring away for a fight, and yelling like a mad bull. With some considerable difficulty I succeeded in getting him below. All hands were now engaged in one general fight on the gun-deck. The master-at-arms, ship's coporal, and sergeant-of-marines were drunk and not able to make exertion to quell the noise. I took my seat, on a shot box on the half deck, and there heartily enjoyed the fun. The tumult had now become quite serious. I saw the captain go from his cabin door forward among the men. I then arose from my seat and followed him along on the other side, and when abreast the berth deck hatchway, was obliged to stop. He had taken the precaution however, before leaving his cabin, to take off his epaulets, so that in the dark he was not recognized. I kept quite near him, but on the other side of the hatchway. Directly an Irish marine that had just come out of a fight, came up to him, squaring away:

"And wid ye like to take a crack wid me, ye spalpeen, ye."

It was very dark, and of course the fellow did not know who he was talking to. Capt. Downes just turned round and went aft, and I also took my old seat again. Sleep for that night was out of the question. My messmates were all sewed up, and I think upon the whole, that it was the most interesting Fourth of July that I had ever passed. But next day all was right again; everything went on as usual, quiet and harmonious.

Having got through with our business at San Blas, we sailed for a port called Moliendo, a very small place communicating with the city of Arequipa. There is no settlement at this place, save only a few Indian huts, and probably about one hundred and fifty souls, who live principally by fishing. Their mode of catching fish is somewhat singular, having no boats or canoes, but instead of which, they take two large seal skins, and make them perfectly air tight; they then blow them full of air and confine them together in the shape of the letter A, with a cross piece in the middle and at the bottom. They then have a pole about six feet long, with a round piece of wood secured at each end, and kneeling on the middle cross piece, with this paddle, they make these (*boltszas*) fly over the water, never mind how rough it is. The fishing line is made of the fibre of some kind of bark, which, however, is very strong. The hook is a piece of bone or shell, with a very sharp point. They go out into the open sea, not far from land, and when they have reached the fishing ground, secure their paddles, then coil the line upon their right hand, holding the hook in their left, with much dexterity throw the whole out in a straight line, then commence hauling in as fast as possible, and in almost every case they hook a fine fish, weighing from four to ten pounds, which they throw into a small net attached to the boltsza. The surf rolls in on the beach in the harbor full twelve feet high, and it is really amusing to see the litttle Indian children of both sexes, run and dive through this almost perpendicular wall of water, and come out on the other side, then wait for the next roller to bring them in on its crest, and then slide down upon the beach again. There is a Roman Catholic Jesuit here, who appears to be a well educated and excellent man. He has a bamboo schoolhouse erected on a hill near by, overlooking the harbor. This building answers for both schoolhouse and church. He invited me to be present at school hours; so I accompanied him up, and we got to the school just as they were about to take their dinner,—each one bringing their own, which consisted of a dried fish, and a bunch of bananas. And before a morsel of food went into their mouths, they dropped on their knees, and with eyes uplifted, repeated, *Gracios Dios—Thank God*, and then went cheerfully to their dinner. The compensation to this good man was one egg a week, which was brought by each scholar every Friday. There were about forty children, chiefly boys, and entirely naked. The letters were pasted upon a small flat board; and the Jesuit told me that they were all bright scholars and behaved remarkably well. The reason why so few girls attend the school is, that they are generally wanted at home to assist their mothers in pounding corn, taking care of the younger ones, &c. And besides, it is not thought to be indispensably necessary for a woman to have an education, as they are generally looked upon as a sort of drudge, made only for servitude!

CHAPTER XIV.

Devotion,—Compensation,—Mode of teaching,—Females not educated,—Prepare to paint ship,—Mix paint,—Propensity for whiskey,—Rather dangerous gratification,—Money,—Comes on board,—Holders,—Temptation,—Cut open a sack,—Steal the money,—Confined in irons,—Punishment,—Jim Innis,—How he was flogged,— Further punishment,—Sail for Callao,—Arrival,—Prisoners in the castle impatient,—Death,—Joy at seeing the Frigate,—Their liberation,—Narrow escape of a prisoner,—Cochrane's wrath at the cutting out affair,—Pleasing manner in which the news was received at Callao,—Repair several merchant ships,—Receive my pay on shore,—Stratagem to secure the money,— Successful in getting on board the ship,—Visit to Lima,—Hotel,—No sleeping room,— Good supper,—Midshipman robbed,—Drunken priests,—Uproarious conduct,—Landlord afraid to interfere, fearing he should lose their blessing—People wish a change in the government,—Ladies all patriots,—Visit the Cathedral,—Description,—Singular manner of treating the dead,—Return to Callao,—Large amount of specie on board the Frigate,—Sail for Valparaiso,—Something about the Baron,—Improvement in Valparaiso,—Murder of an old blacksmith,—Roguery,— Death of a lieutenant,— Pirates,— Sail for home,—Stop at Rio Janeiro,—Singular looking savages,—Visit an orange plantation,—Politeness of a Portuguese lady,—Landing slaves from a slaver,—Feeding them,—Sail for Boston,—Arrival,—Married,—Settle for life,—Commendable freak of a lieutenant,—Remarks.

When we arrived, a messenger was dispatched to Arequipa, to acquaint the merchants of our arrival, also to request them to be expeditious in getting their money on board the frigate. We expected to remain here at least twenty days. The climate being exceedingly dry, it was concluded to paint ship, although it was an uncomfortable place to lie in, on account of a very heavy swell continually coming in from sea, which kept the ship rolling, almost guns under.

As the paint department was under my charge, was ordered to have verdigris enough mixed to paint the inside of the bulwarks on the spar-deck. I took a clean beef barrel, and put in a sufficient quantity of verdigris, and oil enough to mix it;

but having no spirits of turpentine, as a substitute put in five gallons of whiskey. It was stirred up and well mixed to be ready for use on the following morning. At about eleven o'clock, I heard on the forward part of the gun-deck, a dreadful groaning with distressing efforts to vomit. There appeared to be much commotion among the men, I took no more notice of it and went to sleep again. Next morning I found out the cause of the trouble. These fellows who had been taken so suddenly ill, had seen me put the whiskey in the paint, and having a sufficient knowledge of chemistry to know that whiskey was one thing and verdigris another, and of course, after the heavier had settled, the lighter body would remain above, perfectly homogeneous. On the strength of this known fact, after the hammocks were piped down, and all was still, these "jolly Jack tars" stood around the paint barrel, anxiously waiting the time for nature to do her work; but being rather impatient, as the old dame was not to be hurried, they concluded to taste, so in went one tin pot, and then another, and instead of tasting it, when the tin pot was once at the mouth, in consequence of its having oil with it, the good stuff was so slippery, that a good half pint went down each throat, before the pot was removed.

There must have been a great many at this banquet, for in the morning there was not a half a pint of whiskey left out of the five gallons. I made no complaint about it, but drew from the purser's steward five gallons more, and commenced using the paint. About the time we had got through painting, the money began to arrive from Arequipa; we could see the mules coming over the mountain paths, like a string of ants, it came in green hide sacks, each holding about $2,000 and each mule carrying two sacks, there were also cakes of virgin silver, each weighing $1,500. This money was stowed in the spirit room.

There are always men belonging to the hold called "holders," one of which is appointed captain, or, as he is called, "captain of the hold," and their duty is most generally below, getting out beef and pork, serving out water, keeping the cable tiers in order, &c. Then over them is placed an officer, sometimes a midshipman, who is called master-mate of the hold. On this officer devolves the sole charge of the spirit room, which is a part of the hold. No naked light is ever permitted here excepting when it is empty. It was here that the money was stowed. Six men were employed in packing away the sacks; three were in at the further end stowing and the others were passing the bags to them. Now they were all among the whiskey casks, and the smell of the good stuff, had such a powerful effect upon their nerves, that by some means, best known to an old tar, they got a sip of this ever potent essence of life, death and mischief, and now they were all ripe for anything.

"I say, Jack," says Jim Innis, in a low voice, (the master's mate being on the gun-deck striking down the sacks.) "hand us in your knife here. These here dollars belong to the *bloody* Spaniards, and we might as well have a few as not, to pay us for our trouble in working here in this thundering hot hole."

A knife was passed in, and a sack cut, and all helped themselves. They stowed the dollars about their persons in the most ingenious manner, notwithstanding all this caution, they managed to get drunk, and fool-like, one fellow came up on the berth deck, and began to show his money. It soon reached the master's mates ear, and soon it reached the first lieutenant. They were all brought on the half deck, a sentinel placed over them, when they were all searched, and Jim Innis was so drunk that he was brought legs and arms by four men, and when they laid him down, the dollars rolled from him in all directions. These fellows had, I think $192 between them, but the funniest of all was, that one of them positively declared to Mr. Maury that he had brought the dollars with him, and that they were the remains "of his last voyage's pay," but poor fellow, he little thought that the date of the dollar would betray him, for the dollars found on him were new, right from the mint, and dated 1820, and we left Boston in 1818. Notwithstanding these glaring facts, the fellow still persisted that he had brought the dollars with him. They were all put in double irons and under charge of a sentinel, were kept in confinement twenty days, then brought up for punishment. Five of them recieved seventy-five lashes each, but he who cut the bag was to receive a greater punishment, and according to the testimony of the others, this was Jim. He denied it in a most emphatic manner, appealing to the Higher Power to confirm the truth of his assertion. He was stripped and seized up, but his back presented an awful sight. He was with us in the Mediterranean during the Algerine war, was on board the Guerriere when she engaged the Algerine frigate, and during the action, the gun to which he belonged, (the forward gun on the main-deck starboard-side,) burst, killing and wounding all the gun's crew. Jim was among the latter, he was sadly burnt from the neck to the hips, and even now, nearly four years after the accident; the flesh was quite tender.

Under these circumstances, Capt. Downes could not flog him on the back, therefore he must receive his punishment on what is usually denominated the seat of honor. In this case the culprit is not seized up to the gangway, but is brought over a carronade in the following manner. Standing at the breech, he bends over towards the muzzle; his wrists are secured, one on each side the gun, to the forward axeltree, and his legs, to the gun tackle bolts in the carriage. His trowsers are then pulled down, thus presenting to the boatswain's mate, a prominent field for operation. And one lick with the cat here, is worse than a dozen on the back. When all was ready, says the captain to him:

"Now sir, did you cut the bag?"

"Oh, no, sir, I did not."

"Well then, who did? Boatswain's mate go on with him."

And at the first lick, Jim sung out nobly, and fairly made the gun shake.

"Oh, now, my dear, good Capt. Downes, don't lick me any more, and I *will* tell you all."

"Well let us know who did it?"

"Oh, dear! just cast me loose, and then I'll tell you."

"Give it to him, boatswain's mate."

And obeying the order, put on a half dozen. The blood began to run and the flesh to quiver like jelly, and Jim's shrieks and cries fairly made the pigs look aft to see what was going on.

"Now, who cut the bag?"

Poor Jim had nothing more to say on that subject, but continued to beg most earnestly. He took the other half dozen and was let off. Now Jim was a short, chunky, funny sort of a fellow, and notwithstanding the pain he had, and was still suffering, after he was clear of the gun, he turned round among his shipmates, and with a half smile, dryly remarked:

"I've got off with four dozen less than them other beggars after all."

Besides the flogging, they were compelled to carry a 32lb. shot, with 32lbs. of chain attached to their legs, and a wooden yoke about the neck four feet long and nine inches broad, and on it was painted, in several places, in large letters, THIEF. The ball and chain they were to wear during the pleasure of the captain, were also to mess together under one of the gun-deck ladders, and to do the sweeping on the gun-deck.

We were now on our way to Callao, and arrived there, I think about the first of May, 1821.

When we passed St. Lorenzo, we saw the O'Higgins at anchor, passed them however without any further notice, ran up and took our former moorings. It will be remembered that when we left Callao, five months before, we gave the prisoners at the Castle encouragement that we should return in three months, and notwithstanding that their condition had been made quite comfortable through the generosity of our officers and crew, some of them were nearly distracted by the delay, ungenerously charging Capt. Downes with neglect, if not of gross deception. They had numbered the time by making a notch each day with a knife, and when the number had reached ninety, one of them was permitted to go up to the tower to watch the arrival of the frigate, but after ten, fifteen, and twenty days had elapsed, and no Macedonian in sight, they began to despond, and some that were sick when we left, and had been kept alive by the fond hope of being liberated, when they found that the ship did not come, died in despair. Their stock of comforts also began to fail, but what was worse than all, sweet hope had spread her pinions, and was about to leave them forever.

One morning just as the sun was "peeping o'er the hills," the sentinel on the terrace cried out. "*Mira, Mira, frigata Americano.*" In an instant all were up, some wringing their hands, and others crying like children, and all for joy. Those that were able to get from their sick quarters, crawled out, looking as though they had just risen from their graves.* Although Capt. Downes had a great deal of business to attend to, and much of it of a highly important character, yet the first item to which he gave his earnest attention, was that of liberating these unfortunate prisoners. The Viceroy, agreeable to his promise, was willing to give them up if Capt. Downes would become responsible that they should not re-enter the Chilian service. How he managed this part of the negotiation, I was never informed. They were however, all released and brought on board the Macedonian. And as I have before stated, there were many English and Irish among them, and those who were able, obtained employment on board the merchant ships in the harbor. There were three or four among them, whose constitutions had been broken down by their suffering while in prison, who died on board the Macedonian. The Americans all remained with us, until we arrived at Valparaiso. There was one American among the prisoners, who had been severely wounded on board the Chilian brig, Maypo, in the action with the Spanish ship by whom they were captured. A shot cut his bowels out, and broke his arm at the same time. Through the skill of the Spanish doctor he was cured, and while a prisoner, confined to an iron bedstead. He is now an enterprising and wealthy merchant in Boston.

We found many merchant ships lying here, both English and American, notwithstanding the blockade.

Capt. Downes was requested to receive a very large amount of specie on board his ship, both from the shore and from the ships in the harbor. As Gen. San Martin with his vast army were still encamped near the walls of Lima, and

* These scenes were described to us after they had got on board the frigate.

it was generally expected that the city would fall. This was why the merchants and others were so anxious to get their money away. It was also thought that Cochrane had his eye on the merchantmen, who he knew were taking on board large sums of money. And our coming in at this time, was another very fortunate circumstance for them, as Cochrane, no doubt, felt quite sore at the loss of his prize, which we so neatly took from him, a few months previous. There was an American shipmaster here, who had been several months waiting the arrival of his ship from China, and was here when the Esmaralda was cut out. He told us a very amusing story originating from our adventure at Guamas.

When Cochrane first heard of it, his rage knew no bounds. Capt. Guise was immediately arrested, and the command of the ship was taken from him. The poor ship-keeper was sentenced to ten years imprisonment, and the twelve marines most cruelly flogged. Guise was subsequently liberated, and his command restored; the sentence against the officer revoked, and when the story first reached Callao, it caused much amusement. The highest encomiums were passed upon the chivalrous conduct of Capt. Downes, in managing the affair with so much wisdom.

Cochrane, after he had somewhat cooled off, would send for the ship-keeper, and make him recapitulate the whole story; and all this, while he was confined to his cot, in consequence of the gunshot wound in his thigh. While the man was telling his story, Cochrane would burst out into an immoderate fit of laughter at the Yankee trick; at the same time adding, "That Downes is a keen fellow, and I have always felt afraid of him ever since he has been on the coast. He has been the means of taking many thousands of pounds from me."

Many of the merchant ships were somewhat out of repair, and applied to Capt. Downes for the use of his carpenters. As there was not much carpenter work to be done to the frigate, he complied with their requests. I had made a new spar-deck capstan on our passage down the coast, and had put new bottoms to several of our boats; made up all the spars that were required, and now was somewhat at leisure. I took my carpenters on board the vessels that required our service, finished the jobs up in good shape, and charged three dollars per day, all round. I paid the men one dollar and fifty cents each, and was allowed by Capt. Downes to retain the remainder for my own use.

I stripped and coppered a small English brig, while lying off in the harbor. We hove her down by a long-boat filled with water; and having no proper purchases for the occasion, we used common tackles, with luffs, and by a little management, got along firstrate. My bill was two hundred and fifty dollars, which the captain declared he could not pay me on board; I must receive it on shore. This I remonstrated against, telling him what he knew before, the difficulty and danger of bringing dollars from the shore. But on his agreeing to pay me a premium for receiving it on shore, I consented to run the risk. The captain then gave me an order on a merchant who lived a half mile from the outer gate. Next morning, I obtained liberty from Mr. Maury to go for my money, and previous to leaving the ship, put on a pair of white duck trowsers, a blue jacket, and a black silk kerchief round my neck, and made myself look as much sailor-like, and as much un-officer-like as I could, and still retain my respectable appearance as carpenter of the frigate. When I got on shore, I commenced reconnoitering the soldiers, and fixing my plan for a safe retreat with my money, if I should succeed in getting through the gates with it. I passed out through the gates to the merchant's house, presented the order, which he immediately accepted, and asked me if I was aware of the risk I should run in getting to my boat with so much money, as nobody was allowed to have more than twenty-five dollars on their person at one time, and one dollar mere than that sum would be confiscated. I told him that I had concluded to run the risk; so he counted out, I believe, two hundred and twenty-eight dollars, and then assisted me in stowing it away about my person. First, I took the kerchief from my neck, tied up fifty dollars in it, and put it on again. I then put a hundred in the flap of my shirt, and secured it close to my body;

then put twelve in each shoe, and twenty-five in my trowsers, tied up in a piece of cloth given me by the merchant, and twenty-six I carried in my jacket pockets. This was the manner in which I disposed of my money as near as I can remember; and before I left the house, the merchant opened his door, and gave a look round, in order to see if the coast was clear; "for," said he, "every one that comes here, is watched by the police, as they know that they come here for money." Returning, he said to me, "There are two fellows yonder, that may stop you; but if you keep right along, and don't look at them, it may be that they will not notice you." I had not proceeded more than fifty yards from the door, when they both came up to me, and demanded in Spanish if I had money; they took hold of the bosom of my shirt, and tore it open, when, their eyes resting on a crucifix which I had there, closed my shirt bosom again, saying: "*bueno christiano, vamos,*" go, Christian. I had nothing more to fear, until I reached the first gate, guarded by a soldier, with a drawn sword, whose duty was to prevent money from passing through the gate. When the two fellows clenched me, I thought I was gone; but now I began to think I was brought up all standing, sure enough. But "go ahead" was my motto, so when within fifty yards of the soldier, I feigned drunk, reeling and staggering along, and when close to the gate, the fellow stepped back and let me pass. When well clear of him, I assumed my equilibrium again, and kept along rather cautiously, until within about fifty yards of the next gate.

As I had got so cleverly through the first, I adopted the same plan, and those around the gate began to laugh at the drunken sailor, and let me through without any trouble.

The coast was now clear, until I reached the landing-place, which was about one hundred rods from the last gate. I have often read of devotees doing penance by walking with dried peas in their shoes. I think if they should try to walk with twelve dollars in each shoe, over a rough pavement, they would very soon decide that the latter was the greatest punishment; for the effort to keep the shoe upon the foot, and then so to tread as to prevent the dollars from jingling, was certainly very painful. But as I had begun the hazardous undertaking, I was bound to go through with it. When I reached the landing-place, to my great relief our second cutter lay there filling the water breakers. Here was a soldier whose sole duty was to prevent the exportation of specie; he had authority to search persons or baggage, if he suspected any attempt to violate the law. Now here I was, wrapped up in money, and standing on dollars; and my sole-object was to get safely into that boat, and then I should be all right. But how shall I get into her? that 's the question. She lies ten feet below the top of the wharf, and I must get into her here, because if she hauls up to the steps, I shall surely be searched, and if I attempt to *climb* down by the stones, my shoes will come off. and I shall lose my money. I saw that the soldier had his eye on me, so I showed no desire to get into the boat. At present, Mr. Eagle, the midshipman who understood the matter, held on a few minutes, but very soon some gentlemen came to the landing, who for a few moments, drew the attention of the soldier; in an instant, I whipped the dollars out of my shoes, into my bosom, and was into the boat in less than half a minute, and Mr. Eagle shoved immediately off, and I got safely on board with my money.

I had not yet been up to Lima, which lies about six miles from Callao. In company with four midshipmen, we left the ship for a visit to that renowned city, obtained horses at Callao, and got off at about 10 o'clock, A. M. The road is beautifully shaded with tall and stately trees; the entrance to the city is truly magnificent. At the time that we were there (1821) there was but one respectable hotel in the city, which was called *Casa Blanca*, or white house. It was a large establishment, and much frequented by the fashionable portion of the inhabitants, who came there for its excellent coffee. It was also a great resort for the priests, who often remained until one or two o'clock, in the morning, playing billiards, and drinking wine. On our arrival I went to the landlord and requested him to give us a room, but this he could not do as he kept no spare lodging rooms in the house; but said he would provide a sleeping place for us, where we could all be together. I requested him to get us a supper cooked in English style, as we did not like the Spanish mode. He gave us a fine supper of chickens, eggs, and superior coffee; and a dessert of delicious grapes, and green figs. We deposited our money with him for safety, for we were told that the city abounded in rogues, thieves and murderers. One of our young gentlemen wished very much to take a walk after supper just round in the neighborhood of the hotel. We tried to dissuade him from going out, as it was quite dark, and he might lose his way or get into some trouble. Our remonstrances were in vain. He wore his dirk, and had eight dollars in his pocket, and in less than an hour he returned, accompanied by a soldier. He had been robbed of everything except shirt and pantaloons, and would probably have been murdered, had he not been rescued by this soldier. The account that he gave of himself was, that before he had reached the Square, a fellow came up to him, accosting him in Spanish which of course he did not understand. He then stepped round the corner of a house and beckoned the young man to follow him, which he very imprudently did. The fellow then commenced stripping him, holding a long knife in his hand, which he threatened to put into his bowels, if he said a word. After he had got all except his shirt and pantaloons, the guard came along, when he threw himself among them, claiming their protection. The thief made his escape, and our young hero got *safely* back to the hotel, that is, as far as his life was concerned.

It was now past ten o'clock, and we felt sleepy. I went to our landlord, and requested him to show us a place where we could sleep. He said, he "was very sorry that he could not accommodate us, yet; but when those priests are done with the billiard room, I will put some mattresses upon the tables for you, and you can close the doors, and secure them, then you can sleep comfortably." We waited with some considerable degree of patience until the clock struck twelve; felt as though we could wait no longer, went towards the billiard room, to see what the prospect was for obtaining sleep. When near the door, we heard the smashing of glass, and a terrible uproar. We however, opened it, and went in, and such a scene! Here were about twenty bareheaded priests, and jolly fat friars; all blind drunk; throwing broken tumblers and decanters at each other, and making a most hideous noise; the poor affrighted landlord dare not say a word to them for fear of losing their blessing! It was two o'clock in the morning before we could go to sleep, or rather to lie down, as sleep was out of the question, with the noise of the watchmen's bells outside, and the talking over the scenes of evening, left us a small chance for sleep.

We however made out to get a short nap before morning. At sunrise we all roused out, took a light breakfast, mounted our horses, and commenced our tour through the city, Notwithstanding it was on the very eve of capture by Gen. San Martin, everything wore a gay and cheerful aspect. We were told that the ladies of Lima, with but very few exceptions, were in favor of, and highly desirous for a change in the government; and such lengths had they gone in demonstration of their republican principles, that many ladies in the higher circles, had prepared richly embroidered silk banners, which they intended to present to San Martin on his entering the city.

I believe it to be a remarkable fact, which I have ascertained, as the result of my own observations during the course of my travels, that women prefer a *republican form of government to that of a monarchy*; and yet, how many countries there are upon the face of the earth, and which rank among the civilized too, where the voice of woman, or her opinion, however patriotic it may be, is entirely disregarded. There is one privilege however, that she enjoys both in England and in the United States, which no one can deprive her of; *she can write*, and the world will never know the amount of its indebtedness to female writers, and to female philanthropy.

The reader will please excuse my getting off the track, and I will go on with Lima.

Our first visit was to the Cathedral, whose massive columns elaborately carved, and richly plated with silver, ponderous candlesticks, ancient and valuable pictures, rich and very costly crystal chandeliers, Madonna's glistening with precious stones, and many other things, rare and beautiful, rendered the interior of this Cathedral the most magnificent place I had ever seen.

We next visited the great cemetery, covering a large square of ground, and surrounded by a high wall; and in this wall were recesses, or chambers, with shelves on three sides, on which the coffins were placed. These chambers were entirely open to the area, so that the passer-by could easily be reminded of what he must soon become; that is, if he happened to be rich.

But there was another process adopted for the poor, or for those who could not afford to hire a house for their remains, after they were dead. This we also had an opportunity of witnessing, while rambling round this final resting-place. The body was put into the grave entirely naked. It was then covered with quicklime, and immediately two stout negroes commenced with large pounders, pounding the body and the lime into one complete mass. They then threw in more lime, then filled up the grave with earth; so that if a poor fellow should happen to be buried alive, which has sometimes occurred, he would stand a poor chance of getting out again.

We got through with our sight-seeing at about four o'clock, P. M., and returned to Callao, settled for our horses, and went on board the ship. And I am certain, that our unfortunate young companion returned a wiser, but a "robbed" man, and will ever after be cautious how he goes out to "*look round*," on a very dark night, and in a Spanish port. We had now taken on board, lots of dollars, so that our ship sat as deep in the water as a collier, and being all ready, sailed for Valparaiso, where we arrived all well, and found the frigate Constellation, waiting for our arrival; and now we were to get all ready for going round Cape Horn.

It will be recollected that the Baron, to whom Captain Downes showed so much kindness, and who received so much attention from every officer in the ship, besides large sums of money, and many valuable articles, which he was to deliver to their several friends in the United States, this fellow it was now ascertained was a gross impostor, and a notorious swindler. Perhaps some may smile at the credulity manifested by Capt. Downes, in extending to him the hospitalities of his ship, besides doing everything to make him happy. The confidence with which these keepsakes were intrusted to him, together with the readiness manifested in cashing his draft; the respect shown him on all occasions. no one doubting his character; his deportment, being gentlemanly and respectful, any derogatory intimations would be immediately silenced. But let only those smile who are blunted against the finest sensibilities of our nature, and who do not appreciate those noble traits of sympathy which formed so prominent a part of the character of Captain Downes, and which was so fully developed by every officer on board the ship. Here was what all supposed to be an Austrian officer of high rank, he had the confidence of the Supreme Director, at Chili, and also of many of the first officers of the Republic. He was introduced to Capt. Downes as such, and had evidently been very sick, but was sufficiently convalescent, when introduced to Capt. Downes, to accept his kind invitation to accompany him during a short cruise down the coast. Now where was there any room for suspecting either his sincerity or honor? If we go upon the principle of rejecting every man until we have proved him, there would be but little commerce among men. No sensible man will withhold the hand of sympathy from what appears to be a deserving object on account of having been deceived once, twice, or even three times. The obloquy belongs to the deceiver, and not to the deceived. We will now let the Baron " slide," and commence another subject.

There was an evident improvement in Valparaiso since we first arrived there. Many who had set up small places of entertainment and boarding houses, had become wealthy, and owners of large establishments. Many mechanics who came there as adventurers, had now become possessed of much property. There was an old German blacksmith, who commenced in one corner of an old building, who did some iron work for our ship. He had no family, and was somewhat inclined to be miserly; he lived in his blacksmith's shop, and kept his money in an iron safe, under his bed. This old fellow had accumulated a large sum, which he kept in gold; intending, when he had got *enough*, to return to Germany. One morning he was found with his throat cut from ear to ear, and his safe was gone! Valparaiso was overrun with runaway convicts from Botany Bay, and there were many precious villains among them. Some were so gentleman-like in their appearance, and so fascinating in their manners, that they could, and actually did, "deceive the very elect."

There was a ship here from China, with a valuable cargo of China goods; the captain was a pious man, and somewhat advanced in years. He was one day introduced to a gentleman on shore, purporting to be a merchant of Santiago. He managed to get an invitation and accompanied the captain on board the ship. When in the cabin, he commenced overhauling the captain's library, appearing to be much pleased with the collection; observing at the same time, that he had a valuable work, consisting of twelve volumes, which he would be most happy to present to him, as an addition to his library. To this act of generosity our unsuspecting captain very properly responded. The conversation now turned upon the cargo. Having understood that the captain had a well assorted adventure, was desirous of seeing some of the articles, with a view of purchasing. The captain brought out a variety of crape shawls, and several pieces of rich China silks, all of which were pronounced excellent, and well adapted to the Santiago market. Our merchant made a considerable purchase, and the goods were to be sent on shore to his address, where he would then pay the money. He then went on shore, taking leave in the politest manner. The goods, according to appointment, were sent as directed; and in order to relieve the suspense of the reader, I will say that he never saw either merchant, money, or goods again; and as the captain tells the story himself, we must believe it to be true.

Before sailing for home, there were necessarily some interchange of officers and seamen, and among the officers who were ordered to our ship from the frigate Constellation, was a young lieutenant, John B. Cambreling, who, for some slight misdemeanor, had been ordered home. This had such an effect upon his sensibilities, that he became raving crazy, and expired in great apparent agony a very few days after he had joined the ship.

During our absence from Valparaiso, there had been two noted pirates arrested, who were put on board the English frigate Andromache, Capt. Sheriff, for safe keeping, until the return of the Macedonian. They were then handed over to Capt. Downes, who immediately recognized them as old shipmates. They were properly secured, in order to be taken to the United States for trial. The particulars of the act of piracy for which they were arrested, were as follows:

When the U. S. frigate Essex, Com. Porter, was cruising in the Pacific, it will be remembered that she captured several English whaleships; and on board one of them, these two men made part of the prize crew; and in consequence of having manned a number of prizes, Capt. Porter could not spare as many men and officers, as the prizes actually needed; and on board the prize where these two men were put, there were but three officers.

The crew became mutinous, rose upon the officers, and I believe killed one, confined the others, and took possession of the ship. She was subsequently re-taken by an English man-of-war, and carried into Sydney, New South Wales; and on a fair representation of the affair to government, these men, being Americans, were arrested and sent to Valparaiso; while the others, being Englishmen, were retained at Sydney. These particulars I ascertained from one of our crew, who was on board the Essex at the time when the above took place. And it may be truly said, even in this case, that the "way of the transgressor is hard."

These two unfortunate men were confined for some time at Sydney; they were then sent to Valparaiso, confined several weeks on board the Andromache, and were now to go to the United States in double irons, and there to be tried for their lives. Many times I have gone to them in the dark, when off Cape Horn, while they were shivering with cold, carrying a pot of warm tea and other small comforts, which were received with tears of gratitude. They were fast wasting away, and died naturally, a short time after their arrival in the United States.*

We sailed from Valparaiso about the 15th of March, 1821, stopping a few days at Rio Janeiro. While here, I had an opportunity of seeing about twenty strange looking Indians. They were part of a tribe that had been captured in the interior of Brazil, and were kept on an island under charge of a small guard. They were hideous looking savages, having a flat piece of wood, varying from four to six inches in diameter, inserted within the rim of the lower lip, and projecting horizontally. Another piece, and of nearly the same size in each ear, and kept in by the rim of the ear, giving them a hideous appearance. These pieces of wood, when first inserted in the lips and ears of the children, are only small plugs, gradually increasing in size, until by the time the individual arrives at maturity they are of full size. There were several small children and young girls among them, all of whom had the wooden ornaments in the several stages of progression. Some of the children had pretty features, but entirely without expression ; and the old women were the most horrid looking creatures for human beings that I ever saw.

The Bay of Rio Janeiro presents a beautiful panorama throughout the year. After visiting the Indians, we took a turn around the country, and stopped at a farm-house which was the residence of an elderly Portuguese lady. Our company consisted of three midshipmen with myself. The old lady was very anxious that we should spend the afternoon with her, which of course we could not do, as we must be on board our ship by sunset. She insisted, however, on our getting up into her orange trees and helping ourselves to as many oranges as we could carry. We availed ourselves of her generous invitation, and mounted the trees. Whoever has had the pleasure of plucking a ripe orange from a tree

* Full and official account will be found in the next chapter.

SAVAGES SEEN AT RIO JANEIRO.

on its native soil, can alone appreciate the luxury and deliciousness of the fruit.

On our return, we had an opportunity of seeing another sight, which was quite interesting, to me, at least. It was the landing of a cargo of slaves just arrived from the Coast of Africa. They looked like anything but human creatures, and I think that if I had ever had any doubts about the negro belonging to our race, I am sure that such doubts would now be confirmed. Here were about two hundred creatures, their bodies hardly as thick through as a man's thigh; their legs and arms like four projecting spindles, and their countenances a perfect blank. When landed, they were entirely naked, but immediately clothed with a shirt and a pair of trowsers; that is, the males, but the females wore a coarse cotton frock. They were all marched into a square purposely fitted up for their reception. Their food, which was boiled beans, was carried in large copper kettles, which were placed in the middle of the square, a wooden spoon given to each with which to help themselves as well as they could.

We sailed from Rio, and arrived at Boston about July 1, 1821, after an absence of nearly three years. Having sailed sixty-seven thousand miles, during the cruise, and having lost thirty-four seamen and five officers by death. I now considered my ramblings at an end, was married and settled as I then thought for life. I went to work with my old master at his ship-yard, and had been there a few days, when one morning while at work on board of a brig, putting a plank into the deck, forward the windlass, with my back towards it, heard the men (who were at work at the windlass, heaving in a new mainmast,) grumble at some one who could not ship his handspike in time. I turned round for a moment, and behold, the delinquent was one of our lieutenants of the Macedonian, and disguised as a common laborer. I was amazed, not knowing what it meant. On attempting to speak to him he winked at me, which I at once understood. A few minutes afterwards he went on to the wharf, I start-started immediately after him, and when up with him, asked what all this meant.

Said he, "Call me Jones; I have been watching an opportunity to see you alone, in order to explain it all."

As we walked up the wharf, said he to me, again:

"You know that a naval officer has but a small chance for acquiring any practical knowledge of seamanship, and I was determined to devote my three months furlough to the acquisition of what I call practical seamanship." He had assumed the name of Jones, and was entirely unknown, probably, to any one in Boston, except myself, and wished me to keep his secret faithfully, which I did, frequently visiting him at his boarding house as Mr. Jones, and he as frequently calling on me. At the expiration of his furlough he received orders to join another ship. He called on me before leaving Boston, for the purpose of saying good-by. He showed me his tough, sunburnt hands, which certainly did him much credit.

And if every naval officer would devote even a portion of their furlough to the acquisition of some practical or scientific knowledge instead of idling away the time in dull and insipid amusements, our Navy would boast of many more like a Maury, a Lynch, a Stockton, and others who are ornaments to it. And the truly meritorious officer of whom I have been speaking, deserves the highest encomiums of praise even for this one act of energetic perseverance and devotion to his profession, in working like a common laborer, three months, in order to acquire that practical knowledge which could be obtained in no other way. He now ranks among the first in the navy, honored and esteemed by all who know him.

CHAPTER XV.

CAPTURE OF THE ESSEX.

AFTER having been nearly six years with Capt. John Downes, Lieut. J. M. Maury, Doctor Hoffman, and several other junior officers of the Essex, also a great portion of her surviving crew, and a short time under the command of Com. David Porter and Lieut. Edmund Barnwell, and have often visited the scene of her capture, besides many other incidents relating to that gallant frigate, I thought that the official account of her capture might be interesting to the reader.

Copy of a letter from Captain Porter, to the Secretary of the Navy.

Essex-Junior, at sea, July 3, 1814.

SIR:—I have done myself the honor to address you repeatedly, since I left the Delaware; but have scarcely a hope that one of my letters has reached you; therefore consider it necessary to give a brief history of my proceeding since that period.

I sailed from the Delaware on the 27th of October, 1812, and repaired, with all diligence, (agreeably to instruction from Com. Bainbridge) to Port Praya, Fernando de Noronho, and Cape Frio; and arrived at each place on the day appointed to meet him. On my passage from Port Praya to Fernando de Noronho, I captured H. B. M. packet Nocton; and after taking out about 11,000*l.* sterling in specie, sent her under command of Lieut. Finch, for America. I cruised off Rio de Janeiro, and about Cape Frio, until the 12th January, 1813, hearing frequently of the commodore, by vessels from Bahia. I here captured but one schooner, with hides and tallow. I sent her into Rio. The Montague, the admiral's ship, being in pursuit of me, my provisions now getting short, and finding it necessary to look out for a supply, to enable me to meet the commodore by the 1st of April, off St. Helena, I proceeded to the Island of St. Catherines, (the last place of rendezvous on the coast of Brazil) as the most likely to supply my wants, and at the same time afford me that secrecy necessary to enable me to elude the British ships of war on the coast, and expected there. I here could procure only wood, water and rum, and a few bags of flour; and hearing of the commodore's action with the Java, the capture of the Hornet by the Montague, and a considerable augmentation of the British force on the coast, and of several being in pursuit of me, I found it necessary to get to sea as soon as possible. I now, agreeably to the commodore's plan, stretched to the southward, scouring the coast as far as the Rio de la Plata. I heard that Buenos Ayres was in a state of starvation, and could not supply our wants; and that the government of Montevideo was very inimical to us. The commodore's instructions now left it discretionary with me what course to pursue, and I determined on following that which had not only met his approbation, but the approbation of the then Secretary of the Navy. I accordingly shaped my course for the Pacific; and after suffering greatly from short allowance of provisions and heavy gales off Cape Horn, (for which my ship and men were illy provided) I arrived at Valparaiso on the 14th of March, 1813. I here took in as much jerked beef, and other provisions, as my ship would conveniently stow, and run down the coast of Chili and Peru; in this track, I fell in with a Peruvian corsair, which had on board 24 Americans as prisoners, the crews of 2 whaleships, which she had taken on the coast of Chili. The captain informed me, that as the allies of Great Britain, they would capture all they should meet with, in expectation of a war between Spain and the United States. I consequently threw all his guns and ammunition into the sea, liberated the Americans, wrote a respectful letter to the Viceroy, explaining the cause of my proceedings, which I delivered to her captain. I then proceeded for Lima, and re-captured one of the vessels as she was entering the port.

From thence I proceeded for the Gallapagos islands, where I cruised from the 17th April, until the 3d October, 1813; during which time I touched only once on the coast of America, which was for the purpose of procuring a supply of fresh water, as none is to be found among those islands, which are, perhaps, the most barren and desolate of any known.

While among this group, I captured the following British ships, employed chiefly in the spermaceti whale fishery, viz:—

LETTERS OF MARQUE.

	Tons.	Men.	Guns.	Pierced for.
Montezuma,	270	21	2	
Policy,	175	26	10	18
Georgiana	280	25	6	18
Greenwich,	338	25	10	20
Atlantic,	353	24	8	20
Rose,	220	21	8	20
Hector,	270	25	11	20
Catherine,	270	29	8	18
Seringapatam,	357	31	14	26
Charlton,	274	21	10	18
New Zealander,	259	23	8	13
Sir A. Hammond,	301	31	12	18
	3367	302	107	

As some of those ships were captured by boats, and others by prizes, my officers and men had several opportunities of showing their gallantry.

The Rose and Charlton were given up to the prisoners; the Hector, Catherine, and Montezuma, I sent to Valparaiso, where they were laid up; the Policy, Georgiana, and New Zealander, I sent to America; the Greenwich I kept as a storeship, to contain the stores of my other prizes, necessary for us; and the Atlantic, now called the Essex-Junior, I equipped with 20 guns, and gave command of her to Lieut. Downes.

Lieut. Downes had convoyed the prizes to Valparaiso, and

on his return brought me letters informing me that a squadron under the command of Com. James Hillyar, consisting of the frigate Phœbe, of 36 guns, the Racoon and Cherub, sloops-of-war, and a storeship of 20 guns, had sailed on the 6th of July for this sea. The Racoon and Cherub had been seeking me for some time on the coast of Brazil, and on their return from their cruise, joined the squadron sent in search of me to the Pacific. My ship, as it may be supposed, after being near a year at sea, required some repairs to put her in a state to meet them; which I determined to do, and to bring them to action, if I could meet them on nearly equal terms. I proceeded now, in company with the remainder of my prizes, to the island of Nooaheevah, or Madison Island, lying in the Washington group, discovered by Capt. Ingraham, of Boston; here I calked and completely overhauled my ship, made for her a new set of water casks, her old ones being entirely decayed, and took on board from my prizes, provisions and stores for upwards of four months, and sailed for the Coast of Chili on the 12th December, 1813. Previous to sailing, I secured the Seringapatam, Greenwich, and Sir Andrew Hammond under the gnns of a battery, which I erected for their protection. After taking possession of this fine island for the United States, and establishing the most friendly intercourse with the natives, I left them under the charge of Lieut. Gamble of the marines, with twenty-one men, with orders to repair to Valparaiso, after a certain period.

I arrived on the Coast of Chili on the 12th January, 1814; looked into Conception and Valparaiso, found at both places only three English vessels, and learned that the squadron, which sailed from Rio de Janeiro for that sea, had not been heard of since their departure; and were supposed to be lost in endeavoring to double Cape Horn.

I had completely broken up the British navigation in the Pacific; the vessels which had not been captured by me, were laid up and dared not venture out. I had afforded the most ample protection to our own vessels, which were on my arrival, very numerous and unprotected. The valuable whale fishery there is entirely destroyed, and the actual injury we have done them may be estimated at two and a half millions of dollars, independent of the expenses of the vessels in search of me. They have furnished me amply with sales, cordage, cables, anchors, provisions, medicines, and stores of every description; and the slops on board them have furnished clothing for the seamen. We have in fact lived on the enemy since I have been in that sea, every prize having proved a well found storeship for me. I had not yet been under the necessity of drawing bills on the department for any object, and had been enabled to make considerable advances to my officers and crew on account of pay.

For the unexampled time we had kept the sea, my crew had been remarkably healthy; I had but one case of the scurvy; and had lost only the following men by death, viz. John S. Cowan, lieutenant; Robert Miller, surgeon; Levi Holmes, Edward Sweeney, ord. seamen; Samuel Groce, seaman; James Spafford, gunner's mate; Benjamin Geers, John Rodgers, quarter-gunners; Andrew Mahan, corporal of marines; Lewis Price, private marine.

I had done all the injury that could be done the British commerce in the Pacific, and still hoped to signalize my cruise by something more splendid before leaving that sea. I thought it not improbable that Com. Hillyar might have kept his arrival secret, and believing that he would seek me at Valparaiso, as the most likely place to find me, I therefore determined to cruise about that place, and should I fail of meeting him, hoped to be compensated by the capture of some merchant ships, said to be expected from England.

The Phœbe, agreeably to my expectations, came to seek me at Valparaiso, where I was anchored with the Essex, and my armed prize the Essex-Junior, under the command of Lieut. Downes, on the lookout of the harbor; but contrary to the course I thought he would pursue, Com. Hillyar brought with him the Cherub sloop-of-war, mounting twenty-eight guns, eighteen 32 pound carronades, eight 24s, and two long 9s on the quarter-deck and forecastle, and a complement of 180 men. The force of the Phœbe is as follows: thirty long 18 pounders, sixteen 32 pound carronades, one howitzer, and six three pounders in the tops, in all fifty-three guns, and a complement of 320 men; making a force of eighty-one guns and 500 men; in addition to which, they took on board the crew of an English letter of marque lying in port. Both ships had picked crews, and were sent into the Pacific in company with the Racoon of 22 guns, and a storeship of twenty guns, for the express purpose of seeking the Essex, and were prepared with flags, bearing the motto, "God and country; British sailor's best rights; traitors offend both." This was intended as a reply to my motto, "free trade and sailor's rights," under the erroneous impression that my crew were chiefly Englishmen, or to counteract its effect on their own crews. The force of the Essex was 46 guns, forty 32 pound carronades, and six long 12s, and her crew, which had been much reduced by prizes, amounted only to 255 men. The Essex-Junior, which was intended chiefly as a storeship, mounted 20 guns, ten 18 pound carronades, and ten short 7s, with only 60 men on board. In reply to their motto, I wrote at my mizzen, "God, our country, and liberty; tyrants offend them."

On getting their provisions on board, they went off the port for the purpose of blockading me, where they cruised for near six weeks; during which time I endeavored to provoke a challenge, and frequently, but ineffectually, to bring the Phœbe alone to action, first with both my ships, and afterwards with my single ship, with both crews on board. I was several times under way, and ascertained that I had greatly the advantage in point of sailing, and once succeeded in closing within gunshot of the Phœbe, and commenced a fire on her, when she ran down for the Cherub, which was two miles and a half to leeward. This excited some surprise and expressions of indignation, as previous to my getting under way, she hove to off the port, hoisted her motto flag and fired a gun to windward. Com. Hillyar seemed determined to avoid a contest with me on nearly equal terms, and from his extreme prudence in keeping both his ships ever after constantly within hail of each other, there was no hopes of any advantages to my country from a longer stay in port. I therefore determined to put to sea the first opportunity which should offer; and I was the more strongly induced to do so, as I had received certain intelligence that the Tagus, rated 38, and two other frigates, had sailed for that sea in pursuit of me; and I had reason to expect the arrival of the Racoon from the N. W. coast of America, where she had been sent for the purpose of destroying our fur establishment on the Columbia. A rendezvous was appointed for the Essex-Junior and every arrangement made for sailing, and I intended to let them chase me off, to give the Essex-Junior an opportunity of escaping. On the 28th March, the day after this determination was formed, the wind came on to blow fresh from the southward, when I parted my larboard cable, and dragged my starboard anchor directly out to sea. Not a moment was to be lost in getting sail on the ship. The enemy were close in with the point forming the west side of the bay; but on opening them, I saw a prospect of passing to windward, when I took in my top-gallant-sails, which were set over single-reefed top-sails, and braced up for this purpose; but on rounding the point, a heavy squall struck the ship and carried away her maintop-mast, precipitating the men who were aloft into the sea, who were drowned. Both ships now gave chase to me, and I endeavored in my disabled state to regain the port; but finding I could not recover the common anchorage, I ran close into a small bay about three quarters of a mile to leeward of the battery on the east side of the harbor, and let go my anchor within pistol shot of the shore, where I intended to repair my damages as soon as possible.

The enemy continued to approach, and showed an evident intention of attacking, regardless of the neutrality of the place where I was anchored; and the caution observed in their approach to the attack of the crippled Eseex, was truly ridiculous, as was their display of their motto flags, and the number of jacks at their mast heads. I, with as much expedition as circumstances would admit of, got my ship ready for action, and endeavored to get a spring on my cable, but had not succeeded when the enemy, at fifty four minutes after 3, P. M., made his attack, the Phœbe placing herself under my stern, and the Cherub on my starboard bow; but the Cherub soon finding her situation a hot one, bore up and ran under my stern also, where both ships kept up a hot raking fire. I had got three long twelve pounders out of the stern ports, which were worked with so much bravery and skill, that in half an hour we so disabled both as to compel them to haul off to repair damages. In the course of this firing, I had by the great exertions of Mr. Edmund Barnwell, the acting sailing-master, assisted by Mr. Linscott, the boatswain, succeeded in getting springs on our cable three different times; but the fire of the enemy was so excessive, that before we could get our broadside to bear, they were shot away, and thus rendered useless to us. My ship had received many injuries, and several had been killed and wounded; but my brave officers and men, notwithstanding the unfavorable circumstances under which we were brought to action, and the powerful force opposed to us, were no ways discouraged; and all appeared determined to defend their ship to the last extremity, and to die in preference to a shameful surrender. Our gaff, with the ensign, and the motto flag at the mizzen, had been shot away, but "free trade and sailors' rights" continued to fly at the fore. Our ensign was replaced by another; and to guard against a similar event, an ensign was made fast in the mizzen rigging, and several jacks were hoisted in different parts of the ship. The enemy soon repaired his damages for a fresh attack; he now placed himself with both his ships, on my starboard quarter, out of the reach of my carronades, and where my stern guns could not be brought to bear; he there kept up a most galling fire, which it was out of my power to return, when I saw no prospect of injuring him without getting underway and becoming the assailant. My top-sail sheets and halliards were all shot away, as well as the jib and foretop-mast staysail halliards. The only rope not cut away was the flying-jib halliards; and that being the only sail I could set, I caused it to be hoisted, my cable to be cut, and ran down on both ships, with an intention of laying the Phœbe on board. The firing on both sides was now tremendous; I had let fall my foretop-sail and foresail, but the want of tacks and sheets rendered them almost useless to us—yet we were enabled, for a short time, to close with the enemy; and although our decks were now strewed with dead, and our cockpit filled with wounded—although our ship had been several times on fire, and was rendered a perfect wreck, we were still encouraged to hope to save her, from the circumstance of the Cherub, from her crippled state, being compelled to haul off. She did not return to close action again, although she apparently had it in her power to do so, but kept up a distant firing with her long guns. The Phœbe, from our disabled state, was enabled, however, by edging off, to choose the distance which best suited her long guns, and kept up a tremendous fire on us, which mowed down my brave companions by the dozen. Many of my guns had been rendered useless by the enemy's shot, and many of them had their whole crew's destroyed. We manned them again from those which were disabled, and one gun in particular was three times manned—fifteen men were slain at it, in the course of the action! But, strange as it may appear, the captain of it escaped with only a slight wound. Finding that the enemy had it in his power to choose his distance, I, now gave up all hopes of closing with him, and, as the wind, for the moment, seemed to favor the design, I determined to endeavor to run her on shore, land my men and destroy her. Everything seemed to favor my wishes.

We had approached the shore within musket shot, and I had no doubt of succeeding, when, in an instant, the wind shifted from the land (as is very common in this port in the latter part of the day) and payed our head down on the Phœbe, where we were again exposed to a dreadful raking fire. My ship was now totally unmanageable; yet as her head was toward the enemy, and he to leeward of me, I still hoped to be able to board him. At this moment, Lieut. Commandant Downes came on board to receive my orders, under the impression that I should soon be a prisoner. He could be of no use to me in the then wretched state of the Essex—and finding (from the enemy's putting his helm up) that my attempt at boarding would not succeed, I directed him, after he had been about ten minutes on board, to return to his own ship, to be prepared for defending and destroying her in case of attack. He took with him several of my wounded, leaving three of his boat's crew on board to make room for them. The Cherub now had an opportunity of distinguishing herself, by keeping up a hot fire on him during his return. The slaughter on board my ship had now become horrible, the enemy continuing to rake us, and we unable to bring a gun to bear. I therefore directed a hawser to be bent to the sheet anchor, and the anchor to be cut from the bows to bring her head round: this succeeded. We again got our broadside to bear, and as the enemy was much crippled and unable to hold his own, I have no doubt he would soon have drifted out of gunshot before he discovered we had anchored, had not the hawser unfortunately parted. My ship had taken fire several times during the action, but alarmingly so forward and aft at this moment—flames were bursting up each hatchway, and no hopes were entertained of saving her. Our distance from the shore did not exceed three-quarters of a mile, and I hoped many of my brave crew would be able to save themselves, should the ship blow up, as I was informed the fire was near the magazine, and the explosion of a large quantity of powder below served to increase the horrors of our situation—our boats were destroyed by the enemy's shot; I therefore directed those who could swim, to jump overboard, and endeavor to gain the shore—some reached it—some were taken by the enemy, and some perished in the attempt; but most preferred sharing with me the fate of the ship.

We, who remained, now turned our attention wholly to extinguishing the flames: and when we had succeeded, went again to our guns, where the firing was kept up for some minutes, but the crew had by this time become so weakened, that they all declared to me the impossibility of making further resistance, and entreated me to surrender my ship to save the wounded, as all further attempt at opposition must prove ineffectual, almost every gun being disabled by the destruction of their crews. I now sent for the officers of divisions to consult them; but what was my surprise to find only acting Lieutenant Stephen Decatur M'Knight remaining, (who confirmed the report respecting the condition of the guns on the gun-deck—those on the spar-deck were not in a better state.) Lieut. Wilmer, after fighting most gallantly throughout the action, had been knocked overboard by a splinter while getting the sheet anchor from the bows, and was drowned. Acting Lieutenant John G. Cowell had lost a leg; Mr. Edmund Barnwell, acting sailing-master, had been carried below, after receiving two severe wounds, one in the breast and one in the face; and Acting Lieutenant William H. Odenheimer had been knocked overboard from the quarter an instant before, and did not regain the ship until after the surrender. I was informed that the cockpit, the steerage, the wardroom, and the berth deck could contain no more wounded; that the wounded were killed while the surgeons were dressing them; and that unless something was speedily done to prevent it, the ship would soon sink from the number of shot holes in her bottom. On sending for the carpenter, he informed me that all his crew had been killed or wounded, and that he had once been over the side to stop the leaks, when his slings had heen shot away, and it was with difficulty he was saved from drowning. The enemy, from the smoothness of the water, and the impossibility of our reaching him with our carronades, and the little apprehension that was excited by our fire, which had now become much slackened, was enabled to take aim at us as at a target: his shot never missed our hull, and my ship was cut up in a manner, which was, perhaps, never before witnessed—in fine, I saw no hopes of saving her, and at 20 minutes after 6 P. M. gave the painful order to strike the colors. Seventy-five men, including officers, were all that remained of my whole crew, after the action, capable of doing duty, and many of them severely wounded, some of whom have since died. The enemy still continued his fire, and my brave, though unfortunate companions, were still falling about me. I directed an opposite gun to be fired, to show them we intended no farther resistance; but they did not desist; four men were killed at my side, and others at different parts of the ship. I now believed he intended to show us no quarter, and that it would be as well to die with my flag flying as struck, and was on the point of again hoisting it, when about 10 minutes after hauling the colors down he ceased firing.

I cannot speak in sufficiently high terms of the conduct of those engaged for such an unparalleled length of time (under such circumstances) with me in the arduous and unequal contest. Let it suffice to say, that more bravery, skill, patriotism and zeal, were never displayed on any occasion. Every one seemed determined to die in defence of their much loved country's cause, and nothing but views of humanity could ever have reconciled them to the surrender of the ship; they remembered their wounded and helpless shipmates below. To acting Lieutenants M'Knight and Odenheimer, I feel much indebted for their great exertions and bravery throughout the action, in fighting and encouraging the men at their divisions, for the dexterous management of the long guns, and for their promptness in re-manning their guns as their crews were slaughtered. The conduct of that brave and heroic officer, acting Lieutenant John G. Cowell, who lost his leg in the latter part of the action, excited the admiration of every man in the ship, and after being wounded, would not consent to be taken below, until loss of blood rendered him insensible. Mr. Edmund Barnwell, acting sailing-master, whose activity and courage were equally conspicuous, returned on deck after receiving his first wound, and remained after receiving his second, until fainting with loss of blood. Mr. Samuel B. Johnston, who had joined me the day before, and acted as marine officer, conducted himself with great bravery, and exerted himself in assisting at the long guns; the musketry after the first half hour being useless from our long distance.

Mr. M. W. Bostwick, whom I had appointed acting purser of the Essex-Junior, and who was on board my ship, did the duties of aid in a manner which reflects on him the highest honor: and Midshipmen Isaacs, Farrugut, and Ogden, as well as Acting Midshipmen James Terry, James R. Lyman and Samuel Duzenbury, and Master's Mate William Pierce, exerted themselves in the performance of their respective duties, and gave an earnest of their value to the service; the three first are too young to recommend for promotion;

the latter I beg leave to recommend for confirmation, as well as the acting lieutenants and Messrs. Barnwell, Johnston and Bostwick.

We have been unfortunate, but not disgraced—the defence of the Essex has not been less honorable to her officers and her crew, than the capture of an equal force; and I now consider my situation less unpleasant, than that of Com. Hillyar, who, in violation of every principle of honor and generosity, and regardless of the rights of nations, attacked the Essex in her crippled state, within pistol shot of a neutral shore, when for six weeks I had daily offered him fair and honorable combat, on terms greatly to his advantage. The blood of the slain must rest on his head; and he has yet to reconcile his conduct to heaven, to his conscience, and to the world. The annexed extracts of a letter frem Com. Hillyar, which was written previous to his returning me my sword, will show his opinion of our conduct.

My loss has been dreadfully severe, 58 killed, or have since died of their wounds, and among them Lieut. Cowell; 39 were severely wounded, 27 slightly, and 31 are missing; making in all 155 killed, wounded, and missing, a list of whose names is annexed.

The professional knowledge of Dr. Richard Hoffman, acting surgeon, and Dr. Alexander Montgomery, acting surgeon's mate, added to their assiduity and the benevolent attentions and assistance of Mr. D. P. Adams, the chaplain, saved the lives of many of the wounded; those gentlemen have been indefatigable in their attentions to them; the two first I beg leave to recommend for confirmation, and the latter to the notice of the department.

I must, in justification of myself, observe, that with our six 12 pounders only, we fought this action—our carronades being almost useless.

The loss in killed and wounded has been great with the enemy; among the former is the first lieutenant of the Phœbe, and of the latter Capt. Tucker, of the Cherub, whose wounds are severe. Both the Essex and Phœbe were in a sinking state, and it was with difficulty they could be kept afloat until they anchored in Valparaiso next morning.

CAPTURE OF THE ESSEX.

The battered state of the Essex will, I believe, prevent her ever reaching England, and I also think it will be out of their power to repair the damages of the Phœbe, so as to enable her to double Cape Horn. All the masts and yards of the Phœbe and Cherub are badly crippled, and their hulls much cut up; the former had eighteen 12 pound shot through her, below her water-line, some three feet under water. Nothing but the smoothness of the water saved both the Phœbe and Essex.

I hope, sir, that our conduct may prove satisfactory to our country, and that it will testify it by obtaining our speedy exchange, that we may again have it in our power to prove our zeal.

Commodore Hillyar, I am informed, has thought proper to state to his government that the action lasted only 45 minutes; should he have done so, the motive may be easily discovered — but the thousand of disinterested witnesses who covered the surrounding hills, can testify that we fought his ships near two hours and a half; upwards of fifty broadsides were fired by the enemy agreeably to their own accounts, and upwards of seventy-five by ours; except the few minutes they were repairing damages, the firing was incessant.

Soon after my capture, I entered into an agreement with Com. Hillyar to disarm my prize, the *Essex-Junior*, and proceed with the survivors of my officers and crew in her to the United States, taking with me all her officers and crew. He consented to grant her a passport to secure her from recapture. The ship was small, and we knew we had much to suffer, yet we hoped soon to reach our country in safety, that we might again have it in our power to serve it. This arrangement was attended with no additional expense, as she was abundantly supplied with provisions and stores for the voyage.

In justice to Com. Hillyar, I must observe, that, although I can never be reconciled to the manner of his attack on the Essex, or to his conduct before the action, he has, since our capture, shown the greatest humanity to my wounded, whom he permitted me to land, on condition that the United States should bear their expenses, and has endeavored as much as lay in his power to alleviate the distresses of war by the most generous and delicate deportment towards myself, my officers and crew; he gave orders that the property of every person should be respected — his orders, however, were not so strictly attended to as might have been expected; besides being deprived of books, charts, &c. &c., both myself and officers lost many articles of our clothing, some to a considerable amount. I should not have considered this last circumstance of sufficient importance to notice, did it not mark a striking difference between the Navy of Great Britain and that of the United States, highly creditable to the latter.

By the arrival of the Tagus, a few days after my capture, I was informed that besides the ships which had arrived in the Pacific in pursuit of me, and those still expected, others were sent to cruise for me in the China seas, off New Zealand, Timour, and New Holland, and that another frigate was sent to the River La Plata.

To possess the Essex, it has cost the British government near six millions of dollars; and yet, sir, her capture was owing entirely to accident; and if we consider the expedition with which naval contests are now decided, the action is a dishonor to them. Had they brought their ships boldly to action with a force so very superior, and having the choice of position, they should either have captured or destroyed us in one-fourth the time they were about it.

During the action, our Consul General, Mr. Poinsett, called on the governor of Valparaiso, and requested that the batteries might protect the Essex. The request was refused, but he promised that if she should succeed in fighting her way to the common anchorage, he would send an officer to the British commander and request him to cease firing, but declined using force under any circumstances, and there is no doubt a perfect understanding existed between them. This conduct added to the assistance given to the British, and their friendly reception after the action, and the strong bias of the faction which governs Chili in favor of the English, as well as their hostility to the Americans, induced Mr. Poinsett to leave that country. Under such circumstances, I did not conceive that it would be proper for me to claim the restoration of my ship, confident that the claim would be made by my government to more effect. Finding some difficulty in the sale of my prizes, I had taken the Hector and Catherine to sea, and burnt them with their cargoes.

I exchanged Lieut. M'Knight, Mr. Adams and Mr. Lyman and eleven seamen, for part of the crew of the Sir Andrew Hammond, and sailed from Valparaiso on the 27th April, where the enemy were still patching up their ships to put them in a state for proceeding to Rio de Janeiro, previous to going to England.

Annexed is a list of the remains of my crew to be exchanged, as also a copy of the correspondence between Com. Hillyar and myself on that subject. I also send you a list of the prisoners I have taken during my cruise, amounting to 343. I have the honor to be, &c.,

Hon. Secr'y of the Navy D. PORTER.
of the United States, Washington.

During the action, the Essex-Junior lay in the port of Valparaiso, under the guns of a Spanish fort, unable to take any part in the contest. After the action, Capt. Porter and his crew were paroled, and by arrangement permitted to come home in the Essex-Junior, and a cartel, with his crew. Off the Hook they were detained 24 hours by the British razee Saturn, in company with the frigate Narcissus. Com. Porter left the Essex-Junior on the 6th of July, in one of her yawls, with six men, about thirty miles outside of the Hook, and landed on the 7th at Babylon, on Long Island, where he procured a wagon, took on board his yawl and jolly tars, and reached Brooklyn about 5 o'clock, P. M.

The Essex had landed all her specie, amounting to two millions, at Valparaiso, previous to her being captured.

EXTRACT OF A LETTER FROM COM. HILLYAR TO ME.

Phœbe, April 4, 1814.

MY DEAR SIR:—Neither in my conversations nor the accompanying letter, have I mentioned your sword. Ascribe my remissness in the first instance to forgetfulness; I consider it only in my servant's possession with my own, until the master may please to call for it; and although I omitted, at the moment of presentation, from my mind being much engrossed in attending to professional duties, to offer its restoration, the hand that received will be most gladly extended, to put it in possession of him who wore it so honorably in defending his country's cause.

Believe me, my dear sir,
very faithfully yours,
JAMES HILLYAR.

Capt. PORTER.

After some conversation on the subject the following correspondence took place.

Valparaiso, April 4, 1814.

SIR:—Taking into consideration the immense distance we are from our respective countries, the uncertainty of the future movements of his majesty's ships under my command, which precludes the possibility of my making a permanent arrangement for transporting the officers and crew, late of the Essex, to Europe; and the fast approaching season which renders a passage round Cape Horn in some degree dangerous; I have the honor to propose for your approbation, the following articles, which, I hope, the government of the United States, as well as that of Great Britain, will deem satisfactory; and to request, that should you conceive them so, you will favor me with the necessary bond for their fulfilment.

First. The Essex-Junior to be deprived of all her armament and perfectly neutralized; to be equipped for the voyage solely and wholly at the expense of the American government; and to proceed with a proper American officer and crew (of which I wish to be furnished with a list, for the purpose of giving the necessary passport) to any port of the United States of America that you may deem most proper.

Second. Yourself, the officers, petty officers, seamen, marines, &c., composing your crew, to be exchanged immediately on their arrival in America, for an equal number of British prisoners of similar rank. Yourself and officers to be considered on their parole of honor until your and their exchange shall be effected.

In case of the foregoing articles being accepted, the Essex-Junior will be expected to prepare immediately for the voyage, and to proceed on it before the expiration of the present month; should any of the wounded at that period be found incapable of removal, from not being sufficiently advanced in their recovery, the most humane attention shall be paid them; and they shall be forwarded home by the first favorable conveyance that may offer.

I have the honor to be, &c.,

JAMES HILLYAR.

Com. DAVID PORTER,
late commander of the U. S. frigate Essex.

COPY OF A LETTER FROM CAPTAIN PORTER TO THE SECRETARY OF THE NAVY.

New York, July 13, 1814.

SIR:—There are some facts relating to our enemy, and although not connected with the action, serve to show his perfidy, and should be known.

On Com. Hillyar's arrival at Valparaiso, he ran the Phœbe close along-side of the Essex, and inquired politely after my health, observing, that his ship was cleared for action, and his men prepared for boarding. I observed, "Sir, if you by any accident, get on board of me, I assure you that great confusion will take place; I am prepared to receive you, but shall only act on the defensive." He observed, coolly and indifferently, "Oh, sir, I have no such intention." At this instant, his ship took aback on my starboard bow, her yards nearly locking with those of the Essex. I called all hands to board the enemy, and in an instant my crew were ready to spring on her decks. Com. Hillyar exclaimed, with great agitation, "I had no intention of getting on board of you; I had no intention of coming so near you; I am sorry I come so near you." His ship fell off with her jib-boom over my decks; her bows exposed to my broadside, her stern to the fire of the Essex-Junior, her crew in the greatest confusion, and in fifteen minutes, I could have taken or destroyed her. After he had brought his ship to anchor, Com. Hillyar and Capt. Tucker of the Cherub, visited me on shore, when I asked him if he intended to respect the neutrality of the port. "Sir," said he, "you have paid such respect to the neutrality of this port, that I feel myself bound, in honor, to do the same."

I have the honor to be, &c.,
DAVID PORTER.

After the capture of the Essex, Capt. Porter entered into an arrangement with Com. Hillyar, to transport the survivors of his crew to the United States in the Essex-Junior, on parole, on condition that she should receive a passport to secure her from re-capture and detention. On the 5th of July, fell in with H. B. M. ship Saturn, Capt. Nash, who examined the papers of the Essex-Junior, treated Capt. Porter with great civility, furnished him with late newspapers, and sent him on board some oranges; and at the same time made him an offer of services. The Boarding officer endorsed the passport, and permitted the ship to proceed. She stood on the same tack with the Saturn; and about two hours afterwards was again brought to, the papers examined, and the ship's hold overhauled by the boat's crew and an officer. Capt. Porter expressed his astonishment at such proceedings, and was informed that Capt. Nash had his motives. It was stated that Com. Hillyar had no authority to make such arrangement; that the passport must go on board of the Saturn again, and the Essex-Junior be detained. Capt. Porter then insisted that the smallest detention would be a violation of the contract on the part of the British, and that he should consider himself as the prisoner of Capt. Nash, and no longer on his parole; at the same time offering his sword, which was refused, assuring the officer he would deliver it up with the same feelings he had presented it to Com. Hillyar. The officer went on board, returned and informed Capt. Porter, that the Essex-Junior must remain all night under the lee of the

Saturn. Then, said Capt. Porter, I am your prisoner; I do not feel myself bound by any contract with Com. Hillyar, and I shall act accordingly.

At seven o'clock next morning, the wind being light from the southward, the ships being about thirty or forty miles from the land off the eastern part of Long Island, and about musket shot from each other, there appearing no disposition on the part of the enemy to liberate the Essex-Junior, Capt. Porter determined to attempt his escape. A boat was lowered down, manned and armed; he desired Capt. Downes to inform Capt. Nash, that he was now satisfied that most British naval officers were not only destitute of honor, but regardless of the honor of each other; that he was armed and prepared to defend himself against their boats, if sent in pursuit of him; and that they must hereafter meet him as an enemy. He now pulled off from the ship, keeping the Essex-Junior in a direct line between him and the Saturn, and got near gunshot from them before he was discovered; at this instant a fresh breeze sprung up, and the Saturn made all sail in pursuit of him, but fortunately a thick fog set in and concealed him, when he changed his course, and eluded them. During the fog he heard a firing, and on its clearing up discovered the Saturn in chase of the Essex-Junior, who soon brought her to. After rowing and sailing about sixty miles, Capt. Porter succeeded, with great difficulty and hazard, in reaching the town of Babylon, (Long Island) where, being strongly suspected to be an English officer, he was closely interrogated, and his story appearing so extraordinary, none gave credit; but on showing his commission, all doubts were removed, and he met from all the inhabitants the most friendly and hospitable reception.

A gentleman, who took part in the engagement, has related the following anecdotes exemplary of that fearless and patriotic spirit which animated the whole crew of the Essex, and which has characterized our hardy sailors in all their combats with the enemy. To the memory of these brave fellows their publicity is due; and we doubt not many more instances of chivalrous heroism, resulting from a noble love of country, might be obtained and recorded, to the lasting honor of the American name.

John Ripley, after losing his leg, said "farewell, boys; I can be of no use to you;" and leaped out of the bow port.

John Alvinson received a cannon ball (eighteen pounder) through the body; in the agony of death, he exclaimed, "never mind, shipmates; I die in defence of 'Free trade and sailors' r-i-g-h-t-s;'" and expired with the word *rights* quivering on his lips.

James Anderson had his left leg shot off, and died animating his shipmates to fight bravly in defence of liberty.

After the engagement, Benjamin Hazen, having dressed himself in a clean shirt and jerkin, addressed his remaining messmates, and telling them he never could submit to be a prisoner to the English, threw himself into the sea.

SEQUEL OF CAPTAIN PORTER'S EXPEDITION IN THE SOUTH SEA.

On the 19th of November 1813, Capt. Porter took formal possession of the Island, called by the natives Nooaheevah, generally known by the name of Sir Henry Martin's Island, but now called Madison Island. It is situated between lat. 9° and 10° S. and in long. 140° W, from Greenwich.

The following is a letter from Capt. Gamble to Capt. Porter.

Capt. Gamble, the reader will recollect, was left by Capt. Porter with a few men, in charge of two or three vessels and some public property, when he sailed from Madison Island for Valparaiso, previous to his ever memorable battle in the Essex. The following letter comprises all the subsequent occurrences:

SIR, *New York, August* 30, 1815.

With regret I have to inform you, the frigate had not got clear of the Marquesas, before we discovered in the natives a hostile disposition towards us, who in a few days became so insolent, that I found it absolutely necessary, not only for the security of the ships, and property on shore, but for our personal safety, to land my men, and regain by force of arms the many things they had, in the most daring manner, stolen from the encampment; and what was of still greater importance, to prevent, if possible, their putting threats into execution, which might have been attended with the most serious consequences on our part from duty requiring my men to be so much separated.

I however had the satisfaction to accomplish my wish without firing a musket, and from that time lived in the most perfect amity with them, until the 7th May following, when my distressed situation placed me in their power.

Before mentioning the lamentable events of that day, and the two succeeding ones, I shall give you a brief account of a few preceding occurrences, which were sources of great uneasiness to me. The first was the death of John Wetter, marine, who was unfortunately drowned in the surf, on the afternoon of the 28th February, and the desertion of four of my men. They took the advantage of a dark night, and left the bay unobserved by any person, all excepting one, a prisoner, having the watch on deck. They took with them several muskets, a supply of ammunition, and many articles of but little value. My attempt to pursue them was prevented by their destroying partially the only boat (near the beach, at that time sea-worthy.

On the 12th April, began to rig the ships Seringapatam and Sir Andrew Hammond, which, as I calculated, employed the men until the 1st of May. All hands were then engaged in getting the remainder of the property from the Greenwich to the Seringapatam, as I began to despair of your rejoining me at that place.

The work went on well, and the men were obedient to my orders, though I discovered an evident change in their countenances, which led me to suppose there was something wrong in agitation, and under that impression, had all the muskets, ammunition, and small arms of every description, taken to the Greenwich, the ship I lived on board, from the other ships, as a necessary precaution against a surprise from my own men.

On the 7th May, while on board the Seringapatam, on duty, which required my being present, a mutiny took place, in which I was wounded, and the mutineers succeeded in getting the Seringapatam out of the bay. Two days after, when making the necessary preparations to depart for Valparaiso, we were attacked by the savages, and I have with the deepest regret, to inform you, sir, that Midshipman William Felters, John Thomas, Thomas Gibbs, and William Brudinell, were massacred, and Peter Coddington, marine, dangerously wounded. After bending the jib and spanker, we cut our moorings, and fortunately had a light breeze, that carried the ship clear of the bay, with six cartridges remaining out of the only barrel left us by the mutineers.

After getting out of the bay, we found our situation most distressing. In attempting to run the boat up, it broke in two parts, and we were compelled to cut away from the bows the only anchor, not being able to cat it. We mustered altogether eight souls, out of which there was one cripple, one dangerously wounded, one sick, one just recovering from the scurvy, and myself confined to the bed with a high fever, produced by my wound.

In that state, destitute of charts, and almost of every means of navigating the ship, I reached the Sandwich Islands, after a passage of seventeen days, and suffering much from fatigue and hardships. I was there unfortunately captured by the English ship Cherub, remained a prisoner on board of her seven months, during which time my men were treated in a most shameful manner. We were then put on shore at Rio de Janeiro, without the possibility of getting away until after hearing of the peace. I then, by the advice of the physician who attended me, embarked on board a Swedish ship bound for Havre de Grace, (there being no other means of my getting away at that time,) leaving behind Midshipman Clapp and five men, having lost one soon after my arrival in that place with the small-pox.

On the 1st inst. lat. 47 deg. N. long. 18 deg. W. we fell in with the American ship Oliver Ellsworth, from Havre, bound to this port. I took a passage on board of her, and arrived here two days since, after being upwards of an hundred days at sea. I am at present unable to travel, and shall therefore await either your orders, or the orders of the commandant of the marine corps at this place.

I have the honor to remain, with the highest
respect and esteem, sir, your obed't serv't,
JOHN M. GAMBLE.

CHAPTER XVI.

Comment on punishment in the Navy,—Punishment in Queen Elizabeth's time,—Capt. Stockton on the subject,—Present condition of sailors,—Remarks on sea-captains,—They are often swindled,—Hard-hearted wretch,—Kindness, —Benevolent men,—Return to my narrative,—Become a member of the Methodist church,—Strange opinion of pious men,—Unexpected caution,—Conclude to build a house,—Curious manœuvre,—An old miser,—Vigilance committee,—Obtain a lot,—Sickness and death of the miser,—Small business,—Agree with a brother to build a house,—Caution,—Deceived,—Break off with him,—Pay him off.

BEFORE I take leave of the naval service, I wish to indulge in a few remarks on flogging in the Navy, and of the general character of sailors.

I have had occasion several times to mention the witnessing of this brutal punishment, and to repeat the sentiments which I have previously advanced on this subject. Nothing can be more revolting to anything like a sensitive mind, than to see a man tied up, and his back cut into strips; the skin peeling from the flesh, thus leaving it a mass of clotted blood.

I have been told by seamen who have spent nearly their whole lives on board a man-of-war, both in the English and American Navy, that the punishments are more frequent and much more severe in the latter than in the former. This, however, we can give as much credit to as we please.

But I remember while lying at Callao in company with the Hyperion, English frigate, and at one time were quite near her, I observed every morning just after daylight, the upper end of a number of muskets peering over the hammock cloth, and moving fore and aft, or backwards and forward.

One day when one of their boats was along-side our ship, I asked one of the boat's crew what the reason was of their having so many marines on post in the gangway. The fellow looked up to me from the boat, and rolling his quid over, in a good-natured manner, replied:

FLOGGING ON BOARD A MAN-OF-WAR.

"Why don't you let your back get well once, before you get here again. If you will get drunk you must take the consequences."

"Them was fellers as missed their muster. The old man, (Capt. Searle,) don't allow any flogging on board our ship, but what he does himself."

These muskets are all filled up with leaden bullets, chock up to the top, and they are obliged to carry them the whole watch. The penalty for this with us, in the United States Navy, is a dozen or two with the colt. Now, whatever may be the opinion of some with regard to the comparison, one thing is most certain, that the latter is the most brutal, and yet in the English Navy in the time of Queen Elizabeth, the usage was dreadfully severe.

PUNISHMENT OF SEAMEN IN THE REIGN OF QUEEN ELIZABETH.

From the Harleian MSS.

The executions and capitall punishments I finde to be thus in Queene Elizabeth's tyme aborde her own shippes. If anye one mann killed another, he was to be bownde to the dead man and soe thrown into the sea. If anye one drew a weapon wherewith to stryke his captaine, he was to loose his right hande. If anye one drew a weapon within borde in anye waye of tumult or murder, he was to loose his righte hande. If anye one pilfered or stole awaye anye goods or monies from anye of his fellowes, he was to be thryse ducked att the boltsprite and then to be dragged at the bote sterne and sett on shoare upon the next land with a lofe of bread and a can of beere. If anye one practysed to steale awaye of her Majesty's shippes, the captaine was to cause him to be hanged by the heeles until his braines were beaten oute against the shippe's sides, and then to be cutt downe and lett fall intoe the sea. If anye one slept in his watche, for the first time, he was to be headed with a bucket of water: for the second time, he was to be haled upp by the wrysts, and to have two buckets of water poured intoe his sleeves: for the thirde time, he was to be bounde to the mayne mast with plates of iron, and to have some gunn chambers or a basket of bulletts tied to his armes and soe to remaine at the pleasure of the captaine: for the fourth time, he was to be hanged at the boltsprite, with a can of beere and a biscott of breade and a sharpe knife, and soe to hange and chuse whether he woulde cutt himself downe and fall intoe the sea, or hange still and starve. If anye one marryner or soldier stole awaye from her Majesty's service without lycense of his captaine, he was to be hanged. If anye one did mutinye aboute his allowde proportion of victuals, he was to be layde in the bilboes during the captaine's pleasure. As for all petty pillferings and commissions of that kinde, those were generallie punished with the whippe, the offender beinge to that purpose bounde faste to the capstan; and the waggerie and idleness of shippe boys paid by the boatswayne with a rodde, and commonlie this execution is done upon Mondaye mornings, and is soe frequentlie in use, that some meere seamen and saylors doe believe in good earnest that they shall never have a faire winde until the poor boyes be dulie brought to the chest, that is, whipped every Mondaye morninge.

Against flogging in the Navy.—*R. F. Stockton.*

There is one broad proposition upon which I stand. It is this. That an American sailor is an American citizen, and no American citizen shall, with my consent, be subjected to the infamous punishment of the lash. If, when a citizen enters into the service of his country, he is to forego the protection of those laws for the preservation of which he is willing to risk his life, he is entitled, in all justice, humanity and gratitude, to all the protection that can be extended to him in his peculiar circumstances. He ought certainly, to be protected from the infliction of a punishment which stands condemned by the almost universal sentiment of his fellow citizens. A punishment which is proscribed in the best prison government, proscribed in the schoolhouse, and proscribed in the best government on earth— that of parental domestic affection. Yes, sir, expelled from the social circle, from the schoolhouse, the prison-house and the army, it finds defenders and champions nowhere but in the Navy. Look to your history, that part of it which the world knows by heart, and you will find on its brightest page the glorious achievements of the American sailor. Whatever his country has done to disgrace him, and break his spirits, he never has disgraced her. He has always been ready to serve her, and he always has served her faithfully and effectually. He has often been weighed in the balance and never found wanting. The only fault found with him is, that he sometimes fights ahead of his orders. The world has no match for him, man for man, and he asks no odds and he cares for no odds, when the cause of humanity, or the glory of his country calls him to fight. Who, in the darkest days of our revolution carried your flag into the very chops of the British Channel, bearded the lion in his den, and woke the echoes of old Albion's hills by the thunder of his cannon and the shouts? It was the American sailor. And the names of John Paul Jones and the Bon homme Richard, will go down in the annals of time forever. Who struck the first blow that humbled the Barbary flag — which for a hundred years had been the terror of Christendom — drove it from the Mediterranean, and put an end to the infamous tribute it had been accustomed to extort? It was the American sailor. And the name of Decatur and his gallant companions, will be as lasting as monumental brass. In your war of 1812, when your arms on shore were covered by disaster — when Winchester had been defeated and the army of the North-west had surrendered, and when the gloom of despondency hung like a cloud over the land — who first re-lit the fires of national glory, and made the welkin ring with the shouts of victory? It was the American sailor. And the names of Hull and the Constitution will be remembered as long as we have anything worth remembering. This was no small event. The wand of Mexican prowess was broken on the Rio Grande. The wand of British invincibility was broken when the flag of the Guerriere came down. That one event was worth more to the Republic than all the money that has been expended for the Navy. Since that time, the Navy has had no stain upon its escutcheon, but has been cherished as your pride and glory. And the American sailor has established a reputation throughout the world — in peace and in war, in storm and in battle — for heroism and prowess, unsurpassed. He shrinks from no danger, he dreads no foe, and yields to no superior. No shoals are too dangerous, no seas too boisterous, no climate too rigorous, for him. The burning sun of the tropics cannot make him effeminate, nor can the eternal winter of the polar seas paralyze his energies. Foster, cherish, develop these characteristics and stimulate his ambition by rewards. But above all save him, save him from the brutalizing lash and inspire him with love and confidence for your service. And then there is no achievement so arduous, no conflict so desperate in which his actions will not shed glory upon his country. And when the final struggle comes, as soon as it will come, for the empire of the seas, you may rest with entire satisfaction in the persuasion that victory will be yours."

I can fully endorse the sentiments of the gallant Stockton with regard to the noble bearing of the genuine Tar. But when I speak of the sailor, I don't mean every one who wears a blue jacket and goes swaggering through our streets; these perhaps may belong to some wood coaster and too often come under the denomination of sailors. Notwithstanding so much has been said about punishment, it is not often that the real sailor gets into difficulty after all, for he is seldom found guilty of any of the crimes that merit punishment; nevertheless he is *exposed* to the lash and does sometimes catch it. All who know anything of the nature of a man-of-war and of the absolute necessity of a rigid code of laws — such as are expressed in the articles of war — the internal rules and regulations of the ship, know, also, that there *must* be a *penalty*, and that the police regulations of the ship must be undeviatingly adhered to, for a ship-of-war, without complete subordination, would be entirely useless and inefficient in battle; and the characteristic of a sailor is such as that he must be made at all times, and under all circumstances to toe the mark, never mind whether he be one of the crew of six who ply to the West Indies, or of the line of battle ship who number seven hundred; and now what is the penalty? I answer, 'tis the colt, the cat, the irons and confinement, and finally the yard-arm. Can the dignity and discipline of the Navy be sustained under any other penalty? without attempting even the suggestive legislator, I leave the question, with an earnest entreaty to *abolish the whip*. It may answer very well for boys when properly applied, but should never be put upon the back of a man; at the same time, I know that strong arguments can be brought forward in support of the present law; for, here are a crew of four hundred, men and boys, and some from every quarter of the Earth, from the Chinaman to the Laplander, and this heterogeneous mass must be brought under the homogeneous Government, and every officer is responsible for the punctual performance of every item of the law from all those who come legitimately under his charge.

Speaking of the sailor, I have witnessed many an instance of his undaunted bravery and ingenuousness, besides having been told very many noble acts, by those who have been the recipients. I remember, some years ago a ship got ashore near Rockaway, New York; it was in the dead of winter; the ship lay entirely under water, with only the head of her maintop-mast out; nearly all had been swept off and drowned — upon this top-mast head were a sailor and a gentleman passenger; the sailor had lashed himself and the passenger to the rigging to prevent being washed away. The night was dreadful cold — no boat dared come off until morning. The passenger said to the sailor, that his hands were so numb he must let go; he could hold on no longer and must run the risk of being washed off; the noble sailor replied, " here, sir, shove your hands into my bosom and I will hold on to you, " he did so, and the passenger, when telling the story, the tears gushed from his eyes; for said he, "when my frozen hands touched the warm, beating bosom of the noble fellow, I felt relief in a moment; my left hand was directly over his heart, and thought I, here is a heart worth having, and may God bless the owner of it."

What would our country be good for without seamen? How many doctors, ministers and lawyers would it take to reef a top-sail on a dark, stormy night? How many of that mass of nothings, which we daily come in contact with in the *street*, would it take to get a ship's anchor up? The ladies well know how to appreciate the sailor. They show their magnanimity by their generous donations in establishing Bethels, Homes, and the various institutions for the benefit of seamen, who are now properly cared for and respected; are no longer left as a prey to the merciless land-shark, many of whom, after keeping a sailor-boarding house for a few years, come out from poverty, to what are called rich men. Seamen can now go to a church of their own, under the charge of a kind pastor, who, it may be said, in truth too, is to them a father and a friend.

I had now reached a period in my life, when it might be supposed, that I had become pretty well acquainted with mankind, or to use the common phrase, "had my eyeteeth cut." But I regret to say it was not so. The knowledge that a man gains at sea, is quite different from that which he requires for a life on shore. The seaman, may understand the management of his ship on the ocean, perfectly well, and be well posted in all nautical knowledge, well acquainted with their methods of transacting business in most foreign countries. And, even let him come under the appellation of "Model Captain," who has by prudence and economy laid up a few thousand dollars, and now wishes to leave a seafaring life, and engage in some business on shore. He gets into *business*, and at first has many *friends*. But ere long finds himself completely stripped, and must go to sea again. Yes, he must "*hard lee*" again. The landsmen were too many guns for him. He once thought that he knew something; and so he did. He knew what was honest, and if he had dealt with honest men only, would in all probability have been successful, and would have accomplished that for which he left the sea.

But those who were his pretended *friends*, and by whose cunning he has been robbed, now pass him unnoticed, giving him the cold shoulder!

Reader, this is no fancy sketch. Many of those who have been thus victimized, and who are now "*where the weary are at rest, and the wicked cease from troubling*," were well known *every-where*, and whose names now stand registered among the members of the Boston Marine Society, with the prefixed asterisk. And there are, now, among us, living witnesses of the truth of what I have said before. There are now, living among us, some of those threadbare rascals, who would not hesitate, for the sake of gain, to take the last crumb of bread from a family of starving children. These fellows may be seen prowling around State street with a sort of "sneaking, hang-dog look;" the tools of the note shaver, and of the dishonest speculator. Then there are knaves of a higher grade, who stand behind the screen, and when a case of oppression has been perpetrated by the myrmidons in their employ, pretend to know nothing about it! And yet these are looked up to, and *respected?* because they are rich. I once had occasion to meet a gentleman, in State street, at a certain hour. And, at the appointed time, I saw him beside an elegant carriage, in earnest conversation with the occupant, and not wishing to intrude upon the conversation, just passed the open door, and quickly recognized the *old gentleman* with whom my friend was conversing. I stood aside, quietly awaiting the termination of what now appeared to be earnest entreaty. Soon the door was closed, my friend approached me wiping the perspiration from his brow, exclaiming "Oh, dear! it really seems that some men's hearts are harder than flint. I have been half an hour begging him to remit a debt of fifteen dollars, which was due him for the rent of a small tenement, by a widow woman, who washes in my family. She has been confined to her bed with rheumatism for several weeks, which has put her behindhand, and she is not able to pay it. The agent threatens to turn her out of doors, neck and heels, if the money is not paid. He refuses to have anything to do in the matter, saying, 'that his agent *must* collect the rents.' Thus legalizing an act of brutality, that would disgrace a savage. And this modern Dives having in his possession half a million of dollars."

The kind gentleman, who endeavored so hard to alleviate the widow, paid the money, and procured her another tenement. "The rich man also died, and was buried." His property, of course, was disposed of according to the will. Four of the sons turned out to be miserable inebriates, and went off, nobody knows where.

I do not mention these facts through invidiousness, or a desire to be personal. But, like the explorers of the northwest passage, who get among icebergs and icefloes, and who are often in imminent danger, and must quietly await the movements of the waters, which alone can extricate them from the chilling influence of these dangerous neighbors. So must all, who have fallen within the fangs of these unprincipled men quietly wait, until they see what may be slow, yet sure, retributive justice. And yet, I should conceive it to be abruptness to close these remarks, without placing them in a somewhat antithetical shape. We have had a glance at the dark, and now let us look at the bright side.

There are those among us now, and those that have gone to their glorious reward, whose names and memories "will be had in everlasting remembrance." Whose bounties have wiped the tear from many an orphan cheek, and made the widow and the fatherless sing for joy, the couch of the dying laborer, soft and easy, by promising to be kind to his helpless family, giving large sums for the purpose of propagating christian truth, and for disseminating useful knowledge among the indigent, and also of extending the hand of material friendship to those who were needy. The memory of these men draw the tear of affection, while for the others, scorn and contempt.

But to return to my narrative. I was married a few weeks after my discharge from the Macedonian, and then intended to spend the remainder of my days on shore. I became a member of the Methodist Episcopal Church, and as I had now come to an anchor, made up my mind to go ahead with honesty, prudence, and economy. I became acquainted with many of the brethern, and was really happy. As I had about $2,000 which I had carefully saved, it appeared to me that it would be well invested, in the purchase of a small house. I soon heard of one, a short distance out of the city, and on examining it with my wife, concluded to purchase it. It belonged to a prominent member of our church. On my return from it one day, before I had consummated the bargain, I met another prominent member, and to whom I communicated my intended purchase. "Ah!" said he, "my dear brother, be careful how you deal with ——. He will twist you if you dont look sharp!"

"What!" said I, "will *he* cheat me?"

"I don't say that he will cheat you, I only say lookout for him."

I parted with my adviser and went home, "struck all aback," told my wife what I had heard, who was as much astonished as I was. As I never had much experience in buying houses, up to that time, concluded that there must be something more intricate in the sale of a house than I knew anything about, so I let this purchase slide. I could not understand this inferred libel on the Christian character of the seller, notwithstanding it prevented me from purchasing the house. But in justice to this individual, before I proceed any farther, would say that I was subsequently acquainted with him during thirty years of his life; and can further add that he lived exemplary, and continued so until his death. Was a highly respected and prominent member of the Methodist church.

As I had now given up the idea of buying a house, thought I would get a lot just out of the town, and build one to suit myself. I soon found a lot which could be bought at a fair price, but there was something of an ordeal to go through before I could have it. The land belonged to a miserly old fellow, into whose good graces a very popular neighbor had entwined himself. It was for this neighbor to say who should and who should not come into the community, so I found it indispensably necessary to get on the right side of this "vigilance committee," before I could do anything with the old miser. After two or three interviews, he found out who I was, and I was then *unanimously* received. My lot was surveyed off and the deed drawn. When I went to say to the old gentleman that I would call to-morrow morning and pay the money, he, in a tremulous voice asked, *"if the money would be in silver, or gold?"*

I replied he could have it in either, when he preferred gold. Accordingly on the morrow, I carried the money to him in gold. He had a table prepared to count it (twenty-five eagles,) upon, and when his long, bony fingers clutched the pieces, it reminded me of a cat, when she first nabs a mouse, looking round to see if any attempts are made to get it away. This old man was nearly eighty years old, and the sight of this paltry sum was truly electrifying.

He died while I resided in the neighborhood, and on the evening before he expired, the doctor told him he might suck a piece of tender loin rarely broiled. He told the man who attended him to go to the butcher and ascertain how much he asked a pound for tender loin, and to come back and let him know. The man went and found the price to be fourteen cents a pound. The old man turned his languid and dying eyes towards the nurse and said, that was too dear, he could not afford it! He soon died, leaving behind him about seventy-five thousand dollars, which he had scraped together by driblets and privation, much of which after his death went to the four winds. Truly " man heapeth up riches not knowing who shall gather them."

I called the next day to see how the lot looked, now it was mine. I found that the fence had been taken away and on enquiring, was told that my kind intercessor had taken it, which he claimed as his perquisite. I said nothing more about it, as it was too small a matter to make a fuss about. The next business in order was to contract with a builder; and in this I was entirely green. I knew what kind of a house I wanted, and how to plan and build it, but to make specifications, and such a contract as that I should not be cheated, was more than I felt willing to undertake. As for what enquiries I had made among house builders, I found that prices varied in size very much like a basket of potatoes, some mighty large and some mighty small, so my chance of being cheated was in the ratio of the disparity. One of my brethren in the church and with whom I had been on intimate terms since our first acquaintance, was a house builder. I had requested him to give me his estimate, which he promised to. He said to me one day:

" Now, brother, you want to build a house. You have a little money which you want to lay out in the most economical manner. I will build your house by the day, and charge you two dollars a day for my own time; and hire the men as cheap as I can, charging you with just what I pay them. I will purchase the lumber at the lowest cash price, and in building the house will save you a great deal of money."

Now what could be fairer than this. I replied to him immediately, "go ahead." Not many days after, I happened to mention to one of the brethren that Brother ——— was building a house for me. He took me by the button-hole, and with a low, but significant voice, enquired, if I had everything in writing. I replied:

"No; we have nothing but a verbal agreement."

"Ah!" said he, "he'll cheat you, as sure as the world."

"Why, how do you mean?" I asked.

"I mean just this, that he will decieve you."

This completely upset me. I had paid him money when he asked for it, had made no enquiries about the expense already incurred, leaving it all with my good honest brother, who had pledged himself to be faithful and look after my interests. Next day I went over to the building, but he was not there. I began to look round, feeling somewhat alarmed at what had been told me, and under the work bench, there lay a man drunk! one of his smart carpenters. I soon roused the fellow out, and forbade him doing anything more to the house. I found my builder and expressed my dissatisfaction at what I had seen, and the condition of things about the house. I requested him to furnish me with my account up to the present time, which he promised to do. It was several days before I got it, but I found that he had charged me twenty-five cents a day profit on each man, which was contrary to our agreement; nevertheless I let it go without any complaint. On the following day I went over very early, before the time at which he usually came. I took a young man who was a good workman, and had been at work on the house three weeks, and asked him to go all over the building, and make an estimate of what he would finish it up for, and have the estimate ready for me by to-morrow, desiring him to keep the matter entirely to himself. I requested my builder to do the same, which he did. And I believe there was a difference of about eighty dollars between the two. I now said to my good brother, that as the bills had run up much faster than I had expected, I should pay him off, and let the young man finish it at his leisure. He then, as the Western men say, "*rared right up*," declaring he would not be put off so by *friend* or foe. I thought it was time for my "dander to rise a little," so I just recapitulated our first agreement, and compared it with the result, also reminding him that he had completely come the brother over me, and the quicker we dissolved, the better, and after many hard words on both sides, he quit. I settled his bill as I thought, in full, but in a few days he brought me another, additional of twenty dollars, saying he had omitted certain charges. I paid him that also, and we parted, apparently good friends.

CHAPTER XVII.

Commence business,—My father's death,—Start for Vermont,—Amusing incident,—Cold journey,—Arrive at Vermont,—Description of a Vermont family,—Agreeable evening,—Cold lodging,—Well entertained, —Visits,—Agreeable companions,—Happiness of contentment,—Simplicity of living,—Tough goose,—Excellent dinner,—Domestic industry and economy,—Curious idea of a ship,—Supper,—Same old goose. —Remain all night,—Breakfast,—Take leave,—Pleasant travelling companion,—Brief account of my uncle,—Remarks,—My uncle's idea of a fire,—His wish is gratified,—Invitation to go to Europe,—Sail for City Point,—Arrive there,—Visit Petersburg,—Go to church,—Description,—Go to Richmond,—On the way recieve some excellent advice,—Arrive at Richmond,—Hospitality of the people,—Introduction to a minister and his wife,—Dined,—Invited to tea,—Negroes,—Unwilling to join in family worship,—Walk out,—Caught in the rain,—Hospitality of a lady,—Kindness,—Affecting story,—Further attention and politeness,—Allusion to the destruction of the Richmond theatre, —Take leave,—Account of a slave sale.

In 1822, I commenced business on my own account; and as nothing occurred of sufficient interest to record here, pass on to 1824, when my father, who was at my house on a visit, left us early on Monday morning for Vermont, whither he was going on a visit to his brother, who resided in Newfane.

On Monday night, between the hours of eleven and twelve, I had been down the wharf to attend to moving a ship, and just as I had reached my door, a man stood there who had just rung the bell. I inquired what he wanted, and on learning my name, replied:

"I have come in from Lexington to inform you of the death of your father, who died very suddenly at our house, at 4 o'clock, this afternoon."

I had given my father two letters for my uncles, inviting them to call on me, should they ever come to Boston, and in these letters had given my name and residence. When it was ascertained that he was dead, they opened one of them, to know who he was, &c. This was the way in which I was so easily found.

I immediately proceeded to Lexington to make the necessary arrangements for the funeral. The hotel keeper then gave me the following statement:

"Your father stopped at my house about noon, and told me that he was unwell, and unable to proceed any further at present, and wished me to show him a room. I saw he was very weak and sick, and on reaching his room, his strength had entirely failed; he laid down upon the bed, while I went for a doctor. I had hardly reached the stairway when I heard a fall. I hastened back to his room, and found him lying dead on the floor. He was immediately placed upon the bed again, and a doctor was sent for. A post mortem examination was held, and the cause of his death was said to be an obstruction near the heart."

My father observed, on the evening previous to his departure, that it had been his prayer that he might be permitted to see all the members of his family once more before his death, which prayer was thus signally answered.

I had never seen these uncles, and on the following winter, the sleighing being remarkably fine, I took a seat in the mail stage for Brattleboro, Vermont, and from there to Newfane, about 18 miles distant, by private conveyance. The uncle I was now in quest of resided there. The day on which I started from Boston was bitter cold; therefore I went to a clothing store and purchased a thick, drab overcoat to keep myself from freezing. When we arrived at Lowell, I got out, with the rest of the passengers, at the hotel door, and went in to the bar-room to warm myself. The loungers in the room, seemed to eye me closely, and wherever I went, it appeared that I was the object of their attraction. All at once my attention was directed to a placard which read thus:

$50 REWARD.

DARING ROBBERY.

"Last night the house of the subscriber was entered, and the following articles stolen: A quantity of linen and woollen apparel, among which was a drab overcoat, with white mother-of-pearl buttons; the coat nearly new."

Exactly the description of the one I had on. It struck me at once that the coat I had on, was the reason why I was so much looked at, and the cause of the collection of men at the door. I must confess I felt rather awkward, for if they had arrested me on suspicion of being the house-breaker, merely from the similarity of the coat, I should of course have been obliged to have given my name, and residence, and in all probability would have been handed over to the sheriff. Thus I should have lost my passage, besides having my name trumpeted through all the papers, that I had been arrested for house-breaking in Lowell, when I was fast asleep with my wife in Boston; and that I had stolen a coat which I had bought only a few hours before, of Gove & Lock, in Ann street.

When the stage was ready, I walked through the crowd, got in, and we drove off. It was very evident from all appearances, that these people actually thought that the coat I had on, was the one stolen, as it exactly answered the description, even to the velvet collar.

We left Lowell and passed through the southern edge of New Hampshire, over the turnpike, and a more dismal looking region I have never seen in the wildest part of Russia; and in passing through one of the towns, I saw a sign on an old dilapidated shanty, *Elizabeth Saltmarsh*, dressmaker. And in one of the small villages in the northern edge of Massachusetts, was a Mr. E. D. Greenfield, attorney-at-law. I thought if the parties were not married, what a union this would make. A Greenfield with a Saltmarsh; and when the Saltmarsh would be merged in the Greenfield, the cutting and trimming would be done by the Greenfield mowers.

We arrived at Brattleboro late at night. I was nearly torpid with cold, and as there was a good fire burning in the kitchen, we, half frozen passengers, took possession of the fire place, and when sufficiently thawed, ordered a supper, which, in the course of an hour, they gave us. Early next morning, I procured a private conveyance to Newfane, and when we had arrived at the edge of the town, I began to enquire for Squire Robbins' place.

"O, Squire Robbins, the forehanded man. Ain't he—"

"Well, I don't know how many hands or how many feet he has, but I want to find Mr. Asa Robbins of Newfane."

"Well, yes; you see yonder hill with the red building on the side?"

"Yes."

"Well, that's Squire Robbins' farm."

I stopped at a tavern about half a mile from the place, to adjust my dress, and in the operation thought that I should have frozen. And of all the places, in any of the Northern regions, that I have ever visited, I think Vermont is the coldest. As I had but half a mile to go, I started off through the snow, went up to the house, and enquired for Mr. Robbins. He came to the door, I told him who I was. He shook my hand and invited me in, and received me with much cordiality, calling all the family to see their new cousin. He had a rousing fire in the kitchen, over which I had another good thawing, and it being Saturday evening, the unmarried boys and girls were at home. We had a good tuck out of nuts, apples, cider and doughnuts, and such a fire! The great fire in London, of 1666, was somewhat larger, but certainly not much hotter. The fireplace was ten feet long, four feet deep, and from the hearth to the flue was six feet, and this was filled with ignited hickory logs, in full blast, from end to end. As it was very seldom that these people met with any one from the Atlantic States, my visit was rather interesting. We conversed on many subjects, till nearly twelve o'clock, when I began to feel rather sleepy.

My cousin Melissa, conducted me to my room, and bade me good night. After closing the door, I felt a dreadful chill, and on examining the bed clothes, was fearful that I should lie cold. Then there was a shower-bath in one corner of the room, the sight of which made me shudder; and after getting into bed and tucking myself up nicely, began to shake in good style. Sleep was out of the question, and after shivering away two or three hours, I got into a doze and dreamed that I was lying on an iceberg. Although suffering from cold, I could not refrain from laughing at the sudden transition and contrast of life. Last evening I was nearly roasted, and from the time I went to bed till I arose, was nearly frozen. As soon as daylight appeared, I heard a stir down stairs, and was very soon along-side the crater of Vesuvius. I told Melissa that I had been very cold all night. "There, now, cousin Sam, I don't believe you shot your winder down." No, I shut no window; and lo! right at my head was an open window, with just a curtain before it, which, in some measure, accounted for the temperature of my bedroom, which seemed to be many degrees below zero. But we had a substantial breakfast: for my uncle had his larder well stocked with good things. Instead of an ice-house he had a snow-shed, filled solid and packed with snow, in which he kept his variety of meats and fish. As it was the Sabbath, and there being but one meeting-house in the village, and two sects, and each had their minister on alternate Sundays, it not being our turn to-day, we spent the time in talking over miscellaneous matters. Towards noon, I began to look around for some signs of dinner, when my uncle, rather suspecting that I was not acquainted with their Sunday arrangements, observed to me that the dinner hour on that day was six o'clock P. M. We however partook of a good lunch, and at evening, of a sumptuous dinner, after which several of the cousins came in and we had quite an agreeable time.

Next day I visited among their families, and was peculiarly struck with the patriarchal simplicity and happiness that existed among them. I think there were five in the group, and situated on the southern slope of a hill, and all within a few rods of the parental mansion. In each family there were two or three healthy, pretty children. The wives were employed in carding, spinning, or weaving, and one or two grandmothers were comfortably seated and knitting. Each family had two or more cows, a few sheep, pigs, and lots of poultry, and land enough to afford them, with hard work and strict economy, a good living, and some silver change to lay up in the stocking. Another of the cousins, Mrs. Gaffield, lived a little farther off. Mr. G——, when he married was a "*forehanded man,*" a hatter by trade; and owned four acres of land, with a small house containing three rooms, and a hatter's shop ten feet by eight upon it. His whole estate he valued at six hundred dollars, and considered himself independent of the world. He invited me to come over and dine with him on the following day; also to spend the evening, on which occasion he invited his friends and relations. I soon found that in consequence of having come from Boston, and by amusing them with accounts of different parts of the world, that I had become quite a *lion* among them.

Accordingly, on Tuesday, I was on hand at friend Gaffield's, when he showed me round his place. First, I must see the sty where he raised his fat hog that weighed nearly four hundred pounds; then I must see the fine *caows* and lastly, his hat shop, which was a curiosity; and without any attempt at describing it, will only say, that, if a man could manufacture a hat in this pen, then there are no limits to his ingenuity; and yet this plain, noble hearted and honest man, made, on an average, three hats a month, and was now making one for the deacon for which he was to receive three dollars; and all in silver, because these pesky bills were so uncertain. Dinner being now ready, we went in. Mrs. G—— had been flying round; and from the way in which the feathers flew in the morning, I knew that one or more bipeds must lose their lives on my account. And so it appeared, for on the table was a goose, the smell of which was enough to do one good; which alas! was all that I was to have of it. Besides the goose, there was an abundant supply of fine yellow potatoes, apple-sauce, and various kinds of pies, with leather tops and green hide bottoms, excellent sage cheese, the finest bread and sweetest butter I ever tasted. Friend Gaffield now began to sharpen his knife by rubbing two together preparatory to dissecting the goose; which I could see by the manner in which his keen eyes rested upon it, that he knew the nature of his job. At first, with much effort he forced the fork into the breast, and commenced dissecting the leg, but it was of no use, the knife would not penetrate those veteran sinews. He next tried the wing, but might as well have attempted to cut the flukes from an anchor. At length, the kind lady innocently suggested, that she was afraid the goose was tough. The perspiration was now running down poor Joe's face; and he next attempted to hack off a piece from the breast, which he succeeded in doing, and placed it on my plate. I was busy however eating the nice potatoes and goose gravy. The poor fellow now gave it up in despair, freely acknowledging that it was the toughest goose he ever had seen. Notwithstanding, I made an excellent dinner, and we had a good joke over this antiquated bird, that doubtless was the veritable, or a descendant of the cacklers in the temple of Juno at Rome, who awakened Marcus Manlius, in time to pitch the Gauls headlong down the Tarpeian rock, and thus saved Rome.

As we expected company in the evening, and as it was very cold, I remained in the house during the afternoon and spent the time in agreeable conversation with my excellent and industrious cousin, Almost every article of furniture was of her own or her husband's make. Carpets, bed-quilts and every article of clothing in the family, excepting shoes, and her Sunday gown, were of her manufacture. Her pretty calico gown she had bought at "*the store*" for eleven dozen of eggs, and her best shoes for six dozen. She paid twenty-five cents in money to have her dress cut and basted; whether by Elizabeth Saltmarsh, or a competitor, she did not inform me. But it had been worn two summers, and had *not come to wear yet.* At evening, the company assembled. There were about half a dozen *young* men, and one, pretty well advanced. The chief topic of conversation was about ships, how such great things could float on the water; neither of them had ever seen a ship or been out of Vermont.

"Joe Gaffield," says, cousin Sam, "I don't see how a ship can stand up with them great Jo-fired, long masts?"

"Oh," says the old gentleman, "they put in rocks for balancing, then they put the load right on top of the rocks, and then sail along."

"Well," says another, "it must take a deuced sight of timber to make one."

"Oh, yes," replied the old gentleman, "it would take all of Tom Brazier's lot to make one ship." And after a pause of a few seconds, Joe Gaffield, with a very earnest look says,

"Cousin Sam, they tell me, that the *housen in Boston, are all brick. I should think they would all sink right daown; and some of 'em are higher than our meeting-house, and sometimes they ketch fire. I would'nt sleep in one on 'em for all Boston.*"

It was now twelve o'clock, when we were invited to take supper in the kitchen, and by hard squeezing, we managed to sit around the table, and while we were talking, our industrious hostess was preparing a hot supper. She had managed by some means to cut the goose in pieces, and had stewed it with potatoes and onions: it truly was a nice mess, but after all, who ever undertook to tackle a bone with an idea of getting any meat from it, was much deceived; which was easily seen from the manner in which they were slyly laid aside. But the remainder of the fixings were first-rate, and the time passed merrily, and if any of them are alive now, they will remember that night.

I had appointed the next morning for my departure, and as it was quite late, was persuaded to remain there all night. They made a nice bed on the floor for me, and with plenty of rugs and carpets, I slept very comfortable. At daylight my good cousin had breakfast under way, which at seven o'clock, was smoking hot on the table. Here was the old goose stewed up again, and tough as ever. I made a capital breakfast on hot potatoes, sweet butter, and excellent bread and cheese, with a cup of good rye coffee and cream. I took an affectionate leave of these kind-hearted, and happy people, and was to leave Newfane, for Brattleboro in a covered sleigh, and when the driver called for me, was told, that I had a fellow passenger in the shape of a very sociable young lady, who had been keeping school at Newfane, and was returning home to New Hampshire.

Here we were, both of us wrapped up together in a buffalo robe, bouncing over stone walls, stumps of trees, and no matter what, there was no road. All the distance to Brattleboro was one vast sea of snow; but the driver being a good navigator, brought us safe into port at about ten o'clock at night. One object in thus detailing my visit to Vermont, is to show what every one knows, that true happiness does not consist in wealth, popularity, or emolument. Take, if you please, this one family or community, commencing with Mr. Robbins, who, in 1795, having just married, went from Worcester to his present location, with but forty cents left, after his arrival in this, then wilderness, and on the spot where his house now stands, he built a rude hut for present shelter; took up several acres of woodland, which he cleared away, and with some assistance from the neighbors, who were scattered around within 15 miles, erected a house, and cleared a few acres ready for planting, in the following spring, and without entering more minutely into his beginning, he had, when I visited him, several thousand dollars in the Brattleboro Bank, three hundred acres of excellent land, well stocked, and sent large quantities of butter, cheese and pork, annually to Boston. His family were settled around him and all enjoying the height of human happiness, industry and content. And if we should attempt to draw the contrast between this happy community, and the continual and fevered excitement which prevails in our cities,—men rushing headlong to perdition, for the sake of grasping another dollar, tugging and delving through the anxieties of the day, retiring at night upon their downy beds, weary and exhausted, not to sleep, but too often to dread the approach of to-morrow,—we shall see that industry and frugality are twin sisters, who point heavenward, while avarice and covetousness completely extinguishes that noble principle which the Creator gave us, as forming one of the chief elements of our free agency. The covetous and grasping man loves no one but himself. The acquisition of wealth forms the focus of every feeling. The salvation of his own and the souls of his family come not within the sphere of his anxieties. And though he may be aged and his daughters apparently well married to whiskered and moustached *expectants*, and his sons making large calculations on the old man's death, and perhaps at a Thanksgiving dinner party he may look around with much complacency, being the root of these prolific branches, which will flourish more exuberantly when the *root is in the ground.*

Then his miserly and covetous acquisitions soon go to the four winds, and as it often happens in the alternations of fortune that the third generation are doomed to penury and want.

My uncle Robbins, once, in conversation about fires in Boston, enquired if they were easily extinguished, to which I replied that the fire department were probably the most efficient in the world. He replied that he had never seen a house on fire, and were it not for the loss and distress occasioned by it, he should like to see a good large fire. It so happened not long after, that he was on a visit to Boston, when the old glass-house in Essex street was burned. He was at my house at the time. We both went to the fire, and he seemed perfectly frantic with curiosity, and I had hard work to keep him from breaking through the lanes. And, as it was, he got pretty well ducked, for venturing too far.

In May, 1830, business being rather dull, I had an invitation from a particular friend, to accompany his son, (a young gentleman just preparing for college,) on a short tour through England; he having a ship about ready to sail, first going south for a freight of cotton, and then to Liverpool. I accepted the offer, and we sailed on the 15th of May, in the ship Robin Hood, Capt. John Candler, for City Point, on James river, Virginia.

On arriving there, Capt. Candler found his freight ready, and it would probably require ten days to load the ship. I went over to Petersburg to pass a few days, and spent a very pleasant Sabbath in attending the Methodist church for colored people. It stood in a beautifnl grove, a short distance from the town. The day was fine, the birds pouring forth their sweetest notes, and the gentle breeze wafting its fragrance through the fine woods, made it truly enchanting. The preacher was a colored man, and excepting the negro accent and pronunciation, the sermon was as good as I had ever heard in my life. The singing cannct be described, but must be heard to be appreciated. Besides the regular choir, the whole congregation join in. And people may talk of opera, Hungarian, and any other kind of singers, but I had never heard voices so soft and melodious as those of the female slaves at this rural place, and others of which I shall have occasion to refer.

On Monday morning, we took the stage for Richmond, and had, as fellow passengers, a gentleman and his lady, who had just returned from London. On his learning that I was going to England, kindly offered me a few words of advice, which I was very happy to receive, and as the sequel will show, were of essential benefit to me. The gentleman continued:

"My remarks will apply principally to London; before you leave Liverpool, determine on the hotel at which you intend to stop, on your arrival at London; and when the coach reaches its stopping-place, order the cabman to drive you immediately to your place of selection, and be careful not to let any one know that you are a stranger. On your arrival at the hotel, say in a careless manner to the head waiter, who usually receives travellers, 'Waiter, pay the cabman," which he will do, and you will not be cheated; then ask him to conduct you to a room, make your own bargain as to price and location; and when you book your name, say that Liverpool is the place from whence you came; for if you say United States, you will have tag-rag and bob-tail after you, with all sorts of things to sell; besides, your pretty *bar-maid* will be sure to make you pay for seeing London, which you will ascertain when you receive your bill.

"In London, you seldom have any dealings with the landlord, the business being transacted by the bar-maid. Besides all this, when you leave, every individual servant in the house expects a fee from you; and if they know you to be an American, will expect double the sum that they usually receive from an Englishman.

"In passing through the principal streets, probably a genteel looking fellow will approach you with a very polite bow, take your hand, and greet you as if you were an old acquaintance, at the same time assuming a sort of perplexity at not remembering where he had the pleasure of last seeing you, and kindly requesting you just to step in, as he wishes to enquire for a particular friend, with whom he is sure you are well acquainted. Now if you are simpleton enough to enter, the door is immediately closed, and after being robbed, you are passed out of a backdoor into some obscure alley, to make the best of your way out. And when you stop to look at a print shop window, be sure to have one hand on your watch, and the other upon your wallet, for there are always pickpockets at all such places."

I thanked the gentleman very kindly for this piece of pre-information, and it will appear, as I proceeded, that everything was true, and as I said before, of infinite service to me.

At Richmond, I stopped at the Eagle hotel, and directly opposite was an auctioneer's block for selling slaves, or, as they call them, servants. I took a walk through the city, and was much pleased with the people, for they were certainly very hospitable. On Sabbath day, I introduced myself to the minister, after the morning service, when he with much politeness, invited me home to dine. I accepted the invitation, and on arriving there, was introduced to his wife, who was also a preacher, usually supplying some pulpit every Sabbath. We dined on Virginia ham, green peas, and iced milk, and an excellent dinner it was. I was also invited home to tea, after the afternoon service; both minister and wife were so urgent that I could not resist the invitation. After tea, we had family devotion, but the servants would not come in. Mrs. Harris told me that they would never come in to family worship, saying, as an excuse, that they didn't believe in white men's prayers. In sauntering along, one day, it began to rain; as I had no umbrella, and was far from my hotel, I stopped a moment to consider, when a door opened right against me, and an elderly lady very politely invited me in.

It was quite a gentéel house; the lady conducted me into a handsome parlor, expressing herself highly gratified that I happened to be so near her house. I told her I was a stranger in Richmond, and on my way to England. She now evinced quite an interest in my journey, enquiring if I had a family; and when I named that I had a daughter, the good old lady burst into tears, and then told me, that only a few weeks ago, she had lost her only daughter; her darling child. She then related the particulars of her sickness and death. And, although it would be almost as easy to squeeze a tear out of a grindstone as from my eyes, yet the old lady brought them. I could not hear the story of the death of her daughter without a little melting. She was taken suddenly with an obstruction in the bowels, and when the doctor told her that she could not live, she requested that her Sunday scholars might be sent for. They came, she took each by the hand, and in a most affectionate manner, bade them be sure and meet her in Heaven. They all kissed her, when she immediately expired.

The old lady could say no more at present; but after she had become somewhat composed, invited me into her garden, which was fragrant with flowers, and sweet shrubbery. After we were re-seated in the parlor, she related the particulars of that dreadful and fatal disaster, the burning of the Theatre. She named one family that had lost nearly every member. The play was one of unusual attraction. Three lovely daughters, a brother, and the mother, all perished in each others arms; and a young naval officer, who had succeeded in getting out, and was shortly to be married to the eldest, not finding the young lady among the rescued, plunged into the fire, determined to rescue her or die, and poor fellow he perished!

The weather now being fine, I took an affectionate leave of the good old lady, returned to my hotel, and spent the evening with a very intelligent gentleman, from the North, who entertained me with an account of a slave sale that took place a few days before, opposite the hotel. There were two boys, and a young woman, about twenty-four-years of age, to be sold. The woman was a bright mulatto, but had rather a sickly appearance. She was very decently dressed with a white handkerchief over her bosom, and a pink one on her head.

The auctioneer put her up, and the first offer was two hundred dollars, and after hanging on this bid rather over a minute, a man stepped up, and whispered something into the auctioneer's ear. He drew himself up at full length, and with a very solemn look, says: "Gentlemen, *I am informed that this woman, Martha, has religion, and understands the management of children, is a good seamstress, and is acquainted with all sorts of housework. Gentlemen she has religion!* How much am I offered for this valuable servant? I am offered two hundred and fifty, three hundred, three hundred and fifty, four hundred! *Gentlemen, she has religion!* and I am offered only *four hundred dollars* for this pious servant. *Four hundred and fifty,*" and she was finally knocked off for five hundred dollars.

During all this time her eyes were steadily fixed upon the ground, and when an indecent question was asked by a slave dealer, she gently raised her head, and gave the fellow *such a look.* Her new master sent her off in a wagon, probably in the country.

CHAPTER XVIII.

Return to City Point,—Ship not ready,—Screwing Cotton,—Nigger's Song,—Acquaintance with a Slave blacksmith,—He is a Methodist Preacher,—A worthy man,—Ship loaded,—Run out of the Bay,—Pleasant passage,—Go ashore at Hollyhead,—Pleasant trip to Liverpool,—Menai bridge,—Arrive at Chester,—Breakfast,—Arrive at Liverpool,—Walk out on the Manchester Railroad,—Continue at St. Helens,—Well received,—Visit to a Brewery,—Take too much beer,—Leave in rather a bad plight,—Take tea,—Don't like the cream,—Go to the house,—Retire,—Very sick,—Thirsty in the night,—Found water,—Arise early,—Take a cup of tea,—Start off,—Rain,—Disappointment,—Determined to proceed to Liverpool in the rain,—Perseverance,—Arrive at my boarding house,—All right,—Laughable effect of my story,—Take passage for London,—Pleasant view from the top of the coach,—Pass through many interesting towns,—New Castle-under-Lyme,—See the first locomotive engine,—Pass through Wolverhampton,—Interesting sight,—Arrive at Birmingham,—Remain all night,—Start early next morning,—Irish companion,—His ignorance of the United States,—His enquiries,—Left us at Coventry,—Peeping Tom,—Pass through Weeden,—Yankee doodle,—Dreadful,—Arrive at London,—All right,—Call on a gentleman,—Not in,—His visit to me,—Two ladies call,—Their embarrassment,—Explanation,—Accompany them home,—Pleasant interview,—Mr. Henford very attentive,—Pleasant excursion to Deptford and Greenwich,—Pensioners.

I RETURNED to City Point in the steamer. Our ship was not yet full, which gave me an opportunity of seeing how the *niggers* screwed cotton; and think, if I had a ship, that was of any value, she should never be screwed as the Robin Hood was. Curiosity led me into the hold to hear the boys sing, and to see how they managed. The head stevadore, a very intelligent *slave*, took the measure of the space, and selected the bale accordingly; the bales were generally about two feet by thirty inches square, and when the space was but about twelve or fourteen inches, or too small to admit one, two planks were inserted three or four feet, between the two, the outer ends were kept far enough apart to receive the bale, and the inside well greased. A sampson post, which is a piece of timber nine or ten inches square with notches to receive the end of the jack-screw, is placed diagonally at the end of the bale to be screwed; the upper end of the post against the beam and the lower end resting on the bales of the lower tier. The bale is now well greased, entered, and a powerful jack-screw firmly fixed against the sampson post and the end of the bale; and, to any one unacquainted with the process, it would seem impossible that it could ever be forced into that small space, but we shall soon see. The screw is now set taut, and a handspike attached to the crank, and six powerful negroes take hold and give two or three turns, then hold on a minute. The old boss stevadore, by way of encouragement, says, "*Boys, dat bale got to go dar;*" one of the darkies commences in a drawling tone, "*Massa be berry good man.*" The chorus "*whagh,*" round goes the screw, crack goes the beams, and in goes the bale. "*Missey berry good lady too. She biley de eggs and gib nigger de broff; whagh!*" "*Ah, boys you do dat nice.*" By this time the ebony faces begin to shine like a newly blacked boot, and then comes the sweet smelling savor wafting by, like the spicy breezes of Ceylon; but the bale is in though. And when the Irish stevadores in Liverpool get hold of a hard tier, you'll hear them cursing the —— nagers for squazing it so hard.

While we were at City Point we had several small jobs of iron work which the captain wished me to attend to. The blacksmith was a very intelligent negro, and a Methodist preacher. It was really a pleasure to converse with him. He was the property of a widow lady in Richmond, and, in consequence of his excellent character, she had given him permission to work any-where in the State, by paying her a certain portion of his earnings. And truly this *poor, rich* slave was mighty in the Scriptures. He was a finely formed, self-educated man, and what leisure time I had was spent in conversation with him. Yes, reader, I passed many an agreeable hour with this *nigger* and if *you* are as sure of Heaven as he then was, and I may add now is, *you are truly happy. And when unable to work, if his life is spared, after all his toil, he may go to his mistress, and, in the language of King Lear, say to her, "Here I stand, your slave, a poor, infirm, weak, and despised old man."*

Our cargo being now on board, the ship was dropped down the river, we took a fine south-west wind and run out of the bay in fine style. We had a very pleasant passage and arrived off Hollyhead on the Fourth of July. It being foggy, our number could not be distinguished at the signal station therefore a boat came off to us, for the necessary information. I gave them half a guinea to take me ashore; as by landing here I should have an opportunity of going through Wales, and of crossing the strait between the Isle of Anglesea and the main land, on the celebrated Menai suspension bridge, under which ships of the largest class could pass with all sail set. I learned on my arrival ashore that George Fourth had just expired, which caused much excitement throughout the country. I took the coach the same afternoon for Liverpool, 116 miles distant. We rode all night; the weather was remarkably fine and I could see to read most of the time. Arrived early next morning at Chester, a very ancient town, which is on the line of division between England and Wales. Here we took breakfast, changed the coach and started for Liverpool. I had felt for many years a strong desire to see England:

And now on Albion's shore,
I meant to view the landscape o'er.

The railroad between Liverpool and Manchester had just been surveyed, a portion of it graded and the rails laid. As I had a letter of introduction to a gentleman at St. Helens, twelve miles distant from Liverpool, started one morning for a walk on the track, and if not too much fatigued meant to continue on to St. Helens, which I did, and arrived there at 10 o'clock A. M., found the gentleman to whom I was introduced; and was received with much kindness and attention. As I did not intend to remain there but a day, he took me in his chaise for a ride round the country. On our return we stopped at Mr. S——'s brewery, said to be one of the largest in England. I was introduced to Mr. S—— as a gentleman from America; he was a *monstrous big man*, yet he assured me that before he commenced his brewery he weighed but one hundred and fifty-eight pounds, now his weight was over twenty-one stones, about three hundred pounds. Mr. S—— of course took it for granted that as we had no such extensive breweries in the United States, a sight of his would be to me interesting. Accordingly we entered the first room, which contained twelve large vats, holding many thousand gallons of beer, of different ages. Frequently turning to me, and asking:

"*Have you anything like this in America?*"

When about half way through, we were, by his request, seated. He called out:

"John, bring me a gill of four year old Porter."

Conscience! a gill of Porter among three! but I soon found what a gill meant. John came with a quart measure full and foaming, with three handsomely cut glass goblets. He filled one and handed it to me, which I just tasted and returned to him.

"What!" said he, "is it not good?"

"Oh, yes sir, excellent, but my head will not bear it."

"Oh, nonsense! 'tis as mild as milk."

My friend had tossed his off, and like Oliver Twist, held out his glass for more. He too, assured me how *mild* it was. So I drank half the contents of the goblet and pronounced it firstrate. We then commenced our walk again, visiting another apartment, where the bottling was done; here were men, women and children, all at work, in every stage of the bottling process. And now we must try a bottle of Old Stout.

By this time I began to feel how *mild* the four years old Porter was. I really felt about half "smothered," but no excuse could prevail, I must try the Stout. So I drank about half a table glass full, which I feared would be the ounce that was to break the camel's back. I now felt intoxicated, and would have given the world to have been clear of this horrid place.

We were invited into the house, and when seated in a splendid parlor, Mr. S—— rang a small hand bell. A plump Irish girl answered the summons. "*Mary, bring a jug of the old Burton from the further arch.*" So Mary brought up a can of old Burton ale. Mr. S—— began his usual encomium on his good stuff, the "*best in England.*" The Burton glasses were put upon the table and filled. Now I must drink the host's health, which I positively declined, although I had never tasted Burton ale in my life, yet, was fearful it might be too strong. Mr. S——, with much vehemence assured me that it was *smooth* as oil. I gave way again, and put the glass to my lips, and sure enough it was smooth as oil, for half the liquid went down my throat before I was aware of it. And now I had reached the climax, for, be it known to all Johnny Raw's, that Burton ale is little inferior to brandy, especially if it is old. Now I was completely intoxicated, yet my senses were not in the least impaired. I was aware of my condition, and how I came so, and here was my friend rubbing his hand over his vest buttons, and looking towards me and saying, "Oh! how nice I feel." But we had not finished yet. Next came the bottle of brandy, and now we must drink the health of the new king, *William IV.*, which I again positively declined. I was sick as death, besides feeling very faint. The door was only a short distance on my left, but how to reach it puzzled me. Everything appeared to be flying round topsy-turvy, so I waited "till the door came round, and then made a spring, and luckily caught the knob, and reached the outside. The cool breeze in some measure restored me. Mr. S—— came out, insisting on my drinking King William's health. I now began to remonstrate by telling him that I was already intoxicated, and positively refused to take a drop of anything more within my lips. My friend, Mr. Gray, came out and began urging me to try a little brandy. I begged him to take me away from this place, which he said he would do, when he had taken leave of Mr. S——. I managed to get into the chaise, and we drove away from that detestable brewery, and on our way to his house, he stopped at his sister's. As it was about tea time, we were invited to join them. I had an impression that a cup of tea would make me feel better. We were soon seated round the table and the servant handed me a cup of tea, and in her other hand she held a black earthern pitcher, and was about pouring something into my cup. I asked her what she had there.

"*Rum, sir,*" said she, "*'tis very good in tea!*"

"Well, please take it away from *me.*"

The very smell of the rum took away my appetite. After remaining there a short time, we went to his house. I requested Mrs. Gray to show me where I could lie down. She gave me an excellent bed, in a handsomely furnished chamber. At midnight I awoke in a high fever and parched with thirst. I had forgotten where the door was, and knew not how I should obtain water. It was quite dark, and in fumbling round, came across the washstand, and fortunately there was water in the pitcher. Whether it was clean I could not ascertain, but was willing to run the risk. I drank a hearty draught, and went to bed again; but felt very faint. I turned out at daylight, asked the girl in the kitchen to give me a cup of warm tea, which she very kindly did, adding to it a piece of toast. I felt so anxious to get away from St. Helens that as soon as I had taken my tea, requested the girl to give my respects to Mr. and Mrs. Gray, and say to them that I wished to catch the Manchester coach for Liverpool, and that was the reason why I started so early. In order to meet the coach, I had to cross a moor some two or three miles wide, but had not left the house more than twenty minutes before it began to rain most furiously. I had neither umbrella nor overcoat, my shoes were quite thin, and what was worse than all, was quite unwell from the effects of yesterday. When I reached the Manchester coach office there was not room for another passenger until the afternoon. Here I was in a dilemma; wet through, sick, and twelve miles from Liverpool.

I began to soliloquize. "Well, what is to be done now? Among strangers, wet through, and cold. All at once, as though moved by a sudden impulse, I started from the coach office, the rain still pouring, and walked off four miles an hour, until I had reached within four miles of Liverpool. I was weary and hungry, and stepped aside from the road into a cottage where there was a woman and a little child. I sat down a few moments, and found I was growing stiff.

The good woman had nothing to offer me to eat, so I picked myself up again and finished my journey by two o'clock, P. M., and strange as it may appear, when I entered my boarding-house, had completely recovered my strength and felt as well as I ever did in my life, although I had been soaked in the rain since five o'clock in the morning, and had eaten nothing but a little toast. There were a number of shipmasters at our boarding-house, and when I told them the story of my journey to St. Helens and back; they were convulsed with laughter; and it served to make fun for us while we were together. I had now seen as much of Liverpool as I desired, and took a seat on the "*Tally-ho*," for London.

Most travellers in England in those days, rode upon the top of the coach, as it was more pleasant, and less expensive, besides affording the traveller a better prospect of the country. The risk of rain however must be taken into consideration, as it is very inconvenient to hold an umbrella when the passengers are crowded. We left Liverpool for London in high glee, passing through many interesting villages and manufacturing towns. The first town of any note that drew my attention, was New Castle-under-Lyme, in Staffordshire. It stands on a branch of the Trent, and when the coach stopped to shift horses, I noticed opposite the inn a printed bill upon the post of a gate leading up to an extensive machine establishment. The advertisement ran thus: "On exhibition at the machine works on the hill, a steam carriage that will draw — tons on a lêvel road, ——— miles an hour. Price of admittance, one shilling." This was the first locomotive engine that we have any account of. We passed through Wolverhampton just after dark. The atmosphere being rather hazy, it looked like the infernal regions; fires blazing up in all directions from the numerous blasting furnaces. It has also been completely undermined by coal-diggers, and in many instances the earth floors of the cottages have fallen through. We passed many interesting towns, which, on approaching, the guard played most beautifully on the bugle. The coach arrived quite late at Birmingham, where we remained until morning. On leaving B., I had a fellow traveller at my side — an Irish gentleman, who appeared to be well informed on everything but Geography and the History of the United States, of which he was as ignorant as a mule. I have always found the English to be sadly deficient in a knowledge of any other country than their own. This gentleman, on learning that I was from America, appeared to be much interested, enquiring about "that wonderful country." He said to me -

"I suppose you are well acquainted with my brother ?"

"Your brother, sir; what is his name, and where does he reside?" said I.

"Ah! his name is John Nevins, and I think he lives at Swan River."

"Swan River," said I, "why that is in New Holland."

"Ah! indeed; I thought it was in America."

My Irish companion left us at Coventry, and I was really sorry to lose him. By the way, I must say a word about this ancient town. Everybody has probably heard of "Peeping Tom," of Coventry. Leofrice, Earl of Mercia, who was Lord of the place about 1040, is said to have loaded the inhabitants with heavy taxes, on account of some provocation he had received from them; and being importuned by his lady, Godivia, to remit them, he consented, upon condition that she would ride in a state of nudity through the town, which condition she accepted and performed. For being possessed of a long flowing head of hair, she contrived to dispose of her tresses so as to preserve her decency; and at the same time, enjoined the citizens on pain of death, not to look out as she passed. The curiosity of a poor tailor, however, prevailed over his fears, and he ventured to take a single peep, but was struck blind, and was ever after called Peeping Tom. This improbable story is annually commemorated by the citizens of Coventry, with great splendor, and a female, closely habited in fine linen of flesh color, rides through the town, attended by a very numerous and elegant procession. The window through which the tailor is said to have gratified his curiosity, is still shown, with his effigy, always newly dressed for the procession, which is on the Friday preceding Trinity Sunday.

While passing through Weeden, I requested the guard to

give us Yankee Doodle, on his bugle. *Here*, is a large encampment of regular English soldiers, and as soon as the bugle notes echoed through the tents, such a scampering! The whole place was in commotion; and one pretty little girl who was seated near me, was so incensed at the "Yanke National Air," that she put a finger in each ear, determined that such a vile tune should never penetrate her royal head. We entered London through Highgate, and according to the admonition of my Richmond friend, when our coach pulled up at the Bull-and-Mouth, Hyde-Park, I called a cab, directing the driver to take me to the Saracen-Head, Snowhill, Skinner street. I rattled it off so handily that coachee took me for an old Londoner: I entered the hotel with as much assurance as though I had been born on the spot. Notwithstanding my caution, they soon ascertained that I was not an Englishman, in consequence of which, they paid me every attention the house afforded.

Before leaving Boston, I was furnished with introductory letters to several families in England, with whose relatives I was well acquainted, and among whom was a lady whose brothers and three sisters lived in London. Accordingly in a few days I set about hunting up my new acquaintances. My first letter was to a gentleman whose place of business was in the Strand. I called there, but as he was not in, left my card with the letter, and went home, it being near my dining hour.

Just after dining, and while sitting in my room, the barmaid called to me, saying, that there was a gentleman below that wished to see me. I came down and found it was Mr. Herford, the gentleman at whose store I had called in the forenoon.

He seemed somewhat embarrassed, observing "he regretted not being at his *hoffice* when I called; saying at the same time, "that his two sisters were in town, and if I had no objection, would direct a note to them with my address, and that they would in all probability call upon me on their way home."

Accordingly I remained in my room, finishing up some letters, when, at about five P. M., was again called, and informed that there were two ladies in the parlor, who wished to see me; and on entering, perceived two very pretty young girls, neither of whom was far from twenty years of age. After making my bow, and speaking to them, the one whom I took for the eldest commenced a tittering laugh, which increased so fast that she was not able to speak, and holding a handkerchief to her face, began in an inchorent manner to apologize for her rudeness, saying:

"I hope you will excuse me sir." (*tittering again,*) "I don't know what you *will* think of us, sir. While we were on our way here, Maria and I were wondering how we should make ourselves understood by you, having no idea that you spoke English, and then, we thought you were very dark, with long black hair, and when we saw you, were quite amazed, that you so much resembled an Englishman, and spoke the language so well."

"Why? did not your brother tell you that I was not an Indian?"

"Oh; we have not seen brother. He merely wrote a note telling us where you were."

"But did not Mrs. Staniford ever inform you in her letters, that the people in America, were like the English both in appearance and language?"

"No sir, she never said anything in particular about the people, but sent us a book containing an account of the dreadful cruelties practised by them towards the English, and the book is full of their likenesses."

On explanation, I found this description of Americans was a book on the Indian wars, and full of Indian portraits. And, after having a good laugh over our meeting, the girls arose to leave, expressing themselves highly delighted at seeing me, and hinting that it would be very agreeable to them if I would accompany them home. Their place of residence was on the Surry side, just over Blackfriar's bridge, at *Camperdown Cottage.* They resided with their elder sister, to whom I was introduced. We took tea in the garden, under the shade of a venerable oak, and in the evening were joined by the brother. On my return over the bridge, the young ladies insisted on waiting upon me, a short distance, which certainly was quite agreeable. Mr. Herford was very attentive, offering his services to accompany me any-where I wished to go.

Accordingly, one morning, we started soon after breakfast for a walk, stopping first at Deptford, and after looking round the dock-yard a while, went on to Greenwich. Here we saw the jolly, old jack tar pensioners. And it is truly amusing to hear these old salts talk over their slang, and how nicely they will beg a sixpence from you. Here are many of the old Trafalgar's, the Nile's, and Copenhagen's; and just mention the name of Nelson, and you will soon have a crowd around you, some with one arm, another with a timber toe, and there's a poor fellow drawn about in a cart, having lost both legs.

These fellows are all fat and hearty, singing away merrily. They wear cocked hats, blue coats, and large shoe-buckles. When a fellow gets a little too much beer on board, he cock-bill's his old three cornered hat, and begins, perhaps, with the middle verse of some favorite song, but always gives you the chorus.

It is very singular, that every one happened to be right along-side the old boy (Nelson,) when he was shot by the Spanish soger-built-lubber, from the Santisma's maintop.

" *My eyes, Bill, didn't he get it?* Why sir, *there wasn't as much left of* that ere fellow, as would feed a kitten."

" Aye, a brave soul was Nelson, and them ere swabs, he used to wear, is changed into wings, and he's flying about Heaven like a Mother Cary's Chicken."

GREENWICH PENSIONER'S.

CHAPTER XIX.

Story of Greenwich pensioners,—Go to Woolwich,—Its description,—Return to London,—Remarks on seeing London,—My stopping place,—A description,—St. Sepulchre Church bells,—Execution of felons,—British Museum,—House of Lords and Commons,—Meaning of the Woolsack,—Westminster Abbey,—Thames Tunnel,—Tower,—William IV. proclaimed king,—Guests,—Loyalty of citizens,—Visit to neighboring towns,—Windsor,—Windsor Park,—Eton College,—Caricature shop,—Indecent pictures,—Excuse of the printer,—It may do in England,—Horse drinks porter,—Return to London through Hounslow Heath,—Visit St Thomas' Hospital,—King's bench prison,—Description,—Attend church at City road Chapel,—Bunhill fields burying ground,—Smithfield,—Account of Joe Bragg,—Go to Staffordshire,—Potteries,—Dainty Irishman,—Went to Burslem,—Letter to Mr. Ridgeway,—Go through the potteries,—Description of the making of China ware,—Remarks,—Visits to the Foudrenier Paper Mills,—Objection to receive strangers,—Positive Assurance that I had no knowledge of paper making,—Admittance,—Astonishment,—Leave Staffordshire,—Presented with some Staffordshire ware,—Return to Liverpool,—Informed of a Boston captain,—Meet him,—His story,—Urge him to abandon his habits of drinking,—Go to Northumberland and to Newcastle,—Apprise my friends at Newcastle of my intention of visiting them,—Arrival at Newcastle,—Visit anticipated,—Happy meeting,—Convivial party,—Conversation with an old gentleman,—Explosion of the coal mines,—Sail for Leith,—Arrival,—Go to Edinburg,—Fish women,—An old Boston Merchant,—Visit to Holyrood house,—Its description,—Long missing regalia of Scotland,—Edinburg Castle,—Edinburg,—Go to Glasgow,—Arrive.

"WHAT ship was that man on board of in the wagon there, with both legs off?"

"Your honor, that's old Tom Harvey. He lost his pins aboard the Leviathan, when she cut her way through the Dardanelles. Here, boy, *back your cart off this* way, these gentlemen would like a bit of a yarn from old Tom. You see, sir, the Admiralty pays that ere youngster for dragging old Tom about."

We just stepped a few paces ahead, and had a short chat with the old fellow. He was quarter gunner on board the Leviathan, and lost both legs by a splinter, knocked from a gun carriage by a marble shot, weighing over two hundred pounds. He was a jovial old fellow, nearly sixty years of age, and cheerful as a lark. One fellow among the group, took a pride in exhibiting his Sunday leg; he had whittled it out himself, from a splinter of the Victory's mainmast. He had his leg shot off in the action at Trafalgar, with Nelson, and when laying on the table in the cockpit, ready for amputation, the doctor being all ready with his saw and knife, Bill raises himself up a bit, and after taking a fresh quid, says, "please, sir, before you cut off the old stump, just promise me one thing." "Well, what is it, my man?" "Why, that you will save me a piece of the old mast, for a Sunday leg." The doctor promised he would, and fulfilled his promise. These good-hearted fellows would have amused us a week. We made them a small present, and went on towards Woolwich, the most ancient military and naval arsenal in England, and has a royal dock-yard, where men-of-war were built as early as in the reign of Henry VIII. At the eastern part of the town, is the royal arsenal, in which are built magazines of great guns, mortars, bombs, balls, powder, and other warlike stores, a foundry, with three fnrnaces, for casting ordnance, and a laboratory, where fire-works and catridges are made, and bombs, carcasses, grenades, &c., charged for the public service.

Woolwich is seated on the Thames, which is so deep here that large ships may at all times ride with safety. It is about eight miles from London. As it was now late in the afternoon, feeling somewhat fatigued, I concluded not to go any further, but to return to London in the omnibus. The day was unusually fine, and we really had a firstrate time, arriving home in season for tea, and to spend the evening with the girls. In order to see London properly, one must go leizurely to work, provide himself with the latest hand-book, lay out his day's work every morning, and avoid as much as possible being troublesome to friends; for, never mind how much of a stranger you are, anything in London is new to you, and by attending closely to your guide-book, and keeping a sharp lookout for pickpockets, any one can go through London with perfect safety.

My stopping place, as I have previously observed, was situated on Snow-hill, close along-side of St. Sepulchre Church, and very near the old Bailey or New-gate, and not a great distance from the stake at Smithfield, where John Rogers was burnt, or rather the place designated as such. The deep-toned bell of St. Sepulchre has been noted many years for its gloomy and melancholy tones, doling away the last few hours of the miserable felon, soon to expiate his crime upon the drop, in front of that dismal prison. It may have been for stealing five shillings, or for killing a fellow creature in cold blood—the stern law knowing no medium. So the Saracen head is the centre of my every-day's radii.

My first visit was to the British Museum, where, as the boy said, "*I saw everything.*" This unequalled museum is accessible to all, on certain days; and to pass well through it, requires a week. I next visited the House of Lords and House of Commons, and understood for the first time, the meaning of the wool-sack, which was, to let every Englishman know that wool was the life of England. Then to Westminster Abbey, which edifice I shall not attempt to describe, because a much more accurate description than I can give, may be found in many of the library books. Next in order was the Thames Tunnel, which had recently been inundated, and was hardly dry yet; it was not sufficiently finished to make it an object of much interest. I then proceeded to the tower, and was conducted through it by one of the yeoman of the guard. I shall all also omit a description here, for the same reason assigned for the Abbey; and will merely say, that all the localities of any interest were visited, together with the imposing ceremony of publicly proclaiming William Fourth, King of England, which took place in St. James' Park, amidst an innumerable assemblage. There were present as guests, the Duke of Wellington, Prince Frederick of Prussia, and many other noble personages, whose names I did not ascertain. The day was remarkably fine, and everything attending the ceremony passed off in fine style.

As the new king was riding through the streets in his open carriage, he was obliged to stop, occasionally, in consequence of the density of the crowd; when the people would then rush towards the carriage, to kiss his Majesty's hand. Among the loyal devotees were many women, and when they approached the king, he would say, "My hand for gentlemen, but my cheek for the ladies," and suiting the action to the word, held his cheek towards them.

Having travelled nearly over London proper, I commenced visiting the neighboring towns and villages; first, taking the pleasure steamer for Richmond, visiting Richmond Hill, which commands an enchanting prospect over a large portion of the country; then to Windsor. The castle was in mourning for the late king, and had rather a sombre appearance; the *Hatchment*, or *achievement*, still suspended from the front window, facing Windsor Park. This Park, in front of the palace, is lined on each side with some of the most magnificent oaks and elms, in the world. Near the castle is Eton College; I was much pleased with these bright, intelligent scholars. Their play-ground joins the palace grounds. I was told that George IV. frequently played with them when a boy.

Near the palace yard gate, and directly opposite the palace windows, was a caricature print-shop; the windows were filled with all sorts of prints, some of them, I thought, quite indecent; they all had some caricature reference to George IV. and his ladies. I went into the shop to take a survey, and to purchase; and asked the old man who kept the establishment, how it was that he could exhibit these pictures right in the face and eyes of the royal household. "Why," answered the man, with some animation, "I get my living by selling prints; if any man in the kingdom, whether a king or a beggar, can come into my shop, and put his finger on any picture, and say, 'That is me!' then I shall say that I am very glad to have been so fortunate as to obtain such a correct likeness."

The old man's logic was probably sufficient to save him

in England, but in no other European country would such bare-faced caricaturing have been tolerated.

While dining at the hotel, a gentleman came in who ordered the waiter to give his horse a can of porter. At first, I thought it was a joke, but sure enough, the horse drank every drop of it, and then wanted more. I had a mind to recommend the horse to visit Mr. S——'s brewery, at St. Helens.

I left Windsor next morning in the coach, passing over Hounslow Heath, through Chelsea and Kensington gardens; on the same afternoon had an invitation from a gentleman to accompany him on a visit to St. Thomas' hospital, and to the King's Bench prison, both of which were on the Surry side. The prison is chiefly devoted to rich debtors, "*who won't pay.*" We passed through the whole range of the prison grounds, and the yard appeared to be one vast market; and one not knowing that he was in a prison yard, would imagine himself in some popular city market; here were stalls all round the inside of the walls, loaded with every species of game, biped and quadruped. The gentlemen prisoners, with their servants, purchasing whatever their palates desired; for they can live here as high or extravagant as they please, although no spirituous liquors are allowed to be sold on the limits. All along on the side opposite the stalls, are numerous little shops, where small articles are sold, such as stationery, cakes, wearing apparel, and many other necessaries needed by the prisoners, some of whom remain there during their lives. But my companion directed my attention to some shops, over the doors of which the signs read "*Thread an tape.*" "Here," said he, "these gentleman can obtain *anything they want.*"

The King's Bench prisoners are, many of them, noblemen, who prefer lying in prison to paying their debts; their object in so doing being best known to themselves.

In passing out of the prison yard into the office of admittance, your attention is directed by the keepers to a singular piece of wood, about twelve inches square, always exciting curiosity, and it is hung up over the grate; on it is written in large letters:

"*Turn this round and you will see*"
The greeny then turns it round, and on the reverse—
"*Pay for a quart and you'll be free.*"
So all you have to do is to hand over a couple of shillings to pay for the quart, and you can then go out.

Next day being Sunday, I attended church at the City Road Chapel, where Rev. John Wesley formerly preached; and heard an excellent sermon from the Rev. John Watson, a very celebrated Methodist preacher. After service took a walk through Bunhill-fields burying ground, was shown the graves of Watts, Bunyan, and of many others, "*who, being dead, yet speaketh;*" then proceeded to the place said to be where the stake was erected for the burning of John Rogers at Smithfield.

[I mentioned in a former chapter about the crew of the Indiaman, that many of them were subsequently ship-masters. Joe Bragg, afterwards sailed out of England, and in London the following appeared on the police record.]

ALLEGED MURDER ON THE HIGH SEAS.

Joseph Bragg, master of the brig Valiant, lying in the East India Docks, was on Tuesday, April 11, 1827, examined at the Thames Police Office, charged with the murder of Francis Williams, a black man, the cook. Several of the crew were examined; but as their evidence was corroborative of each other, we shall only give the evidence of Robert Harris, who stated, that he was a seaman on board the Valiant, and that during their passage to the Isle of France, the prisoner was in the habit of kicking the deceased, and knocking him on the head; and on the 16th of September the prisoner asked where the black rascal was. He was told that he was aft. Prisoner then went aft, and saw the deceased with a bone of beef in his hand. He desired him to go to the round-house, and told him to eat the bone. Deceased made no reply. Prisoner began to cut his clothes off, leaving only his frock shirt. He then fastened a rope round his body, and dragged him to the hatchway, aud threw him down upon some barrels. The deceased lay some time insensible. The prisoner then ordered him on deck, which, he not immediately complying with, he hauled him up. Deceased begged a drink of water. Prisoner called the cook of the day, ordered him to get a panican of beef pickle, and actually forced a large quantity of it down the deceased's throat; and on his attempting to resist, he dashed him against the boom, and struck him several times; deceased fell on the deck; he then dragged him towards the head of the ship. Prisoner then told the deceased to take a bucket and fasten the bottom of it: but he seemed quite unable to do it. Prisoner then snatched up a hammer, struck the deceased on the head and knocked him down the hatchway; deceased fell on the barrels, and groaned dreadfully. Prisoner then said, "Oh! the black rascal, I'll take the sulks out of him." Prisoner then called the deceased to come on deck, but he was unable; he then went and struck him. Deceased fell, and prisoner took a shovel and began to cover him with the ballast, as if in the act of burying him alive. When he had nearly covered him, he flattened the ballast on his chest. He subsequently took the ballast off, called for a rope, made it fast to the leg of the deceased, and dragged him forward. He then called out to the people to haul away, which they did; but on perceiving it was the deceased they were hauling, they refused. The prisoner, with one of the crew, hauled the deceased on deck. Deceased was quite unable to stand, and his head lay upon his shoulder. He inarticulately begged a drink of water. Prisoner replied, "Fetch him a panican of pickle." It was brought and he put it into deceased's hand, who endeavored to put it to his lips, but was unable, and let it fall upon the deck: deceased also fell down; prisoner said, "You sulky rascal, I'll make you stand up;" and he desired Bill Cassan to put the poker into the fire; Cassan refused; prisoner did it himself; all this time the deceased lay insensible. When the poker was red-hot, he applied it to the back of the deceased, and deceased shrunk a little. Witness saw the steam come from the burning back of the deceased! Prisoner then hauled deceased on his feet, swearing he would take the sulks out of him; a rope was then made fast to the deceased, and he was slewed overboard; he was hauled up on the larboard side; while he was hauling up, one of the iron hooks struck him on the throat, and lacerated it dreadfully; he then lay on the deck groaning. Some of them said, the best thing was to put the man down below; prisoner replied, "Let him lie there—the rascal; I'll take the sulks out of him before I have done with him;" he lay there until the evening. Prisoner then told the mate to put him down below, and he was lowered down and placed on the water casks; there was then very little appearance of life in him, and he groaned occasionally; they then put him into his hammock, placed him upon his back, and found him dead on the following morning in that position. The prisoner said, he never knew a black man to die of the sulks before. The body was laid out on deck. Prisoner desired that it should be sewed up in his hammock, and heaved overboard, at the same time ordering the mate to give the crew half a tumbler of rum each. This was the first spirits they had ever got from the prisoner. While they were drinking, the prisoner asked them if they saw any marks on the body. No answer was given, apprehensive they should be served so themselves. The body was then sewed up in a hammock, a bag of sand put in with it, and it was hove overboard. The crew were then called into the cabin, and prisoner asked them if they would sign a paper, certifying that the deceased died by the will of God. They refused. Prisoner then asked if they would sign—"Accidental death?" They did so, but through fear. When the vessel arrived at Port Louis, prisoner employed an attorney, and he asked the crew to swear that the deceased died in his hammock; and on the crew going to explain to him, the attorney replied, that he did not wish to hear any thing about the matter—all he wanted was for them to swear that the deceased died in his hammock, which they did. The prisoner was then remanded for further examination.

Monday morning, took the coach for Staffordshire, as I had letters to one of the most extensive pottery proprietors in the shire. I left the coach at the Red Lion, at Hanley, preferring to walk to Burslem, the town at which I intended to stop. Here I had one of those delicious mutton-chops, such as cannot be found any-where else in the world; and while thus enjoying my repast, an Irish laborer came in to beg something to eat. The kind landlady cut off a good sized piece of Cheshire cheese and a large piece of bread to match which she gave him. The fellow took it, and crossing over to the other side of the road, threw it over the hedge. The old lady happened to see it; she ran over, and clenching him by the collar, made him pick it up and carry it over to the house again. His excuse for throwing it away, was,

"An sure it was 'nt bread and cheese hungry that I was."

The good landlady was a powerful English woman; she gave him a pelt in the back of the neck, and with her foot helped him out of the door.

I walked over to Burslem and found Mr. R——, and if there is a place in the world where you find true and disinterested hospitality, it is with the English. As soon as Mr. R—— had ascertained from my letter who I was, he conducted me to his mansion. Mrs. R——, and in fact the whole family, were determined to make me happy. I was conducted through the potteries, and each process for making the beautiful china and other wares, was explained to me, commencing with the calcination of the flint and bones, all through to the ornamental painting on the beautiful tea sets, which is done principally by young ladies, and I am sure that a visit to the Potteries is worth a journey to England. Here you see a bright-eyed little fellow at the bench, and in an apparently careless manner, with a grin on his dirty face, catches up a ball of clay, puts it on the horizontal wheel which he turns with his toes, and in the most dexterous manner, with a little flat stick and his nimble fingers, turns out a pretty cream pitcher or a sugar bowl, as the saying is, "in no time." I thought of that passage in the Scripture, "behold we are the clay and thou art the potter." God moulds us into any shape he pleases; then we must pass through the furnace, and if we come out from that ordeal unbroken, he then in infinite goodness, puts on the enamel, and we are fit for the master's use.

Mr. R—— took me over to see Mr. Foudrenier's paper-mills, the largest in the world. No persons are admitted, however, without *special* permission. We went up to the large gate, in which there is a hole about six inches in diameter, and through this aperture all conversation is held with those inside. Mr. R—— enquired for Mr. F., and after a few minutes he came to the hole. Mr. R—— observed that he had with him a friend from America, and to whom he wished to show the paper-mill. Mr. F. at first very politely objected, saying that he had suffered much by the introduction of strangers, but after a little parleying, the door was opened, and I was admitted. As soon as I was inside the gate, and before entering the mill, Mr. F. asked me in a very serious manner, if I had any knowledge of paper making. I assured him that I had no further knowledge than that which I had gained from the encyclopedia, and my object for wishing to see this establishment was, that I had heard much of his powerful steam-engine, and the surprising rapidity with which paper was made. He then told me why he was so cautious. That not many months ago, two gentlemen travellers from the United States, had obtained an introduction into the mills, pretending great ignorance about paper making, when it subsequently turned out that these gentlemen were paper makers, located near Philadelphia, and that they while looking round, had stolen some of his plans, and introduced them into their own establishment.

In passing through the spacious warerooms of the potteries, I noticed a beautiful pattern of plates very much resembling china. I remarked to Mr. R—— that I had never seen anything of the earthernware kind, that so nearly resembled china. On the morning of my departure from B., I found a box with my name upon it, placed near my carpet-bag, and ascertained that I had been presented with four dozen of these plates, with the compliments of the donor.

From Staffordshire, I returned to Liverpool. Next morning at the breakfast table, I was told that there was a Boston brig lying at the Salt house dock, and on hearing the captain's name, recognized him as an old friend. After breakfast I went up to the dock, and there he was, standing up against the dock house, so drunk that he could not move.

As soon as he recognized me he gave a dreadful exclamation of surprise, and began to weep like a child; saying that he was ruined, had made a bad voyage, and that his owners would kick him out of their employment. He begged me not to mention what I saw. I took him by the hand and assured him that I would not, and urged him to cheer up, and by no means to resort to drinking as a palliative against trouble. "If you have done your duty, and the voyage is adverse, the fault is not yours." I also urged him to shift his dress, to come down to our house and make himself cheerful. I believe he got a good freight from Liverpool, and on his arrival home everything went off firstrate. I saw him in Boston many times afterwards, but we never exchanged a word about Liverpool, and there was not in Boston a handsomer formed man, nor one more highly respected than Capt. ——. His owners esteemed him highly, and I have never divulged his secret.

My next move was from Liverpool to Newcastle-on-Tyne, passing through York and Durham, into Northumberland. I had letters to a family residing in Newcastle, and when in London I wrote to them that I should soon be on my way to the North. From Liverpool to York, I had a very pleasant companion in the person of a young Quaker. He was very communicative and intelligent, and gave me much valuable information about England, and was also very inquisitive in his enquiries about the United States and its government. I was quite sorry to part with him.

On my arrival at Newcastle, I saw a gentleman standing at the coach door, enquiring of each passenger his name. I concluded that this was the gentleman in search of me; so, when I got out, said I:

"Is your name Rutherford?"

"Yes, sir."

"All right; go ahead."

He knew in a minute that I was the man. We were quickly at his house; and as it was his wife with whom I had been acquainted in Boston, our meeting was rather a cordial one. That night, a party was got up, and we had a tall time; and according to English fashion, did not separate until daylight; all appeared social and happy. One of the gentlemen showed me round Newcastle, which at this time was wrapped in gloom, in consequence of a dreadful accident which had occurred only a few days before. An explosion had taken place in a coal mine, near by, by which 129 lives were lost, and many others maimed, some of them for life.

In walking one day, I was introduced to an old gentleman, who, as we passed along the street, pointed to a row of buildings which once belonged to him, but were now the property of another. He stopped short, and taking my hand, observed:

"Now I am poor, and a poor gentleman is the most useless being in creation; he is of no use to himself, or to any one else."

I did not exactly accord with him there; for, notwithstanding his remark might apply in many cases, yet it was not generally true, as the future usefulness of a man bereft of his property, very much depends upon circumstances. I parted with my good friends in Newcastle, and took passage in the Steamer —— for Leith; there were several cabin and a number of steerage passengers. We left Newcastle early in the morning, passing Shields and Sunderland. After we had left the Tyne, a gale sprung up, which continued with much violence, until we reached the Frith of Forth.

On arriving at Leith, next morning, I went ashore and looked around among the shipping. Here were female stevedores, with canvas petticoats, and a large canvas jacket over all, rolling casks on board the ships, and lowering them into the hold as handily as any men that I had ever seen. And it was amusing to see the long string of Scotch fisherwomen, with their broad backs, and a two bushel basket of fish on their shoulders, all dripping down over their leather jackets, going up the Leith road to Edinburgh; the distance is one mile. On the way, there is a large gin palace, where they stop to get a nipper, and woe be to any man who says an insulting word to them; they would all drop their baskets, and pommel him so that he could hardly walk. As this has happened several times, every one gives them a wide berth.

I had an introductory letter to a gentleman, who was an

extensive book publisher. He very kindly left his business, and devoted himself entirely to me while I remained in Edinburgh. I stopped at the Prince hotel, Prince street. At the dinner table I recognized an old Boston merchant, who formerly kept on India wharf; he sat opposite, and repeatedly urged me to take a glass of wine, which former experience induced me to decline. I soon found that nearly all at the table were a set of blow-hards, and my old friend was not a whit behind them.

According to Scotch etiquette, it is indecorous to leave the table before all have finished. I remained until they had drank wine, Scotch ale, porter, and had called for brandy. I then arose, went to my room, which was directly over the porch, and set there awhile, waiting for my Scotch friend to call for me. I heard them arise from the table, and saw my old Boston friend leave the room, hardly able to stand upright; he staggered through the alley, and went into the street. I saw no more of him after that day.

My first visit in Edinburgh was to Holyrood house, once the residence of Mary, Queen of Scots. The keeper of the place, an old lady, conducted me through all the rooms. Mary's sleeping-room, with the bed and oaken bedstead, remained as she left them; also, her work-table, work-basket, with needles, thread, and many et ceteras belonging to a lady's sewing establishment. We were shown the chamber where Rizzio was killed, while playing by her side, her favorite air on the guitar. Lord Darnley's boots and many household articles, were not allowed to be touched. The rooms, particularly the suite appropriated to her own use, were richly hung with French tapestry; but I was told that the oaken floors were never carpeted.

I was next shown into the chapel, which is without a roof; the floor is covered with weeds and grass; much of the stone work retains features of former grandeur. The vault where the remains of the Scottish Kings are deposited, which consists of white marble, is now in a state of decay.

From the top of the hill called Arthur's seat, there is a magnificent and expansive view of the city, and far beyond, showing some beautiful scenery. There is also a fine view from Calton hill, and in fact, Edinburgh has a beautiful appearance when viewed from an elevated position.

My next visit was to the Castle; here I saw the newly discovered and long-lost Regalia of Scotland, once belonging to *Robert Bruce, King of Scotland.* The sceptres are silver gilt, and headed with a crystal globe; the crown is small and inelegant, set round with emeralds, rubies, topazes, and pearls. The Castle itself is a congeries of very rude, ill-planned buildings, and has no security but from its walls, and naturally strong situation.

On the whole, I was highly gratified with the beauty and situation of Edinburgh; yet it is only in reference to its external appearance, that the mind is fully satisfied. When you look into the houses, the shops, the streets, either for their furniture, their merchandise, or even for persons, or equipage suitable to the grandeur of the buildings, you are utterly disappointed. Everything appears out of proportion with these majestic edifices, and must either be passed by unheeded, or if noticed at all, must be with dissatisfaction. After seeing all the sights in Edinburgh, I took leave of my kind friend, and proceeded to Glasgow, which is also a beautiful city, and not exceeded by any in Europe.

CHAPTER XX.

Glasgow,—Its description,—Go to Greenock,—Heavy gale,—Perilous condition,—Frantic girl,—I had my fears,—Meet an old acquaintance,—Difficulty in finding my goods,—Disclosure of an imprudent captain,—Get ready for sailing,—Meet an old companion,—Traitor,—Mr. Tialo, —His history,—Falling out with my old acquaintance,—Incident on the passage,—Arrive home.

THE four principal streets which intersect each other, at right angles, divide the city into nearly four equal parts. The high church is a magnificent Gothic structure. There are several splendid churches and other edifices, not surpassed by any in Europe. The city is situated on the north bank of the Clyde; the suburbs extending to the opposite side, connected by three elegant stone bridges. Although introduced by letter to this magnificent city, I did not call upon any one, but rambled about with no other companion than my guide-book. After seeing all that was desirable in Glasgow, I took the steamer for Greenock, and as there was nothing very attractive to me there, excepting the Dry-docks, I left in the next steamer for Liverpool. It was late in the afternoon when we started. After entering the Frith, it came on to blow hard from the north-east. We were now fast drifting on to the coast of Ireland. When between Donaghadee and Port Patrick, the gale was terrific. It was quite dark, our coals were nearly expended, and we were quite near the rocks on the coast of Ireland. I stood most of the time near the captain, and putting his hand on my shoulder, "now," said he, "if the engine holds out, we shall get by; but if a screw gives way, or anything stops the engine, we are gone. We can break up the chairs, tables, and any of the wood-work about the ship if the coal gives out: but my only fear is, that the engine will not last. The passengers were much alarmed, but by good management, most of them were kept below. There was a girl about twenty years of age, who got upon deck, and seeing the state of things, became frantic. She clenched hold of me, saying:

"Oh, dear! dear! what shall I do? I have something on my mind that I wish to confess before I die. Oh, mercy! Oh, mercy!"

With some trouble I got her below, and shut the cabin door; so that if we went on the rocks, they might as well die there, as any-where else, for death would be inevitable, and to tell the truth, I was not without my fears. Here we were, close on to the rocks, in a small steamer, with rather an equivocal engine, a furious gale and a heavy sea. As the captain said, if the engine stops for a minute, we are gone. If it had been so, my fate would not have been known, for no soul except those on board, knew where I was. My friends at Newcastle knew that I had gone to Leith, and that was the extent of their knowledge of my whereabouts. When in London, I had purchased about one thousand dollars worth of goods which were sent to Liverpool, subject to my order; these would have been lost to my family. But an overruling and kind Providence had ordered it otherwise and we were saved; the wind shifted a few points, which very much abated the danger. By daylight we were under the lee of the Isle of Man, and scraped up fuel enough to carry us into Liverpool. And when once on terra firma, again, I assure you I felt glad. I fell in with an old acquaintance, captain of a ship bound for Boston and to sail in two days; he invited me to take passage with him, which invitation I accepted.

My first business was to see about my goods, so I went to the Canal office with my number and description. The clerk looked over the list of names; I had given him my name which began with H. Now as the English seldom sound the H, he looked among the O's, and after running the list over carefully, he says:

"There are no goods here for you."

"Well, how can that be? You have the goods on your freight list, and here is the ticket."

"Well, truly, this is mysterious; there must be some mistake; your goods must have been left at Manchester."

Now here was a fix; my passage in this ship was vetoed. In the afternoon I called again, and almost the first things I saw in the freight room, were my goods. And when I told the clerk that my goods were there, he asked me again, what name? I told him. I then saw him looking under the O's, and I reeled off a little bit of my mind to him. Said I, "what kind of a clerk are you? don't you know how to spell a name? I told you Holbrook, and just look upon your ticket.

"O, I beg your pardon, I was looking for Olebrook."

"Well, you had better go and learn English before you set yourself up for a clerk."

I spent the evening with several Yankee Captains. One of them who had a fine ship, began telling me how much it had cost him for frolicking money since he had been in the Liverpool trade; it was an enormous sum. I replied:

"How can you support your family? It must take all your wages and primage."

"O, nonsense it don't cost me a cent. I get it out of vegetables, ship chandlers and stevedores' bills."

"But don't your owners overhaul your bills?"

"No, they never look at my bills; I just hand in my account and that is all I ever hear about it."

I observed he had been drinking, so the old adage holds good, "When liquor is in, wit is out," if it had not been so, he would never have exposed himself in this manner, for he knew I was well acquainted with his owners. Next morning I had everything belonging to me on board the H— T—, Capt. B——. There were two other passengers, one of whom I recognized as an old schoolmate and a near neighbor. His father was one of the tories who took no part in the revolutionary war, although he was born in Boston. He had escaped, by some means, the general fate of the tories found in Boston, after the conclusion of the war. They were carried out of the town in a charcoal cart, amid the hooting and pelting of the boys, and forbid ever showing their heads in B. again. This aristocratic gentlemen managed to escape his just due, until the excitement was over. His family lived near our schoolhouse, and, although a boy, I could not help observing what a proud, haughty fellow he was; and the boys (this passenger and his brother) were too proud and haughty to associate with the others. And what was worse than all, they were poor, living entirely on the pension allowed them by the British government, which was also allowed to all who remained during the revolution. So I had some idea of the chap who was to be my companion for thirty-five or forty days. I had frequently met this man in Boston, and our recognition was hardly ever more than a slight nod. I had not seen him for many years before we met on board the H—— T——. At the dinner table I spoke to him of our former acquaintance, but it was easy to see that the old, assumed loftiness, was still there; however, as we were to be together for a weeks, I intended to pass the time as agreeably as I could. The other passenger, Mr. Tialo, was an Englishman, and a very fine, sociable fellow. Very early on the voyage I observed that my Boston friend had a habit of speaking very sneeringly of everything that was American; frequently alluding to the "Tavistock" as the most fashionable hotel in London, and the place at which he had stopped, and then drawing the contrast between the society of England and that of the United States — passing very high encomiums on the former, and heartily running the latter. I enquired where his elder brother was?

"He is in the army and stationed in India."

"O, then, he is not in the American army?"

"A-m-er-i-c-an army? No, indeed, I hope not!"

I received all this without showing any symptoms of uneasiness, reserving it until another time. In the course of conversation he told me that he had been to England to receive his father's pension, which amounted to four thousand dollars, which he had in Spanish dollars, in the box in his state-room.

Mr. Tialo was much afflicted with the rheumatism, which he acknowledged was brought on by excessive drinking. He belonged in Nottingham, was an extensive dealer in lace, and very wealthy. He managed to get his goods into the

United States by smuggling, and was now on his way to New Orleans to meet a quantity of lace which had been smuggled from St. John, N. B.; he being very sociable and communicative, I became quite attached to him. He gave me much information about England, and many amusing anecdotes about Lords and Noblemen with whom he had lived. He had risen from a poor servant boy to a gentleman of fortune, and one moonlight evening he gave me the following extract of his history:

His parents were very poor; he went to live in the family of a Lord somebody as under-scullion, which was to attend on the cooks, bring coal, and perform any duties that were required; after a while he was promoted to a whipper-in; that is, to see that the hounds were all in the kennel. He told me many amusing anecdotes about hounds, some of which quite surprised me. He said, that when a hound showed any disposition to fawn, or as we would say, to be docile, he was immediately killed, no matter how valuable he was, for as soon as there was any perceptible relaxation of his savage nature, he was useless. He next obtained a situation as chief butler to a nobleman, who was so eccentric in his habits that he allowed no one but his wife to see him. No other eye had seen him for eighteen years; he made all his bargains and transacted all his business through a screen. He lived with this nobleman seven years, and as he had now nearly five hundred pounds in his possession, concluded to try something on his own hook.

There was at this time an auction sale of mattresses that had belonged to the English army; after the Battle of Waterloo these beds were ordered to be sold. They were stuffed with wool; he bought the lot, on which speculation he realized eight hundred pounds profit.

He confessed that he was frequently intoxicated, and "now," said he, "the foundation of my fortune I attribute to a drunken freak. I had been drinking all night with some friends, and was quite intoxicated when I left them. In the morning, on going home, passed a crowd of persons who were listening to the auctioneer. I stopped and bid something over the last, when the auctioneer knocked it off to me, and asked my name. I was sober enough, however, to behave well, and to give my name and residence, not knowing what I had bought; and after reaching home and becoming cool enough to remember that I had purchased something at an auction, began to be alarmed, feeling certain that I had been cheated."

"While ruminating over what I supposed to be my folly, two gentlemen called upon me with a roll of papers as large round as my arm. I assure you I felt ashamed and considered myself ruined. The gentlemen began to congratulate me on my good purchase, and I soon ascertained the nature of my bargain; and the first payment took more than half of all that I owned."

As it was getting late we went below. He finished his story by saying that the purchase was a lot of land containing about 22,000 feet, and I think he told me that he had paid one shilling sterling per foot, and that he had sold one small lot for ten shillings per foot; the residue was now worth thirty — would soon bring a guinea; and on the strength of this purchase, he had engaged in the lace business and had been very successful. But the poor fellow died in New Orleans, and that was the last of poor Tialo.

One day the Boston gentleman was not at the dinner table in time to commence with us, so the captain sent the steward up to find him, when he came down, quite indignant that we should have began without him. I knew what was coming and felt glad that an opportunity would soon offer when I could give vent to my feelings. I asked him why he was offended? "If you did not hear the bell it was not our fault; we heard it and came down, and when we found that you did not come, the captain sent the steward for you, and as far as I am concerned, don't consider your conduct or conversation has been such as to merit much attention on board an *American* ship. Your remarks in many instances have been highly derogatory to the character of an *American citizen.* Remember, sir, that neither you or any of your family are *Americans*, although born in Boston. You have in that box the price of American blood; you have enjoyed all the benefits of a free country, while that box contains the reward of a dastardly opposition, when our country was struggling for freedom! I am a passenger with yourself, and know my position too well to make any trouble on board this ship; but if ever we meet on shore, I may remind you of your sneering epithets during this passage."

We arrived in Boston, Oct. 4th, 1830, in thirty-eight days from Liverpool. On our passage, an accident occurred which resulted rather differently from what any one would suppose. Two men went aloft to send down the main-royal yard, as it looked very much like a blow, and the captain wished to have everything snug before night. The men had just got upon the yard when the ship gave a heavy roll and away went the royal-mast, yard and all, and the two men came tumbling down; one went overboard clear of everything, and the other came down head foremost through the mainsail, and was jammed in between the pumps. The man that went overboard fell flat upon the water but did not sink. I caught a coil of rope from the belaying pin and threw it over his head, and thus saved him. He was hauled on board, was quite black, and unable to speak; while he that fell on deck was hardly hurt, and in a few days went about his duty; the other was unable to leave his hammock during the passage.

CHAPTER XXI.

Description of a certain class of men,—Build a dock,—Have to deal with curious characters, and consummate villians,--Make the best arrangement in my power,—Sycophants,—Eastern land speculation,—I get into it, —Romantic calculations,—Get handsomely cheated,—A visit,—Incident,—Meet a squatter,—Previous description of him,—Arrangement, —His history,—Mosquitos,—Stop with a private family,—Interesting, —Scarcity of Gospel preaching,—Incidents,—Leave for Bangor,— Visit the Indians at Old Town,—Politeness of a Squaw,—Return to Boston,—Go South for timber,--Make an acquaintance at Washington,— Conversation on the South,—Slavery,—Bitter against the North,—His niggers better off than many white men at the North,—Method of punishing his slaves,—Gives me much information about his plantation, — Slave dealer and slaves, — Description, — Arrive at Richmond, — Have a view of the slaves,—Price of servants,—Finds out I am from the North,—Indignation towards me,—Some difficulty in Wilmington, —Adjusted,—Go on board the boat,—Reflections,—Arrive at Charleston,—Think of purchasing,—A pompous down east captain.—His mistake,—Arrive at Savannah,—Attend Sabbath School,—Former worship, — Attend Marshall's church, — Description,—Some account of Marshall,—Solemnity of his worship,--Return to Charleston,—Travel North with Henry Clay,—Sail for Wilmington.

In the former part of this book, I had occasion to speak of a certain class of men, whose principle aim was to defraud and impose upon all who came within their power. But there are others, who, under the garb of sanctity, would draw every drop of the vital fluid from your veins in order to subserve their own purpose. They always approach you with the bland smile, and the outstretched hand. But always suspect a man who affects great softness of manner, an unruffled evenness of temper, and an enunciation studied, slow, and deliberate. These things are all unnatural, and bespeak a degree of mental discipline into which he that has no purposes of craft or design to answer, cannot submit to drill himself. The most successful knaves are usually of this description, as smooth as razors, dipped in oil, and as sharp. They affect the innocence of the dove, which they have not, in order to hide the cunning of the serpent which they possess. And I will venture to say, there is not a man, who has reached the age of fifty, that has not come in contact with men of the above description.

The longest life is but one series of experiments, or developments which cannot be recalled, and can only be used as beacon lights for others. We hear much said of friendship. I doubt whether a man or woman lives, that can properly define this ambiguous term. The bee is the friend of the honeysuckle while its petal contains the sweet; but after that has ceased, he buzzes by, searching for another. The deceitfulness of friendship has ruined thousands. There does not exist upon earth, either community or fraternity, where it disinterestedly predominates over the baser passions. Yet, in every sphere, and in every grade, we find isolated instances of pure friendship, that needs no transformation; it comes in its own celestial garb. Oh, yes; amidst the dearth of this deceitful world, it comes like the sweet note of the skylark, which directs the eye upward. "Yet verily the man is a marvel whom truth can write a friend." Did selfishness induce a Howard, a Lawrence, a Miss Fry, and a host of others, who lived only to dry the tear of affliction? Oh, no; contrast these, with those grovelling wretches, stationed upon the curb-stone or seated behind some office table who, with palsied hands and watery eyes, are greedily devouring from some morning print, the price of stocks, and rate of interest; who are waiting the application of some needy individual whom they may, as an act of *friendship*, completely fleece; thus carrying distress and mortification into the bosom of a once lovely family.

It may be that I have dwelt rather long upon a subject which it may well be said, "every body knows." But as I shall have occasion to show up some of these "chaps" before I get through, it will do no harm to introduce them now.

In 1833, through the suggestion of the captain of a Norwegian vessel, I made the model of a dry-dock, such as were in use in Norway. As the nature of our business required the workmen to be much of the time in the water, a dock of this simple construction, would obviate much of this unpleasant exposure. Not having a suitable place in which to locate it. We did nothing about it until 1835. My partner being an active and intelligent young man, remained at the yard, while I selected a place on which to build the dock. Having collected the materials, commenced it amidst the sneers and foolish remarks of many who pretended to have a great knowledge of hydraulics and hydrostatics, and many other things that they were totally ignorant of.

After commencing the dock, a gentlemanly-looking man came to the yard, and introducing himself as one well versed in the sciences, remarked to me, he had understood I was building a floating dry-dock. "Now," said he, "allow me to say to you that your plan will never succeed." He then began a long, rigmarole story about the pressure of water, the immense strength that would be required to prevent its destruction, and the great injury which would result to the vessel it contained. My reply was, that I also had some knowledge of hydraulic pressure, and felt fully satisfied on that score, and at the same time should be happy to receive any information or suggestion that might be of service. As I turned to leave him, he remarked that he felt afraid it would prove a failure. I went about my business, not in the least intimidated by any remarks which had been made by this gentleman. Although I knew that the whole thing was an experiment, which if it failed, would be a serious loss to me. There were many, besides the gentleman alluded to, who gave adverse opinions, and sometimes I felt rather unpleasant. When the dock was nearly completed, a man came to me with whom I had been acquainted many years. He looked pale and agitated. After going round the dock, and examining everything very minutely, said to me in a very excited manner:

"Did you know that Mr. F——d had a patent for this dock?"

"No, sir, I knew nothing of any patent, nor did I suppose that there could be anything of the kind, as it is not a new invention. Docks of this kind have been used in Norway for more than fifty years."

"Well," said the man, still very much excited, "I have had his model two years, and he has heard about this dock, and will put an injunction on you, unless you make some arrangement with him."

As I then knew but little about law, or the nature of an injunction, I made an enquiry, and was told that if the man who held the patent right could make it appear that we had infringed on his right, he could commence a lawsuit, and at the same time forbid the dock being used until the case was decided, which might be one or two years, besides feeding a parcel of *miserable, hungry pettifoggers.* I felt very bad, not being at all acquainted with law, and having spent much of our money on the dock, and now to have to lie, and perhaps rot before the case could be decided, besides the expense of the lawsuit, appeared too hard. I have no doubt that this poor trembling man who had the model for two years, not having pluck enough to build it, and seeing the thing right before him, was the cause of all his trouble, and evidently the cause of ours. I accordingly went to Portsmouth where Mr. F—— resided, and made an arrangement with him, although I knew the patent was invalid, yet by this agreement the dock could be launched and put into operation without further trouble. Notwithstanding this difficulty was obviated, the very paper which I supposed was a protection appearing perfectly simple in its form, has ultimately proved a source of much litigation and expense. After the death of the original, Mr. F——, the agreement fell into the hands of some such *fellows* as I have before described. The paper contained more technical meaning than I was at first aware of. It has been the cause of much subsequent annoyance and expense. One more remark about the dock. It was launched successfully and performed admirably, answering every purpose for which it was intended, and these same *very wise men,* who predicted a failure and would have liked to have seen their prediction prove true, afterwards came to me, and had the impudence to say:

"*There, Mr. H., I knew when you were building that dock, that it was on the best plan that could be adopted; how perfectly simple, and how exceedingly well it answers the purpose!*"

I turned away from these *contemptible wretches*, merely remarking that they had better attend to their own business and leave me to manage my own.

In 1836 the great Eastern land speculation came up, when so many "*lucky*" (?) individuals made their fortunes. I remember to have seen it stated in some popular work, that there has been from as far back as the tenth century, and up to the present time, some periodical, prevailing delusion, such as the Dutch tulip mania, South Sea bubble, morus multicaulis, Eastern land, &c., and they will continue to come, despite the sagacity and wisdom of the present, and probably of coming generations. As I had a little touch of the Eastern land epidemic, will say a few words about it, and if the reader happens to be one of the *lucky* ones, I hope his feelings will not be hurt if he should happen to see it mentioned at this time. All who remember the event know how suddenly it came up, like the Aurora Borealis; all at once the whole North-eastern hemisphere was lighted up, newspapers teemed with the *sudden* rise of Eastern land!

From Boston to New Orleans, all was commotion, bonds for townships changing hands, and at each change a profit of forty, fifty, and in some cases a hundred thousand dollars was "*not*" realized. I kept out of it until toward the last, when *every body* else had made their fortunes. One day I read a paragraph in the paper, something like this:

"*Lucky speculation.*"—Our fellow-citizen, D—— being at Bangor, bought a bond of a valuable timbered township, for which he was to pay (*and had given his notes*) fifty thousand dollars. He sold the bond the same day to a Philadelphia company for two hundred thousand, thus in a few hours, realizing a profit of a hundred and fifty thousand dollars!"

This poor fellow was ultimately ruined by this hasty and unfortunate transaction. Before this affair came out however, I was into it, in company with several others, who were considered to be very shrewd, and there was really, as we thought, a *fortune* before us.

"Why," says V—, who was *the sharpest one in the company*, "just look here;" and with his pencil had it all figured out on his memorandum book, thus: "The land costs so much, — now, allowing so many thousand feet of boards from each acre, so many acres at —— and allowing for expenses and contingencies, it leaves the enormous sum of —— millions of dollars! Why, gentlemen, here it is right before you; figures can't lie you know; we shall make a hundred thousand dollars apiece, sure as the world."

Not one of us had ever seen the lot, having purchased it by the plan. Col. Humbug, from whom, and when we purchased it, showed us a bundle of certificates purporting to be from surveyors and explorers, who all gave the most flattering accounts of the luxuriant growth of timber upon it, stating also that it bordered on a bay where a vessel could haul along-side the bank, and take in the lumber. Then there was an abundance of black bears, and a splendid pond where a man might sit all *day and fish;* besides, there was to be a great military road cut through which would very much enhance the worth of it. About a month after the purchase, when things began to leak out a little, a gentleman of our acquaintance was going down east to *look* at a lot that he had purchased. As he was to go directly through *ours*, we asked him to take a look and tell us what he thought about it. We were anxious to see him on his return, expecting to hear a good report of our purchase; but what was our chagrin and dismay when told that he had not found it! and that he had spent nearly two days, with two men who were familiar with every inch of the country, and no such place as our plan designated could be found! We now began to suspect; and would have taken *fifty thousand dollars each for the speculation!* We felt a sort of an inkling that we had been sold; so one of our party with myself started off for the promised land. First, stopping at Bangor in order to have a conference with Col. Humbug, from whom we had made the purchase, and by much enquiry, found where our lot ought to have been, but it *was'nt there!* for instead of bordering on a bay as it was described on the plan, and where we expected to find it, we were told by the land agent that no such lot existed, but there was one bordering on *the pond*, that probably was the lot we were in search of, and after climbing over rocks, hills, dismal smamps, and pine forests, half devoured by mosquitos, reeking wet with perspiration, our clothes torn by brambles, and suffering much from thirst, came to a house. The door being open, we entered. Here were two cut-throat looking fellows, seated beside a table, drinking whiskey. There was no furniture in the room, but against the wall were two rifles with powder horns, and a few articles of ragged clothing. We asked for a drink of water, which was brought us by a woman who looked the very image of distress. After obtaining what information we could get from these men, went off in the direction pointed out by them, and kept on through myriads of large, blue flies and mosquitos, dense woods and bogs, and at last found what we supposed to be the place.

On a high and verdant hill was an old squatter who had cleared about forty acres, and built two log-houses. He had reared a family of good looking young men, and the place looked very fine. This man had been in the habit of cutting the timber and wood from any part of the lot and selling it on his own account. We were told on our arrival at the village in the vicinity, that this old fellow had understood the land had been sold, "but," said he, "let any one enter my house, and order me off, I 'll shoot him as quick as I would a bear." As the farm was at the top of the hill, and it being quite a walk to reach it, we concluded however, that as we were to be shot on reaching the summit, to take it very moderately.

The pathway, though somewhat meandering, was very steep, and the journey fatiguing. We at length reached the house, and came suddenly upon them. In one house, Mrs. C—— was washing, and when we entered the door, she turned quite pale, and left her work. I told her not to be alarmed, assuring her that we were friends. We then enquired for her husband; she at first hesitated, and then said he was in the next house. We went into the *next house* and found him, sitting as though in deep meditation. We saluted him, with, "How are you, sir?" He responded, bade us be seated, and after the usual prefatory talk had subsided, we said to him that we were the purchasers of the lot, and had called on him to arrange about his farm. He seemed much agitated, and in order to suppress any unnecessary fear I told him that we were not disposed to trouble him or to distress his family; that we had called on him to request that he would not cut off any more timber or wood from the place, and as he had never paid anything for his farm, we required him to pay two dollars per acre for the one hundred and sixty, which he then held in possession; giving him seven years in which to pay it; to which he cheerfully agreed. His good spouse had in the meantime tidied up a little, and brought us some fine strawberries and cream. In a joking manner, I alluded to the shooting story, at which he laughed very heartily, declaring that he had not owned a gun for five years, observing that he knew the villagers did not like him, and he believed that their dislike was occasioned on account of his having the best farm in that vicinity. He appeared to be an intelligent man, related the hardships he had endured in raising his family. "Every slab," said he, "in these houses, I brought from the mill on my shoulders, and many a time have gone several miles through the snow for a bag of meal. I cleared away the place with my own hands, and made all the improvements you now see."

After having made our proposition to the old man, with which he appeared perfectly satisfied, we left him, and descended from this fair mount again into the world of mosquitos, monstrous blue flies, bogs, briars,and reached the village late in the evening. As the next day was the Sabbath, we concluded to remain here until Monday morning. We stopped with a private family, consisting of a man, his wife, and two children. There was no place of worship here, and I think the nearest meeting-house was seven miles distant. There were perhaps twenty families, and quite a number of interesting children. This good lady told me that once in a great while, a preacher would come along, and when notice was given that there would be religious services for but one evening, the news would spread round the country, and those who lived on the borders of the river, if they could not obtain canoes or boats, would come down on logs, and get back the best way they could. And she had known them to come ten miles on a single log, greedily devouring every word the preacher said, and eagerly entreating him to come again.

I gave her my Bible, which she received with much pleasure. Notwithstanding what I have said about the scarcity of religious instruction here, it happened that for a few weeks past, there had been a man from Bangor, who had preached once on Sabbath morning, and in the afternoon held a Sabbath school. As he intended to preach in the schoolhouse, I very gladly attended, but was sorry to observe the behavior of several young men—fishermen, which was indecent and unbecoming. The preacher, 'tis true, was not only uneducated, but quite illiterate, and what may be termed a vulgar man. His speech was bad, and before commencing his sermon, took from his pocket a plug of tobacco, opened his knife, cut off a quid, and commenced his sermon. Notwithstanding this evident breach of what we, in a more civilized part of the country, call propriety, he preached the truth, and I believe him to have been a good man. On Monday morning, we left this place for Bangor, determined, although we had been cheated, to have a little ramble through *down east.* We visited the Indians at Old Town or Orono; they appeared to be quite numerous, but very filthy in their habits. One old squaw invited us into her wigwam; she was engaged in basket making, and had a pappoose nicely stowed away in a birch bark cradle.

This show of politeness was evidently intended to get money from us; but she was so disgustingly dirty, we did not give her a cent, and her earth floor was so filthy that I was glad to leave it. In one corner, was a piece of fresh meat upon the ground, nearly covered with dirt, which was probably to be her next meal. We left these aboriginal descendants, returned to Boston, and commenced a suit against the fellow from whom we had purchased the moonshine, recovered a part of the money, and let him run with the rest of these Eastern rogues. Everything relating to our business continued prosperous. In 1842, we were in want of a quantity of hard pine timber, and as it could be purchased more advantageously from first hands, I went to Savannah for that purpose, and for expedition, chose the land route, as far as Wilmington, and from thence to Charleston and to Savannah by steam-boat. On my way, and when at Washington, I became familar with two southern gentlemen, who were planters, and resided in the south-western part of Georgia. The youngest of the two, and with whom I had the most conversation, was very intelligent and agreeable in his manners. Our principal conversation was about the South. The topics were varied, but mostly on the subject of slavery.

He was bitter against the North for their interference, and declared that his niggers were better off than one-fourth the population of Massachusetts. I asked him if it was true that slaves were whipped, and as cruelly treated as we sometimes read of. He replied, "That on some estates, where they have a bad driver, the hands are abused; but then no gentleman will keep a fellow like this on his farm, when he is known to abuse his slaves. I never whip my niggers; I've got a better mode of punishing than cutting them to pieces with a cowskin. In my barn, I've a box about six feet high, and just big enough for a good-sized fellow to stand upright in, when the door is closed. This box is driven through with sharp pointed nails, as thick as they can stick; and when a nigger commits a fault, never mind whether man or woman, they are stripped and put into the box, where they remain all night. If they become sleepy, the sharp nails keep them awake; and in the morning they appear quite tame. When a fellow has the sulks, I just remind him of the box, and it works upon him like magic. He says 'Oh, massa, don't put me in dat box; I rudder you kill me.'"

At first, I thought he was hoaxing me; but on his assurance that what he had stated was true, I let it pass. He imparted to me more information about his plantation, most of which was of too indecent a character to remember, much less to publish.

At Washington, an addition was made to our baggage list in the shape of thirty-five slaves, of both sexes, from the boy of seven years, to the old man of fifty. They were in charge of, and I believe owned, by two of the meanest looking rascals I had ever met. The one that appeared to have the most to say, was a thickset, swarthy looking fellow, with red hair, that hung about his head like sea-weed round a rock; face thick with freckles, and the most wicked looking eye, probably, that was ever placed in a man's head. He wore a broad-brimmed straw hat, a hunting jacket, and long boots; he had an enormous mouth, and when he laughed, his head was nearly off. This fellow looked like just what he was, *a slave dealer.* I was told that he had bought up these *servants* (for you must know that the southern people seldom say *slave*; they are all called either *servants* or *hands*) in Maryland, and was going to Louisiana, to sell them there, unless he could peddle them off on the way. When we arrived at Richmond, which was early in the morning, the cars stopped in front of a large hotel, and remained nearly half an hour. Immediately on their stopping, he procured a half gallon measure of whiskey, and served to each one a half gill. They were chained and handcuffed, except the children and one good looking mulatto woman, who was permitted to stand on the platform with a little boy. When I looked into the baggage car, and saw these poor creatures, I felt a sensation which I cannot describe, and observed that he spoke rather kindly to the woman, who looked very sad and downcast. Said I to him:

"What do you ask for that woman?"

"*Well, now, look here; I will sell you that ere woman for seven hundred dollars; she'll bring me double that sum in Mobile; she's rather sulky now, because they took her little gal away and sold her to an Alabama feller, and she has'nt got over it yet.*"

"What do you ask for that boy?"

"*I'll take two hundred dollars for the little cuss. I don't like children; the little devils get away, and then we kan't whip 'em as we do a big feller.*"

Not feeling much like purchasing, I declined the offer; and as it was about time to start, I took my seat in the car again, beside my former acquaintance; and when the driver came in, sat beside him, and endeavored to get into conversation about his nefarious business. I commenced by asking if he ever separated families, or bought children that were taken from their parents. All at once he gave me a disdainful look, and asked me if I was not a "Northern man?"

"Yes, I am from Boston."

He then uttered a horrid oath, and replied, "Well, I thought so," and turned immediately from me. I crossed over to my old friend again, as the slave merchant had now cut my acquaintance, and given me the cold shoulder. Often, when on board a man-of-war, I have seen a poor fellow seized up to the gangway, and receive three or fonr dozen, and perhaps only for getting intoxicated; and how I have pitied him; but could have danced for joy to have seen this scamp tucked up, and a hundred lashes neatly put into him. *But never mind; let him go.* He had some difficulty in Wilmington, in getting his *cattle* through the Custom House, which I hoped would have detained him there, so that we might have been clear of his company; but, they were all marched on board the steamer, *with the chains of liberty clanking as they go.*

While on board the boat their irons were removed, and they had one side of the forward deck allotted them. And now, let any one possessing the thousandth part of a soul, just take a seat on the opposite side of the deck and begin first with his eyes, and look upon twenty-eight poor, unfortunate adult wretches, chained and doomed to slavery, cruelty, and outrage, during their natural lives, and for no other crime than being born black. And see that sorrowful well-formed, bright mulatto woman, her child torn from her and carried, she knows not where, and in all probability herself reserved for the most diabolical and basest of purposes. And can it be possible that we are in the United States? oh, no, it cannot be so; *we are descending the Nile, with Nubian slaves for the Cairo market.* What! such a sight as this in the only land of *liberty* on earth; a land whose insignia is equality surmounted with the liberty cap, and whose Latin motto is: "*E pluribus unum,*" what an antithesis! On our arrival at Charleston, they were all bound with irons, and marched off somewhere, probably to the jail-yard, for safe keeping.

I had an acquaintance here on whom I called, and through

his politeness was conducted round the city, and introduced to a number of gentlemen who were affable and courteous, and with whom I was much pleased. As my errand to the South was to purchase timber, I commenced looking round among the immense rafts in the river here, and probably should have obtained what I wanted without proceeding further, had it not been for a development of that characteristic which we find every-where, and too often with the shrewd Yankee, which is: "*leaving the substance to grasp at a shadow.*" I had concluded to take the timber if I could find a vessel bound East that would carry it for anything like a reasonable price. There were several eastern schooners discharging granite at the breakwater, that would soon be ready, and one that was already to receive a frieght.

I procured a boat, with two negroes, and pulled off to her. The captain was walking the quarter-deck, and when nearly along-side, we lie on our oars. The skipper came to the break of the deck, with both thumbs placed in the armhole of his vest.

"Good morning, sir," said I, "are you bound East?"

"Yes, sir, I am."

"What will you take a cargo of timber to Boston for?"

"Well, I don't know; I expect freights are good now, and don't like to set a price till I have looked round."

"Well, sir, I can assure yon that the merchants on shore tell me there is not a ton of frieght in Charleston for the East, and as I am in haste to get back to Boston, will give you seven dollars per thousand, which is fifty cents more than the usual rate."

"I guess freight is good or else you wouldn't have come off. I can't give you an answer now."

"Shove off, boys," said I, and we went on shore.

I remained in Charleston three days, and frequently saw this captain driving through the streets with his hat off, and wiping the perspiration from his face and looking for me, but he was too late, and went East entirely empty. I have mentioned this apparently trifling circumstance, merely to show how apt we are to leave a surety for an uncertainty, and most of our losses and perplexities occur from an inordinate desire to get more, and we often discover, when too late, that our calculations required a little shrewdness as a counterpoise.

Now the point of failure with this captain was not in refusing to take up with my offer at once, for he was bound to get the highest freight that could be obtained; this was a duty he owed to himself and to his owners. But here was a tangible offer over the common rate, and he should have gone immediately on shore with me, when he would have learned there what he afterwards found to be true, that there were no freights for the North, and could have earned seven hundred dollars rather than to have gone home with nothing.

In conversation with a wealthy merchant once, on this very subject, he remarked that he owed his success to one established principle on which he had always acted, (with only one exception,) which was, never to refuse a good paying offer, under an expectation that the article would rise. And the exception was, once he had a lot of hides, for which he had a good offer before they were discharged from the vessel. His broker told him that they were on the rise, and that he had better store them. He did so, and lost the whole.

I took the steamer for Savannah, and arrived there late on Saturday night, took up my residence at the Pulaski House, and an excellent hotel it was. On Sabbath morning I attended the Baptist Sunday School. It was well attended, and well conducted. There were many colored children, but chiefly females. The Baptist preacher, whose name I have forgotten, was a very energetic and off-hand man, and after the services, the ordinance of baptism was administered; and in his address to the audience, remarked in a very feeling manner, that there were those before him that were kept back by diffidence and unbelief from following the example of those who were shortly to be buried with Christ by baptism.

"Yes, my beloved friends, there are those before me that I would give worlds to dispel their doubts and baptize them, but there are also those whose lives and example is such that I would give worlds to unbaptize them."

The house was densely crowded, and a marked solemnity

pervaded the whole. In the afternoon I attended the Baptist church for colored people. The house is well situated and very commodious. I went early and was offered a front seat. The house was soon filled to its utmost capacity, and all were neatly dressed, particularly the women, who were generally clad in calico gowns, with either a white or a colored handkerchief on their heads, and with snow-white aprons neatly tied. Although the choir was quite large, containing some of the sweetest voices in the world, yet the whole audience joined in the singing. The preacher was the celebrated "*Old Marshall*," and was then upwards of eighty years old. He was brought from Gambia with his mother when quite a child, and had been nearly seventy years a slave, but by industry and frugality had saved enough of his little earnings to purchase his freedom. He was an early convert to the Christian faith, and for many years had been a preacher, had picked up his own education by close and assiduous application. He had been free about ten years when I heard him; but the poor fellow, notwithstanding his age, had only a few months before been tied up and whipped with a cowhide for buying from a slave a few bricks which he told Marshall were his own property; but the law strictly forbade a colored man from buying anything from a slave under a penalty of a certain number of lashes. His text was, I think, the whole of the fourteenth chapter of John. His reading was clear and distinct and his enunciation excellent, excepting the negro pronunciation of "brederen," for "brethren." He went through the chapter with much spiritual feeling and simplicity, during most of the time seemed much affected. At the close of the sermon the communion was celebrated. Very few went away, they merely retiring from the body of the house, leaving that for the communicants, whom I should think numbered about three hundred. This was the most interesting scene of the whole. After singing a hymn in perfect time, and in most solemn melody, another colored preacher engaged in prayer, after which Marshall commenced breaking the bread.

All was still as death; my eye was steadily fixed upon him, watching every emotion, and when the bread was broken, he raised his venerable head, the tears stealing down the furrows that grief had ploughed for them.

"*My dear beloved brederen and sisters, dis is de broken body of our blessed Lord and Master. He know what it is to have de cow-skin on his blessed back; but he was whipped for our transgression, dat we might be happy and go where he is, where dar is no more slave.*"

At this last sentence, his watery eyes beamed with a heavenly lustre. Neither the pen of a ready writer, nor the most eloquent speaker, could have done justice to describe this communion season in all its pathos.

After having finished my business in Savannah, I took the steamer for Charleston, on my return homeward. On arriving there, ascertained that Henry Clay had left the city only the day before for Wilmington, N. C., having been South on an electioneering tour. There had been great times in Charleston on his account, and probably the excitement would be great all through to Washington. Not having any business to detain me in Charleston, I proceeded to Wilmington.

CHAPTER XXII.

Gamblers,—Their description,—Plays,—A young man made a victim,—Incident,— Result of desperation,—Arrive at Wilmington,—Great preparations for Henry Clay,—Description of the road,—Speeches,—Enthusiasm,—Ludicrous conduct,—Arrive at Weldon,— Introduction to Mr. Clay,—Arrive at Washington,—Ship to be blown up,—Torpedo,—Meet Mr. King,—Invitation to visit House of Representatives,—Great Excitement,—Account of the blowing up,—Exciting scene in the house,—Laughable story,—Confusion of members,—Nothing occurs for several years,—Myself and friend visit a tract of land in Athens,—Conversation with a negro,—His story,—Learns to read,—Employment on board a packet,—Runs away,—Is detected,—Sold,—Secreted on Board a Boston ship,—Arrives in Boston,—Sails as cook,—Married,—Settled,—Arrive at Portland,—Take stage for Augusta,—Leave Augusta for Skowhegan,—Incident and story on the way,—Arrive at Skowhegan,—Further about the affair.

On board the steamer, there were a set of fellows which I at once set down for gamblers, nor was I mistaken; they are generally known by their rig and habits, and any one who has travelled through the Southern, or Western states, can always distinguish them by certain unmistakable signs, viz: Inveterate chewers of tobacco, great smokers, large, bushy whiskers, when they can raise them, and sometimes only the moustache, hair, nice and sleek, generally curled or frizzled, a massive ring on the little finger of the right hand, with two or three others distributed among the digits; a very large and apparently valuable watch establishment, with a very poor watch attached.

Real gamblers are seldom addicted to drinking ardent spirits, reserving their wits as their stock in trade, and when together, often have some trifling incident which elicits the broad, silly laugh.

Among the passengers was a young man about twenty years of age, who had with him a black leather valise, which he put in his state-room, opposite where I was then sitting; then came into the cabin, locked his state-room door. After the supper table had been cleared, preparation was made for playing cards. I took a seat near by, determined to watch the proceeding as closely as possible. The young man with the valise made one of the party, three of the gamblers making up the rest, while two others were apparently careless lookers-on. Now for the villany.

Each of these lookers-on had a small, ivory-headed cane, which I could plainly see was in continual motion against the back of his comrade. When they had played nearly an hour, the young man arose, completely fleeced. Champagne was freely supplied of which he frequently drank. I thought of the many gambling scenes that I had read of, but here was one directly before me. The young man took from his pocket a cigar, and with trembling fingers attempted to light it, but suddenly remembering that smoking was contrary to the rules in the cabin, replaced the cigar, arose, and pacing the cabin a few times, went to his state-room, brought out his valise, threw it upon the table, saying, "gentlemen, there are seven thousand dollars; the money is not mine, it belongs to my employers; produce a like sum, and I am your man." In a few minutes they declared that the money was ready.

Although there were a number of gentlemen present, not one of them possessed magnanimity enough to interpose and rescue the young man from impending ruin. It may be asked why I did not interpose, and sure enough, why did I not? But the sequel will show that it needed the interference of more than one. Just as he had thrown the valise upon the table, as though struck with a sudden impulse of conscience, took it again, restored it to his state-room, and closed the door.

I left the scene and went upon deck. Not long after I had left the cabin, one of the passengers came up, and told me there was trouble below; that one of the gamblers went to the young man's state-room, and presenting a loaded pistol, told him as they had been bullied into the stake, he must come out and put up his money or he would blow his brains out. He rushed to the table, played, lost his money, and was ruined! *Young reader, do you ever play cards? if so, remember the fate of this young man!* Before finishing my narrative, I shall have occasion to refer to other scenes similar to the one just described and of which I was also an eye-witness.

On arriving at Wilmington, found the place "*alive with Henry Clay!*" They had prepared an extra train of cars to convey him and a large company of volunteers, to Weldon. On the rear car, a gun was mounted with which to announce his approach to the several stations, where the inhabitants, having been notified, collected in order to greet the great statesman. Banners and mottoes were streaming from every car, and his reception at the stations was quite enthusiastic. The people were collected in large groups, dressed in their best attire, particularly the ladies; and when Mr. Clay alighted, there went forth a shout that made the welkin ring. They immediately formed a circle round him, expecting a short speech; he first shook hands with the ladies and gentlemen, and then addressed them for ten or fifteen minutes. As I was in the mail train we could not, at all times, stop until he had finished; but usually met at the next station. At one of the towns at which we stopped, before arriving at Weldon, a very large crowd had collected, who appeared to be of a different character from those we had previously met; there were few ladies among them, and when our cars stopped, the other train was not yet in sight. Among the crowd there was an old fellow, whose hair was perfectly white; he held his hat in his hand, and was running on in the most extravagant manner against Mr. Clay. His voice was sharp and shrill, and he was surrounded by a gang of men and boys, and crying out, "*Henry Clay, the —— traitor, if he comes near me, I'll just put my fist in his face; don't let him come near me, the scoundrel;*" then up goes a cheer. At first I thought the fellow crazy, but it appeared that he was perfectly rational, and I feared that when Mr. Clay arrived, there would be trouble. The cars were now in sight. The moment they stopped, Mr. Clay was surrounded by the crowd, in the centre of which was this noisy old fellow, who immediately approached him, and grasping his hand, says:

"Mr. Clay, bless your good old soul, you shall be our next President; yes, you shall, and show me the man who dares to say aught against it!" Up went three hearty cheers for Henry Clay, who in a brief manner thanked them for their good feeling. As it was getting late, the Clay party gave these equivocal patriots a gun, and we all started for Weldon, where we arrived at two o'clock, P. M. A large collection were there from many miles around to participate in the dinner; flags were flying, and guns firing in all directions, and deputations were continually arriving to greet the Presidential candidate.

I had an introduction to him as from Boston, when he with much apparent amazement asked me how I happened to be there. "I replied, I came here to see you, sir." He laughed, and we were all crowded into the dining rooms which had been fitted up for the purpose, and partook of an excellent dinner, but we of the mail cars, were obliged to retire before the others, as our hour for starting was four P. M.

On arriving at Washington, I learned that on the afternoon of that day, a torpedo experiment was to be tried upon a ship of four hundred tons; it was to take place within about two miles of the Navy Yard. As I had a desire to see how they managed matters in Congress, concluded to remain a few days.

While on my way to the Capitol, I met Hon. Mr. King, who had been our speaker in the Massachusetts legislature for the last year. He politely invited me to accompany him to the house; but as the ship was to be blown up in a few hours, deferred my visit to *Congress* until the following day. It was evident from the movement of the people, and the enormous price of carriage hire, that the blowing up affair was to be something great. I started off at an early hour and secured a good place very near the torpedo buoy; the collection of citizens on both sides the river was immense, and at half past four, the ship came round the point with all sail set, right before the wind. She was a fine looking vessel, but was *doomed to destruction:* and when she had approached within a hundred yards of the buoy, the lieutenant in charge raised his hat to the multitude, and with his boats' crew went over the side. Now was a moment of excitement. Her bow had just touched the bucy, and in another moment she was a mass of fragments; the destruction was so instantaneous that it was impossible to describe it in detail. I could perceive that she broke off amidships, and both ruptured ends were considerably raised; but in an instant all was flat, floating on the surface, hardly two pieces of wood remaining together.

Immediately after the destruction of the ship, three other torpedoes were discharged, raising a huge column of water, two hundred feet high, very much resembling a shaft of crystal, rising suddenly from the bed of the ocean; the smoke, beautifully curling into a pyramid, added much to the grandeur of the scene. Next day, by invitation, I visited the House of Representatives, took a seat in the gallery opposite the speaker. The House had been called to order, but everything appeared to be in the utmost confusion. The speaker sat in his desk quietly reading a newspaper, when suddenly a voice called out, "Mr. Speaker," then another, still louder, "Mr. Speaker," and another louder yet, "Mr. Speaker." The Speaker then gave a rap on his desk announcing the name of the gentleman who had the floor. The subject which had occupied the House on the day previous, was an appropriation for some improvement in the condition of our western frontier. It had been warmly discussed, and was likely to go by the board, but the gentleman now announced being in favor of the measure, and in the face of all opposition, was determined to put it through. He commenced thus:

"Mr. Speaker, allow me sir, to relate an anecdote which occurred in the town from which I came. "A young man, with whom I was intimately acquainted, had paid his addresses to a lady with whom I was also acquainted, and for a season all went on very well. Suddenly something transpired which put an end to the intimacy for the present, and the gentleman was forbidden ever to enter the house again. He was much distressed and earnestly sought an interview with the offended lady; but was denied the privilege of seeing her. He at length determined on the last effort of reconciliation. He went to the house, rang the bell, was admitted, and wished to see the lady for the last time, (unless they could make the matter up.) She came, and he thus addressed her. 'My dear, we have been acquainted for some time; our acquaintance has ripened into friendship and love; you have discarded me for an evident misunderstanding. Now let us blot everything from the page of remembrance, and begin anew.' They mutually embraced, renewed the acquaintance, and were finally married. Now, Mr. Speaker, this is my position; let us act as wisely as this young couple did, and commence anew." This created a general laugh throughout the house.

I had been two years in the Massachusetts Legislature, and had witnessed some things which I considered rather derogatory to the character of respectable men, and now plainly saw that I had not seen everything. All around the floor were groups of men, busily engaged in noisy conversation, apparently regardless of the subject under discussion, and others were debating a point, evidently under much excitement, and interlarding their remarks with dreadful oaths, apparently regardless of anything like decorum. I left this babel, and to change the scene, took a walk in a flower garden. Comment on the *City of Washington* is unnecessary now; I leave it for those more capable of faithfully delineating the true character of the Capitol during a Session of Congress. I left Washington for Baltimore, and on arriving there learned that a mob had just destroyed a printing-press, the excitement of which had hardly subsided; took my seat for Boston, and arrived home on the 10th of June.

Several years passed without any event transpiring worthy of note, except that during this time I had received from a man who was indebted to me, a deed of a tract of land in the town of Athens, in Maine. One of my neighbors had also received a deed from the same source, and under the same circumstances. We had mutually promised that at some convenient season we would go and examine our newly acquired estate. At length the time came. We took the steamer for Portland, on our way to Athens. We left Boston, late in the afternoon—had a pleasant night. I was out very early next morning, in order to get a look at the land. I went amidships, leaned over the rail, and as we were close in shore, I had a good opportunity for gratifying my desire. Along-side of me was a negro, who was also scanning the shore along. I remarked to him that here would be a nice place to raise grapes. He turned to me with an indignant smile.

"Grapes! sir? These people raise grapes?" Why, sir, they are too lazy to make a hoe handle, but will send to Boston to buy one. If you are going down East, you will see two or three lazy lubbers spend a whole day in a boat, and catch twenty-five cents worth of fish, rather than go to work, as they might do, and earn a dollar apiece. There is no more soul in these eastern fellows than there is in a sculpin."

"Do you live here?"

"Yes sir, I reside in Bangor, and have a wife and two children. I own a small house, a good sized pig, a cow, and a lot of chickens. I have just returned from Porto Rico, in a Boston brig, and am now returning home. I was speaking of these eastern fellows not having any spunk; on the passage home we had a couple of chaps that belonged to Ellsworth. The mate flogged them every day, and they had not spunk enough to resist him; and even after we had got in, they were as meaching to him as kittens. I don't think much of these down-easters, anyhow."

"How long have you lived here among them?'!

"Well, sir, I have been married about three years; am a runaway slave, and think I shall have time to relate to you my story. I believe I was born in Richmond, but am not certain, nor did I ever know anything about my parents. The first thing I ever knew was, of being a little boy in Tappahannock. My master had a little son near my age, whose name was William, but they called him Billy. My master died when I was quite young, and Billy taught me my letters, by making them in the sand; it was against the law for any one in Tappahannock to teach their slaves to read. Billy and I were good friends; my mistress was a nice woman, and I seldom got a whipping.

"When I grew a big boy, my mistress let me out to a man that followed packeting form Norfolk to Richmond. On board this packet I learned to read, by taking the letters off the boxes, and getting Billy to show me how to put them together, and very soon could read a chapter in the Bible, and reckon figures. When I was old enough, my mistress allowed me to marry. I had been acquainted with a nice girl, that belonged to a man up river. I paid him seventy-five dollars for her for three years, and at the end of that time, if I paid two hundred more, I might have her altogether.

"The captain of the schooner had a job to supply a steamboat that run to Philadelphia with coal; we carried two loads there.

"One day, one of the men at work with us, says to me, 'Bill, why don't you cut sticks now? You are in a free State, and now is your chance!'

"This was the first time I ever thought of running away. There was a colored family that lived a little way from where we discharged our coal, and the old man was one who waited on parties. I told him I had a mind to run away, but had left my wife and some money at home, and the next trip would manage to bring my wife and money, and be a free man. When I got back to Richmond, I got a fellow to bring my wife up to the schooner, and the captain consented to let her go with me to Philadelphia. I took her ashore, and my old colored friend got a place for her in the country. I then made tracks for New York, got a voyage as steward of a packet ship to Havre. Was gone four months, and on my return to New York, went to Philadelphia to see about my wife. My old friend was mighty glad to see *me*, but told me bad news about her. She had a place in an abolition family, but they treated her so bad, she went back and gave herself up to her old master. I believe" *continued the negro*, "that the slaves at the South would have been much better off if the Northern people had let them alone, and not troubled them at all.

"I went back to New York, and got a voyage to New Orleans. I knew I was a fool for doing so; but perhaps it is just as well now. When we reached the city, I was marched off to prison for safe keeping, till the ship was ready for sea. As I went along with the policeman, who should I fall in with, but a man that lived the next house to my mistress; he knew all about my running away, so I was put in irons, and was confined as a runaway slave. Information of my arrest was sent home, and in two weeks Billy had arrived at New Orleans, and came to the prison to see me. When I saw him, these eyes *began to leak*, and he was a baby too, and in a few minutes, says, 'Bill, as soon as mother heard you were here, she sent me to tell you if you would come back with me, she would overlook all; but if you refuse to return on these terms, I have orders to sell you.'

"I told him that as I had now tasted liberty, couldn't think of being a slave any longer.

"'Well then, you must be sold.'

"He advertised me in the newspaper, and gave me a first-rate character, and brought me one to read. When my wife went back, her master did not whip her, nor even say a hard word to her, but my mistress claimed her, because she was my wife. I was sold to a tobacco merchant, and put in the packing house to take account of the shipments, and in thirty-seven days from the time that I was sold, I was in Boston. I had got acquainted with the steward, while in prison, and the night before the ship went from the levy, I was stowed away between two bales of cotton behind the pantry, and lie on my side the whole passage; the steward fed me through a small hole in the boards.

"At midnight, after the day of our arrival, when all was still, the steward hauled me out, and with a good deal of trouble carried me on deck, but I was totally blind. There were two colored men that kept a shop in Brattle street, waiting for me with a wagon. I was taken to a house, washed, and a suit of clothes were given me. They kept me with them a few days until I could see. I then got a voyage on board a Bangor brig for Havana, and have sailed out of Bangor ever since, and that is three years ago."

This was Bill's story, and I have endeavored to repeat it just as he told it to me.

We left Portland, and according to directions, proceeded

to Augusta in the mail stage, where we were to enquire our way to Athens. Augusta is a pretty place; we remained here two days, and took the mail stage for Skowhegan. The weather being warm, and the inside of the coach somewhat crowded, I took a seat outside with the driver. While riding through this barren region, I observed to a man who was sitting beside me, that a large farm of such land as this, would give a fellow the horrors. He turned to me, and said:

"Did you ever have the horrors?"

"Yes, many times."

"Well, then, you know how to pity me."

"Why, what 's the matter?"

"Well, sir, I will tell you. I am under charge of the sheriff; he is inside, and I am going back to Skowhegan."

He then related the following story:

"I live about eighteen miles from Boston; (I have forgotten the name of the town, although familiar to me for many years after.) One of my neighbors came to me and said he wanted to raise two hundred dollars to meet a payment due on his farm. 'Now,' said he, 'I have a note against a man at Skowhegan, Maine, for one hundred and sixty-five dollars, for a shingle-machine that I sold him, a year ago this month. This note is now due, and I am sure that he can pay it immediately. I will sell you the note for one hundred dollars cash, and must have the money in three days. I gave him the hundred dollars and took the note. I had never seen any part of Maine, and thought I should like a trip to the eastward; so I commenced my journey, and arrived at Skowhegan four days ago; found the man that owed the note. He was a gallows-looking rascal, and at first was going to strike me, and asked me what I meant by bringing him a forged note. Said I to him, 'What do you mean by a forged note? I bought it of that man,' pointing to the name. By this time I was surounded by a dozen real, vagabond-looking fellows; the man swore he had paid the note, and said that he could produce it; and the next morning brought a note which he swore was the genuine one which he had paid; still swearing that mine was forged. Seeing how matters stood, I took the stage for home, to lay the matter before the man from whom I had bought it. I reached Augusta in the evening, intending to leave next morning; but just as I had seated myself at the breakfast table, the sheriff came in, and arrested me on a charge of forgery and am now on my way back to Skowhegan."

By this time, we had arrived at Waterville; the coach drew up to the tavern, for the passengers to dine. The sheriff took charge of his man. I followed them into the parlor, and remarked to the sheriff:

"I see you have a prisoner there, sir. We sat together on the coach, and he has related to me the circumstances of his detention; I think there is some mystery about it."

"Yes, sir; it is a hard case for our friend here, anyhow."

Dinner was ready, but the prisoner would not eat. I urged him to take some food, as he had eaten no breakfast, and it would be late in the afternoon before we should arrive at Skowhegan. He still refused, saying that his distress was so great, he felt no desire for food. Away from home, among strangers, arrested for forgery, and without means to defend himself. I partook of a hasty dinner, and returned to him.

"Now" said I, "if your statement to me is true, I will be your friend, and remain by you until we see the result. If you are in want of money, I will give you enough to pay your expenses; so now cheer up; you may rely on me as your friend."

Hearing this, he seemed much affected, took my hand, and thanked me kindly. The stage being ready, we mounted to our seats again, with the prisoner by my side. He appeared to be an honest, simple-hearted man, owned a small farm, and had left a wife and one child at home. He said that the greatest cause of his distress was, that when he left home, he did not expect to be absent but a few days, and now he feared that his farm and stock would suffer, and his wife would also feel alarmed for him.

"Don't let that trouble you," said I; "keep a stiff upper lip, and never be frightened, if you are innocent. If you *are* an innocent man, you have *nothing* to fear."

At five, P. M., we arrived at Skowhegan. In front of the tavern was a long piazza, crowded with a gang of bloated, ragged, state prison-looking loggers, and the most conspicuous among them, was the hero of the shingle-machine. He was about half clad, and little more than half intoxicated. My friend, the prisoner, myself and sheriff went into the sitting-room, and closed the door.

CHAPTER XXIII.

Termination of the shingle-machine affair,—Obtain a horse and chaise and start for Athens,—Description of the roads,—Sentiment,—Stop to rest,—Dismal appearance of the country,—See a house,—Get to it,—Happen to hit on the right man,—Explain our visit,—Kindly treated,—Description of land speculators,—Describe our lots,—They are valueless,—Remarks on Athens,—Remain all night,—Affecting story,—Reflections,—Early breakfast,—Depart,—Ride up to a tavern, —Plentiful supply,—Arrive at Skowhegan,—Description,—Start for Boston,—Disposal of our land.

I INFORMED the sheriff that I was the prisoner's friend and should not leave him until justice had been done. "If this man has come all the way from Boston with a forged note against that 'cut-throat looking villain,' with an expectation of getting money from him, then he deserves the highest punishment that the law can inflict. But, sir, if on the other hand, it turns out that all this is a scheme to defraud this man of the genuine note, I am determined to put him through and have that fellow punished."

The gentleman who was my fellow traveller to Athens was also a sympathizer with me in behalf of the prisoner, and was willing to remain until the case was decided. The first thing now to be done was to procure able counsel, if such could be found in these regions, and it must be done immediately.

The sheriff recommended me to a squire somebody, who resided in a village seven miles distant. I accordingly made preparation to go for him, and went out on the piazza among the people who, by this time, had considerably increased. They gathered round me, enquiring what was to be done with the forger. I now explained to them my position; that after hearing the man's story, I believed that a plan had been arranged to defraud him out of the note and probably to extort money from him. "Now, gentlemen, I am his friend to any amount, and am determined that the guilty party shall be punished." Turning to the miserable object who was the cause of this trouble, said I, "how is it that there are two notes alike, unless you wrote a duplicate for this very purpose? And I wish to ask another question. You say you paid the note two months ago; why did you pay before it came to maturity? you don't look as if you were over-run with money." And while talking with the fellow, the landlord beckoned for me to come in; he then took me aside and said:

"I think, sir, this matter can be adjusted without further trouble. That fellow is now under bonds for stealing logs, and is not worth a red cent. I think if you will come in and see the sheriff with me, the whole matter can be settled without further trouble."

And now, reader, *what do you think flashed across my mind? could it be possible that the landlord was at the bottom of the whole transaction, and when he found that the man had a friend he was glad to back out?* And to end this villanous affair it was adjusted that night; and in the morning our quondam prisoner came to me with a cheerful countenance, saying that all was right; he had been remunerated and was going home in the next stage. Although this story may appear like fiction, yet I assure the reader it is strictly true.

We ascertained that Athens lay in a northern direction about twelve miles distant. Obtained a horse and chaise and commenced our journey very early next morning; previously partaking of a hearty breakfast. The first few miles was through a decent country, bearing a luxuriant growth of stunted pine trees; the road, however, was richly lined with bushes, and here and there a few *red and green blackberries.* Our path now lay up the side of a young mountain, the top of which looked as high as the clouds. The sun shone brightly, imparting much warmth. And the old horse showed evident signs that his pores were not in the least obstructed, and in order to relieve the poor brute, we both got out and walked behind, pushing the team ahead with all our might. We soon discovered that going to Athens was altogether up-hill work, and after four hour's drag, we reached the summit and stopped to rest, for we had actually pushed the horse most of the way up. I sat down and began to *sentimentalize.* I cast my eyes around to catch a sight of Athens, either of Mars Hill or the Acropolis, crowned with the majestic Parthenon, but saw nothing before me but one vast desert of white rocks. My companion was a whole-souled fellow, and we really enjoyed this scene of desolation. All at once I fell into a *reverie.* What is life in nine cases out of ten, but what is here so clearly illustrated? Youth starts out into the world with fine and flattering expectations. The road for a few years is balmy and pleasant, but he soon finds that many of his prospects, like the pine trees, are stunted, and that gold does not grow on bushes by the roadside. In climbing the hill, he not only drags his own weary limbs along, but often has to push others ahead, and after all this fatigue, when at the top, what does he see but a dreary waste of barren rocks?

All *three* of us now being sufficiently rested, we bipeds got into the chaise and concluded that as we had pushed the old horse up hill, it was no more than fair that he should drag us down. We began to descend, and very soon lost sight of land. Here we were now on a sea of rocks, of every species, reaching quite round to the horizon. The road led to a deep valley.

After riding an hour, we saw in the distance a green spot, when on a nearer approach discovered a house and barn near by, surrounded by some well cultivated land, and when within a quarterof a mile of it, I got out, went over to make enquiry of the people in what direction Athens lay. I jumped over the fence and saw a good looking old man in the barn yard, whom I saluted.

"How do you do, sir? will you have the kindness to direct me the road to Athens?"

"*Why, sir, you are in Athens now!*"

"Do you call this Athens?"

"Yes, sir, this is Athens."

I went back a short distance, waved my hat to my friend in the chaise, when the farmer kindly offered to pilot him in. I had not yet made known my business to him, but as we were now all together, told him that we had come here to hunt up two tracts of land, having the deeds with us, and asked him if he could direct us to any one that could point out the lots to us.

"Oh, yes, sir, I am the register of deeds and commissioner for Athens. If you will show me your deeds I can inform you of their location. Gentlemen, walk into the house, and I will take care of your horse."

We entered and he introduced us to his wife, a fine, healthy, lady-like looking woman, and a family of six rosy, chubby-looking children the very picture of health. The lady was extremely kind, and immediately made preparation to get us some refreshment. In a few minutes a table was spread with an abundant supply of good things. After partaking of them, the old gentleman sat down with us, giving an entertaining account of the Eastern land speculation, relating many anecdotes of half-mad purchasers who came there with large, and well-drawn plans, having upon them broad and rapid rivers, excellent mill sites, with a gigantic growth of pine trees, none of which had ever been found, nor did they ever exist.

He knew about our lots, and said he could point them out if we would walk to a small hill a few rods from the house. When we had reached the summit with the plan in hand, he commenced with me.

"You see that farthest ridge yonder? You observe there are two?"

"Yes, it looks like a little streak along the horizon."

"Yes; well your lot lies beyond that!"

"Why, that is beyond sundown!"

"Yes, 'tis a long way off, but there is a large swamp just this side, and it would be rather difficult to reach it now, the mosquitos are so thick they would devour a man in a few hours."

"What kind of land is it?"

"Well sir, it is rather stony, and there is some *wood* there, but there is no way to get it off."

"What do you think it is worth?"

"That is rather hard to say, for nobody wants it. You might possibly get twenty-five cents an acre by giving a long credit."

Having obtained all the information, and much more than I desired, about *my* lot, my companion wished his pointed out.

"Oh, your lot lies just here; you have passed over a great part of it in coming here."

"What! all those rocks?"

"Yes sir."

We both burst into a hearty laugh.

"Halloo, Ben," said I, "your fortune is made, sure. All you have to do is, to notify the King of Holland that you can supply him with granite for building his contemplated city on the grand bank. And now, you have the advantage over me, for you can walk over your ground, while I can't reach mine, without going to it in a balloon. We have now seen 'where our possessions lie,' and are standing on a hill in Athens, which might have been called Mars Hill; but I think that *Cecrops* was not the founder of this modern city, neither will it ever become a seat of kingly authority, under another Codrus, nor the capital of a modern Greece; and if another Paul should ever come here to preach, he would probably choose the words of his predecessor for a text, 'Finally, brethren, farewell,' for I hardly think he would ever visit it again."

We returned to the house. As it was late in the afternoon, we were politely solicited to remain all night, as it was seldom they saw strangers, and particularly those that were all the way from Boston.

We consented to stay. He then invited us out, and showed us around his farm, which was like a beautiful oasis in the desert. It consisted of about forty acres, and was under excellent culture. He had resided on it ten years; had formerly lived in New Hampshire, but meeting with a heavy loss, retired with his family to the wilderness, selected this spot, and by hard labor and rigid economy, had made his farm what it was. "But," said he, "I am like a man on a rapid river in a boat, pulling against the current, if I stop one minute, my boat is swept down, and it is hard work to regain my former position. We have excellent health, and have lost but one child since we have been here. Our eldest daughter died in March, which was a heavy stroke for us, and I thought it would have carried my wife off too." Previous to retiring, the lady again alluded to the last illness and death of this amiable girl: she very imprudently went a short distance from the house early in the morning, while the ground was quite wet; her shoes being very thin, she took a violent cold, which led to rapid consumption. She pined away very fast, so that her hip bones protruded through the skin.

She begged her father to remove her from the soft bed, and let her lie upon the floor; the father, to gratify her, complied, but she could not endure it a minute, and wished to be put back again. She then called her parents, little brothers and sisters to her bedside, kissed them all, and dropped sweetly away into the arms of her Saviour.

This recital was somewhat similar to that of the old lady in Richmond, and was equally affecting. I could not avoid mingling my tears with theirs. How strong are the ties of parental affection, which often seem made up and woven with our very life-strings.

We retired to rest, and notwithstanding I was quite weary with my day's journey, it seemed as though I could lie awake, and contemplate this solitary, yet lovely family.

Here, but a few days ago, was a lovely blooming form, just ripening into usefulness, her mother's solace, her father's hope, and on whom the little ones doted to the extent of their capacities. It was to save her mother's step that she went out in that unguarded manner, as the errand required despatch.

Although this young lady was the picture of health, with ruddy cheeks and ample form, how applicable here are Tupper's lines on death:

"Keep silence, daughter of frivolity—for Death is in that chamber!
Startle not with echoing sound the strangely solemn peace.
Death is here in spirit, watcher of a marble corpse—
That eye is fixed, that heart is still—how dreadful in its stillness!
Death, new tenant of the house, pervadeth all the fabric;
He waiteth at the head, and he standeth at the feet, and hideth in the caverns of the breast;
Death, subtle leech, hath anatomized soul from body,
Dissecting well in every nerve its spirit from its substance;
Death, rigid lord, hath claimed the heriot clay,
While joyously the youthful soul hath gone to take its heritage."

Early next morning we partook of an excellent breakfast, and bade adieu to this hospitable Athenian family. And were it in my power, would heap blessings on their heads, and strew their paths with happiness and peace.

It was a lovely morning, and at about nine o'clock we made the land, and were soon clear of *Ben's lot.*

At noon, we rode a short distance out of our way, in order to reach what we thought to be a tavern; both ourselves and horse wanted some refreshment. On reaching it, we found a collection of people outside the door, and there seemed to have been some trouble around the premises; we soon ascertained what the difficulty was. Two men had swapped horses, and it appeared that the swapper had cheated the swappee, who wanted to annul the trade, and get his horse back; to this the fellow would not listen, consequently they had a small fight. How it ended, I don't know; am certain that I did not feel interested enough in them to care.

We called for dinner, when a great, tall slab of a girl came in to know what we would have, whether *meat wittals*, or bread and milk. We replied, "beef steak, if you have it, or a piece of ham." After waitng a long time, Dolly informed us that our dinner was ready in the next room; and true enough, it was a dinner. Here was a large pudding dish, with meat enough for ten hungry men, and the meat fairly swimming with melted grease; then there were two large pies, a loaf of bread, a plate of butter, a piece of cheese, a dish of potatoes, and a saucer of pickles.

Now Dolly knew we were hungry, and governed herself accordingly. She waited upon us very attentively, and seemed much afraid that we had not made a dinner, because we left more than half she had placed before us. Our bill for this dinner was twenty-five cents each.

We started in good spirits for Skowhegan, and arrived there about sundown, on Saturday.

Next morning, at Sunday School time, I took a walk towards the meeting-house, and must say that in no country town have I ever seen a prettier company of young ladies and children, nor those that were more fashionably dressed. The town is prettily situated, containing some fine farms and a beautiful waterfall in the centre.

We were out early on Monday morning, as the stage left at nine o'clock, for Augusta. I saw no more of the shingle-machine fellow, although there were a number of loggers hanging round for their morning dram, which consists of New England rum and half a pint of molasses. I entered into a joking conversation with some of them, while on the piazza. Said I:

"You appear to be a hard set of fellows here."

"Yes, sir; they 'll take your eyeteeth out, unless you look sharp, and keep your mouth shut."

"How do they dispose of log-stealers here?"

"How do they dispose of them? Why, they must ketch 'em first. There are fellows here that will steal a log directly before your eyes, and you won't know it. There 's Ned Sprowl; he 's the slickest thief in the whole State of Maine. I 'll tell you what he did.

"One of our lumber dealers had over a thousand logs in the booms, waiting a chance to get 'em over. Every morning he missed a number of his logs, and was determined to watch 'em himself. He put on his big coat, took his gun, well loaded with duck shot, a bottle of stuff, and straddled a big log. It was a bright moonlight night; after a while he gave a look round, took a swig from the bottle, and fell asleep. In the morning he awoke, and found himself astride the bark. Ned Sprowl had been there and hauled the log out from the bark, and never waked the fellow."

The stage being ready, we jumped in, and were soon safe and sound in Boston. Perhaps the reader would like to know what disposition we made of our property. I gave our kind host a power of attorney to sell mine for one cent an acre; and if he could not obtain that, give it to somebody, and pay them something for owning it. My comrade did the same, and if it is true, as some geologists say, that stones grow, Ben must have a powerful crop by this time.

CHAPTER XXIV.

Allusion to a previous chapter, relating to the fate of my fellow apprentices, —My attention again drawn to the subject, on meeting one who had been a convict in the State Prison,—Several years a teacher in the prison,—Remarks,—Meet an old acquaintance,—His rapid downfall,—His son,—Downfall and ignominious end,—My friendship for my friend, —His behavior,—Dies miserable,—Become acquainted with the history of two young convicts,—Disposition to hide their sins,—Remarks of an old sinner,—His honest confession,—Murder of the Warden,—Discharge of one of my scholars as evidence,—His genteel appearance,—Recommitment to prison, — Liberation of another,—Calls on me,—Supply him,—Goes to New Bedford,—Returns,—Is the same Villain still,—Ungrateful conduct,—Arrested,—Sentenced to House of Correction,—Advice to the young,—Always willing to help the poor and afflicted,—Sometimes treated with ingratitude,—Assist an old drunkard,—His happy reform, and peaceful family,—Supply him with necessaries,—Another State Prison story,—Hypocritical rogue,—His apprehension, and history,—Thefts,—Appeals to me for sympathy,—Have nothing to do with him.

In a previous chapter, I alluded to the fate of some, who were apprentices with me, and of others, who were my contemporaries. In walking down Washington street one day, I met a certain character, who, to use the common phrase, is coining money, in a most nefarious business; who usually mingles in the best society. I could not refrain from looking back to the place where I first saw him, though on no consideration, would I ever mention his name. I will however relate a few *incidents* which rather conclusively show that *State Prison conversions* do not often amount to much.

For several years, I had in company with others, at the solicitation of a Society of benevolent individuals, visited the State Prison, at Charlestown, on alternate Sabbath days, for the purpose of teaching the convicts, who were divided into classes, and invariably gave the greatest attention to the instruction. The chaplain, *Mr. Curtis*, was apparently a man of exemplary piety, who did all that lay in his power for the present, and future welfare of the prisoners, and was sure to mark the incipient signs of repentance in any with whom he conversed, was also faithful in promoting its growth, which in some instances he felt satisfied, was consummated in genuine conversion, which in two other cases was the means of obtaining executive pardon, and premature discharge.

At the early part of my services at the prison, while looking round the chapel I saw a man among the convicts, who, during his apprenticeship, was one of my most intimate companions, a steady, industrious, and respectable youth. He became a man, left his mechanical profession, followed the sea, became master and owner, married into a respectable family, had two children, a son and a daughter. The boy was well educated, and also followed the sea. Now, mark the *downfall, and tell me how it could be.*

Capt. S., enjoyed the confidence and respect of those who knew him. But, all at once, like the gathering of a thunder-storm, or the destructive tornado, he fell, like Lucifer from Heaven, passing rapidly through all the grades of vicious delusion, until he was locked up in the State Prison for stealing.

During the first two years of his imprisonment, his son was faithful and affectionate to his mother and sister, throwing in his earnings toward the support of the family. But as suddenly as did father, so did he fall; became a drunkard, was discharged from his employ, and finally hung, as a mutineer, on board the U. S. brig, Somers.

The chaplain of the prison felt encouraged from what he saw, that this unfortunate man was a true penitent. His sentence was for three years, and at its expiration, on the day of his release, I met him, and proffered my friendship. He told me that he had seen his wife, who was willing to receive him again, and to live with him. In order to encourage the reform, and to assist him until he could get into some employment, I furnished him with fuel, groceries, and a supply of clothing, for all which he appeared very grateful. He was a skilful turner, and told me that he only wanted a small lathe and some tools to commence with, and he would then earn a good living. I felt much pleased with his deportment, and furnished him with all he wanted, and with money, with which to purchase stock; all went on well for several weeks. One evening, his daughter came to my house in tears, and begged me to come to the house, for her father had abused her mother shamefully, saying, "it was impossible for them to live together."

I went immediately over, saw them, expressed my surprise and regret, that, under the favorable circumstances with which they had met, that they could not banish the remembrance of the past, and look at the future, under God's blessing, as the bright sunset after a stormy day. To be brief, he turned like the "dog to his vomit, and the sow to her wallowing in the mire," gave himself up to intoxication, and died a drunkard! Notwithstanding the prospect before him, of seeking God's blessing, and ending his days in happiness and peace.

My visits to the prison, were on alternate Sabbaths; and for several months I had the same class, which consisted of six young men, neither of whom were over twenty-five years of age. It was not allowed for a teacher, to hold any conversation with a convict scholar on any other subject than that which concerned his lesson, or the application of it to the present case. But I could not resist the temptation, to digress from rule so far, as to enquire of each one his name and term of sentence. I commenced with the one opposite to me, and in a low voice asked his name, and the above particulars. He gave me *a name*, whether true, or an *alias*, I could not tell. He belonged to a town near Worcester, Mass., and when arrested, was doing a prosperous business, had been married a year, and had one child. Said he: "I am *entirely innocent* of the crime alleged against me, and for which I am now suffering; it was for forgery. I was in company with some young men one evening, when the conversation turned on *beautiful hand writing*. I was asked if I could imitate *that name*. I did it so well, that none of the others could distinguish the original from the copied. Next day, I was arrested on charge of forgery, tried, and sentenced for five years in the State Prison."

This was the sum of his story, which might do to tell to *marines*, for sailors would not believe it. I showed no signs of *unbelief* about his story, merely observing that if I were living at the expiration of his sentence, I should like to see him.

I could not help noticing the cast of this young man's head, his high, and well-formed forehead, brilliant and penetrating eyes, together with a fine manly form; but, alas! what does all this amount to? *he is a State Prison convict*, a stigma, which time may partially cover, but is never forgotten.

The next case was a youth from the country, he was also *innocent* of the crime for which he was imprisoned! What an outrage upon society, when an *innocent man* is arrested for an alleged crime, tried, and found guilty by twelve impartial jurymen, and then in cousummation of this act of *injustice*, the stern judge pronounces the appalling sentence, two days solitary confinement, and five years hard labor in the State Prison! "*Woe unto you also ye lawyers! for you lade men with burdens grievous to be borne, and ye yourselves touch not the burdens with one of your fingers.*" This young man very *briefly* told me his story; which was, that some stolen property was found in his possession, *but he could not tell how it came there!* he had been in prison two years, and had three more to serve. Neither did I intimate to *him*, that I disbelieved his story, and was sorry to find that neither of them had ingenuousness enough to openly confess their crimes and manifest some signs of repentance. But mark the contrast; the third man on the seat, who was a rough, highwayman-looking fellow, with short wiry red hair, face full of large freckles, and a wicked looking eye. During the time that these innocent youngsters were telling their stories, he was reaching forward, and attentively listening to their statements. He was an entire stranger, probably never having seen them before meeting in the class. After the boy had got through with his story, this fellow very deliberately straightened himself up, and giving *me* a sort of leering look, said he, in a low voice, of course, "I wonder, sir, how it is that these two innocent chaps are allowed to sit with me. I *acknowledge that I am a big villain*, and I deserve to be here. I broke into a house and helped myself to a fine lot of silver, but I got drunk one day, and told of the robbery, and they just nabbed me, and put me here for ten years. But never mind, I'll be a good blacksmith when I get out."

There was one other, whose term of imprisonment would expire in a few weeks, and to whom I merely remarked, that I should like to see him after his liberation, gave him my address, and said no more. A very short time after this *private interview*, Mr. Lincoln, the warden of the prison, was murdered by a convict in the workshop, where our young forger was employed, who was an eyewitness to the assault. One day a gentleman called on me, neatly clothed in a handsome suit of black, with white gloves, gold watch elaborately chained, and making a very polite bow, "*How do you do, sir? perhaps you* don't recognize me; you remember your class at the prison." I immediately recollected that fine countenance, took him by the hand, and enquired how it was that he was at liberty. He replied that he had been pardoned in order that he might give testimony against the murderer of the warden. Our interview was short at this time, but he called on me again, saying, that when the trial was over, he was going home, and hoped to pass the remainder of his life in an honest endeavor to get a good living, also to regain a respectable standing in society. But alas! how frail is man, and how weak are resolutions when made in our own strength. It was only a short time after this interview, that I read the arrest of this innocent young man for a larceny, that would, without any doubt, send him back to his old quarters, where he might have the *pleasure* of putting on his uniform and sitting again beside his old friend, the red haired burglar. According to appointment, the young man who was to be liberated in a few weeks, came to my house, and then informed me that he belonged to New Bedford, and would like to go home; but had neither money nor clothing. I supplied him with a suit of clothes, and gave him five dollars to bear his expenses, and for which he seemed very grateful. Not many days after his departure, I received a letter from him, in which he said he was so persecuted by his old acquaintances, on account of having been in the State Prison, that it was impossible for him to remain there, and should return to Boston, which he did, and came to me for advice and assistance. He said that he had worked a few years in a cabinet maker's shop, at the prison, and thought that he understood the business well enough to work at it for a living. Accordingly, with the assistance of two others, we procured him a situation in a cabinet maker's shop; procured him several jobs, such as making work-tables, and benches for some benevolent ladies, who were willing to pay him a generous price for the articles. He had not been many days in the shop, when the workmen began to miss their tools. At length the young man was suspected as being the thief, was accordingly watched, and caught in the act of pocketing a nice gauge; he escaped from the shop, and from the young man who detected him. Complaint was immediately made to the police officer, who ascertained his boarding-place, which was in Broad street, near the old Custom House.

The officer was on the lookout for him, when by-and-by the gentleman came along, and the policeman made an attempt to nab him. The fellow sprang from his grasp, ran to the wharf and jumped overboard. But unfortunately for him it was nearly low water, and there he was nearly up to his arms in mud, "steadfast and immovable." After a great deal of trouble in getting boards and ropes, and amidst the jeers of a crowd of Irishmen, he was hauled out, rinsed off, and carried to jail. By some means he had got hold of a miserable tool of a lawyer, who had been made acquainted with the true character of the fellow, and his dastardly treatment of those who had so kindly loaned him shop-room and tools; for on searching his trunks, over twenty dollars worth of stolen property was found. This pettifogger knew all this, and yet was trying to get him clear! He came to me to know if I would use my influence in behalf of the prisoner.

"O, yes, you shall have all my influence to get him back

to the State Prison, where all such fellows ought to be, during their natural lives."

He was sent to the House of Correction for one year, and I never saw him again. Now, young readers, you perceive that I have been rather explicit in narrating these State Prison incidents, and my reasons are:

First, that you may see the danger of petty thefts, which are most generally insipient big ones. Secondly, pernicious influence of bad companions, and the certainty that your sin will find you out. Bad habits, of whatever class they may be, when once imbibed, are hard to be eradicated—often continue to grow until the committing of some great crime brings the perpetrator either to the gallows or the State Prison, the ignominy of either, lasting through a whole generation.

I have often been laughed at for showing sympathy, and endeavoring to assist the wretched. It is true, I have given hundreds of dollars to alleviate the condition of the poor—of which there are three kinds, viz: *God's poor, the devil's poor, and poor devils,* all of which I have endeavored to do toward them as I should wish to be done by, were I in their condition. In some cases I have met with base ingratitude and abuse. But never mind, the balance is on my side; what I have given in *true benevolence* is not lost, but will come back with ample interest. The narrow-souled wretch who withholds his hand from assisting a fellow-creature in distress will surely get his pay. I have said that in some cases I have been requited with ingratitude, but one pleasing instance of appreciated kindness, such as I will now mention, goes to offset a dozen of the other.

During the Washingtonian movement in 1845, there was a man who lived in a neighboring town, for many years a notorious drunkard. His family had suffered much, being often destitute of a morsel of food. Early one morning, a man said to me:

"There goes old ——, he is just come in for a regular drunk. He gets a few dollars, and then, instead of providing food for his family, keeps drunk until his money is gone, then goes home and abuses them."

I ran out and caught hold of him. I saw that he had already made a beginning. I caught his arm and asked him to step in with me for a few minutes. At first he resisted and began to show fight, but after much persuasion he sat down with me. I took his fevered hand and looked him in the face. Said I, " now you have come to Boston to pass your time in beastly intoxication. You have a family who want the money that you are going to throw away for rum. Now, my good fellow, go immediately home, but before you go, my friend here will take you to Washingtonian hall where you can sign the pledge, and I am sure that if you leave off drinking, you will yet become a happy husband." The old man listened with attention; he then grasped both my hands, and commenced weeping like a child. He declared that no one had ever talked to him in that style before, but had called him a drunken villain and various other insulting epithets. Said he, "I will sign the pledge!" My friend conducted him to the hall — he signed, and went home a sober man.

A week after this interview, I ascertained where he lived and went out to see how he got along. When near the house, I passed by on the other side, to ascertain if I could see him, and what he was about. His regular business was that of a wheelwright, and could have constant employment if he would keep sober. I observed that he was busy at work, so I crossed the road, and went into his shop. At first he did not recognize me, but in a minute he caught my hand, and invited me into the house, and there was a scene for an artist. At a window, sat a half-clad girl making a check shirt. The neighbors, having heard of his reform, now commenced assisting the family. A younger girl sat knitting with neither stocking nor shoe to her feet. She was also poorly clothed. But the most affecting scene of all, was the wife, sitting with an infant at her breast. The poor woman looked the very picture of sorrow, her eyes sunken, face pale, and furrowed, as though the tears had frequently coursed their way from those lustreless orbs. The nursing infant bore the very lineaments of its mother's grief, looking emaciated and sickly, as though it could hardly find sufficient nourishment from nature's fountain to sustain its equivocal existence, and when introduced to the emaciated wife, she received me with a sort of melancholy joy, as though she had said, "*Oh, sir, I fear 'tis too late!*" In a few minutes she seemed to brighten up, and said she felt rejoiced that her husband had signed the pledge, "*and oh! I pray that he may keep it.*"

I saw their wants, bade them good-by, and went home. Early next morning I packed up a two bushel basket full of provisions, with some articles of wearing apparel, and sent it to them, and had the pleasing satisfaction of hearing some months afterwards that they were all right. The old man was a thorough teetotaller, the family were all comfortable, and continued so the last time I heard from them. Reader, there is no fiction about this story, 'tis true, and do you think that I shall ever lose the value of the provisions that I gave this family? I have one more State Prison story to tell you, and will then go about something else.

I think it was in the Autumn of 1835. I attended the Baptist Church in Federal street, under the pastoral care of the Rev. William Hague. Several times at our vestry prayer meetings I noticed a very gentlemanly looking young man who usually wore a large broadcloth cloak, his hair fixed off in the first style. He was a regular attendant on Sabbath days, as well as at all the prayer meetings. He frequently visited the pastor, conversing chiefly on the subject of religion, and became familiarly acquainted with the deacons and the leading members of the church. He frequently took an active part in the conference meetings, and one Sunday evening he arose, and with a drawling, melancholy voice, said that he had been very much shocked at the wickedness of a young lady at the house where he boarded. She had actually played a march on the piano during the intermission, and it made him feel so bad that he was obliged to retire to his room and go to prayer.

After a few weeks, he proposed himself for membership, and really, all thought him an exemplary and pious young man. But not wishing to be thought egotistical, or of arrogating to myself any superiority in a knowledge of human nature, will just say, that during this time, I had not the least confidence in him, for I caught him in a falsehood to begin with. He appeared to be very much attached to me, saying that he was in the Mediterranean with me. He had probably heard me say that I was two years there, and thought that he could manufacture a sort of intimacy out of it. Neither did I wish to make known my scruples, fearing that possibly I might be mistaken, in which case my remarks might be injurious to him. At the same time I felt well satisfied that he was a *fire-ship in disguise.* Another thing excited my suspicion, he frequently asked me if I knew of any employment that he could engage in. Now, here he was, rigged out like a nabob, boarding at an expensive house, and no employment. He passed the regular examination, as to his Christian experience, was baptized, and received as a member of the Church. But somehow, I could not feel towards him as I should. I *knew* nothing about him derogatory to the Christian character, and as a matter of duty, should have felt the same cordiality for him as for any other, but it was not long before the true character of our newly-initiated brother came out. About three weeks after his reception into the Church, at one of our evening meetings, the pastor requested the male members to remain after the meeting was dismissed. He then said that he had some unpleasant intelligence to communicate, which filled him with distress. It was, that the young man of whom I have been speaking, had that day been arrested for stealing. A committee was appointed to investigate the affair, and report at the next church meeting. On the following day I ascertained the particulars of the theft, which were that, in passing along the south side of Quincy Market, he fixed his eye on six tubs of butter, and very adroitly, with a piece of chalk, wrote his initials upon them, then stepping off a short distance, called a hand cart, and told the man to take that butter and follow him. He put it on his cart, no one asking any questions, and went off, the fellow leading him up to Cunningham's auction room, corner of Milk and Congress streets. The butter was put into the store. Our gentleman, with his large cloak and dangling tassels, stepped up to Mr. C, saying, that he was to leave in the eleven o'clock train, and he had the remains of a large invoice of excellent butter, which he wanted sold for cash, as soon as possible. While waiting for the sale, a police officer, accompanied by the hand cart man, stepped up to him, put his hand on the gentleman's shoulder, "How do you do, sir? How do you sell butter?" He at first denied any knowledge of it, but it was no use to deny it, he was marched off to Jail, and locked up. On the same afternoon on which I had ascertained these facts, a paper was brought to me, on which was written, with a piece of charcoal, "*My dear friend, please call and see me as quick as you can; I wish to see you very much.*" I thought probably, that he might have some disclosures to make, which might benefit somebody, so I went, and obtained permission from the jailor to talk with the prisoner through the grates. As soon as I saw him, he commenced a regular *boo-hoo*, sobbing away, at a great rate, held his delicate hand through the bars for me to shake, and begged me to do him one favor, which was, to be his bondsman for two hundred dollars, before he came up for trial. Not wishing to add irony to misery, nor to multiply words, I declined having any further conversation, excepting only a few words of advice, and left him.

I noticed while looking into his cell, that there were two savage looking villains as his companions, who seemed to *laugh* at the tears of this hypocrite. I learned further, about the history of this unhappy man, that he had been for many years a consummate villain.

When he came to our church, he had just been liberated from the Thomastown State Prison, having served two years for stealing a quantity of watches in Portland. On leaving Thomaston, the first thing he did was to procure a suit of sailor's clothes, and by representing himself as a seaman, who had just left the hospital, excited the pity of a benevolent captain, who shipped him for a short trip to the South. He made out to rob this kind captain, and purchased the genteel suit he then wore, with the stolen money. On searching his trunk, after his arrest, a number of books, belonging to Mr. Hague, were found, which he had stolen when on his pious visits to that gentleman's study. What disposition was made of him I don't know, but about two years afterwards, he again came to me, but I positively refused to have anything to do with him.

CHAPTER XXV.

Return of my son from California,—Comply with his request,—Arrives safe—Unjust tariff,—Falls into the hands of villains,—Discovery of gold,—Become interested in California speculation,—Determine to go to California,—Prevented by sickness,—Recovery,—Embark on board Empire State,—Description of the passage,—Arrive at Chagres,—My companion,—Engage a boat,—Detention,—Start,—Strong current against me,—Stopping place for the night,—Difficulty in procuring shelter,—Sleep in a pigsty,—Description of my lodging,—Unceremonious leave of my fellow lodger,—Meet my companion in the morning,—Get underway,—Chagres river,—Next stopping place,—Description of our entertainment,—Our hostess,—Another day dawns,—Off again,—Arrive at Cruces,—Amusing scene,—Sickness and death,—Miserable fare,—Difficulty in obtaining mules,—Engage them at high rates,—Pass a miserable night,—Morning dawns,—Poor breakfast,—Start for Panama,—Dreadful road,—Exciting scenes,—Suffer from hunger,—Leave my mule.—My condition,—Exhausted,—Animated by God's promises,—Arrive at Panama,—Description of the country,—Sick man,—Effect of kindness,—Remarks on dying,—Story,—Remarks on Panama,—Much sickness,—Embark on board the steamer Unicorn,—Description of the Passengers,—Incidents,—Card playing on the Sabbath,—It is stopped,—Villanous character of the passengers,—Arrive at Acapulco,—Difficulty,—Origin of the trouble,—Arrival at San Francisco,—Appearance on entering,—General character of the population,—Enquiring for my son,—Found the scoundrel who cheated him,—Miserable accommodations,—Cases of sudden transition from prosperity to beggary,—Secure a passage to Sacramento,—Perilous adventure,—Gale,—Arrival at Sacramento,—Result of companies,—Auction sales,—My business apparently all right.

In 1849, my eldest son returned from San Francisco, having gone there from the Sandwich Islands. It will be observed that this was some time before the gold discovery.

California had just been taken possession of by the United States, but not yet received into the Union. My son gave such a flattering account of San Francisco, I was induced to comply with the request, which was the object of his return.

He wished an assortment of goods, and a small, fast-sailing vessel, which he felt sure would turn to a good account.

I furnished him with the vessel and goods; he sailed, and arrived safe at San Francisco.

But notwithstanding the United States had possession of Upper California, the old Mexican tariff was still in force, which on some articles was very high, and considerably reduced the profits; but the goods, taken altogether, paid a fair profit; and after the discovery of gold, the vessel was sold for a good price. The young man would have done well, had he not subsequently fallen into the hands of a consummate villain.

When the California fever began to rage, and had become absolutely an epidemic of a most contagious character, I became connected with others, in parts of voyages, which we supposed would do well, for we had no reason to think otherwise.

I felt much anxiety about the result of my son's business, and had determined to go to California, calculating to arrive there in season to meet the vessels in which I was concerned; but was detained in consequence of an attack of cholera, which confined me to the house about six weeks. After my recovery, however, the determination to go not having abated, I obtained a passage to Chagres, in the steamer Empire State, Capt. Wilson.

On board this steamer there were about three hundred cabin and steerage passengers, among whom were about forty regular New Orleans gamblers, together with several ladies, of doubtful reputation.

There were also some who had run away from their families, and some who were fleeing from their creditors.

It usually happens, that men, or rogues, who possess cunning enough to evade justice, most generally bring themselves out by boasting of their success; and so it was with these men, who seemed to take a pride in telling how they dodged the constable. One of these worthies was two days and nights stowed away in the coal bunker of the steamer, while two constables were in search of him; one of whom took a station on the steamer's deck, the other at the head of the wharf. There were among the cabin passengers, however, several gentlemen of the highest respectability.

We arrived at Chagres in eight days from New York. There were four of us who had been previously acquainted with each other, and it was our intention to travel together, until we reached San Francisco.

As I had some little knowledge of the Spanish language, I went on shore and bargained for a boat to take us up the Chagres river to Cruces.

This being at the early part of the emigration, there were many more inconveniences and difficulties to encounter, than at a subsequent period. The negro boatmen were very saucy and obstinate, notwithstanding the price for taking passengers up river was ten times as much as it had been before the gold fever broke out.

After agreeing for the boat, and having our luggage on board, and as we supposed, everything ready for a start, we found the niggers had gone off, nobody knew where; at length, by searching, I found one of them, and demanded the reason why we were not on our way, as several boats had already started. The fellow replied they were getting their food, and would soon be down. After waiting with much impatience for nearly two hours, and threatening to take out our trunks, they made their appearance, and started.

There was a strong current against us, and it was with much difficulty that we made the least headway; but by keeping close in with the bank, and with a vigorous use of the poles, they managed to make a little progress ahead. After sundown it soon became quite dark. We had now reached a miserable stopping place, which they called Gattoon. There were no sleeping places here, nothing but a few bamboo negro huts. I was aware that to sleep in the open air in this region, was very dangerous. What was to be done? I tried among the huts, and could see no place fit for a dog to lie in. There were several other boats that had stopped here, and on the beach were groups of passengers, that intended to pass the night in drinking, smoking and singing. The reason why I felt so anxious to get under cover, was, that I had hardly recovered from my late illness; and felt afraid that exposure might produce a relapse, which of course in a place like this, would end in death. I had missed my companions, and as the night air become chilly, was determined to get in somewhere.

A short distance from the boat was a large pigsty, built of bamboo, and over the swine there was a sort of chamber where the husks were kept. I managed to crawl into this *chamber*, but the floor was so slight, I was fearful that it would give way and let me down among the grunters; at any rate, I was under cover. I had not been here long, when I heard one of my companions enquiring for me. He was a very heavy man, and I knew that the floor would not hold him, so I lay perfectly quiet.

There were six large hogs in the sty, and they knew that some lodger had taken possession of the upper part of their domicil; whether they were afraid of losing their provision, or were indignant at my impudence in thus intruding upon them, I cannot say, for they kept up such a hideous squealing and grunting through the night, that sleep was out of the question; and if my bamboo floor had given way, *O shocking to relate, what would have been my fate?*

At daybreak I left my lodgings, without saying even good-morning, *to any one down stairs;* went over to the boat, and there they were strewed along the beach, some asleep, and some half drunk, trying to sing. I found my companion, who had managed to get along, somehow or other through the night. We began now to muster up our niggers, who were not far off, and were soon under *poles* again. Notwithstanding the rapid current against us, and the little headway we made, the balmy air, beautiful prospect on each side the river, and the sweet singing of birds, altogether made it a most delightful morning.

Chagres river, for beautiful and picturesque scenery, is not surpassed by any other in the world. We had an ample supply of provisions but were somewhat cramped for room, being obliged to sit or lie in one position nearly all the time. We passed the day very pleasantly, and at night stopped at "Dos-Hermanos," or two brothers. Here was but one hut, occupied by an old, decrepit negro woman, that much resembled an orang-outang; there were also, two sharp-snouted, half-starved pigs, and a few miserable looking chickens, in the hut with her. We obtained permission to lodge in an old shanty belonging to the estate, which was nothing more than a few bamboos stuck in the ground, with others across, and the roof thatched. Poor as it was, it afforded a shelter from the night air.

We had not been long on our backs, before we found that there were others there who claimed a pre-emption right, and had assailed us from the crowns of our head to the soles of our feet. I went into the old orang's hut, and asked for a candle, but such a thing was unknown to her. At last, however, by rummaging over her traps, she found a piece of sperm candle about an inch long, which she had kept as a curiosity, not knowing either its use or value. I bought it, and when I cut the wick clear and lighted it, she was much astonished that she had not made the discovery before. This brief light enabled us to clear away the rubbish, so that we made out to live till morning.

As soon as day dawned, we were out, breathing the noxious and miasmatic air, and listening to the songs of the paroquets, which were flying around in myriads. Rather than to be on the river another night, we told our boatmen if they would get us into Cruces, during the day, we would give them five dollars extra. This offer seemed to have the desired effect. They pulled and tugged, and in order to assist them, when we came to a bend in the river, all got out and walked across, which very much facilitated the passage. At sunset, we arrived at Cruces.

This had been a feast-day in honor of some tutelary Saint. The natives, young and old, male and female, were nearly in a state of nudity, dancing, singing, and carrying on at a great rate. We got into a tent with some others who were going to California, and were told by the man who kept it, that there were many cases of the Isthmus fever in our immediate vicinity, that there had been many deaths, principally Americans. The food here was miserable, consisting chiefly of rice, and dried fish, which was abominably dear. Here were a number of villanous operators who had established themselves at this post to rob all who came in their way.

Our next business was, to procure mules, which had also become a monopoly. A few designing fellows had bought them all up, and let them out to emigrants at enormous rates; but there was no help for it, we must get to San Francisco at *any rate*, so we .engaged our mules at sixteen dollars each, for Panama. After passing a miserable night, and partaking of a poor breakfast, mounted our mules, and started for Panama.

I had been told that the road was dreadful; but soon found both occular and physical demonstration of the truth of all that had been said about it. Our caravan consisted of about forty: we were soon among the rocks, and commenced the ascent through the tortuous gorge, then coming down into a sea of mud, where the animals sunk, in some instances, quite up to their bodies. In these cases, the rider must dismount if he is not *thrown* off, and obtain the assistance of others, to extricate the poor beast; to do which, is always a difficult matter, and in some cases impossible. And then the poor animal must either be killed or left to perish in the mire.

I met a man who had been obliged to leave two mules in this dreadful condition: he said he was unwilling to kill them; as it was impossible to extricate them, he knew of no alternative, but to leave them to their fate, fearing that he might get mired himself. While he was telling the story, the tears were trickling down his eyes, in compassion for the miserable animals; offering any man fifty dollars that would go back and shoot them. I was pitched into the mud several times, and once thrown off on the rocks, and providentially escaped injury.

These animals are remarkably sure-footed, if the rider will allow them to take their own course, they get along much better. It was very evident now, that my mule could not hold out for the whole journey. Several had already given out, and were left standing in the road. The *riders, however poor they may have been at home*, now found themselves on their legs again.

I had taken some articles of provision at Cruces, which were put in a small basket, and hung on the mule's back, but by some means it had fallen off, so I had nothing to eat, and no way of getting anything until my arrival at Panama. My poor beast now came to a stand, and if he had been a descendant of Balaam's ass, and had inherited his power of speech, would in all probability have told me, that he could go no further, and that I must shift for myself; and would also have asked me to look at his back, which I accidentally did, and found it completely raw.

I was now six miles from Panama, the company had all gone ahead, except those pedestrians who had been unhorsed, and who were scrabbling along as well as they were able. I was quite exhausted, and my feet much swollen. I took an affectionate leave of my poor animal, and left him to *his* fate, while I calmly resigned myself to *mine.* My shoes, in consequence of being saturated with mud, were almost useless. I found it hard work to get along. But that ever-abiding talisman and watchword *go ahead,* which has cheered me in many subsequent difficulties, gave me a new impetus.

I found it necessary to sit down and rest quite often, and though hungry and thirsty, that cheering promise contained in God's word, *fear not, for I am with thee,* inspired me with strength and courage; and at eight o'clock in the evening reached the *shanty hotel,* called Oregon House.

It was full to over flowing; but no matter for that, *I am with thee,* rung in my ears. I applied to the landlord, who very kindly gave me a small cot bedstead, without bed or bedding upon it, and on which I threw my weary body, and after resting a while, obtained some food, and again lie down, but not to sleep. For, overhead, there were crowds of half drunken fellows, who kept up such a hideous roaring, that to sleep was impossible.

My cot was within two feet of a sick man, who had been taken down with fever. At midnight, he began to groan in a most distressing manner. I spoke to him in a soothing tone; he was evidently in much pain, and was fearful that he was going to die.

I arose, and asked if I could assist him in any way, he answered, no. I then began to cheer him up; offering my assistance in any shape, and told him not to *think* of dying in this wretched hole. I got him a swallow of brandy, which soon relieved his pain, and in the morning he was much better. I afterwards saw him in San Francisco. He was then a great strapping fellow, big enough to eat part of an ox.

And, to digress a moment from my narrative, I would remark, that I firmly believe many die before their time. I do not wish to enter into an argument on this point; for, perhaps the reader may stop here, and ask, how any one *can* die before their appointed time. Neither do I *now* have any reference to suicides, but wish merely to state my position, and then leave the subject, after relating one or two examples that have come within my own observation. In the course of my narrative, I shall have occasion to mention several instances which may be relied on as facts.

It is well known, that the nervous system has a great deal to do with animal life, and those who possess weak nerves, are easily excited. Many cases have occurred, where persons have dropped dead under sudden excitement, either from fear or joy.

The nervous system is the balance wheel which regulates the physical and mental powers, and when that is deranged, we are comparatively good for nothing.

Now let us apply this to a sick person, who, probably, may have been previous to their illness, of what is usually called a nervous temperament. Sickness having rendered what was weak before, still weaker.

Suppose it to be a young lady; she is taken suddenly ill. Relatives, friends, and acquaintances, will naturally call to see her, and though her sickness may not be of a fatal character, yet, one of these intruding visitors, may be an old Granny, who, with spectacled eyes, and a look of horror, declares that the "*poor, dear creature*" is going, just as her *dear Betsey* did. She sees the *same deathly look, and she* must die *whether or no;* and she does die.

Now, as I have before observed, without going into an argument, say, that if this young lady had seen a few cheerful companions, or a judicious clergyman, in all probability she would not have died, or at all events her life might have been prolonged.

This is not a fancy sketch, and I could name parallel instances, were it not for taking up too much time, at the present stage of my journey to California. Will only add one case where resolution on the part of the patient, kind and encouraging conversation by the visitor, has produced a speedy recovery, and radical cure.

Some years ago I had an intimate friend, who had been taken suddenly ill; he had been a strong, athletic man, having previously enjoyed excellent health.

As soon as I heard of his sickness, which was some days after he was taken ill, I called at his house, and on entering, was met by his wife, who, as soon as she saw me, burst into tears, saying, "she was going to lose her dear husband," and immediately gave vent to a paroxysm of grief.

She took me to his bedside, when I at once saw that his *dying*, was all in my eye. What, with the doctor, who was intent on a good bill, and the old women, who were fast frightening him to death, I have no doubt he *would* have died of inanition. For, neither doctor nor nurse would allow him any food, except a little weak tea, and a very small piece of toast, twice a day.

My first salutation was, "halloo, William! What are you doing here?"

He rolled up his eyes like a dying calf, shook his head, "*O! I am very weak.*"

"What's the matter?"

"*O! I dont know.*"

"Have you eaten anything to-day?"

"O! no sir;" says his wife, "the doctor won't *allow* him to eat anything."

"Well, now look here," said I to his wife, "you are starving him. Send immediately, and get two pounds of tender loin, broil it well, and give him a small piece at a time, and when that is gone, get more, and I will insure you that he will live, and soon get well."

She did so, and in a few days I called again; he was up, and dressed, walking about the room quite cheerful, and in a few days more, he was about his business. He is now, 1856, stout and hearty, and likely to live many years.

To resume my journey, I had been twice at Panama in 1820, and there was a marked difference in the population, between that year, and 1850. Then, there were only a few Spanish citizens and about one thousand soldiers, and at siesta time in the afternoon, all was quiet as the grave, but now, the place was one continual scene of fights, rows, drunken yells, and every species of confusion. Nights and Sundays were no alleviation. The police regulations were wholly inefficient, the authorities not daring to imprison an American, let the offence be what it might. And here might be seen a specimen of the future population of San Francisco and the mining districts.

There were many cases of Isthmus fever, many of which terminated in death. The very idea of dying in this place, was worse than death itself.

As our party all had through tickets, the company provided us with a passage to San Francisco in the steamer Unicorn, Capt. Porter. She sailed from New York some three months previous, with passengers for California, stopping at Panama for provisions and coal.

We had among our cabin companions a number of Western *bowie knife* fellows, who were gambling night and day.

On the first Sabbath after leaving Panama, they got their cards out the first thing after breakfast, and commenced playing. I went to the captain and asked him if he allowed gambling in his cabin on the Sabbath. He replied that the passengers from New York had continued to do so since they left there, and he doubted whether he *could* stop it now.

"Then," said I, "you are no longer master of your own ship, if your authority does not extend far enough to stop what is not allowed on any other American steamer, that I have ever been on board of, and if you do not stop it, you are not the man I took you to be."

He was willing to make the attempt, however, went below, and requested them to abstain. They at first showed symptoms of refusal, but finally concluded to put away their cards.

They were down on me, in rather an underhanded manner, making frequent allusions to Methodists, picking out particular passages in the Bible, reading them aloud to the female passengers. Notwithstanding all this, I was treated respectfully by all, being cautious not to come in collision with them, for I saw that they were a set of villanous desperadoes, each carrying a bowie knife, or a revolver fully charged. One day an innocent sort of a fellow made a remark which one of these wretches did not happen to relish. The latter drew out his knife and made a plunge at him. Fortunately he dodged the knife, jumped up and ran among the crowd, and the murderer after him. My blood fairly chilled, for I expected to see that horrid looking knife plunged into his body. He was rescued by the others, but there the fellow stood, trembling with rage with his knife in his hand, swearing he would have the fellow's heart's blood.

At Acapulco, there was a row with the authorities on shore, which resulted in the imprisonment of one of our steerage passengers. Here was a time; there were two other steamers in the harbor, full of passengers for California, many of whom were of the same class with ours. The news of the imprisonment of this man caused a great excitement. A meeting was held on the beach, and resolutions passed to rescue him at any rate. The cause of his imprisonment was for grossly insulting a Spanish officer, and I do not hesitate to say that in nearly all the difficulties that have taken place between these natives of Granada and California Indians, from the commencement of emigration to the present time, 1856, where lives have been lost, and men have been maimed and robbed, that some turbulent, unprincipled Western men, have been the agressors, who, being better armed, and possessing more bodily strength, have robbed and otherwise insulted these harmless people, who of course will seek for retaliation, and then the whole country is up in arms for revenge. I have been an eyewitness to many of these scenes.

The man before alluded to, was liberated on the payment of a fine of fifty dollars, and on the morning of sailing, the officer who had been insulted, having business on board, was met in the gangway by this fellow who had before insulted him, and here he added another cowardly assault, which might have stopped the steamer had it not been settled on the spot.

We sailed from Acapulco for San Francisco, where we arrived after a passage of thirty-five days from Panama. All over the hills, as far as the eye could see, were white tents. The bay was crowded with every sort of a thing in the shape of a vessel, the flags of every nation under heaven floating in the breeze.

San Francisco was filled with gamblers, rogues of every species, cut throats, highway robbers, Sydney convicts, villanous commission merchants and bankers, fraudulent auctioneers, hypocrites, apologies for courts, and some of the most miserable and contemptible pettifoggers that could be scraped together from every section of our country. Every sort of government official, from the Collector to the Harbor Master, looked out to feather their own nests, and succeeded in getting a pretty good pile of Uncle Sam's money. I have given a pretty good catalogue of characters, every one of which I think can be identified by others as well as myself, as it happened that I was simpleton enough to get into the *fangs* of some of these worthies. Notwithstanding the broad sweep I have taken, I don't wish to be understood as saying that there were no honest men among them, for there were men who were honest then, and have continued so up to this time, and with whom I would trust millions, whose reputation for honesty remains intact. I shall pass over this description of California men and manners for the present, and mention a few incidents that occurred during my residence there, then leave the country in possession of its ruler and owner, the Devil, and would say to *any* who may see their own characters among those that I have drawn, as the caricature printer said to me at Windsor, Chap. xix:

"I have a right to make a print or a picture, *if not obscene*, on any subject I choose, and if any one sees their own likeness there, they must call me a clever painter for making so good an imitation."

My first object, after I landed, was to find my son; and on enquiry, ascertained that he had gone to the Sandwich

Islands. I found the fellow who had cheated him, and to all appearances was, when I saw him, fast going to perdition; notwithstanding, only a few months before, he was receiving $190,000 a year for his gambling houses and brothels. And when I *last* saw him, he was a worthless vagabond; just what others, *whose names I could call*, must surely come to, according to the retributive justice of Heaven. I have already seen the fate of some, and others are sure to come along in their turn.

Capt. B., myself, and one other of our companions, took up with a temporary residence in a half-built shanty, and continued to live there as well as our circumstances would permit.

All sorts of provisions were abominably dear, besides being very scarce. Capt. B. and I were waiting at San Francisco for the arrival of vessels from Boston, in which we were concerned. There was a brig at Sacramento, which had been there a few weeks, owned by a company of which I was unfortunately one. I was obliged to wait several days before an opportunity offered of getting up from San Francisco, as no steamer had yet been put on the river, although there was one fitting for that purpose, by a commission house, that were thought to be somewhat richer than the Rothschilds; but they run along a little while, and finally funked out, and became beggars. This boat was advertised to sail next day, at 4, P. M. The weather was rather cold and rainy. I went down to the landing with a heavy pea-jacket on, and a very heavy pair of boots, for which I had paid fifty dollars.

When I came to the beach, the last boat had gone off; but as there were four others beside myself who were passengers, the agents hired a boat with two men to take us on board. The boat was soon piled with trunks, so that there was scarcely room to stand, and a very poor chance for the men to row. The steamer lay more than a mile from us; it blowed furiously, beside a heavy tide setting against us.

When we got out into the strength of the wind and tide, our case appeared almost hopeless. Both boatmen were intoxicated, their thole-pins broken, and here we were fast drifting out to sea. I felt so provoked with the drunken scamps, that I wanted to beat them over the head with the oar. And in addition to our comfort, we were drifting broadside across the chain of a large English ship; which, had we struck it, our fate would have been sure death. But providentially, when within a few feet of the chain, we saw a whale boat coming round the bow, in which were two Chinamen and a Swede, besides a man with a steering oar. They were pulling with all their might to get ahead; the boat was half full of water, and they dare not stop to bail her. I sung out to them to come towards us; we were at the same time, working with all our might to keep our boat off the chain; and when the whale boat got near enough to venture it, I made a spring, and reached her, but soon saw that my condition was very little better than before. The whale boat was fast sinking; the man that was steering her, declared that it was impossible to get anywhere, and we must drift out to sea.

"O, I think not," said I. "Pull away, boys." I turned to with my hat, bailed away, and very soon found I was gaining on the water.

About a hundred yards from us, I saw a small shore boat pulling along under the lee of a ship. I hailed her at the top of my voice; finally, the fellow edged off towards us, and when she was near enough, I made a leap into her.

"Now," said I, "my dear fellow, I want to get on board that steamer."

I sat down, backed his oars, and by pulling up under the lee of the vessels with incessant labor for more than an hour, we got near enough to catch a rope from the steamer, and was soon safe on her deck, and I assure you, I was thankful. The boat I left first, I believe was saved, but do not know the fate of the whale boat. It blew so hard, that the steamer could not get underway until next morning. We made a short stop at Benecia, and arrived at Sacramento on the following night.

There were quite a number of vessels there, but many of them were valueless, as it was impossible to make any repairs, or obtain a crew, even to get to San Francisco. These vessels had been owned by companies, who had, in almost every case, exploded, sold out everything for a song, and cleared for the mines.

I was much amused, one day, on hearing the crier, who goes round on horseback, advertising the fixtures and furniture of a barque, for sale at auction. He cried out in a long, drawling voice:

"*To be sold this day, at the levee, the cabin furniture, beds, bedding, and a lot of stuff belonging to the brig Jane. The company have all burst up, and gone to the devil.*"

I believe there was not one out of the numerous companies that were formed in the Atlantic States, that arrived in California with the unanimity with which they started. Many of them having previously drawn up the most rigid police and moral regulations, making it penal to use any kind of profane language, or to engage in any sort of gaming. Then, previous to sailing, they must all go to some public place of worship, and a farewell sermon preached to them; *subject, Gold Diggings.*

But, alas! these very exemplary young men soon found how evanescent is that happiness, where gold is at the bottom. Many of them, before they got up with Cape Horn, were in open rebellion against all discipline; and as soon as the vessel reached her anchorage at California, the whole concern was dissolved. The brig that I went up to see, was all right; they were selling her cargo, and everything was then apparently doing well.

CHAPTER XXVI.

Return to San Francisco,—Purchase a lot on which to erect a house,—Condition of the streets,—Opinion of the climate,—Caution,—Voyages,—Land purchase,—Price of lumber,—Another owner,—Result,—Arrival of the brig,—Difficulty with an upstart,—Difficulty of getting up the river,—Trouble with the men,—Go up the Sacramento,—Purchase a steamboat,—Preparations for going down the river,—Description of the crew,—Fears excited,—Reach the brig,—Conclude to improve the steamer,—Return to San Francisco,—Condition of San Francisco,—Villanous outrage,—Entire absence of justice,—Hypocrites,—Downfall of nabobs,—Effects of intemperance,—Miserable scoundrels calling themselves lawyers,—Description of a California court,—Summoned as a witness,—Decision,—Murders and robberies on the increase,—Inefficiency of the Municipal government,—Vigilance committee organized,—Trial and execution of Jenkins,—Pusillanimous wretches object to these noble fellows.

I REMAINED only a short time at Sacramento and returned to San Francisco, to await the arrival of a brig which was daily expected. And as our shanty was rather incommodious and out of the way, we concluded to purchase a lot and put up a coop, just large enough to shelter two of us.

The streets were in a deplorable condition; scarcely any part of San Francisco, (except on the narrow sidewalk), that was clear of mud, which, in many places, was over knees in depth. It was with much difficulty that carts could be drawn along with only one or two hundred pounds weight. Being the rainy season there was no chance for the mud to dry.

I had frequently heard of the beautiful climate of California, but if this is a sample of it, I prefer Nova Zembla, at once. From November until May, it is one continued series of hard gales, and rain, with a tremendous current continually running down the bay. And during what is called the summer months, from May till October, after 10 o'clock A. M., a cold, deathly wind comes in through the heads, which makes it necessary to put on a thick pea-jacket, and in many cases a fire is by no means uncomfortable. At night two good blankets are indispensable to keep you from freezing, and a sheet-iron case to prevent being devoured by fleas and rats. Also a sharp look-out or you will have your skin taken off by some smooth-faced rogue.

I had some misunderstanding with a man concerning a bargain, and on perceiving his drift, named the matter to a friend who gave me the following advice:

"If you wish to escape with one breath of life, whatever your trouble may be, don't go near one of those despicable wretches, called lawyers."

I find that I have unconsciously slipped from the indicative to the imperative mood. So, if you please, we will go back to the *lot*, on which we intend to build the small house. My companion, Capt. B., had selected a location, containing about 8000 feet, for which he agreed to pay twenty-eight hundred dollars. The pretended owner seemed to be a very conscientious man, saying that he could get a much larger sum for it, if his conscience would allow him to ask it. Now was not he an honest man? Well, we agreed to take it and pay him his cash in ten days. So we got a *little* lumber together, for it could be purchased then for the very liberal sum of nine hundred dollars per thousand feet! We calculated, that when finished, our house would be about the size of a common camboose house, with very much the same inside finish.

On the third day after the commencement of our mansion, while Capt. B. was busily employed on the premises, a gentlemanly looking fellow came up to him, and demanded what right he had to build on his premises?

"I have *purchased* the lot," said B.

"Of whom, pray?"

"Of a man named Ross."

"Well, sir, I am the owner of this property and you must move your traps very quick."

He had got hold of the wrong chap if he undertook to frighten him. B. replied civilly, that he should see the man from whom he had purchased the lot, and if he was not the legal owner he then would leave it. The fellow was satisfied with this, and went off.

Capt. B. went immediately to Ross, and very quietly told him the story about the man who claimed it, &c., adding, "Now, if you don't pay me three hundred dollars damages immediately, I'll haul you up before the Judge in five minutes." The fellow began to turn pale, and to stammer out some kind of excuse. Capt. B. was determined. The villain paid over the money and here the matter ended. Subsequently, I found it to be a common occurrence for one man to sell another's land, or rather, what another man claimed. As to the true ownership that was as hard to decide, as it was to determine where the first negro came from.

The brig that I was waiting for had now arrived. She had stopped at Valparaiso, and brought some fifty or sixty bags of flour on freight, consigned to a house in San Francisco. The brig was bound up the river to Sacramento. We had the flour brought on shore, and safely piled on the wharf. The consignee was notified. Very soon an upstart of a youngster came down with his cart to take it away, but just as he commenced loading. it began to rain. He then in a very pompous manner, declared he should not receive it, and if any of it was wet, he should hold the brig for damages; because, said he, it should not all have been landed at once.

The young man who was supercargo of the brig informed me of the difficulty. I hastened immediately to the wharf. The boy was there when I arrived, and had just ordered the cart off. I said to him, very pleasantly, "What's the matter, sir? He began to stretch himself out, assuming a very dignified air, and very impudently told me that he should not receive the flour. I replied, the brig is bound up the river, and as the bill of lading specifies, the flour is to be landed immediately on her arrival at the port of San Francisco, and here it is, and while you are taking it away, if it rains much, we will cover it with a sail. He still used impudent language, at which I got provoked, and just went up to him: said I, "If you say another word I'll throw you into the dock, you good-for-nothing puppy! there is your flour; now go tell your master what I have said to you." The result was, that every bag of it was moved before sunset. We procured a pilot, and the brig started off for Sacramento. By some carelessness she got on to a bank, fifty miles below, and in all probability the river would not rise for some time, so she was likely to lay there a month. I felt much troubled at the circumstance, as her cargo was lumber, and in consequence of the daily arrivals, it was fast falling in value.

We had another trouble, the men were intent on leaving the brig, and it was with much difficulty that they could be kept on board. I went up to Sacramento again, to make some arrangement about taking off the deck load, and securing it against the bank of the river until some means could be devised for getting it to the city, but I found it difficult to procure men to do this, without paying them enormous wages. I finally, as the last resort, purchased a small steamboat that belonged to a California company. She was to be sold to settle up the voyage, but some of the owners wished to retain an interest in her which was agreed to.

I had her immediately prepared to go down river for the brig as they had succeeded in getting her afloat, and she then lay in deep water.

The steamer was a small concern, not much larger than a common pilot boat, although her engine was to all appearance a good one, and of sufficient power for a larger boat. We wooded up, made the necessary preparation, and started early next morning.

The crew, consisting of myself as captain, a broken-down lawyer for a fireman, a half-and-half mechanic who had some slight knowledge of a steam-engine, for engineer, and a broken-down schoolmaster for cook and general assistant. Thus manned and equipped, we started off, to tow a deep loaded brig against a strong current, and a head wind. While going down river, I had my fears as to the capacity and power of the engine, whether it would move the brig against such a powerful resistance. I was also aware that neither myself nor the engineer, knew much about steam, but was certain that the whole matter devolved on me, and was determined to make the best of it.

We reached the brig on Saturday night, lay by on the Sabbath, and at 12 o'clock, midnight, roused all hands out, got up steam, and with most intense anxiety watched for the decisive moment. We started the engine, and to my inexpressible joy, she went ahead!

I jumped on to the hurricane deck over the engine, cheering up my legal fireman, who occasionally broke out into a moan, declaring he could not stand it any longer, holding up his delicate, lady fingers, to show me how they were scratched.

"Never mind that, my good fellow," said I, "give her the resin; stir up the fire. Engineer, how much steam have you?"

He tried the cock, "*whiz! whiz!*"

"As much as she will bear, sir."

"Never mind, give her a little more. Stir up the fire! Go ahead, boys!"

I kept on the forward part of the deck, expecting every moment to find myself high up in the world, but found it was as necessary to cheer them up, and encourage them, as it was to hold up the arms of Moses when he was fighting the Amalekites, for as soon as my voice stopped, they began to flag, and look very serious. We found it was now necessary to anchor, in order to fill up the boiler.

At three o'clock P. M., we partook of some refreshment, examined everything about the engine, found it good, got up steam and off again. I found by the movements of my poor lawyer, that he had much rather have entered a *nolle pros.* and given up the case, than to have gone on with it; and my schoolmaster-cook-and-maid-of-all-work, was much given to *declining*, which made it necessary that he should be addressed either in the potential or imperative mood. And to keep matters along, the crew of the brig were employed in running out the kedge, and hauling ahead, which kept them continually grumbling, and to add to the variety of the scene, the mate and pilot got into a fight, and take it altogether, it was a funny mess.

Nevertheless I kept my steamer all right, encouraging the fireman to throw in the resin, and stir up the fire, now and then enquiring of the engineer how much steam he had. "Whiz! whiz!" was the answer. The fore part of the boiler was red-hot, still we went along slowly against the current. I was afraid to stand over the engine, expecting every moment that something would happen. But there was no alternative, "Go ahead!" was the motto.

I thought of some lines which I remembered to have read when a schoolboy, and which I applied to my engine:

"*Limbs, do your office and support me well, bear me to her, then fail me if you can!*"

We passed a number of vessels bound up to Sacramento, but they could do nothing, and were obliged to lie at their anchors, until either a favorable wind or the abating of the current would give them a chance to get up. At night we could see the mast heads of the vessels lying at the levee, which was twelve miles distant. We let go the anchor, and took our dinner, after which we turned to, cleared up, filled the boiler, and felt quite encouraged. The fireman had got over his fright, and

> "Whate'er in docile childhood or in youth,
> He had imbibed of fear or darker thought,
> Was melted all away."

We had now arrived near our journey's end. The strength of the current was much diminished, and it being necessary that some arrangement for a berth should be made at Sacramento, I concluded to cross the prairie on foot, a distance of about fourteen miles, and thought that I could do it in five or six hours easily. At daylight, the following morning, I went ashore, taking with me some beef and bread, the captain's gun, and a few charges of powder and shot. After passing through the forest that lines the river, found myself on an extensive prairie, bounded by the horizon.

Kept along in the right course, four or five miles, but found it so muddy, with pools of water from the recent rains, which were too deep to wade through, that I concluded to alter my route, which brought me into a much worse condition. All at once I found myself among the tulies, where the water was over my head, and a noted place for grizzly bears. Immediately turned about, in order to retrace my steps, but was soon bewildered, and uncertain which way to go.

I struck out into the prairie again, to take a look round; the sun was obscured, and there was nothing by which I could direct my course. Though much fatigued, there was no place to sit down, except in the mud.

It was now getting towards noon, and I began to have some slight fears that I must pass the night "*out doors.*" While stopping a few minutes to rest, I saw an animal start up just ahead of me, attempted to cock my gun, and, behold, there was no spring to the lock! I took it by the muzzle, and made it fly through the air. In my trouble, I could not help comparing that gun to some *men* that I have come in contact with, though they look very well, and are well *charged*, yet, when required to perform any special duty, *they have no spring to their lock*! Was now relieved of this useless weapon, and went ahead, my eye intently fixed on the horizon. I saw something in the distance that looked like a man on horseback, and following out the law of incidence, changed my course, and in an hour we met, and ascertained that I was going directly away from the point I wished to go to. He, pointing to a little lump of something in the distance, said that it was a load of hay, that not broken down, I must go up to it, and then be sure to follow the cart ruts, which led into Sacramento. Was very much fatigued, and should have esteemed it an act of *politeness* if he had given me his horse.

Continued along, and at last reached the load of hay, from which I took my departure with joy. How true it is, that in life, never mind what our trouble may be, or how deeply we may be afflicted, if we can but find a friend that will point us to an object, from which we may travel joyfully on to deliverance, how sweet is that friendship? *and that friend is God.* I now placed myself between the ruts, and where they were not clearly defined, cast my eyes behind, until I caught the line, and kept straight ahead, when they soon appeared again.

My fatigue was excessive, yet nothing could be seen ahead but the dim line of earth, bounded by the sky. To my great joy, I came to a stone about as large in diameter as a peck measure. Robinson Crusœ was not more astonished at the foot print in the sand, than I was at the sight of this rock. I sat down. You who loll upon divans, and downy cushioned chairs, know nothing of luxury, compared to mine, on this hard seat upon this prairie of mud, but we are never satisfied; soon I wanted something to lean my back against, and then probably should have wanted a pillow. I had no time to spare, as it was verging toward sundown, and after dark it would be impossible to discern my guiding lines.

I started off again, much refreshed, and after travelling an hour, thought I could discern a white speck, that looked like a tent, and on my right there was a lone tree. Soon the village of Suterville hove in sight. Now I was safe! and walked over to the tree. Strange as it may appear, this tree was truly, solitary and alone, not another within four miles, and only a few feet from the ground there was a large limb that grew out horizontally from the trunk, with smaller ones, so arranged, that it made an excellent couch. I lay down upon it, and had a good sleep.

When I awoke the lights were a sufficient guide, and soon found myself in a good tent, with a pot of hot coffee, and a fine beef steak. Rubbed myself down with a coarse cloth, went to bed, and next morning was good as new. The brig arrived that afternoon, and the crew left her as soon as they could get ashore. Lumber was now rapidly on the decline, and by the time the brig was discharged, it had become quite dull.

Our little steamer having performed so well, we concluded to lengthen her out, which would make her much more valuable. Our steam crew, however, were part owners, and concluded to give up steamboating, and try something more congenial with their comfort and education. They sold out their interest. We then took her down to San Francisco, and added thirty-five feet to her length. After doing this, sold her. San Francisco was now in its zenith of imaginary wealth, and of *real* wickedness: for, though there were ministers of the Gospel, judges and juries, and a regular municipal government, yet, it might in truth be said, there existed neither law, gospel, or order. The greatest outrages against individual right were not only tolerated, but *sanctioned* by the law.

Immediately, on the arrival of a ship, the crews, in open violation of the contract which they entered into, by signing the articles, deserted, even before the ship had anchored; this, too, in open defiance of captain or mate. The law not only sustained them in this villanous act, but obliged the master to pay them their forfeited wages.

Murders and robberies were committed in open daylight, and the perpetrators, if arrested at all, were, by bribery, suffered to escape. The polls were guarded with bowie-knives and pistols, in the hands of reckless and profligate scoundrels. Candidates for office, who could furnish the greatest quantity of intoxicating, liquor and continue it the longest, were generally successful.

If a stranger died, who had no one to look after his effects, the public administrator was sure to get the whole. There were many who made great pretensions to piety, who kept up a system of espionage over others, writing to their friends at home, making statements highly derogatory and injurious to their reputation; and these same fellows were violating the Sabbath and doing many things under a cloak which they dare not do openly. Verily they have their reward. Among the ministers of the gospel, there were some who were godly, praying men, but there were others, who had assumed that sacred calling, that cared more for gold than for the immortal souls of men, and they proved it too, for some of them became gamblers. There were also men who had *managed* to get posssesion of a large amount of gold, who became so proud and overbearing, that they could hardly be approached by any one who were not as wealthy as themselves.

During my short stay there, I witnessed the downfall of some of these mushroom nabobs, who were glad to take up with the most menial conditions, rather than starve. One or two instances of this came under my immediate notice. A young gentleman with whom I had transacted business in Boston, came out to San Francisco, arriving shortly after I did; and certainly, for uprightness, gentlemanly deportment, and business tact, I knew not his superior. As fast as prosperity lifted, dissipation lowered. To my utter astonishment he called on me one day, intoxicated. I took him by the hand, with a view of giving him some friendly advice, at which he was highly indignant, as though he entertained the idea that his condition was not apparent. When I said to him, my dear fellow, you have been drinking, he very rudely replied, that it was none of my business, he should drink when and as much as he pleased!

His career was short. The last time I saw him he was nearly in a state of nudity, and looked miserably. I believe he was taken to the hospital, where he shortly after died. His parents were wealthy, his father one of the most active and enterprising merchants in Boston. There were other cases of a similar character which also came within my business sphere, but will not detain the reader by naming them. Shall pass over many occurrences which would only substantiate what I have just written, respecting the general character of most of the population of San Francisco, at that time. I have spoken of lawyers, or rather a set of black-guards, who assumed that title, and will relate one affair in which I had an opportunity of witnessing the modus operandi of a Californian Court. A gentleman who was my intimate friend, had a barque arrive, on board of which were a number of passengers. Among them was a squirt of a fellow who called himself a doctor. On the passage to San Francisco, this chap had given some of the fellow passengers advice about the best method of relieving constipation and diarrhœa. The ship was furnished with the best medicine chest that could be obtained, and the captain freely dispensed whatever was necessary.

Very soon after the arrival of the barque, some fellow put the doctor up to making a demand on the owner for medical service, rendered during the passage. The owner at once, refused to acknowledge any such demand. The other then, according to the direction of his advisers, put an officer on board the barque and commenced a suit.

I was summoned as a witness or evidence for the defendant. The court was held in a shanty made of a few joist, and rough boards. I appeared, agreeable to the summons. The desk for the judge was a rough pen something like what we see at Brighton for the temporary security of hogs during the sale. There sat a horsejockey looking fellow, with a cloth cap on one side of his head, a cigar in his mouth, and his feet raised some two feet above his head, upon a crossbar. When I entered the *Court-room* (?) there stood a tall, rawboned fellow, the prosecuting attorney, laying down the case to the horsejockey judge, occasionally lifting up his arm to give vehemence to his argument, when it was easily seen that he had come out unprovided with needles or thread, for under both arms, the sleeve was torn nearly off, and no signs of a shirt anywhere. This genius was laying down what he called Iowa law, and when he got off a pretty good grist, the judge would remove his cigar, and remark, "*Well, I reckon you are right!*" and when he had closed his *powerful* argument, my friend's lawyer arose, and he was a greater jackass than the other. He undertook to quote Missouri law, and neither judge nor lawyer knew any more about a ship or the usuages on board, than a California Indian. I was called on the stand to give my testimony, as to what I knew, regarding these matters; and really as to any respect for such a court as this, or anything that could be construed into contempt, was out of the question.

His honor wished me to explain to the Court what I knew relative to such cases in the Atlantic States. I briefly stated to the jury, that the law required all vessels to be provided with a medicine chest, with an ample supply of medicines for the voyage, but there was no law that *obliged* the owners to furnish a physician — and in the present case I ventured to give my opinion, that a passenger, who was a doctor, had no more claim against an owner for medical advice or attention, towards a fellow passenger, than a shoemaker would have for mending a passenger's shoes. The Court now adjourned for a few minutes to liquor up, and the judge, to get a sufficient head of steam on before he charged the jury on this momentous case. The sum claimed, was one hundred and seventy-five dollars, and from the movements, I was inclined to think that they were determined to have it, which with the costs, would probably amount to three hundred dollars: and that it would be equally divided between the plaintiff, lawyer, and judge. The jury were a set of rag-a-muffins collected from the street by a constable. The case was decided against the defendant, and all he had to do was to fork over the money, which, including the keepers and expenses, was five hundred and seventy-five dollars. This was California justice.

Murders and robberies were now so common, as to be perpetrated at noonday. The constituted city authorities were wholly inefficient. There was no secure place in which to confine prisoners, a small bribe would break shackles and bolts, and set the rogues at liberty again, who, emboldened by their success in evading justice, were ten times worse than before. But thanks to that band of heroes, the vigilance committee; it was to them that the citizens owed their lives, and the preservation of their property from robbery and fire. I witnessed five destructive conflagrations, which were without doubt, in every case, the work of incendiaries. Yet through the faithful watchings of the vigilance committee, they were checked. The first decisive act of the committee, was the execution of Jenkins, a notorious burglar, and an escaped, Sydney convict. He entered a store in open daylight, knocked the owner down, and carried off a small iron safe. He was apprehended, tried, convicted, and hung upon the flag-staff, on the Plaza, and all within forty-eight hours from the theft. This summary act of justice seemed to strike a terror among the evil doers, and for a short time, things went on well, expect, that a parcel of milk-and-molasses fellows began to make loud complaints against the vigilance committee, "*for taking the law into their own hands.*" And I am sure from my own observation, that had not these noble fellows arisen and organized, in defence of life and property, San Francisco would have swarmed with robbers, murderers and incendiaries. As for efficient laws to punish crime, there was none, neither was there energy enough in the municipal government, to detect a murderer, or to secure him, if apprehended.

CHAPTER XXVII.

Affair with a miserable scamp calling himself a lawyer,—Vigilance committee regularly organized,—Another culprit,—Prompt decision,—His execution,—Arrest of two notorious burglars,—Trial,—Attempted rescue by the city authorities,—Incidents of their reception and execution, —Dreadful conflagration,—Fickleness of fortune,—Tour through the Mines,—Desire to see all that was going on,—Scene at a gaming table, —Results,—Meet an acquaintance,—Remarks on California,—Cruelty of the Indian quack doctor,—Leave my business with two "nice young men," at Panama,—Propose to return home,—Cross the Isthmus,—Arrive at Jamaica,—Imprudence of the passengers,—Arrive home,—My "nice young men," burst up,—Start again for San Francisco,—Sailed from New York in the Cherokee,—Arrive at Chagres,—Took boat for Gorgona,—Arrive safe,—Procure mules for Panama,—Thrown off my mule,—Take passage in the Tennessee for San Francisco,—Taken down with fever,—Death of a passenger,—Escape death by avoiding medicine,—Recovery,—Arrival at San Francisco,—My property squandered by these "nice young men,"—Live on board the Susan Drew,—Villanous treatment towards Capt. Constant, by an execrable wretch called a "Lawyer,"—Terrible fire,—Assist in building a store,—Assist a young man in going ahead again,—Remarks of a Boston gentleman,—My anathema,—Leave for San Francisco,—For San Juan del Sud,—Arrive, —Description of the place,—Difficulty in getting ashore,—Incidents,— Previous trouble with Spanish soldiers,—Affair with a Missourian,— Trouble with the agent,—No mules,—Obtain them and start,—Difficulty commences.

THE morning after the execution of Jenkins, there was an attempt to get up an indignation meeting, and a pettifogging lawyer undertook to make a speech, setting forth the *inhumanity* of the act, and various tender-hearted remarks. He had not proceeded far in his sympathizing speech, when he had to make his escape, or he would most surely have been lynched. The idea of a lawyer telling about *inhumanity*—a fellow who would suck the last drop of blood from an unfortunate man, and leave him gasping, tell about inhumanity!

Necessity compelled me on a peculiar occasion, to call upon a *lawyer* to get a paper drawn which would probably contain about twenty-five lines. This paper was to be signed by two others besides myself. The lawyer that I employed had been a Western judge. After the instrument was written he wanted his pay, which he said was fifty dollars, but would take something less. I told him that when the other parties had signed it, which would be as soon as I could get them together, we would then pay him. Not being able to find but one of the others, the paper remained with him several days. As I was walking on the plaza one day, I met this lawyer and another. They were walking together. In a very abrupt manner he called me by name, and said:

"*You know the number of my office, sir, and if you don't call and get that paper, I'll sue you?*"

Unfortunately for me, I never had philosophy enough to bear an insult. I approached, and told him if he opened his mouth to me again in that insulting manner, I would knock him down. He turned pale as death, and said no more. The gentleman who was walking with him had gone off ashamed of his company. I went immediately to his office, related the affair to his partner, who in a very gentlemanly manner wished me to take no further notice of it, saying, he knew V——e was a close-fisted fellow, and wanted all he could get, adding that when the parties were ready, just come in and we will make it all straight. I met the other fellow a few days afterwards, in Well's banking house. He was then as polite as a French barber.

The Vigilance Committee were now perfectly organized, with regularly appointed officers in every department, with ample and convenient rooms for trial and confinement. Many of the most respectable and influential men in San Francisco were members.

The next culprit was an English highway robber, who was taken in the act. The alarm bell was rung, the court immediately assembled, the robber was tried, condemned, and received his sentence to prepare for death, in one hour. Preparations for the execution of the sentence were made at the end of the wharf. A clergyman kindly volunteered his services to attend him to the place of execution. At first the criminal began to curse and swear, fairly abusing the good minister who continued faithfully exhorting him to repentance. The poor deluded convict was apparently inexorable until a few minutes before he was run up, then in a faint voice asked the clergyman if *there was a hope for him.* He kneeled, made a brief prayer, and was launched into eternity.

Everything was conducted in the most orderly and solemn manner, the whole crowd seemed impressed with the solemnity of the scene. Next was the arrest of *two* notorious burglars who were tried fairly, having every advantage they could desire respecting evidence, in their favor. They were however condemned and sentenced to die. One night a possee of city officers came unawares upon the guard, at the committee rooms, rescued these prisoners, and removed them to the half-built city prison. But the gallows was not to be robbed, as the sequel will show. The city authorities seemed to exult over this, what they called triumph of law over a mob. The Vigilance Committee showed no signs of disaffection, expressing themselves perfectly satisfied if justice was done to the burglars. But it very soon became manifest that after a short imprisonment they would be set free. A deep, and what proved to be a successful plan, was laid by the committee to take these villains from their place of confinement, and put the sentence which had been justly passed upon them, into execution. Accordingly, on Sunday morning, which occurred only a few days after they were taken, every preparation was made at the rooms, the halters were rove through the blocks outside the door, a suitable number of persons on the spot ready for duty, a carriage with four resolute men well armed, and another containing six also well armed, proceeded to the prison, forced the doors, threatening instant death to any who should oppose, seized the prisoners, put them into the carriage and drove off.

At the same moment the committee's alarm bell was rung, and in less than ten minutes, over four thousand persons were at the place of execution. I arrived in time to get a position near to these unfortunate men. On the arrival of the carriage, they were hurried out, the rope put on their necks, and they were immediately strung up.

It certainly could not have been more than thirty minutes from the time they were taken from the city prison, before they were in eternity, or in a fair way for it. One of them died without a struggle, but the other, in consequence of the rope having slipped round, so as to bring the knot on the back of his neck, struggled very much, and after hanging nearly an hour, was lowered down, and a doctor with a lancet, ascertained that he was not dead; he was then strung up again. While they were hanging, two Chinamen came along, one of them looking up with a smile, "*hiyah, dat do em good.*" They were both cut down, and delivered over to the coroner.

A few weeks after this last execution, San Francisco was visited with a dreadful conflagration, thought to be the work of an incendiary. This fire was the ruin of many, and in which many lives were lost; but by that indomitable energy and perseverance which was characteristic of the place, in a few weeks it was again rebuilt, and everything going on as before.

Several incidents occurred during my first residence in San Francisco, some of which related to my own pecuniary affairs, which would not be interesting to the reader, so I pass them by. The others only went to show the fickleness of fortune, which was fully demonstrated in many instances which came within my own notice. One gentleman *became so rich*, that it was a difficult matter for him to stand still. He was usually seen posted at a corner, with both thumbs in the armholes of his vest, occasionally raising himself on his toes, assuming such a look of importance, that no one could touch him with a ten foot pole. This man *became so poor*, only a few months from this zenith, that he had no place in which to lie his head, that he could call his own.

Another millionnaire? died in an old long boat. There were others who were connected with a famous banking establishment, and cut a mighty great figure, burnt up, and no doubt twisted many an honest man out of his hard earnings; and if I should attempt to call these fellows by name, it would make a book as large as the London directory. Of course these remarks do not apply to honest men.

It had been my intention before leaving California, to make a tour through the mines. I had promised to visit a company of young men, who were working a claim on the Oregon gulch. I took the *wagon* for that region, first stopping at Mormon Island, which had been a very productive mining locality; but *now* was a nest of rum holes, and gambling dens.

It was my principal object, to see everything that belonged to the miner's life and characteristic, I mingled with them in groceries, gambling houses, tents and diggings. Philosophers may talk of studying out human nature by those developments which they accidentally come in contact with in civilized life, or an occasional visit to the poor, but let a man spend a week in a mining region, where there is no sort of moral restraint, but on the contrary, a full display of the very worst passions that human nature is subject to. He there sees the full scope of human depravity.

I went into a gambling saloon where there were six monte tables, notwithstanding, there were probably two hundred persons lounging round the bar, and hovering round the card tables, it was still as a church, hardly a word was spoken; such was the intense eagerness with which the motions of the card players were watched.

At the table where I first stood, there were but two players, and those were Western miners, one was quite aged, probably, sixty-five, the other a young man; the latter seemed rather cautious, while the former was bent on destruction.

There was a full peck measure of gold coin upon the table, which is always exhibited as a lure. The old man had been a heavy loser; the monte dealer, had kept him well plied with liquor, and though intoxicated, his eye was keen. While I stood there, his last coin was lost, he then drew himself up, took another drink, hauled out from his bosom a leather bag containing about a thousand dollars, threw it upon the table, and in an exulting manner, accompanied with a horrid oath, declared that he was not broke yet. Here were gold scales, all ready to weigh out the dreadful stakes! The keen eye of the gambler villain, his marked politeness, delicate fingers, studded with rings, beautifully curled moustache, with the glistening end of a revolver peering from his bosom, made an impression on my mind, that probably will not be erased while I live. The old man's bag was evidently fast melting away. I left him and passed over to another table.

Here were three players, this monte dealer was a different looking man from the other, for it happened to be a very pretty *wo* man, with two ruffian looking scoundrels on each side, to guard her from insult. Here too, was a hugh pile of glittering manmon; one of the players, who by the way, I recognized as a Boston man, had been quite successful, had about his person, over seven thousand dollars that he had won in two hours, having commenced with eighty-four dollars. I stood aside, so as not to be known.

He had a friend who took a position behind him, and was earnestly urging him to stop. He continued turning down the champagne, swearing he would not leave until he had burst the bank.

I left the house in order to procure a sleeping place, which I found to be a hard matter, but succeeded in getting a chance with a miner, in a bunk without bedclothes.

Next morning, I saw the Boston man, when a mutual recognition took place. I then referred to *last evening*, he was somewhat surprised when he learned that I was there. He told me however, that the *lady* stripped him — he left the table without a rial, "and," said he, " here I am without money enough to get my bitters."

The prominent part of the story was, he wanted me to loan him a hundred dollars! *That man had a wife and two children in Boston.*

I left this place and proceeded up to where my young friends were, passed a few days very pleasantly with them, then took a range off in another direction, mingling with the miners, some of whom I found to be very intelligent men, others again, were miserable and dissipated.

The mines and gold diggings having been so often described, I shall omit anything of a descriptive character here, and merely add, by way of closing up my California tour, that in *my* mind, the ultimate success and prosperity of California yet remains a problem; and I think it was a great mistake on the part of the government, ever to have admitted it into the Union.

It does not require much penetration to see that the acquisition of that territory never can be of any pecuniary advantage to the country at large. There will always be contentions and troubles, which will finally end in a revolt.

Some portions of the upper country, with much labor and expense, can be made highly productive; while a great portion of it, for agricultural purposes, is entirely useless. As long as gold continues abundant, or sufficiently so to pay, the population will always be great; but when that ceases, Upper California is done.

I noticed that in the immense forests along the Sierra Nevada range, not a young tree is to be found. I have seen splendid oaks, which, to appearance, contained sufficient timber for a ship of three hundred tons. I measured a pine tree that had fallen, it having been undermined by gold diggers. This tree was three hundred feet long, and eight feet through at the butt; and another that was standing near it, was as long, and twelve feet through, and either of them would square eighteen inches at the top end.

The snow lies in the upper valleys nearly all the year, and in some places it is more than twelve feet deep, in the summer months. Many of the Indians go entirely naked, and I believe would never trouble a white man, if the latter were not the aggressors. I have met them on the road while travelling alone, and they have invariably returned my salutation with true Indian politeness.

There was much sickness throughout the mines, and many deaths. The most fatal disease was diarrhœa, which was caused chiefly by laboring in the water, and a too frequent use of ardent spirits. I administered relief to some who were sick, and admonished others who were pursuing the right course to become so; quack doctor's fees were enormous and in no case would they come nigh a sick man that had no money.

One amusing incident occurred, that really pleased me. An Iowa man had suffered much from toothache. One of these man-killers came along, and was applied to to extract the tooth, which he made out to do in a bungling and painful manner. He then says to the man:

"Your teeth want cleaning; by doing which, it will prevent the toothache."

"Well, go ahead."

So the man sat down, and the doctor went to work, scraping and filing a set of teeth that had never been through the operation before. After he had finished, and both had taken a nipper of whiskey:

"Well, now doctor, what's to pay?"

"I shall *charge* you eighty dollars."

"What's that, stranger?"

"Eighty dollars is my price for taking aeout a tooth, and cleaning aeout a mouth."

The miner looked at him a few moments, and then stepping on a block, took down his rifle, capped and cocked it, and with a savage look and a western oath, ordered the fellow out of his tent, and with a stentorian voice, swore that if he was not out of the reach of his rifle in five minutes, he would shoot him. The doctor gathered up his leather bag, started, and was soon over the hill. By this time, two of the miner's comrades had come in, and to whom he related the story. He was a good-natured, clever fellow, and said that if the charge had been ten or fifteen dollars, he would have paid it willingly, as the whole operation occupied but an hour and a half. I thought the *doctor* (?) was served just right.

During my tour through the mining region, I was much interested in the Geological formation of the country, a graphic description of which would make a book of itself. I returned to San Francisco, and made arrangements for returning home.

I left my business with two *nice, young* men, at least, as I thought, for I certainly had a right to think so. They were both apparently pious men, members of Christian churches in Boston, and with whom I had been previously acquainted, before leaving San Francisco. It was understood between us that remittances should be made to me by every steamer, until the business was closed.

I sailed from San Francisco in the Tennessee. Several passengers were sick, and one died before we reached Panama. We crossed the Isthmus safely, although part of our train was robbed, and some of them murdered. We arrived at Chagres late in the evening, and with much difficulty got on board the Crescent City, then lying three miles out.

On our way home, we stopped into Jamaica for coal. Many of the steerage passengers went ashore, drank freely of Jamaica rum, were taken with cholera and diarrhœa, and died like fools, after having withstood the hardships of the mines for two or three years, and having also, a considerable amount of gold dust about their persons, of which, probably, their friends knew where it went.

I arrived in Boston in October, and after waiting two months and not receiving either letters or money, felt suspicious that something was the matter. I started off again for this land of scoundrels, in the steamer Cherokee. We had a regular north-west gale, until up with St. Domingo. Our boat groaned and creaked like an old basket; but she carried us safe to Chagres, and that was all we desired. We took boats for Gorgona, as it was thought at this time of the year to be the best road. Arrived safe, and took mules for Panama.

About four hours out of Gorgona, my mule, a vicious animal, threw me on to a ledge of rocks, which knocked the breath out of my body for a few minutes, but fortunately, escaped without broken bones. I was soon horsed again, though in much pain; went on my way rejoicing, and arrived at Panama by sunset.

I took passage in the Tennessee, and sailed for San Francisco. On the third day after leaving Panama, began to feel premonitory symptoms of fever. Several were already down with it, and one poor fellow, a German died along-side of me. I was taken early in the morning, was so much debilitated, that I could not stand. My friends took me to my berth, and called the doctor, who came, saw my condition, and prescribed. The medicine was brought to me, but as soon as the boy had gone I managed to throw it out of the air-port, feeling certain that if I took his stuff, should as surely die as the others did. He called again, and enquired how the medicine had operated; I answered him in rather an incoherent manner, telling him that it was all right. "Yes, I perceive your pulse is better, I will send you two powders; take one immediately, and the other at twelve o'clock." The powders came, but they went where I should have gone, had I taken them. I was very thirsty, the water was so warm I could not retain it, so I took a glass of ale, and felt immediate relief. I perceived that I had gained strength, and commenced rubbing myself with a coarse cloth, and instead of water, used the ale. I had been confined to my berth two days, which is about the time it takes one to die. I thought the matter over seriously, and was determined not to die, unless it was God's *will* that I should, and felt sure that if I took medicine, my days were numbered.

I began to stretch myself out, rub my joints and body with the coarse piece of canvas, and on the third morning, asked the doctor for a bowl of chicken broth, which he allowed me to take, at the same time feeling my pulse, and expressing his surprise at my rapid convalescence while so many were still very low!

Of course, it would not do for me to tell him that I had not taken his medicine, for he certainly was very kind and attentive, and it would, no doubt, have hurt his feelings. I am certain that my cure was effected by *hard rubbing*, *pale ale*, [illegible]*solution*, for before the week was out I was on dec[illegible]e surprise of many, and though my appearance was deathly, yet the old fellow missed me this time.

On my arrival at San Francisco, I was very weak, but rapidly gained strength and entire recovery, soon ascertained that my *nice, young men* had burst up only a short time after I left San Francisco, and had included all my property in their assets: and neither of the principals nor the assignees, could give me any satisfactory account of it. And to sum up the whole matter, it was a regular California failure, which means a total annihilation of money, papers, reputation and principle.

During my stay at San Francisco, the second time, I lived on board the ship Susan Drew, owned by Capt. Victor Constant, of Boston, one of nature's noblemen, a veteran shipmaster in whom it may be truly said there was no guile. And yet these heartless wretches, contrived to involve him in a lawsuit. His lawyer, a Boston man, since dead, and gone to the ——. Excuse me reader, I came near using an improper expression. This same lawyer told Capt. Constant in my presence, that his case would surely be decided in his favor; at the same time requesting the captain to hand over a few hundred, on account; which he did, and to the astonishment of my good friend the captain, this infamous lawyer turned right about, and favored the case against him, by which means he has lost his ship and cargo.

I have said in another place, that there were many incidents relating to my business matters, which would not be at all interesting to any one, but I wish to be indulged in naming one, which goes to show a principle, or spirit which I shall leave for the reader to name.

After the great fire, as I was passing by the ruins of a store, I noticed five or six men trying to haul a stick of timber out of the water. I saw that they were unacquainted with that business, so I went where they were at work, showed them how to proceed, and assisted in getting one piece up; was going away, when a gentleman hailed me and enquired if I would assist in building the store, the wages, I think, were twelve dollars per day, and as I had nothing to occupy my time, told him yes.

We built the store, and my wages for that and another job, amounted to three hundred dollars. The morning after the fire, before I commenced on the store, I was walking among a collection of half-burnt goods, and saw a man with whom I had been previously acquainted, sitting and mourning over a little pile of stuff, that was hardly recognizable.

"Halloo," said I, "what are you doing here?"

"Oh, I have lost everything that I had in the world, and this pile of rubbish is all I possess, my money is lost, and here I am a beggar."

"Nonsense, man, don't sit here, you see every body all

around you going ahead again, come, I will lend you a hand."

So I went on board the ship, changed my dress, brought some tools ashore; we both went to work among the smoking timber, and soon cleared away enough for a small shanty, which we raised, and boarded with scorched *blankets!* I bought some coarse cloth, and covered the roof, and gave him a *hot-coffee* machine, with which he went ahead, and in a few months had two thousand dollars.

During this time, there was a Boston gentleman who was continually running round, telling how strange it was that a man in my position should lower himself by working as a common journeyman. He addressed himself in this manner to an old ship-master, who was my particular friend. The latter turned towards him with an indignant look. Said he:

"You good-for-nothing scoundrel, that man has been robbed by just such fellows as you are; and now, because he is trying to retrieve himself by working like an honest man, you are running round, trying to injure his reputation. Fix up my account; I want no more business with you."

My friend was kind enough to call and apprize me of this conversation, and early next morning, I met the fellow on Long wharf; he held out his hand for a shake; I gave him a look which I think he remembered till he died, which was very soon after.

Of all the characters in the world, I think a hypocrite is the m[illegible]testable. Therefore I wish to have it known, that, [illegible]r much I lament it, and my earnest prayer is that I may overcome it, *I am vindictive*, and will only repeat upon those who have injured me, the language of Jeremiah, *Lamentations*, 3d *Chapter, and the last three verses*, and of David, 109th *Psalm*, 1*st to the* 16*th verses*, and there I leave them.

Having nothing more to do in San Francisco, I took passage for home in the steamer Independence, for *San-Juan-del-Sud*, which was the Nicaragua route, it having been cracked up as the most expeditious. She was an old, rickety thing; notwithstanding which, three hundred passengers were willing to risk their lives on board of her. We had a fair passage to San Juan, but on the day of our arrival, (Sunday) it blew a smart breeze, attended with much rain.

There is no harbor, the whole bay lying exposed to the open sea. The surf was rolling in furiously, and it continued to rain hard all day. The word was passed throughout the steamer for all passengers to get their baggage ready for going on shore; and as all were anxious to get across the country, the rain was not considered an obstacle. But landing in the surf was the trouble; the boats could not approach the shore within twice their length; the negroes waded off, and took the passengers upon their shoulders, which was little better than swimming ashore, for all were drenched through as soon as they left the boat. The trunks and bags were also taken from the boats on the heads of the negroes, many of whom were drunk, and there they were, negroes and trunks rolling over in the surf; some of them were knocked open, and scarcely one was landed without damage.

The principle place to receive the passengers was a long shed, with only the roof covered; and this was a regular, stinking rum hole. Here we all gathered, like so many drowned rats. Among the passengers was a lady, a sea captain's wife, who was in rather a delicate situation. She was quite wet, and must remain so during the night, as her trunks were soaked in salt water, and of course all her apparel wet. I rendered her husband what assistance lay in my power, and finally succeeded in getting a part of the shed screened off for her accommodation.

There was one other house, but it was too small to accommodate more than twenty persons. It had been nearly destroyed only a few nights before our arrival, by the Spanish soldiers, in consequence of some misunderstanding between the latter and some forty or fifty Americans. A serious fight occurred; the Spaniards, about two hundred in number, assailed the house and fairly riddled it with bullets. Several were killed on both sides. These soldiers were quartered a short distance from our long shanty, and there was some talk of punishment; but as we were all anxious to get away, the matter was dropped.

It was now night; there were about two hundred steerage passengers in the building, and nearly all of them were drunk. The place was a perfect bedlam, and the air fairly rang with drunken yells. I procured a grass hammock, and hung it up away in the further corner of the shed, as I thought out of the way of everybody. One of the men who was employed in the building, cautioned me about snakes. He said there were any quantity of them, of the most venomous kind; and if I did not hang my hammock very high, they would crawl into bed with me. However, snake or no snake, I turned in, and fell asleep. Just as I began to dream about sweet home, I was aroused by some one throwing themselves across my body. I jumped out, it was very dark, and demanded what the fellow meant. He showed no inclination to move, so I cast off one end of my hammock, and let him down. The first I knew was a vivid sight of the sun, moon, and seven stars. He was a powerful Missourian, and hit me between the eyes, such a blow, that completely capsized me. I picked myself up, and got hold of something. They say that "a drowning man will catch at a straw;" but I rather think that I caught something heavier than a *straw*, by the looks of his cheek next morning. Several of my friends who happened to be near, came to the rescue, and took him away; he dropped his hat in the fray, which I picked up, and at daylight next morning heard him enquiring for it.

"Here is your hat, sir," said I; "and do you know how you abused me last night?"

"Well, now, look here, stranger, I was drunk. You see this cut on my face."

"Yes, and if I had had a pistol, you would never have worn your hat again."

He was a gentlemanly fellow, after all, and made every sort of acknowledgment. We shook hands, and made the matter up.

We had another trouble to encounter; there were no mules to be had here. At San Francisco, we had paid our fare to Greytown, and were allowed eighty pounds of luggage free; all over that was to be paid for to the transit agent, at the place where we now were, and were also to have mules in readiness immediately on the arrival of the steamer.

There were three persons attached to the agency, who transacted their business under a tent, a short distance from the beach. Much discontent was manifest among the passengers, on account of the delay. The agents had sent out muleteers in all directions, to search for mules. In the meantime the luggage was weighed and paid for. No one thought of looking at their ticket; but one man happening to look at his, saw that 84 pounds were allowed free of charge. This caused a general discovery. The fact was made known to the agents, and the money demanded back, which they refused, saying that the agent in San Francisco had no right to frank a pound of luggage. The tent was now surrounded, and the immediate destruction of everything belonging to the concern threatened, if the money was not paid. They very prudently rectified the mistake, and this matter was settled.

The next trouble was about the mules, which, contrary to specification, were not ready. The agents were again threatened, and were told that they would be held accountable for expenses while we were detained. They were evidently much frightened, seeing who their customers were.

On Monday evening, twenty-four mules were brought in, and I was lucky enough to get a very poor one. Our luggage was in charge of the agents, who were to forward it immediately to Greytown. At 12 o'clock, Tuesday, twenty of us were ready, and started on our journey to Virgin Bay. We were advised by those who knew the country, not to start until next morning; but being anxious to leave the miserable hole, we pushed ahead, and soon came on to the mud region, previously crossing a rapid river about twenty yards wide.

CHAPTER XXVIII.

Find that we were mistaken in starting so late,—Horrid road,—Party stop,—Difficulty in turning my horse,—Pass an uncomfortable night,—Dreary prospect,—Mules get mired,—My mule gives out,—On my legs again,—Unpleasant position,—Cheered by the promise of the Almighty,—Unexpected deliverance,—Groundless fears,—Arrive at Virgin Bay,—Wash and bathe myself,—Burgo's miserable steamer,—Incidents,—Uncomfortable night,—Fort Carlos,—Break our Rudder,—Make a Substitute,—Rapids,—Interview with female passengers,—Their ignorance of the journey,—Advice,—Start for Greytown,—Find the steamer Daniel Webster,—Baggage not arrived,—Poor accommodation,—Sail without our luggage,—Stop at Havana,—Arrive at New York,—Bad treatment at the transit office,—Build a schooner,—Sail for Australia,—Wrecked,—Taken off and carried to Hamburg,—Particulars in my letter,—Visit to Kiel, Duke of Wellington,—Blockading fleet,—Interview with Sir Charles Napier,—Return to Hamburg,—Start for Berlin,—To Hanover,—Bremen,—Return to Hanover,—Take the cars for Cologne,—Go up the Rhine,—Return to Cologne,—Start for Brussels.

It did not take long to convince me that we had made a mistake in leaving at midday, as night would overtake us before we could reach a suitable place to sleep. Owing to the recent rain, the road was almost impassable, our mules were fairly wallowing in the mud, and there was not one in the party that had not either been thrown off, or obliged to dismount, in order to extricate his animal. In some places we were under the necessity of leaving the mule to scrabble out the best way he could, while the riders did the same, and when, within half an hour of sundown, on coming to a dry spot, I proposed to stop for the night. It was then raining quite fast, and darkness would soon be upon us.

But no; the word was, go on as far as we can, while we

have daylight. Being somewhat in advance of the company, and some distance up the side of a rock, beneath which was a deep precipice, and the pathway was so narrow, that the mule could scarcely get foothold, and now so dark that the animal refused to advance another inch.

Just at that moment, I heard the Indian yell, which I knew was a signal for a halt. Here I was, a mile ahead, on the edge of a rock; an attempt to turn my mule would be sure destruction to both. To my great joy, I heard the footsteps of the guide close by, and called him. With his assistance, dismounted, and with good management turned the mule round.

I rode back to where they halted, and if they had tried, could not have selected a worse place. No shelter, except a large tree, which, upon the least agitation, poured the water down upon us in torrents. We had nothing to lie upon except the bare mud, although we contrived to haul some small boughs under us, which, however, immediately sunk in the mud.

Our animals remained during the night immovably fixed, poor creatures, without food or drink. I think this was the longest night I ever knew. I was somewhat afraid of cramp, or fever, but escaped both. It was with much difficulty that we extricated our mules from the miry clay. We endeavored to be as cheerful as possible, being well aware of the unpleasant journey before us.

We abandoned the idea of keeping together, as every one seemed intent on looking out for himself. We had not been more than an hour under way, when I heard a loud screaming some distance behind, which was from an Irish boy, hailing his father, who was just behind me. The fellow was singing out, "Father! father! I am stuck fast." I stopped, while the father went back, and sure enough, his poor beast was so firmly mired that it was impossible to get him out, and there he must die.

My poor brute began to tell me, by unmistakable signs, that he must stop. My position now, was anything but agreeable. If I could get to Rivas, I was safe, but that was impossible. The Irishman and his son were far behind, literally swimming through the mud. Very soon my mule stopped, entirely exhausted. I dismounted, and left him to *his* fate, feeling somewhat doubtful about my own. It was noon, and I was entirely ignorant of the distance, or of the right road, hungry, thirsty and weary, I scrabbled, having lost my hat and one shoe. My shoe, however, after much labor, I found again. My strength failed me, and I sat down on a rock.

Remembering God's promise, started again, and after wallowing an hour, came to an old hollow tree, and thought of crawling into it, just leaving my head out, and if I died there, some one, probably, might recognize me. Again, *I will be with you*, sounded in my ears, so I concluded not to die yet. And but a few minutes after, a negro came along on a strong horse. I made a bargain with him for the use of the animal, for which I was to pay him ten dollars, on our arrival at Virgin Bay. What a sudden transition! Only a few minutes before I was wallowing in the mud, expecting to die, and here I am now, mounted on a fine horse, and with a guide too!

Reader, never distrust your ever-watchful Father, who careth for you, never mind what the trouble is. Put your trust in God, and don't give up the ship. But there are times when Faith must be kept continually on the stretch, as it will appear in my case. My negro was a stalwart fellow, naked as he was born, except an old rusty sword, fastened to his body with a leather belt. Soon after I had mounted, he struck off from the main road, into the forest, cutting away the underbrush, with his sword, to make a passage for himself and horse, but not cutting high enough for the rider, often did I have to dodge very quick, to prevent sharing the fate of Absalom. He was a surly fellow, and took no notice of my complaints. All at once, it seemed to flash across my mind that the fellow was leading me into the woods, to rob, and probably to kill me, everything about his movements looked so suspicious. In order to be prepared for the worst, I kept my hand upon my knife, to be ready in an instant. He knew I had gold upon my person, for, in adjusting my clothes, he had seen it. My fears, however, proved groundless; he was leading me along through a better and a shorter road. Soon we emerged into the highway again, ascended a hill, and there was Virgin Bay, beneath us, with a few temporary hovels, and a diminutive steamboat lying about a mile from the landing.

The first thing, after getting into the town, was to make the best of my way to the water side, strip, wash my clothes, wring them well, and put them on again. It now began to rain like fury. On going a short distance, got into a rough house, and obtained permission to go into the chamber, then stripped myself again, bathed from head to foot, with cold water, commenced rubbing with a coarse towel, until I felt a glow throughout my body, put on my wet clothes, purchased some refreshment, and followed the crowd to the landing, ready to embark for the steamer. Many of our party had not yet arrived, and I had cause to fear that some of them had met with a sad fate.

It seemed as though my troubles would never end. Here were two hundred and seventy persons to be crammed on board a cockle shell of a steamer, not large enough to accommodate fifty persons comfortably. We were all to be carried to the steamer in a miserable dug out, called a bungo. We must also be carried to the bungo on negroes' shoulders. It takes but a very little to capsize one of these tubs.

It may be recollected that but a few years since, we received intelligence that one of them had been overset when full of passengers, and over fifty persons were drowned, some of whom were not recovered until many days after, having a large amount of gold dust about their persons, which kept their bodies down.

When on board the bungo, I at once assumed the command, insisting on every one keeping himself seated on the bottom. Notwithstanding my exertions to prevent accident, it seemed as if they were resolved to upset her at any rate, as many of them were intoxicated. I finally succeeded in getting her out into deep water, so that no more could get on board. We then went out to the steamer, and when all the passengers were on board, her deck was only a few inches from the water. We were huddled together so close that there was not room for any one either to sit or lie down.

The night was cold, and being wet felt very uncomfortable, in addition to which we were obliged to stand ankle deep in the water until morning. By squeezing along among the crowd, I got near the boiler, but was driven away by an Irishman who belonged to the boat. Resistance was out of the question.

Early the next morning, we were abreast Fort Carlos, the sun rose beautifully, and the morning was charming. How gratefully did I receive his radiant beams upon my wet and shivering body.

But here was another difficulty, the commanding officer at the Fort, forbid our passing. They had their guns manned all ready to fire into us. Our captain, a drunken, swaggering fellow, swore he would go by at any rate, but was persuaded to anchor the boat, go ashore, and arrange matters with the commanding officer. This Fort is at the entrance of the Nicaragua river, and the right to navigate it had not been negotiated. Matters being settled, we went on our way, and through the carelessness of the captain, the boat struck the bank, and broke off the rudder. We rigged a Kentucky oar over the bow, and went along firstrate. Our boat could go no farther than the rapids, over which it is extremely dangerous to attempt a passage. Preparation is always made to check the boat before approaching too near.

The boat that followed us was carried among the rocks, not being checked in season, she was nearly destroyed, and many of her passengers were drowned. Our boat was stopped in season, and hauled safely along-side the bank. We were now to leave this boat, and take the one on the other side, or below the rapids. She had just come up from Greytown, with passengers who were to pass over the road we had just left, being bound to San Francisco. The distance between the boats was half a mile. I went on board the upward steamer, expecting to meet a friend, en rout for California. Went into her cabin, and there were about thirty ladies, of all ages, sizes, and complexions, who were rigged out in their finest dresses, and who appeared to be preparing for a ball, rather than a tramp through the mud. My appearance seemed somewhat to startle them; I apologized for my intrusion by saying that I was looking for a gentleman whom I expected to find on board.

There seemed to be two matron looking ladies, who appeared to have some control over the rest. So I addressed myself to these: "Ladies, I see you are all preparing to go on shore. Allow me to give you a few words of advice. I have just come from San Juan, and advise you all to change your rich dresses for the very poorest you have; you will find no accommodations for ladies on board the other boat, and your road from Virgin Bay to San Juan, will be one continuous sheet of mud. You can procure no refreshment on the way, and on your arrival at San Juan, if the steamer is not ready, your condition will be extremly uncomfortable."

They appeared much surprised at this information, saying that the agents at New York, had given them quite a different description of the road, representing it as a *beautiful ride, more like a pleasure excursion, than a journey.* I assured them that it was quite the reverse, the road was in a most miserable condition, adding, the moment you leave this boat your trouble commences. Even from here to the other boat, which is but half a mile, you cannot avoid sinking ankle deep in mud, and on board the other, there are no accommodations for you whatever, nor a morsel of anything to eat. When you arrive at Virgin Bay your lives will be jeopardized in landing, and then if you don't look sharp you will be robbed by villanous agents. There are few ladies' saddles to be had, the mules are miserable, and if they give out on the road, what will become of you? You may rely on what I have told you. I am very glad that the friend I was looking after is not here.

The ladies began to unrig. No passengers were allowed to go on board until they had finished their newly arranged toilet. In a short time they came ashore, metamorphosed into *novitiates for a nunnery.* I saw no more of them. At 4 P. M., we started for Greytown, and arrived next day at 2 P. M.

The steamer Daniel Webster was lying ready for us, and was to sail in two days. Our luggage had not yet arrived, there seemed to be a general anxiety among the passengers whether it *would* arrive in season for the steamer. There were no accommodations here for sleeping except at the rum holes. Myself and three others hired a bamboo shed, and slept upon the ground; we having no beds were glad to take up with what accommodations we could get.

The steamer would allow no passengers on board until the morning of sailing, and on that day our luggage had not arrived and were obliged to sail without it, the agents at Greytown assuring us that it should be forthcoming by the next steamer, which in some measure relieved our suspense. I never saw mine after landing it at San Juan.

I called on the transit agents at New York, for indemnification. They refused to do anything about it unless compelled by law. I told them that my loss was $175. I did not wish to go into a lawsuit, and if they would refund what I had paid for its conveyance to their own agents, which was eight dollars, I would trouble them no more, which they also refused, and ordered me out of the office. Such was the treatment I received from this transit company's agent.

But to my narrative. We stopped at Havana for coal. It was but a short time after the filibustering executions, the excitement against the Americans had not yet subsided. An officer came off from the shore to furnish passengers with permits for landing, for which we paid one dollar. I had a pleasant ride around the country, and think there is no place where an invalid could pass the winter more pleasantly than at Havana.

I arrived home early in December, 1851. In 1854, I built a small schooner, which I called Sheerwater, put a cargo on board, and Sept. 8th, sailed for Australia. On the 10th, a gale sprung up from the S. E., which continued to increase until the night of the 11th, when it turned into a furious hurricane. We were capsized, taken from the wreck by the Hamburg ship, Hampden, and carried to Hamburg. Immediately on my arrival there, I sent the following letter *home, which briefly* describes the disaster.

Hamburg, October 16th, 1854.

DEAR SIR:—I am sorry to be under the necessity of dating a letter from this place, so opposite to that of my destination. But God has so ordered it, and we must submit to his will. I am also extremely unhappy that it devolves on me to relate a dreadful disaster which has befallen the Sheerwater.

On the 10th ult., it commenced blowing hard, with a heavy sea, and continued to increase until Tuesday, the 11th. The schooner had behaved nobly, riding over the sea like a bird, her deck dry, and everything all right. On the morning of the 12th, at daylight, the mate who had the watch, called all hands to shorten sail, or rather to take in all, except a small piece of the mainsail, to lay her to under.

We now lay to perfectly dry, but from the appearance of the Heavens, feared that the worst was yet to come, and so it unfortunately proved. The gale, by 10 A. M., had become a perfect hurricane, with a sea that seemed to reach the very Heavens, accompanied with floods of rain that for a moment would smooth the sea, but it soon rose again like mountain-peaks, not one of which came on our decks.

But now came the blast that was nigh sending us into eternity. The schooner was thrown down, her masts nearly parallel with the water, the cargo shifted, the water was pouring into her, and we thought we were gone.

She righted during a lull, which brought her deck out of water. Directly it came on again, and down she went. We sprung to the weather rail, in order to get upon her side, which might prolong our lives a short time. She again righted a little, but left us no hope; and with much trouble we obtained an axe and cut away the foremast. This was a difficult job, as it blew so heavy that it was almost impossible to make a stroke with the axe. We succeeded in getting it over the side which immediately relieved her. Still hung by the lee-rigging, which could not be got at; but at length we succeeded in getting it clear.

It then swung round under the stern, knocked away the rudder, and injured the stern post. We cut the weather-rigging of the mainmast, but it blew so hard we could do nothing more. The mast, on account of the heavy roll, broke partly off in the wake of the deck, and split up about fifteen feet; it being a tough stick was loath to go. We now lay with our deck out of water. Everything in the hold had shifted, our water casks stove and empty, provisions wet and spoiled, (except our meats). The gale had now somewhat abated. We set to work to put things to rights. The sea was still running very high, which made it difficult to accomplish much; but if we could get anything on her to keep her steady, we might possibly remain on board a few days and run a chance of being taken off. We were quite exhausted, not having eaten anything for nearly twenty-four hours. All were anxiously scanning the horizon to catch a glimpse of anything that looked like a sail; when the joyful cry, of "sail ho!" saluted our ears. A little speck was just discernible apparently coming towards us.

Every eye was now intently fixed upon the stranger, and soon discovered to our grief that she was edging off from us; probably we had not been seen. Our feelings may be easily imagined. We soon hit upon an expedient which was the means of our preservation. There was a cannon on board, that lie just under the hatchway, which we succeeded in getting up; there was also a tin case of powder, that had been hermetically sealed, which we were fortunate enough to get, and one of the men had some dry matches.

We fired our gun three times, when the ship run her colors up, and immediately tacked and stood for us. She hove to about half a mile from us, lowered her boats, and came to us, notwithstanding it blew very fresh. We all got safely on board the ship Hampden, of Hamburg, Capt. Ariansen, from the Bay of Mexico bound to Hamburg. She had been thrown on her beam-ends in the same hurricane, and were upon the point of cutting away their masts, but by staving their water casks, she righted. Capt. Ariansen stated to us, that they saw something black, but could not make out what the object was until he saw the smoke. We were on board the Hampden thirty days, during which time we were treated with much kindness,

Very respectfully, yours,

SAMUEL F. HOLBROOK.

WRECK OF THE SHEERWATER.

I will just add here, that on my return to the United States, I made a statement to the Department at Washington, of our rescue and kind treatment by Capt. Ariansen.

The Secretary of the State immediately ordered an elegant gold chronometer and chain, to be sent to the Consul at Hamburg, to be presented to Capt. Ariansen, also a handsome present to Robert Sloman, Esq., the owner of the ship, for refusing any compensation for our passages. I received the following letters from the Secretary, apprizing me of the present.

DEPARTMENT OF STATE,
Washington, January 17th, 185[illegible]

SAMUEL F. HOLBROOK, ESQ.,
No. 44 Purchase street, Boston, Mass.

SIR:—Your letter, of the 13th inst. addressed to the Secretary of the Treasury and referred by him to this Department respecting the wreck of the schooner "Sheerwater" of Boston, in which vessel you were a passenger, and acknowledging the kindness extended to you by Captain Ariansen of the ship "Hampden," and Mr. Bromberg the acting United States Consul at Hamburg, has been received. You will perceive, from the enclosed copy of a communication addressed to Mr. Bromberg on the 21st ult., that your suggestion in regard to a recognition of the valuable services of Mr. Sloman and Captain Ariansen has already been anticipated by the Department.

That part of your letter relating to provision afforded by the United States to destitute seamen, has been referred to the Fifth Auditor.

I am, Sir, respectfully,
Your obedient servant,
W. L. MARCY.

DEPARTMENT OF STATE,
Washington, December 21st, 1854.

SAMUEL BROMBERG, ESQ.,
United States Consulate, Hamburg.

SIR:—You will receive with this despatch, a bag containing a gold Chronometer, with a heavy gold chain attached, which the President of the United States has directed to be presented to I. I. Ariansen, for his humane and gallant conduct in rescuing from shipwreck the Master, passengers and crew of the schooner "Sheerwater" of Boston; and also five packages, enclosing a copy of "Mitchell's Universal Atlas," and the "National Portrait Gallery of Distinguished Americans," for presentation to R. Sloman, Esq., the owner of the ship "Hampden," as an acknowledgment of his humanity and generosity in refusing compensation for the passage to Hamburg in that vessel of shipwrecked American mariners.

The Department has learned that the risk incurred by Captain Ariansen in rescuing these unfortunate persons was very great; the kindness and attention shown to them by him is spoken of in the highest terms of commendation.

You will transmit a note to the Senate of Hamburg, expressing in suitable terms, the high regard which the President entertains for conduct so noble and disinterested, and requests that these presents may be delivered in the name of the United States to the individuals for whom they are intended.

I am, Sir, &c.,

(Signed.) W. L. MARCY.

I now take leave for a few days, when I shall resume the narrative, and endeavor to amuse the reader with my journey through Europe to Sebastopol, Asia Minor, Syria, Palestine, Egypt, and the Carnival at Rome.

www.ingramcontent.com/pod-product-compliance
Lightning Source LLC
LaVergne TN
LVHW011257110826
845149LV00001B/162

* 9 7 8 1 4 1 8 1 8 8 7 1 9 *